THE BLACK STUDENT'S GUIDE TO GRADUATE AND PROFESSIONAL SCHOOL SUCCESS

THE BLACK STUDENT'S GUIDE TO GRADUATE AND PROFESSIONAL SCHOOL SUCCESS

EDITED BY VERNON L. FARMER

Foreword by
Carol Moseley-Braun

GREENWOOD PRESS
Westport, Connecticut • London

Library of Congress Cataloging-in-Publication Data

The Black student's guide to graduate and professional school success / edited by
Vernon L. Farmer ; foreword by Carol Moseley-Braun.
　　p. cm.
　Includes bibliographical references and index.
　ISBN 0-313-32311-9 (alk. paper)
　　1. African Americans—Education (Graduate)—Handbooks, manuals, etc.
2. African American graduate students—Handbooks, manuals, etc. 3.
Universities and colleges—United States—Graduate work—Handbooks,
manuals, etc. 4. Professional education—United States—Handbooks, manuals,
etc. I. Farmer, Vernon L.
　LC2781. B4658　2003
　378.1'55'08996073—dc21　　　　2002029588

British Library Cataloguing in Publication Data is available.

Library of Congress Catalog Card Number: 2002029588
ISBN: 0-313-32311-9

First published in 2003

Greenwood Press, 88 Post Road West, Westport, CT 06881
An imprint of Greenwood Publishing Group, Inc.
www.greenwood.com

Printed in the United States of America

∞™

The paper used in this book complies with the
Permanent Paper Standard issued by the National
Information Standards Organization (Z39.48-1984).

10　9　8　7　6　5　4　3　2　1

The Black Student's Guide to Graduate and Professional School Success is dedicated to my son, Vernyatta L. Farmer, and all other Black students who seek to embrace their heritage, hoping that they will strive in all aspects to develop their fullest intellectual capacity and that they will be inspired to explore the true heritage of their own people. I hope that they will realize that education is essential if they are to claim their rightful place in this nation and the world. For this reason, Black people have always stressed educational achievement at all levels of the learning continuum, and through perseverance, sacrifice, faith, and struggle they have managed to remove many of the educational barriers that stood in their way. Black students must understand that life is what they make it. Struggling is the real meaning of life; success and failure are in the hands of God. Shun not the struggle because it is God's gift. Therefore, obtaining a graduate and/or professional degree is a major step that Black students must take in making this claim.

Black students, you must understand that education is the great equalizer that will give you the power to balance the scale of inequality. However, you must also be cognizant of the great achievements of Black people who traveled the road before you and who paved the way for you to obtain an education. Your recognition of the past experiences and contributions of Black people to the nation and the world will strengthen your pride and self-esteem and provide you with the tenacity to achieve even more than they achieved. May you continue the struggle for a graduate education and for the power that knowledge manifests, and may you draw inspiration from the past, a sense of understanding from the present, and hope from the future. Black students, as you witness the beginning of the new millennium, you find yourself part of a proud tradition, walking in the footsteps of your ancestors and blazing a path for those yet to follow. In this sense, the struggle toward equality for Black people in the world reaches backward as it strains forward.

Finally, you must never forget where you came from, what made it possible for you to get to where you are today, and what it will take to get to where you want to be in the future. You must never forget that God, or whatever name you choose to call the Omnipotent, has been and remains the one essential fact that has guided Black people in their struggle for equality in the world. Finally, you must recognize the privilege, seize the opportunity, fulfill the responsibility of learning, and become committed workers in the daunting task of making a new world, contributing to the improvement of Black people and the nation.

Contents

Foreword

There was a joke circulating around the law school of the University of Chicago when I was a student that went something like this: What happens to the "A" students? They become professors. What happens to the "B" students? They get rich practicing law. What happens to the "C" students? They become politicians. Neither I nor the president of the United States contradict the gist of that joke.

I have been blessed to serve in our nation's highest legislative body—the U.S. Senate—and to travel to faraway places as an ambassador, but I remain in awe of the scholars who exemplify lifelong learning. Some of those scholars have contributed their observations and experiences in chapters and essays to *The Black Student's Guide to Graduate and Professional School Success*. The only issue is whether the advice and guidance they offer will be received and understood by the people for whom it is written.

I hope this book will reach its target audience. Many of its contributors have not only trod the path prospective graduate students are considering, but some of them have also had to carve that path where none before existed. Their observations are too valuable to pass up, and I hope this generation of graduate and professional students will have the wisdom to stop long enough to harvest the wisdom that is offered.

I will not take the time here to tell my own story or to extol the virtues of education to the readers of this foreword. You already appreciate the latter, and the former could not begin to add to the thoughtful, erudite, and insightful guidance that this book provides in its entirety. It is singularly perceptive about a broad range of issues and challenges uniquely faced by men and women of color. It is in that regard a tool to help tap the full capacity of people who might otherwise be precluded from contributing to the benefit of all society. This guide, in the end, serves the interests of all Americans, because our country is stronger when the talents of all can be brought to bear on civil society.

This guide is therefore a recipe for transformation. If one path is made easier, if one student is inspired, if one life is changed, then *The Black Student's Guide to Graduate and Professional School Success* will have fulfilled its mission. I have no doubt, however, that this guide will achieve its goal and more and will be a source of hope and renewal for America.

Carol Moseley-Braun

A SPECIAL TRIBUTE TO CAROL MOSELEY-BRAUN

After the death of A. Leon Higginbotham Jr., who was initially asked to write the foreword for *The Black Student's Guide to Graduate and Professional School Success,* choosing another author was a daunting task. Finally, because of her unwavering commitment to equal justice for all members of our society, Ambassador Carol Moseley-Braun was chosen from among a cadre of esteemed scholars to write the foreword. Ambassador Carol Moseley-Braun, a graduate of the University of Chicago Law School, made political history when she was elected to the U.S. Senate in 1992. She has the distinction of being the first woman from Illinois elected to the Senate, being the sole African American in the Senate from 1992–1998, and being only the second African American to serve in the Senate in this century. She was the first former U.S. senator to hold the post of American Ambassador to New Zealand. Carol Moseley-Braun also has the distinction of being the first woman to serve as a permanent member of the powerful Senate Finance Committee. She fought hard in the Senate on issues of minority rights and education, amassing a solid legislative record. A notable Senate victory came after Ambassador Moseley-Braun made an impassioned speech arguing for the defeat of a patent on the Confederate flag, a symbol of slavery in the pre–American Civil War South. She served on the Judiciary Committee, the Banking, Housing, and Urban Affairs Committee, the Small Business Committee, the Aging Committee, and the Bipartisan Commission on Entitlements and Tax Reform.

Throughout her tenure in the Senate, she commanded attention for her legislative leadership in sponsoring progressive bills on education and other issues and for her ability to build successful coalitions in the Senate. Among her legislative initiatives were the innovative Education Infrastructure Act, the Women's Pension Equity Act, and historic preservation for the Underground Railroad. Senator Moseley-Braun was also a strong voice for requiring the armed services to enact effective procedures to combat racial and sexual discrimination within the military.

Finally, I am especially indebted to Ambassador Moseley-Braun for accepting the invitation to write the foreword for *The Black Student's Guide to Graduate and Professional School Success*. Ambassador Moseley-Braun's outstanding scholarship and solid legislative record make her a role model for many students pursuing or desiring to pursue a graduate education.

Vernon L. Farmer

A. Leon Higginbotham Jr.

I was greatly saddened by the death of A. Leon Higginbotham Jr., chief judge emeritus of the United States Third-Circuit Court of Appeals, who had been asked just prior to his death to write the foreword for *The Black Student's Guide to Graduate and Professional School Success*. Although Judge A. Leon Higginbotham Jr. died before he had the opportunity to respond to my request, this is a special tribute to the intensity of his commitment to equality and civil rights. Neil L. Rudenstine, former Harvard University president, said, "He was a powerful presence and voice, a voice that has influenced our legal and judicial world for decades." A. Leon Higginbotham Jr., an internationally known advocate for human rights, was chosen to write the foreword because of his commitment to equality and civil rights and his uncompromising record of service and advocacy for equal justice.

A. Leon Higginbotham Jr., a graduate of Yale University Law School, was a public service professor of jurisprudence at Harvard University's John F. Kennedy School of Government and a lecturer of law at Harvard Law School. He also taught at the law schools of the University of Michigan, New York University, Stanford University, Yale University, and the University of Pennsylvania. A. Leon Higginbotham Jr., both as a judge and as a prolific writer, defended civil rights with great passion and eloquence. His scholarly works consist of a multivolume series of books on race and American law considered by many scholars an American classic. The series includes *In the Matter of Color: Race and the American Legal Process* and *Shades of Freedom*. The first volume, *In the Matter of Color*, is a definitive history of slavery, race, and constitutional law, which received several national and international awards. The second volume, *Shades of Freedom*, provides a history of the African American struggle for racial equality in America. Judge Higginbotham's scholarly works also include *Race, Values, and the Early American Legal Process* and *African Americans and the Living Constitution,* which he coedited with John Hope Franklin and Genna Rae McNeil. In addition to these books, he published numerous research articles and legal papers. Prior to his death, he was writing the third and fourth books in the multivolume series, a book titled *Race and the American and South African Legal Process,* and an autobiography. Finally, the legacy of A. Leon Higginbotham Jr., one of America's most prominent and influential judges, should inspire Black students not only to achieve academic excellence but also to become human rights advocates for all members of society for generations to come.

As part of this special tribute to A. Leon Higginbotham Jr., Hilary Hurd, editor of *Black Issues in Higher Education,* granted me permission to reprint Ronald Waters' article entitled "Judge Higginbotham's Legal Legacy" in *The Black Student's Guide to Graduate and Professional School Success.*

Vernon L. Farmer

Judge Higginbotham's Legal Legacy

The passing of Judge A. Leon Higginbotham Jr., one of the most distinguished African American jurists of this century, has left a gaping void in the leadership of our community that will be difficult to fill. I say this because, even though as a lawyer and judge he dealt with many civil matters, nevertheless, the deep intensity of his commitment to social justice and its expression in his pursuit of equal rights for Blacks was nothing short of legendary.

Indeed, at the time Thurgood Marshall resigned from the Supreme Court on June 27, 1991, there was considerable hope that someone in the Thurgood Marshall tradition would be chosen to fill that vacancy someone whose legal qualifications were outstanding, whose record of service to the cause of equal justice was deep, and whose views were in the sync with the Black community. Thus, Leon Higginbotham's name was prominently tossed up, along with others who also held the values of the civil rights movement close.

Higginbotham was a natural to be considered for the Court and not only because he was a graduate of Yale law. From the time he was named to the federal bench in 1964 at the age of 36, to 1989 when he was elevated to Chief Judge of the Court of Appeals, he had put together an outstanding record of achievement.

So, it was with utter shock and dismay that one witnessed the cruel spectacle of the elevation of Clarence Thomas to the Supreme Court by the right wing conservative element of the Republican Party. With this appointment, the Thurgood Marshall tradition of commitment to civil rights was broken. A Black lawyer who acts as a proxy to the White conservative movement was installed and a voice for the majority of the Black community on the highest court of the land was vitiated. This was a step that has profoundly wounded Black America.

One of the promises of our participation in the political system through the civil rights movement was that our view would be fairly reflected in the political system through men and women who respected that tradition and that legacy. The respect for this legacy is due because it was purchased at the price of personal and collective insult and injury that was meted out solely because of race. Leon Higginbotham was of the generation that experienced such insults directly. He often spoke of the difficulties that he faced while an undergraduate at Purdue University, as a student at Yale law, trying to get a job as a lawyer, in the practice of law—in short, at every step of his development. The experienced men and women of his generation fueled their strong determination to end racism by joining the collective efforts by a variety of groups fighting it.

While Leon Higginbotham Jr. was insulated from direct involvement in the Civil Rights Movement during most of the 60s and 70s as a sitting federal judge, he nonetheless mentored some of the most accomplished civil rights lawyers today.

He went to great lengths to try to call Supreme Court Justice Clarence Thomas to historical accountability. One of his most cited works is his "Open letter to Judge Clarence Thomas from a Federal Judicial Colleague." In this legal memorandum framed as letter, he attempted to remind Justice Thomas of his legal legacy. Thus, he wrote: "While much has been said about your admirable determination to overcome terrible obstacles, it is also important to remember how you arrived where you are now, because you didn't get there by yourself."

So I as many other Americans, Black and White are saddened by the fact that this Titan of the law and champion of the oppressed will no longer be among us. His passing depletes the ranks of those who are uncompromising in their use of the law to oppose racist practices in society. And it does not appear that the avocation of civil rights law is as attractive to the younger generation. As such, the ranks of civil rights law advocates are not receiving the replenishment that is needed to continue to fight against both old and modern racism. There needs to be a fitting memorial to Judge A. Leon Higginbotham Jr. that would insure that the ranks of those trained and committed to civil rights law will continue to grow.

In this, the need for civil rights lawyers is not merely an American avocation related to Blacks. Almost anywhere in the world one travels as an African American, he or she is aware that the world respects the monumental struggle that we have waged for human rights. We should build on this legacy—both domestically and, increasingly, as a part of the global community where the need for human rights is urgent and critical. I believe that this would help to continue to move his community forward—even in his absence.

Dr. Ronald Walters
Professor of Political Science, University of Maryland
Reprinted from *Black Issues in Higher Education 15*(23), 120, January 7, 1999

Acknowledgments

I have had a long-standing commitment and interest in increasing opportunities for Black students to obtain a graduate education. Therefore, it was with enthusiasm that I undertook the task of editing *The Black Student's Guide to Graduate and Professional School Success*. I am greatly indebted to many individuals for their advice, encouragement, and support during the various phases of this research project. A very special debt of gratitude is owed to the sixty-two distinguished scholars, including sixty Blacks, one Native American, and one White American, who wrote chapters and essays for this book. I also owe a great deal of gratitude to the twenty-seven Black students who wrote essays about their personal trials and triumphs in pursuit of their graduate and professional degrees. It is truly the stories that these students describe in their essays that help bring this book to life.

A special thanks is extended to Greenwood Press and Lynn Taylor, Jane Garry, and Marcia Goldstein, for giving me the opportunity to publish the third Black Student's Guide for Greenwood. I am particularly indebted to them for their sustaining support, editorial suggestions, and overall assistance with the manuscript throughout its various stages. I am deeply indebted to Ernesta P. Pendleton and Robby Lindsay for their editorial comments and advice, for without their input this book most certainly would have stagnated at some point. My deep appreciation and thanks are extended to Evelyn Shepherd-Wynn, who worked tirelessly during the three-year span of this research project. Her intelligence, good judgment, and editorial expertise helped to improve the final manuscript considerably. A very special note of appreciation is extended to Octavia Daniels, Angela Morris, and Xanthe Seals, student research assistants, for helping to carry out some of the research and logistical tasks essential in preparing the final manuscript for publication.

I would like to acknowledge with gratitude the editors of the first two Black Student's Guides published by Greenwood Press: William J. Ekeler, editor of *The Black Student's Guide to High School Success,* and Ruby D. Higgins, Clidie B. Cook, William J. Ekeler, R. McLaran Sawyer, and Keith W. Prichard, editors of *The Black Student's Guide to College Success.* Their scholarly work served as a catalyst for *The Black Student's Guide to Graduate and Professional School Success.* Finally, I would like to acknowledge with gratitude all of the Black scholars who came before me and who inspired me to publish this book.

Introduction

This book is the product of the editor's commitment to increasing opportunities for Blacks in graduate education. *The Black Student's Guide to Graduate and Professional School Success* is an informative book designed and written specifically for Black students to help them structure graduate and professional careers. The book provides background information critical to helping Black students make informed decisions about graduate education. In addition, the book guides them through the process of preparing for standardized tests; negotiating admission; finding a faculty mentor; choosing the right field of study; selecting the best curriculum; obtaining teaching, administrative, and research assistantships and internships; adjusting to the campus environment; adjusting to technology; engaging in research and publishing; developing a global identity; maintaining Black pride and self-esteem; interacting with other racial and ethnic groups; and focusing on the overall importance of graduate education. The book draws Black students' attention to the advantages and benefits as well as to the problems and roadblocks they may encounter enroute to a graduate and/or professional degree.

In laying the foundation for writing *The Black Student's Guide to Graduate and Professional School Success*, the editor and his research team examined hundreds of issues of Black publications, including *The Black Collegian, Black Enterprise, Black Excellence, Black Issues in Higher Education, Crisis, Ebony, Jet,* and the *Journal of Black Higher Education,* to identify Black authors from different types of higher education institutions and from varied professions and regions in the nation to make the book a nationally oriented publication. Evidence of exemplary research and publication, teaching and other creative work, community and public service, and career field contribution were the criteria used to identify the authors. The authors selected are viewed by the editor as role models that Black students can emulate in their pursuit of a graduate education. Therefore, in reading the chapters in this book, Black students should look for authors who have succeeded in achieving educational and career goals similar to their own and with whom they can personally identify. All of the contributing authors in this book have been successful, and so can Black students!

The Black publications identified above were examined to develop a number of themes and titles for chapters and essays to be included in this book. In addition, the editor and his research team participated in several National Black Graduate Students' Conferences to solicit input from members regarding the relationship of the themes and titles to the main theme of the book. As a result of the examination of the Black publications and the dialogue with Black graduate students, authors were selected to write chapters and essays addressing the themes and titles of the book. In addition, the authors who wrote chapters for this book were asked to help identify outstanding Black students to write essays describing their experiences in graduate and professional school. All of the authors were given considerable latitude in expressing their own ideas and thoughts. They were asked to be straightforward in sharing their experiences and in offering their advice to Black students. More specifically, they were asked to write from an intellectual and analytical perspective, drawing upon their experiential base of knowledge in easy and understandable language and providing advice and information to Black students on how to prepare for and succeed in graduate and professional school.

The Black Student's Guide to Graduate and Professional School Success is organized into three major parts. In Part I, "How to Become a Successful Student in Graduate and Professional School," twenty Black scholars and one White scholar wrote chapters about how to prepare for and succeed in graduate and professional school. In Part II, "How I Succeeded in Graduate and Professional School and in My Career Field," thirty-nine Black scholars and one Native American from varied professions wrote essays to share experiences that led to their graduate and professional career success.

In Part III, "How Contemporary Students in Graduate and Professional School Are Succeeding," twenty-seven outstanding Black graduate and professional students wrote essays of an autobiographical nature describing their accomplishments. These student essays personify much of the advice and information provided in the chapters and essays in Parts I and II and humanize, personalize, and reinforce the main theme of the book by giving credit where credit is due. In cases where parents, teachers, counselors, coaches, religious and community leaders, or other significant individuals were especially helpful, the students were encouraged to note their contributions. In these essays, Black graduate students recount their problems, their solutions, and their successes.

It is no doubt that in the past, many Black students have been successful in graduate and professional school without being exposed to much of the information in this book. Perhaps, though, many of the problems and roadblocks they may have encountered could have been avoided or minimized had they been able to draw upon the experiences and advice of the authors in *The Black Student's Guide to Graduate and Professional School Success*. Meanwhile, Black students who were not successful in the past may have benefited from it, too.

Finally, the editor strongly recommends that Black students in undergraduate, graduate, and professional school as well as those in other educational levels read this book seriously. It is conceivable that you may wish to read Parts II or III or both before reading Part I because these parts are more inspirational while Part I is more action oriented. Parts II and III should certainly inspire and encourage you to consider a graduate or professional degree. In reading Parts II and III, you will find that the essays written by the authors are so structured that they can be used as road maps describing various routes on your journey to a graduate education. You will undoubtedly discover one or more essays that you can choose to help guide you toward a graduate or professional degree. You will also find that some of the essays as well as chapters will be more beneficial to you than others. Although you may initially choose to read the book in parts, it would be extremely wise to read it in its entirety to become familiar with the process required for entry and success in graduate and professional school as described in Part I. Reading the entire book will help you develop the right questions and arrive at the right answers required to make informed decisions about graduate education. Read them all; make note of what you find to be appropriate and helpful and use it. It is my hope that the chapters and essays in this book will inspire and encourage you to strive for excellence.

In addition to identifying various road maps to follow, you will notice that many of the authors had help along the way and are quite generous in acknowledging the help they received from others during their graduate education. In these chapters and essays, the authors are now attempting to extend a helping hand to you. While reading this book, keep in mind the positive strides that Black students have made in graduate education over the past decades. Read the book not only for the important information it offers but also for the inspiration it provides. Remember, success cannot be achieved without struggle. Therefore, I challenge you to make the sacrifices and the tough decisions necessary to be successful. Finally, *The Black Student's Guide to Graduate and Professional School Success* will help you make intelligent choices in structuring your graduate education. But above all, as you read the chapters and essays, remember, if they could do it, so can you!

Vernon L. Farmer

PART I

HOW TO BECOME A SUCCESSFUL STUDENT IN GRADUATE AND PROFESSIONAL SCHOOL

CHAPTER 1

Making Sure You Have the "Right Stuff" to Be Successful in Graduate and Professional School

ANNE PRUITT-LOGAN

Scholar-in-Residence, Council of Graduate Schools, Washington, D.C.

TIME AND PLACE

A discussion takes place in my office with an undergraduate who is contemplating graduate study. If there is one overriding reason for you to consider graduate or professional study, it is because you have an inquisitive mind and love to learn. You might ask yourself, Why do I want a graduate degree? What can I do with it that I can't do without it? What will it do for me? Is it the earning power that I am seeking? A certain lifestyle? Options for a variety of jobs? Is it that I want to be a role model for other Black students? Do I just want to delay commitment to a career? Am I considering it because my favorite faculty adviser thinks I should? Should I go for a master's degree or a Ph.D.? For an M.D. or an MBA? Do I have what it takes to succeed—in other words, do I have the *right stuff?*

Tom Wolfe's book *The Right Stuff* is about American heroism. It is said that Wolfe began writing it at a time when it was unfashionable to contemplate heroism. He was writing about test pilots in America's manned space program. These were men who lived fast lives with dangerous machines. Wolfe had the reader to understand that these men and their wives were brave beyond compare. Some Black students would contend that at the beginning of the twenty-first century it is unfashionable for them to contemplate graduate study. After all, the economy is good; people are making big money without a graduate degree. Those who are skilled in the use of computers are in demand, and to get a job in that area, one does not need a graduate degree. Besides, affirmative action programs are under attack, multi-cultural scholarship is repudiated, and the need for ethnic studies departments is heavily criticized. So, why should I even think about it?

Consider this: making big money and just getting a job are the wrong reasons for considering graduate study. So is the status of affirmative action. The question has to do with achieving admission to graduate study. It is not about whether one should attend graduate school. And ethnic studies constitute only one academic area of study. It is more about curriculum and pedagogical issues, and not whether to attend. So if you have an inquisitive mind and love to learn, then you are ready to consider whether you have the right stuff to succeed.

A graduate student is distinguished from a professional student. Graduate students are enrolled in graduate degree programs in pursuit of master's or research doctoral degrees that will prepare them for careers in academe, business and industry, or government service. Professional students on the other hand are typically enrolled in degree programs preparing them for practice in fields such as medicine, dentistry, and law. The nature of the programs determines the milieu in which the student matriculates. Yet the demands are sufficiently similar that a discussion of the right stuff can apply to both kinds of study. Both are tough, demanding, and mind-stretching. You never imagined that there would be so much to learn; you never knew that so many people had created vast amounts of knowledge that you are required to learn before you can go further than they went. Course work is intense, concepts are more complex than those presented in your undergraduate education, you have a shorter time for learning, and it seems that you must use every waking hour in this singular pursuit. When I use the term *graduate study,* I will be referring to both academic and professional programs.

Let's consider what's involved in the right stuff—what qualities are required?

ABILITY

Check out your college grade point average. Do you meet the minimum required for the graduate programs that interest you? You should also examine your entire college transcript. Both pieces of information will help you to determine whether you have prepared yourself for the intellectual rigor required for graduate study. They will show not only that you have the intelligence but also that you are focused and goal-oriented—that you can survive some pretty turbulent years.

Notice that I did not specify looking at your grade point average alone. Student performance can vary over the college years depending on a variety of factors. Sometimes the early years are ones of floundering, when there is little interest in a specific course of study. This can change once you select a major and become intensely interested in a field. A situation such as this can be reflected in an overall GPA that is lower than required for graduate study. Examining the grades in your major might reveal a different commentary on your ability. Such a scenario will require some explaining once you apply for admission, but it is important for you to understand this.

Your scores on entrance tests also indicate ability. In the admission process, there is considerable variability in the weight given to scores on tests such as the Graduate Record Examination (GRE). They are the great bugaboo, with much of the research on tests suggesting that Black students—as a cohort—consistently score lower than other students do. This need not be the case, for the great responsibility is on you the student to invest your intelligence—your time and energy—in your studies. You have to produce. If you want to go to graduate school, learn all you can and take advantage of all the resources available to do so. If such tests are required by your intended department, make sure that you learn all you can about the test and prepare well, including taking advantage of coaching opportunities provided by the test makers themselves. (For example, see the GRE Web site: *http://www.gre.org.*)

FINANCIAL RESOURCES

Graduate study is expensive. Depending on the field, you can matriculate on either a part-time or a full-time basis. Those who elect to study part-time tend to do so because of limited financial resources or related obligations. Thus they hold full-time jobs and spread the time for earning the degree over a comparatively longer period of time.

Large numbers of students prefer to study full-time where tuition, fees, books, and materials are only one part of the demands on resources. Housing and travel become added ingredients. If there are family members who depend on you, they must be considered also. Just as graduate study requires money, however, money is available. You should begin to plan early. Apply to the university and academic department that you contemplate attending, and inquire into a select number of financial aid resources outside the university.

Financing for graduate education can take many forms, and it is different from financial aid for undergraduate study. Whereas undergraduate support is based primarily on need, graduate aid is most often based on academic merit. Here again your performance in undergraduate school is significant. Remember that a fine academic record can help you to secure funds for further study.

Financial support for graduate study varies with the degree you pursue and your field of study. Substantially more funding is available for doctoral study than for master's degrees, some fields—such as the sciences—have more funds available than do the humanities and education, for example. The type of support also varies, including assistantships, grants, and fellowships. Some students value a grant or fellowship much more highly than an assistantship because the former suggests that you are not obligated to do any work. In my view, the best of all worlds would include a combination of these types of support. Because assistantships obligate students to interact with professors and other students, they go a long way toward preventing isolation and creating the kinds of networks that are invaluable in graduate study. Take advantage of the opportunity to work in your department. Even if you receive a fellowship, being a research assistant or a teaching assistant puts you in contact with professors and other students. It helps you to become an integral part of the graduate environment. A teaching or graduate assistantship is very helpful because either one helps to socialize you—if you are interested in becoming a college professor—to various aspects of the job.

Have you chosen your field of study? The certainty with which you apply for a field—along with the grade point average mentioned above—is also considered in the award of financial support.

YOUR PROSPECTIVE DEPARTMENT

The administration of graduate study is decentralized. For one contemplating admission, in reality this means that you apply to an academic department that interests you rather than to the university. Graduate departments vary in specialties and emphases. For example, a department of psychology at one university could offer a degree in counseling psychology, whereas a department at another would not. One department could be strong in experimental psychology while weak in clinical. It is important to be able to match your interests with the strengths of a given department so that upon application you can make a strong case for admission based not only on the department's strengths but upon your preparation and interests as well.

Search for departments and universities where the presence of Black students is valued. A diverse faculty is one sign, although such diversity might not be present in your department. Faculty mentoring is another sign to look for. A caring attitude among faculty over and beyond advice on courses to take lets students know that they will be regarded as developing professionals, not just as vessels for the receipt and production of knowledge. Examine notices on the bulletin board about such things as departmental activities for students, content of courses, student organizations, field trips, and visiting lecturers. All of this will give you an idea about the environment that Black students will find at the institution. So do your homework; just as the department is examining your credentials, you should be examining the environment.

YOUR BACCALAUREATE INSTITUTION

Another aspect of *right stuff* belongs to the institution that conferred your bachelor's degree. It should be accredited and should possess a strong record of preparation of students in your major. Professors at your institution should be known—at least by reputation—to colleagues in the department to which you are applying.

Most graduate institutions are pretty large. If you are graduating from a small college, consider your ability to be comfortable in a much larger, perhaps less personal environment. If you are graduating from a single-sex institution—women's college or men's college—consider your ability to be comfortable in a heterogeneous setting. Visit graduate institutions and talk with other graduate students who attended similar undergraduate institutions about their transition.

DELAYING GRADUATE STUDY

Consider whether you have had experience working in your chosen field of study. This might work both for and against you. In some fields—such as education—experience as a teacher goes a long way in solidifying in your own mind that this is an appropriate field for you. In one of the sciences—such as chemistry—a job could work against you if in the intervening years you have failed to keep up with developments in your field. Although there might be good reasons for delaying entry into graduate study, consider what it will take for you to get back into the habit of being a student. After all, being a student will likely reduce your income, and you might then have dependents that you did not have as a college student. Also, your mind might be reluctant to buckle down and study.

REFERENCES

Whether we like it or not, the individuals you have asked—as well as some whom you may not have asked—to support your application for graduate study play a crucial role in your acceptance. These include former professors, supervisors of your fieldwork or internships—persons who can speak about your performance as it relates to your chosen field; they can cite examples of your work with them—they have firsthand knowledge. They should be individuals who are willing to make a prediction about your success in the future. Letters from your minister, neighbors, and the like won't cut it.

YOUR AREA OF STUDY

A variety of experiences can assist you in deciding what your field of study should be. These include course work, internships and fieldwork, and discussions with professors, persons working in the field, and students already enrolled in graduate study. The more certain you are about the area of study, the more convincing you can be in your application for admission.

YOUR HEALTH

Do you have the stamina needed to take the long nights and missed meals, to satisfy faculty expectations at the same time you are trying to satisfy family expectations?

When you get beyond the right stuff discussed above—ability, financial resources, references, and certainty—you should ask yourself whether you have courage enough to stay the course and to be self-directed. Are you focused? Do you know how to organize your life and be goal-oriented? Do you have the ability to delay gratification—to put off those extra activities that are just fun to do or interesting? They can be as varied as attending all of the season's football games or chairing a committee in your Greek-letter organization. The dropout rate is pretty high and is often attributed to the lack of the *stuff* listed above. What I am suggesting is that graduate study involves stress of the kind that you might not have experienced before. Be sure that you listen to you body and take care of yourself. That includes rest and relaxation, exercise, and proper nutrition. Most students master these demands and graduate as stronger individuals. However, if you ever suspect that you are having emotional problems, seek help immediately from campus medical and counseling services.

WOMEN STUDENTS

Although the number of women enrolling in graduate school is increasing, their numbers compared with those of men make them a minority. There are some fields, however, where the number of men and women is about equal and some in which there are more women. Pressures faced by women graduate students are a subset of those faced by all graduate students. Besides the possibility of being in a minority, some women question their fit. Some feel as if they don't belong. They question their competence and doubt their ability to do independent work. Some report problems finding mentors. For some, having to balance the demands of family, work, and school adds to the ordinary stresses of graduate study. Where advisers are concerned, women sometimes feel more comfortable with women faculty members than with men. If you are a woman, it is certainly important to have women to whom you can turn. When considering a prospective graduate department, especially one in a traditionally male field, determine whether there are women present on the faculty to serve as advisers, mentors, and role models.

BEING A BLACK STUDENT

Let me turn to a discussion about being a Black student studying for a graduate degree. This is another subset of more general consideration of the *right stuff* and in some respects parallels my earlier comments about gender. Black students do not constitute a homogeneous group, and whatever I say must be understood in that context. To talk about being a Black student seems to assume that individual identity and group identity are the same. You cannot be identified by a single characteristic. You are a member of multiple groups at the same time. Your blackness will be important depending upon the setting. It will also become salient depending upon, for example, whether you are the only Black student in your department. Graduate study is a demanding undertaking, regardless of race. Yet a Black student will have to deal with the emotional impact of being different. Let's face it. Most institutions granting graduate degrees are predominantly white, and most graduate academic departments are smaller than undergraduate departments you are leaving. Being in the minority may not be new to you, which means that you know how to deal with it. For some others, it will come as a new struggle that must be addressed.

Remembering that racism is practically a hallmark of American society, faculty members and students bring with them the biases that permeate their societies. Even well-meaning individuals offend inadvertently. Nevertheless, offenses do affect the learning environment and thus must be discussed here. I probably do not need to explain stereotyping and discrimination as it pertains to relationships between majority and minority people. They color our attitudes toward ourselves as well as the attitudes of others toward us. What about an attitude that some minority students hold about themselves? It's the belief that we need to be models of some idealized perfect student; we don't need any help. This is demonstrated in unwillingness to take part in study groups, unwillingness to ask faculty members or peers to help for fear of revealing a stereotypic "weakness" or "lack of knowledge." Clearly this attitude will have a negative impact on your achievement. Of course, some or your peers will not invite you to join study groups, in which case you should invite yourself, or start your own. By all means confer with faculty members. They are there to teach; if you don't consult with them, they can't assist you. Have confidence in yourself, but don't be afraid to ask questions. This set of attitudes is often played out in putting pressure on yourself to succeed because you are a minority student. You might find it helpful to confide in your network of friends who are in the same boat as you.

The attitudes of individuals of other races toward you might be influenced by the way they understand affirmative action. Predominant views of affirmative action characterize all Black students as inferior in ability, academic preparation, and financial resources. Fellow students and professors sometimes will say things that reflect these beliefs. I advise you to have confidence in your own ability in order to keep such comments from derailing you.

Some people believe that Black students are admitted under affirmative action guidelines. This means that they believe that admission requirements have been lowered so that you can matriculate. Faculty members who believe this might hold Black students to lower standards of performance. If this happens, you might not be given tough assignments or responsibilities that are given to majority students because it is not expected that you can handle them. In other words, expectations are low.

An attitude that affirmative action has spawned among some Black people (to our detriment) is that we deserve to be held to lower standards—we ought to be given a break, as it were. Nothing could be further from the truth. There is no goal that is worth shoddy preparation or doing just enough to get by. Always strive to be the best that you can be. At the same time, however, realize that you do not have complete control of your destiny. In part, your fate is indeed controlled by others, and some of what happens might, indeed, be the result of racist beliefs.

Although I mentioned your undergraduate college in remarks above about securing admission, there is another aspect that might be especially important for Black students who are graduates of predominantly Black colleges, most of which are in the southern part of the United States. You will find that some of the mores and habits are different in predominantly white institutions—especially those outside the South. Making the transition may result in culture shock. Because a period of adjustment could detract from the ordinary transition to graduate study, it is wise to take advantage of opportunities to visit your future university before you matriculate.

Some Black students believe that White professors cannot adequately meet their needs. It is very important for Black graduate students who feel this way to find a support system and a Black mentor, particularly a Black faculty member. Let me share with you comments from a recent Black Ph.D. recipient from a predominantly White university. She told me that "there was no Black faculty member in the department—someone to give you that sense that you belong there and that there is someone you can go to with your fears, concerns, ideas. It can be very isolating at times. I was fortunate to have had persons like Professor X, Y, and Z across campus that didn't mind listening to me. Personally, I think Black students will need that, because they are usually going into alien territory where they are often given subtle and not so subtle messages that say 'You don't belong here and we don't want you here.' "

It is necessary that you feel that you belong, and it might be your association with Black faculty that helps you to reach that point. On the other hand, you might go to graduate school with a comfortable sense of self and therefore experience little anxiety about your sense of belonging. The key is to develop a good relationship with someone whom you respect and who has your best interests at heart, regardless of race.

Create your own community. If being isolated gives you pause, you can also reach out to Black students in other departments. Even national gatherings of Black students offer community. One example is the National Black Graduate Student Association (e-mail: NBGSA@ccaix.jsums.edu). Take advantage of opportunities to attend national gatherings in your academic discipline. You are likely to meet other Black students who are specializing in your area and thus plant the seeds for a network of scholars. You can share your experiences and thus support each other.

A broader, more carefully developed community is sometimes needed to validate your purpose for engaging in graduate study. Family and friends, for instance, do not always understand the purpose of graduate study—in contrast to professional study like medicine or law. Some might question the time, expense, and forgone income, and even question your sanity. To say the least, these questions become detractors. In order to stay the course, you will have to cultivate a community of supporters—those people who you know are pulling for you.

Some of these folk can be regarded as mentors. To be sure, you will need more than one. Your research adviser will be one. That person will see you through completion of your thesis or dissertation and is likely to help you get a job, write references for you, and guide you in organizing your time. Another mentor might be the one who takes an interest in you and your family or helps you think through a personal crisis. Some mentors will sit and listen to you as you recite your dreams and aspirations, your disappointments, and your quandaries. Each one is critical to your making it through graduate school.

Your community need not be limited to your department or institution; it could be spread over several institutions, and it could involve townspeople in the university community. Many Black graduate students participate in local churches and thereby strengthen their spiritual life. Know that there are people pulling for you. They may not necessarily be those you expect to do so. Include faculty. People who might become supporters don't always approach you; you must take the initiative. Cultivate a community of supporters who will serve your needs in a wide range of ways.

If things are not working out, change majors or even schools. Graduate study is difficult, and there may be very good reasons to shift to a different department or even to drop out altogether. It's one thing to shift directions because you have reevaluated your life situation. It's another to be anxious over one of the many hurdles placed before you. The former reason is reasonable; the latter—the hurdles—with some help, can be taken in your stride. In either case, don't burn bridges behind you. You will benefit from good references from former advisers and professors.

DO YOU STILL WANT TO PURSUE GRADUATE STUDY?

Now that you have considered what it takes—*the right stuff*—I challenge you to remember that we need you—a Black intellectual—among the leadership in academe, in business and industry, in politics, in communities—in every walk of life. The good news is that in the fall of 1997 approximately eighty-two thousand Black students were enrolled in graduate school. That is a substantial group of individuals who had the courage to take such a giant step. It's all about heroism and resolve. The bad news is that they represented only 9 percent of all enrolled U.S. citizens and permanent residents. Furthermore, Black students were only 9 percent of all degree recipients. Note also that most Black people earn degrees in the fields of education, business, and the social sciences. Although it is essential that they serve well in their chosen fields, we need to play catch-up in other fields such as biological sciences and engineering. So don't shy away from study in those fields.

In sum, *the right stuff* includes ability, your prospective department, and your baccalaureate institution. It also includes your decision as to whether you will delay study, the financial resources available to you, the people you invite to serve as references, and how certain you are about your chosen area of study. You must give special attention to your attitude about yourself as a Black person and the way you deal with race in America. If you can say "Yes, I have the right stuff," it doesn't matter whether it's fashionable; it's heroic. You will swell the numbers of Black degree recipients. And besides, you'll have a great time.

CHAPTER 2

Negotiating Admission to Graduate and Professional Schools

WILLIAM E. SEDLACEK

Professor of Education and Assistant Director of Counseling Center,
University of Maryland–College Park

You will receive a great deal of advice on many useful topics in this publication. I am going to concentrate on advice to get into school. I will lead into what to do after you are in school, but that will be dealt with in more detail elsewhere.

YOUR REASONS FOR POSTGRADUATE STUDY

Why do you want to do postgraduate study in this particular area? This may seem like an obvious question, but it is one that you and other applicants will be answering in one way or another in the application process. Have you thought about your answer? Have you read publications or checked the Internet on the field? Have you talked to an adviser or career counselor about the area? Have you consulted with students currently in school in your proposed field to get their reactions? Have you discussed what it's like to work in the field with someone currently employed in it? Do all these things and more before you do anything further. If it looks good, proceed to the next step.

ASSESSING YOUR STRENGTHS AND WEAKNESSES

Do you know your strengths and weaknesses? This is a particularly difficult question for a Black student for a number of reasons. First, you may have less clear information about your potential than applicants from other races have. One of the long-term legacies of racism is that we have not developed measures that are as valid in telling us about your potential as we have for other students. Tests such as the Scholastic Aptitude Tests (SAT), the Graduate Record Examination (GRE), and the Medical College Admission Test (MCAT) don't work so well for you, but many schools will employ them anyway out of habit or ignorance (Sedlacek,1998a,b). So you need a way to figure out how first to evaluate yourself honestly and then to present that information to the school(s) to which you are applying.

I recommend that you evaluate yourself on a set of what I call noncognitive variables. Nearly all schools in all fields will be interested in how you look on such variables, but they will vary in their manner and specificity of assessing them. You may work them into an essay, an interview, a letter, a recommendation, or a phone call, but get them into your application file somehow.

NONCOGNITIVE VARIABLES

Why should you care about noncognitive variables? Because they may help you present some of your outstanding qualities that would otherwise be missed. Sternberg (1985) has suggested that there are three kinds of intelligence: analytic, which is verbal and math problem solving such as we measure on standardized tests; experiential, which is the ability to be creative or adaptive; and contextual, which is the ability to negotiate a system. You may not show what you really can do through your analytic ability and may need to stress your experiential and contextual intelligence in your application. Why? Because dealing with racism in your life has probably caused you to develop those other abilities in order to survive and succeed. It's not fair, and most schools do not understand this or have a systematic way to get at your true abilities, but that's the way it is. This is one of the best examples of racism we currently have in our education system. But you can beat it by making sure *all* your abilities get presented. Table 2.1 describes some noncognitive variables that get at your experiential and contextual intelligence. Many schools in different fields use this list or a similar one (Sedlacek,1998a,b). So check yourself on the list to see whether you are on the high or low side on each scale. Since we are not always so honest with ourselves, have someone who knows you well and can "give it to you straight" evaluate you on the dimensions as well. *Don't hustle yourself.* A key strategy for handling a system is self-knowledge. You may not choose to share your limitations, but you should know what they are. Once you have figured out your strengths and weaknesses, you are ready for the next step.

IMPROVING YOUR NONCOGNITIVE VARIABLES

Can you work on your weaknesses? Yes, the noncognitive variables were designed to provide for your improvement on each. They are changeable characteristics. Work with an adviser or a counselor, a good friend, or a family member whenever possible in order to improve yourself on the noncognitive variables. It's tough to go it alone (see "Strong support person" in Table 2.1). The more time prior to application you have to improve your shortcomings, the better applicant you will make. I will give some advice on working on each of the dimensions, which may be helpful.

Positive Self-Concept

Try to imagine yourself as a student in the program you wish to enter. Is it you? Will you seem out of place? These are common concerns of Black students in graduate and professional school. The key here is not that you feel generally good about yourself but that you feel good about yourself as a student or professional in your field. Discuss these questions with any Black students or professionals you know, and see what things came up for them and how they handled them. Also, remember your strengths. You have gotten this far on your ability. Where do you show it? All those noncognitive dimensions are forms of ability.

Realistic Self-Appraisal

Using feedback to improve yourself is an important positive attribute. The biggest problem you may have is that because of racism not all the feedback you get is accurate. Some will intentionally mislead you; others will not understand the experiences you have had or your cultural context and will give unintentionally uninformed feedback on your abilities. This feedback can be overly positive as well as overly negative. Many who are uncomfortable with you or have lower expectations of you will give you more praise than you deserve. You have to have the ability to sort through the "noise" in the system and know what is useful and what isn't. This is where knowing yourself and having a strong support person who can be honest with you become important.

Understand and Deal with Racism

I have used the word *racism* several times; now I will define it. Racism is action taken by individuals or institutions (e.g., social systems) that results in negative outcomes for members of a certain group, independent of other considerations. Results, not intentions, count here. If an individual or system has the power to influence you, what happens to you is what is important, not

Table 2.1 Evaluating Noncognitive Variables

	HIGH SCORE	LOW SCORE
1. Positive Self-Concept or Confidence	Feels confident of making it through graduation. Makes positive statements about him/herself. Expects to do well in academic and nonacademic areas. Assumes he/she can handle new situations.	Can express reason(s) why he/she might have to leave school. Not sure he/she has ability to make it. Feels other students are better than he/she is. Expects to get marginal grades or challenges. Feels he/she will have trouble balancing personal and academic life. Avoids new challenges or situations.
2. Realistic Self-Appraisal	Appreciates and accepts rewards as well as consequences of poor performance. Understands that reinforcement is imperfect, and does not overreact to positive or negative feedback. Has developed a system of using feedback to alter behavior.	Not sure how evaluations are done in school. Overreacts to most recent reinforcement (positive or negative), rather than seeing it in a larger context. Does not know how he/she is doing in classes until grades are out. Does not have a good idea of how peers would rate his/her performance.
3. Understands and Deals with Racism	Understands the role of the " system " in his/her life and how it treats nontraditional persons, often unintentionally. Has developed a method of assessing the cultural/racial demands of the system and responding accordingly; assertively, if the gain is worth it; passively if the gain is small or is ambiguous. Does not blame others for his/her problems or appear as a " Pollyanna " who does not see racism.	Not sure how the " system " works. Preoccupied with racism or does not feel racism exists. Blames others for problems. Reacts with same intensity to large and small issues concerned with race. Does not have a method of successfully handling racism that does not interfere with personal and academic development.
4. Prefers Long-Range to Short-Term or Immediate Needs	Can set goals and proceed for some time without reinforcement. Shows patience. Can see partial fulfillment of a longer-term goal. Is future and past oriented, and does not just see immediate issues or problems. Shows evidence of planning in academic and nonacademic areas.	Lack of evidence of setting and accomplishing goals. Likely to proceed without clear direction. Relies on others to determine outcomes. Lives in present. Does not have a " plan " for approaching a course, school in general, an activity, etc. Goals which are stated are vague and unrealistic.

16

	HIGH SCORE	LOW SCORE
5. Availability of Strong Support Person	Has identified and received help, support, and encouragement from one or more specific individuals. Does not rely solely on his/her own resources to solve problems. He/she is not a "loner." Willing to admit that he/she needs help when appropriate.	No evidence of turning to others for help. No single support person, mentor, or close adviser can be identified. Does not talk about his/her problems. Feels he/she can handle things on his/her own. Access to previous support person may be reduced or eliminated. Is not aware of the importance of a support person.
6. Successful Leadership Experience	Has shown evidence of influencing others in academic or nonacademic areas. Comfortable providing advice and direction to others. Has served as mediator in disputes or disagreements among colleagues. Comfortable taking action where called for.	No evidence that others turn to him/her for advice or direction. Nonassertive. Does not take initiative. Overly cautious. Avoids controversy. Not well known by peers.
7. Demonstrated Community Service	Identified with a group which is cultural, racial, and/or geographic. Has specific and long-term relationships in a community. Has been active in community activities over a period of time. Has accomplished specific goals in a community setting.	No involvement in cultural, racial, or geographical group or community. Limited activities of any kind. Fringe member of group(s). Engages more in solitary rather than group activities (academic or nonacademic).
8. Knowledge Acquired in a Field	Knows about a field or area that he/she has not formally studied in school. Has a nontraditional, possibly culturally or racially based view of a field. Has developed innovative ways to acquire information about a given subject or field.	Appears to know little about fields or areas he/she has not studied in school. No evidence of learning from community or nonacademic activities. Traditional in approach to learning. Has not received credit-by-examination for courses. Not aware of credit-by-examination possibilities.

the intention of the perpetrator. For example, if you do not get fairly evaluated in your application to school and get rejected, the effect on you is the same regardless of whether the rejection was intentional or unintentional. Also, the society may lose an able professional in the field.

I believe you will encounter racism in a variety of forms wherever you apply or ultimately attend. Some forms will be less important than others. The idea here is how you handle the racism you will encounter. If you see racism everywhere and spend a great deal of time and energy on it, you will probably have little time for study and will burn out and leave or flunk out. On the other hand, if you do not see the racism around you, you will probably not understand the system and how it works and leave it for that reason. Your best position is one where you try to stay ahead of things by watching for examples of racism and then deciding what, if anything, to do about it.

A brief example might be useful here. I had a light-skinned African American male graduate student who was having a tough time figuring out what was going on. Sometimes those around him did not realize that he considered himself Black, and certain derogatory comments about Blacks would come up directly or indirectly. How should he act? Should he call people on their comments? Should he somehow make it clear he was Black in most (some, all) situations? Were his social relationships based on his race? We eventually worked out a system whereby he made a determination of how people were reacting (or not) to his race, and then he would decide what, if any, action to take based on his perceived best interests. The decisions were his and might be completely different for someone else. For example, he decided to argue with a fellow student over what he felt were racist remarks about campus diversity programs, but he chose to overlook departmental policy on choosing a dissertation topic, which he felt made it difficult to study race-related issues. His adviser was a mentor to him but was head of the faculty committee on dissertation procedures.

Some of you might be asking, "Aren't those problems all graduate students have?" While all students must negotiate the system, Black students typically must also factor their race into the equation, which requires more sophistication in dealing with that system. What about historically Black institutions? Surely I don't have to worry about racism there? Unfortunately racism may take different forms, but it is potentially present there also. For example, a program at a historically Black school may be trying particularly hard to show its peers at predominantly White schools that it uses the same high standards and may avoid using more appropriate admissions measures. Make no assumptions about racism. If it's there, deal with it. If not, move on.

How about trying to eliminate the racism? If you have the time and inclination, great, we need it. However, such activity may not help you get into and get through school, which is the focus of this article. For those interested, see Sedlacek & Brooks (1976) and Sedlacek (1995) for some ideas.

Long-Range Goals

Do you plan ahead? Or are you spontaneous and like to see how things will work out? Having a plan, even if you have to change it, is the best strategy in your academic or your social life. Because the system is in many ways set up not to be in your best interests, you must plan and try to stay ahead of it or it may do you in. Make an assessment of your typical planning time and try to stretch it out with some goal setting and evaluation as to accomplishment. Goals can be academic, personal, social, and so on. Keep your goals realistic and realize that you may need a number of smaller, shorter-term goals to reach a bigger, longer-term goal. For example, the goal of finishing medical school would require many subgoals; for example, passing a chemistry course. Those who are selected and succeed in graduate or professional school see interlocking links among their goals. What if you haven't been thinking of postgraduate study in a particular field for a long time? Help the admissions committee see that your interests have been moving in that direction for as long a time as you can. Early school projects, family interests, hobbies, and the like can all be tied in. *Show, don't tell,* whenever possible. Everyone says they are interested at application time. Show some past behaviors whenever possible.

Strong Support Person

Do you have a history of turning to others for help? Or are you a loner? Seeking help and making use of it is a positive attribute. Faculty in professional and graduate school expect it. If you don't look for assistance, it will be assumed that you are doing fine. Here we have another by-product of racism. You may feel that asking for help shows weakness and that someone may say, "What are you doing here?" It may happen, but it is an even greater risk to assume you can handle it alone. In fact, it is common for the very best students to use tutors, advisers, and other resources more than other students do. Find one or more people who can give you the advice and perspective you need. Very often it is useful to work with a mentor who is of another race as well as someone Black. White people may know the system they created and be particularly helpful in enabling you to understand how to work that system.

Successful Leadership

Do others turn to you for advice? Do you influence others in ways you may not think of as leadership, such as in your family or community? Don't only think of formal leadership titles or situations. Be sure to assess as many nontraditional forms of leadership in which you may engage as possible. In order to get some leadership experience, put yourself in situations where you can influence others, such as clubs or groups. A big part of this dimension involves being assertive. One reason leadership experience is so important is that because of racism you may not have had the same opportunities as nonblack students to be a leader, especially in a formal sense in a group. Also, assertiveness is required to work a system that is not going to do well by you unless you call attention to yourself on your terms. Get involved, take action, and develop your leadership skills. Admissions committees love leaders.

Community Service

Community service is really a support variable, but it's turning to a group rather than an individual. Do you have a group (formal or informal) to which you can turn for advice and direction? Is there a group that cares about your development? The group can be a family, a geographically based group, a group based on your race (e.g., a Black student group), or a group with any other basis, but it should function as support for you. Some groups, including families and race-based groups, require more of you than you get back in support. Such groups may meet other needs of yours, but make sure that you find one or more that provides support and that you can access the group while you are in school. This may be an important part of your decision as to where to attend school. If you are away from your support community and cannot turn to it or develop another one on or near the campus, you may have difficulty. Don't rule out e-mail, telephone, or other ways to get the support you need, but make sure the means you have of obtaining support are practical for you.

Knowledge Acquired

What have you learned outside the classroom? Of what you have learned, does any of it apply to your field of study? Think creatively about how it might apply and make the case in your application. This is an important point for people making admissions decisions. An example I knew of involved an African American student who was applying to medical school but had never worked in a hospital or driven an ambulance, two common ways of showing medical interests. However, there were no hospitals near the applicant, and family and community issues occupied her spare time. By detailing her work with community food programs, she was able to show some long-term medical interests. But she needed to package and present her experience in a way that the admissions committee could interpret. She did this in her personal statement and in her interview.

DECIDING WHERE TO APPLY

What schools should you apply to? The answer to this complex question will vary depending a number of considerations. Some are obvious, such as financial concerns. However, don't just go to a school because you are offered money. The school could be a bad fit for you, and the admissions department could just be trying to buy you. Some schools operate a version of slavery by offering money but little else to Black students. Check the situation out carefully. The type of program offered is another important dimension to your decision. Are you interested in counseling or clinical psychology? Law or business? Programs vary considerably, so get all the information you can.

Geography can be important in many ways also. For example, one of my African American female students from the East wanted to study in a small town in the Midwest, but she also was interested in meeting Black males in order to have a social life and possibly find a mate. There were few eligible Black men in the community surrounding the Midwestern school. She eventually chose a school based near a city where there were some Black men. Again, because of racism, there are not always equal opportunities for developing a positive situation for a Black student.

Racial climate of the institution or program is something else you should consider. I tell my Black students to place the racial environment in one of three categories. One such category would be a place with few Black students (or students of color), where people are unaware of race or uncomfortable with it. Is race mentioned at all in the literature or during your visit or by other sources? Do you have to bring up the topic of race and the environment for Blacks in the department or town, as opposed to the issue being raised in a constructive way? A second level of racial environment is one where there are some Black students and faculty and individuals may raise race in a positive way, suggesting that they are attempting to increase the numbers of students of color but are not yet where they wish to be. A third level of racial environment is one where race and racial issues come up naturally in a multi-racial environment. People understand racism and are comfortable discussing it. It is important for you to assess your own interest and ability to prosper in each environment. I have seen Black students be successful in each, depending on their abilities to deal with the respective environments, their expectations, and the other considerations that are involved. I recommend that you check Helms (1992) for a discussion of racial identity and think about how it might apply here.

The last variable in selecting a school I wish to mention is the selectivity of the program. Programs vary a great deal and again you should find out all you can about the credentials of the applicants and see how you fit. Keep in mind that you may be emphasizing things about yourself other than test scores and grades, so don't rule out schools that look out of your range until you determine how they might view your other attributes.

A basic strategy is to think in threes. On each dimension (e.g., selectivity) divide the schools you are considering in three categories (high, medium, and low). Then be sure you apply to one (or some) in each category. Don't apply only to selective schools, those in a certain area, and so on. Applying to a broader range will give you more choices and enable you to avoid having more homogeneous schools all make the same decision about you.

FINAL THOUGHTS

I hope I have given you some new thoughts and ideas to consider in applying to a postbaccalaureate program. I suggest you use the information here, along with everything else in this publication, in pursuing your goals. Good luck! We need you.

REFERENCES

Helms, J. C. (1992). *A race is a nice thing to have.* Topeka, KS: Content Communications.

Sedlacek, W. E. (1995). Using research to reduce racism at a university. *Journal of Humanistic Education and Development, 33,* 131–140.

Sedlacek, W. E. (1998a). Admissions in higher education: Measuring cognitive and noncognitive variables. In D. J. Wilds & R. Wilson (Eds.), *Minorities in higher education* (pp. 47–71). Sixteenth Annual Status Report. Washington, DC: American Council on Education.

Sedlacek, W. E. (1998b, Winter). Multiple choices for standardized tests. *Priorities, 10,* 1–16.

Sedlacek, W. E., & Brooks, G. C., Jr. (1976). *Racism in American education: A model for change.* Chicago: Nelson Hall.

Sternberg, R. J. (1985). *Beyond IQ.* London: Cambridge University Press.

CHAPTER 3

Graduate School Admission in the Era of Hopwood

ELIZABETH K. DAVENPORT

Assistant Professor of Education and Coordinator of Center for the
Professional Development of Teachers, Texas A&M–Kingsville

As a college student in the 1970s, I was faced with the same questions that you are asking yourself now: "Are my grades good enough to get into the graduate school of my choice?" "Should I have participated in more extracurricular activities?" "Whom should I ask for a reference?" "Will my college admission scores be high enough?" It was a personal nightmare—choosing, applying, taking tests, and then waiting for that letter—the letter that would allow me entry into my chosen profession. Applying to colleges and waiting for the admission letter is a college student's rite of passage, a crossroad in your life, an event that marks the change from college to graduate school. It is also an indication of your own promise as a student and scholar. As your wait for vindication of your hard work, congratulate yourself—you have earned it! Remember that many of your peers have not made it this far or have been unable to traverse the educational terrain as well as you have. What happened to Johnny, who sat next to you in kindergarten, or Cindy, who took your boyfriend away from you in middle school? Better yet, where's Freddie, who was so good in chemistry in high school? Finally, what happened to all your friends who entered college with you? Over 50 percent of those students are no longer on college rolls. Each year thousands of promising individuals apply to graduate school, but only a small percentage get in. Some are discouraged when they see the ratio between graduate spaces and applicants, which is twenty-five to one or higher for some programs. Others are turned away or discouraged by the current perceived hostility in academia to the admission of African Americans, Hispanics, and Native Americans to institutions of higher learning. Daily, in newspapers and on television, we are seeing one challenge after another to the concept of affirmative action in college admissions. Therefore many of you will begin this process wondering, "Can I attend the graduate school of my choice in the era of Hopwood?" I answer this question with a resounding *yes.*

AFFIRMATIVE ACTION AND ME

Having been a student in the 1970s, I cannot discount the important role that affirmative action played in my career. I was admitted to the University of Michigan Law School, class of 1975. Although I had applied to other law schools, being a Michigan native, I was always certain that if admitted to U of M, I would attend. I was admitted into what was probably U of M's most ethnically diverse freshman class ever. In my class, the student population was approximately 50 percent female and 7 percent African American. And we, the African Americans, came from everywhere—Houston, Chicago, Detroit, and Miami. After suffering through the Black Action Movement (BAM) strikes I and II, the University of Michigan had embraced cultural diversity by creating an affirmative action policy that included admission criteria that considered race along with a multitude of other factors such as socioeconomic status, extracurricular activities, and whether members of your family were U of M alumni. In the 1970s, civil and racial injustice led to a commitment by U of M, and other universities, to remediate past discrimination in the admission of minorities to this nation's colleges and graduate schools. This social unrest also led to a revived commitment from the federal government to enforce the constitutional provisions of the Fourteenth Amendment of the U.S. Constitution. Therefore I owe my professional career, to a very limited degree, not only to affirmative action but also to the racial and social unrest of the time.

I say "to a limited degree" because, like you, I was in no way guaranteed admission to graduate school. I graduated from high school in 1970 and graduated with honors from the University of Michigan College of Education in 1972. Although my law school admission test scores were low, compared with those of many members of my class, my 3.57 was still impressive. I had also participated in many extracurricular activities. My older brother had also entered U of M Law School the summer before. Finally, like you, because of challenges to the graduate school affirmative action policies happening at that time, I had to wonder whether I would get into the graduate school of my choice.

Once these policies were created, challenges to the affirmative action policies had come quickly. One such case that was discussed during my law school years was *Bakke v. Regents of University of California* (1978). *Bakke* involved the medical school of the University of California at Davis. The medical school had opened in 1968 with an entering class of fifty students. In 1971, the entering class contained one hundred students, a level that remained until the time of the lawsuit. U of C—Davis's first entering class had Asians but no Blacks, Mexican Americans, or Native Americans. To solve this problem, the faculty devised a special admissions program that embraced an applicant rating system that included the candidates' overall grade point average in science courses, scores on the Medical College Admission Test (MCAT), letters of recommendation, extracurricular activities, and other biographical data. Allan Bakke was a White male who applied to the Davis medical school in both 1973 and 1974. He sued, claiming reverse discrimination. The Supreme Court decided that the university must be accorded the right to select those students who will contribute the most to the "robust exchange of ideas," stating that no racial infirmity exists in an admission program "where race or ethnic background is simply one element—to be weighed fairly against other elements—in the selection process." Therefore, despite *Bakke* and cases like it, I was able to graduate from a top law school and attend three other quality graduate schools (New York University, Temple University, and Michigan State University), and you can too.

AFFIRMATIVE ACTION AND YOU

Although I believe that affirmative action programs remain a vital safeguard for protecting equal opportunity, *Bakke* was not the last challenge to these programs. Two events have converged to make minority admissions difficult. In 1995, the University of California system's Board of Regents voted to drop affirmative action in admissions beginning with next year's entering class. In Texas, the U.S. Court of Appeals for the Fifth Circuit, in the *Hopwood* case, barred public colleges in that state from considering the race of prospective students.

Cheryl J. Hopwood et al. v. State of Texas et al., like *Bakke*, concerned the admission of students to a professional school, in this case law school. The plaintiffs—Cheryl Hopwood, Douglas Carvell, Kenneth Elliott, and David Rogers—applied for admission to the 1992 University of Texas law school freshman class. All four were White residents of Texas and were rejected despite having grade point averages of 3.8 and LSAT scores of 39 (equivalent to a three-digit LSAT score of 160). The plaintiffs sued primarily under the Equal Protection Clause of the Fourteenth Amendment. The plaintiffs' central claim was that they were subjected to unconstitutional racial discrimination by the law school's evaluation of their admissions applications. After a bench trial, the district court held that the school had violated the plaintiffs' equal protection rights (861 F. Supp. at 579).

The district court recognized that the proper constitutional standard under which to evaluate the admissions program was strict scrutiny (Id. at 568). The court concluded that it was undisputed that the school had treated applicants disparately based upon the color of their skin. Using the strict scrutiny test, the court posed two questions concerning the law school's admission process: (1) whether it served a compelling government interest, and (2) whether it was narrowly tailored to the achievement of that goal. Under the first prong of the test, the court held that two of the law school's five reasons offered in support of its graduate policy met constitutional muster: (1) "obtaining the educational benefits that flow from a racially and ethnically diverse student body," and (2) "the objective of overcoming past effects of discrimination" (Id. at 571).

However, the Fifth Circuit overturned this decision in 1996 with Judge Jerry E. Smith writing the opinion, as follows:

With the best of intentions, in order to increase the enrollment of certain favored classes of minority students, the University of Texas School of Law ("the law school") discriminates in favor of those applicants by giving substantial racial preferences in its admissions program. The beneficiaries of this system are blacks and Mexican Americans, to the detriment of whites and non-preferred minorities. The question we decide today in No. 94–50664 is whether the Fourteenth Amendment permits the school to discriminate in this way. We hold that it does not. The law school has presented no compelling justification, under the Fourteenth Amendment or Supreme Court precedent, that allows it to continue to elevate some races over others, even for the wholesome purpose of correcting perceived racial imbalance in the student body. "Racial preferences appear to 'even the score' ... only if one embraces the proposition that our society is appropriately viewed as divided into races, making it right that an injustice rendered in the past to a black man should be compensated for by discriminating against a white." (City of Richmond v. J. A. Croson Co., 488 U.S. 469, 528, 1989, Scalia, J., concurring in the judgment)

These events and others (the admission policies of the University of Michigan and the University of Washington are currently being challenged by the Center for Individual Rights) have resulted in fewer African Americans and other minorities being admitted to the University of Southern California, the University of Texas, and many other institutions of higher education. The Wall Street Journal (April 17, 1997) noted that twenty-one African American students have been selected for next fall's class at UCLA's law school—an 80 percent drop from the previous year and the lowest number of African Americans offered admission since about 1970. In Texas, nearly four hundred fewer Black and Hispanic students have been offered admission as undergraduates—a 20 percent decline. However, despite legislation and court challenges, African Americans graduate from college and are being admitted to graduate school daily, and you can too.

MY SUGGESTIONS

Affirmative action, or the lack thereof, will not eliminate your chances of getting into the graduate school of your choice, but poor planning can.

While you are still an undergraduate student, get as much practical experience as possible in the area in which you wish to concentrate; establish good relationships with professors who can later support your graduate school ambitions; and maintain good grades.

I would also like to offer a few suggestions to assist you on your graduate school quest. First, find the higher education program that fits your needs, goals, and objectives. Finding the right school will require research by you and the setting of both short-term and long-term goals. You must set long-term goals, starting in your freshman year, if your goal is to attend Harvard, Massachusetts Institute of Technology, University of California, or any other prestigious graduate school. It will be too late to decide to go to these schools in your senior year. Short-term goals, such as creating an application strategy, can be developed in your junior year if you are a good student and have a pretty good idea about the type of graduate school you want to attend. Finally, if your scholastic record is not quite up to par, you may want to find schools with liberal admission policies—they still exist. In any event, to help you on this quest, you should ask yourself some questions. You can group these into four areas: your goals, your record (grades, recommendations, activities), your finances, and your flexibility.

Your goals may be the easiest to ascertain. You want to be admitted to the graduate school of your choice. However, this choice maybe limited by your record, your finances, and your flexibility. Choosing the right program to apply to is at the heart of every successful application strategy. This decision not only influences your chances of gaining admission to graduate school but also affects the probability of your success in obtaining your degree. Therefore, before selecting the graduate school of your choice, organize your training, qualifications, and program preferences. Once you have chosen a program, match your qualifications. Will your grade point average get you into this school? Will you need a higher score on your graduate admission test? Do you have the financial aid resources to allow you to attend this school?

Geographic location may be important to you also. For some students, family status, friends, relationships, and the like have a bearing on geographic preferences. Do you want to remain in your native state, where tuition may be a bit cheaper, or do you want to apply to other schools where tuition costs are potentially higher? This flexibility or lack of flexibility in geographic location will have a direct bearing on your choice. Finally, there are still colleges and universities with admission criteria that consider race along with a multitude of other factors, such as socioeconomic status, extracurricular activities, and your graduate admission scores. You might do some research in your school library to locate these schools and see whether they fit into your career goals and objectives. Second, once your choice is made, familiarize yourself with the type of financial aid that is available to you. Most graduate student financial aid falls into one of four categories: tuition waivers; scholarships, grants, and fellowships; research and teaching assistantships and traineeships; and loans. Most universities offer tuition waivers (full or partial). They discharge the student from paying tuition and fees and often come in conjunction with other financial aid or a graduate assistantship. Scholarships, grants, and fellowships are based on academic merit, financial need, or both. At Michigan State University, I received a Martin Luther King–Cesar Chavez–Rosa Parks graduate assistantship, and a friend of mine, who is White, did too! For me, the graduate assistantships meant guaranteed employment and free tuition; for my friend they meant in-state tuition, which was then waived by her department. Customarily, research and teaching assistantships and traineeships require some work. The number of hours involved will vary depending on your department. Finally, loans are a fourth source of graduate support. These funds are borrowed from banks, educational institutions, and the like.

Finally, despite *Hopwood* and the action in California, most graduate programs still have specific financial aid funds available for most minorities and students from lower socioeconomic backgrounds.

Third, visit the school. Familiarize yourself with the staff. Determine whether there will be one or more mentors in your program. A good mentorship is the key to a rewarding graduate career. Mentors serve as guides and have interpersonal, organizational, and systems functions (Gilbert & Rossman, 1992). Mentors are important to African American graduate and professional students who face unpredictable fates in the graduate process. For example, according to Claude Steele (1992), from 1977 to 1990, though the number of Ph.D.s awarded to other minorities increased, the number awarded to African Americans dropped from 1,116 to 828. Steele further noted that African Americans also need more time to complete the graduate process. Therefore, you should make sure that your graduate program offers emotional and professional as well as financial support. Mentoring activities in the interpersonal sphere include being a role model and offering acceptance, confirmation and empowerment, counseling, and friendship. At the organization and systems level, mentoring may include sponsoring, coaching, protecting, and introducing the student to others who can advance his or her career.

Fourth, remember you, and you only, are your best salesperson. When creating your graduate admission plans, do not discount the importance of scheduling interviews or the academic purpose or autobiographical part of your application. You know what you are capable of doing. In your application, make a strong case for your admission. If you can schedule an interview, do so. I know of several incidents where a strong interview and a well-written application got students into the graduate school of their choice.

Therefore, never underestimate your own faith and tenacity. I began this chapter by telling you to congratulate yourself for your accomplishments. Always remember that you and your determination are vital components in your graduate career. According to Claude Steele (1992), you, like most of your peers, began school with test scores that are fairly close to the test scores of Whites. However, you are not like most African American students, who the longer they stay in school, the more they fall behind.

[B]y the sixth grade Blacks in many school districts are two full grade levels behind whites in achievement. This pattern holds true in the middle class nearly as much as in the lower class. The record does not improve in high school. In 1980, for example, 25,500 minority students, largely Black and Hispanic entered high school in Chicago. Four years later only 9,500 graduated, and only 2,000 could read at grade level. The situation in other cities is comparable.

Even for Blacks that make it to college, the problem doesn't go away. 70 percent of all Black students who enroll in four-year colleges drop out at some point, as compared with 45 percent of whites. At any given time nearly as many Black males are incarcerated as are in college in this country. And the grades of Black college students average half a letter below those of their white classmates. ... Tragically, low grades can render a degree essentially "terminal" in the sense that they preclude further schooling. (Steele, 1992, pp. 70–71)

Current data reveal that although our representation in higher education has grown in the past decade, it still is significantly below the percentage we represent in the general population. This is especially true at the more prestigious research universities and the most expensive four-year colleges and universities. The data also reveal that many of our educational gains over the past decade are due to the huge increase in the enrollment of African American women in institutions of higher education. Twice as many African American women as men obtain bachelor's degrees and master's degrees. The number of African American women obtaining first professional degrees also increased by 219 percent during the past decade. African American women achieved these performance gains despite lower SAT and ACT scores, more frequent remedial course work, and a greater percentage being first-generation college students than our peers.

Today my journey has taken me to teaching at a Hispanic serving institution. Daily I meet students who, like me and many of you, are the first generation of their family to attend college. They have beaten the statistics, and so have you. You are the exception to the rule; a twenty-first-century version of W. E. B. Du Bois's "Talented Tenth." Let no one set limits for you. You, and you alone, can determine your destiny.

REFERENCES

Gilbert, L. A., & Rossman, K. M. (1992). Gender and the mentoring process for women: Implications for professional development. *Professional Psychology: Research and Practice, 23*, 233–238.

Steele, C. M. (1992, April). Race and schooling of Black Americans. *Atlantic, 269*(4), 68–78.

CHAPTER 4

What It Takes to Be Successful on Standardized Tests

GRE, GMAT, LSAT, and MCAT

BRENDA JARMON

Associate Professor of Social Work, School of Social Work,
Florida A&M University

In a 1997 gathering with members of the press, the presidents of a handful of top research universities were discussing their commitment to diversity. As if with one voice, they said that standardized test scores play only a small part in their admissions processes. Their institutions, they pronounced, are virtually uninterested in SAT and ACT scores. The high-powered buzz of insistence ended abruptly, however, when the presidents were asked whether their institutions issue press releases whenever their average freshman SAT scores go up. The embarrassed silence illustrated the central paradox surrounding standardized test scores—that even though higher-education professionals understand their limitations, especially as an aggregate measure of groups of students, they also know that the general public is impressed by high test scores and considers them of paramount importance (Chenoweth, 1997).

Therefore, this "central paradox" has led me to ask, what are we really measuring? Or, measurement of what? Although "reliably constant," experts say standardized test scores are often misunderstood and misused. I tend to agree. Whether it is the GRE, GMAT, LSAT, or MCAT, a standardized test score should not be the only measure for deciding whether a student will be successful in graduate school. While preparing a chapter for the book *Black in America: When a Ph.D. Is Still Not Enough,* I interviewed a number of individuals with Ph.D.s from across the country to determine what they thought about the GRE. When asked whether the GRE was a significant factor in determining success in graduate school, 95 percent answered with a resounding "no" (Jones, 2002). Some of these leading African American scholars' comments are summarized below.

According to Niam Akbar, professor of psychology at Florida State University, "No one I know has been able to demonstrate its [the GRE's] usefulness." I agree with Dr. Akbar. In fact, one of the things that happened in the early 1970s, when the Association of Black Psychologists (ABP) challenged the American Psychological Association (APA) about its admission criteria for graduate schools in psychology, was the questioning of the relevance of test scores for graduate admissions training. At that time it was found that people were being excluded from graduate school because of GRE scores, but there was no demonstrated evidence that the GRE actually predicted performance. From that challenge, the ABP was able to get the APA to encourage all the programs that they had in fact certified to *waive* the requirement as a major criterion for admission. Please note that this was almost thirty years ago, and the bottom line is that still no appreciable consequence of including the GRE as a part of the criteria has been shown, particularly for African American students. There is some question about how "predictive" the test is for all students, and certainly when it comes to African American students, it's predictive value is even less than it is for others.

Dr. Freddie Groomes, executive assistant to the president of Florida State University, believes that the GRE can be significant as it relates to general screening because it shows the areas that need to be strengthened. However, the score is not a predictor for whether a student will succeed and should not be used in this way.

The Honorable Judge Verne A. Hodge, Territorial Court of the Virgin Islands, indicated similar views related to the LSAT. Judge Hodge stated that back in the 1960s it wasn't so much so that Howard University refused to make the LSAT a prerequisite for admission. It was felt that the exam was biased against African Americans and people of color and could not predict a person's ability to do well and blossom in law school. Judge Hodge took the exam though and noted that Howard University to date requires it for admission. But it is not the only criterion considered.

Dr. Israel Tribble, president and CEO of the Florida Education Fund, uses the McKnight model as an example of why the GRE is not a good predictor of success in graduate school. The McKnight doctoral program was designed to recruit, retain, and nurture Black Ph.D.'s for the state of Florida. In his book, coauthored with S. David Stamps, *If You Can Walk, You Can Dance; If You Can Talk You Can Sing* (1995), the McKnight model data reveal that the McKnight model works, in that it is an effective mechanism for graduating minority and other financially disadvantaged graduate students. For example, data show that many of the traditional assumptions, such as an overriding value placed on GRE scores and the devaluing of graduates from historically Black colleges and universities, do not hold true. Graduate and candidate students in this study came to their graduate programs with GRE scores ranging from a high of 1350 to a low of 550. Further, when graduates and candidates of predominantly White colleges and universities were compared with those from historically Black colleges and universities, no significant differences were found. I agree with Stamps and Tribble's (1995) assessment:

As we move into the 21st Century, it is going to be essential that America provide educational opportunities for all of her citizens from kindergarten through graduate school. Granted, all Americans will not attend graduate school, but it will be necessary for graduate schools to move away from the paradigm that has traditionally favored the white male student with the highest GRE scores and those who have graduated from predominantly White colleges and universities. (p. 135)

As a McKnight graduate, I will use my own case as an example to further illustrate why I believe " 'I will' is more than IQ." I became a McKnight doctoral student in August 1986. I left a job as director of an alternative school for pregnant and parenting teens to attend Florida State University's School of Social Work as a McKnight doctoral fellow. This was a major career change for me, as I was making a decent salary, owned my home, and had successfully completed the M.S.W. program at Delaware State University. Why on earth would I want to leave my job and home, move to Florida, and live off of ten thousand dollars a year to pursue a Ph.D.?. For me, it was about the opportunity to live on a college campus, and to have someone else pay for it. Living on a college campus was important to me because I had dropped out of high school at fourteen due to pregnancy. In short, I was the mother of two children by the time I was fifteen years old. Additionally, my A.A., B.S., and M.S.W. degrees were obtained while I worked full-time and raised my son and daughter. I spent ten years of night school earning the A.A. and B.S. degrees and two more years of night school to earn the M.S.W. By no means was I the "traditional" college student. Therefore, when the McKnight opportunity came and I was selected as one of twenty-five students in the country to receive this generous fellowship, I accepted. Little did I know there was more to accepting the fellowship than agreeing to come to Florida.

As a former high school dropout and pregnant and parenting teen, who took her first college entrance test in 1970, I had self-doubts about being successful in higher education. Though I am not able to recall my exact test score in 1970, I do recall that it was below the average, and there was much discussion regarding whether I could do college work. My heart sank. Immediately, I made an appointment to talk with a counselor. After I finished telling him that I had dropped out of school at the age of fourteen and was the mother of two children by the time I was fifteen years old, the counselor developed a deeper understanding that persistence, patience, dogged determination, and commitment were present. His attitude changed, and I was granted the opportunity to pursue an undergraduate education as a continuing education student. Interestingly, in 1992 I was one of five persons in the country to win the Outstanding Adult Education Award from the U.S. Department of Education—another testament to my belief that " 'I will' is more than IQ."

Certainly I did not see any reason not to attend college, especially since I was a secretary at Delaware State University and I could take college courses for free. Survival to me was making sure that my son and daughter had every opportunity to learn the importance of an education. In order for me to show my son and daughter the value of an education, I had to demonstrate to them that getting an education was important—so important that I was willing to attend night school to obtain my degrees. Yes, my test scores may have been low, and those who determined whether or not I got into Delaware State University may have misunderstood or misused my low score, but my determination, my drive, and my will to succeed overpowered that low score!. I say to you today that adopting an "I can" attitude is one way to propel you to the next level. However, let's be clear here that adopting an "I can" attitude is not the only thing you need to do to be successful on standardized tests. This was my test and challenge because prior to being accepted for the McKnight Doctoral Fellowship Program, my GRE scores were a sum total of 750 and my graduate school GPA was 3.7. I am told by the McKnight program that when Florida State University was making a decision about my admission application, my GRE score became a serious issue and doubts abounded about whether I could be successful in the Ph.D. program. It is my understanding that Professor Merrill Hintaka took them on. She insisted that the committee review my record from a holistic perspective, noting from whence I had come and my high GPA, not to mention the fact that I had already acquired three degrees. But more important, she thought the fact that I had persevered, persisted, and coped with some extraordinary situations in life warranted more consideration, despite my low GRE scores. She believed beyond a shadow of a doubt that I would be an asset to Florida State University. Dr. Israel Tribble echoed her sentiments and advocated for me as well. Guess what? The committee made a decision to put me on the "alternate list" for acceptance. In doing so, they listed me as the number one alternate. I was accepted as a full McKnight fellow in May 1986, and in August 1986 I began my Ph.D. journey. I successfully completed the Ph.D. in 1992—a prime example that " 'I will' is more than IQ."

Since standardized tests have been the norm for many admission committees in colleges and universities around the country, and it appears that they may be a part of the criteria in the twenty-first century as well, being successful on standardized tests will require early intervention from the African American community and the education community in general. Based on my twenty-five years of experience in education, I agree with Dr. Tribble's basic assumptions about the African American community and its stance toward education:

1. African American children, as well as other socially disadvantaged children, come into this world capable of learning—barring brain damage or some other debilitating social, psychological or physical infirmity.
2. The African American community cares deeply about education and possesses an abiding commitment to the process and the institution. Our community understands that the progress of individuals and the collective community depends almost unilaterally on educational achievement.
3. The Black community has demonstrated the ultimate in "religious faith" about schools and expects them to do the best possible for their children. (1992)

I believe these three assumptions are essential to educational success. To restate, schools and teachers must believe that Black children can learn. In fact, the communities from which Black children come are steeped in historical supplication regarding the importance of education. For example, Mary McCleod Bethune built what is now Bethune Cookman College with $1.50.

Finally, the strong faith exhibited by the Black community can be harnessed to assist the schools in being more successful at providing a positive and productive education experience for each child. In short, we must help the education community to see Black children from a "strengths perspective." It is difficult when one is labeled in kindergarten as a "slow learner," incidentally from a standardized test score. That label is likely to follow that student throughout his or her primary education days, so that by the time he or she arrives to take the GRE, GMAT, LSAT, or MCAT, he or she may lack the confidence and self-esteem to be successful on the test. Early intervention becomes paramount in terms of preparing our children for standardized testing. This type of intervention should begin in the home; however, the schools can play a significant part as well. For example, the issue of nature versus nurture is one that we understand and recognize, and it is clarified by the realization that it is time to wipe clean historical inaccuracies about minorities so that accurate information can produce new ideas and new understandings. For example, a multi-culturally based curriculum that recognizes the contributions of African Americans and other minorities is absolutely essential in a pluralistic society. When children cannot relate not only to the subject matter but also to the purveyors of that subject matter, the inability leaves a negative effect on their ability to learn.

New strategies for improving achievement and performance have to be bolstered, nurtured, and reinforced from outside the school setting. Therefore communities must initiate and develop strategies for motivating, mentoring, nurturing, and loving all of their children. Short of some massive efforts on the part of caring adults and communities, many of our Black children will still not be prepared for standardized testing. The African proverb "It takes a village to raise a child" is critical to this effort. For example, as a young child growing up in Selbyville, Delaware, in the 1950s and 1960s, I attended an all Black elementary and middle school. All of the teachers were Black, as were the pastor, the counselor, and the gym teacher, all of whom lived in my neighborhood. But more important, the *expectations* each had for my academic performance operated from a "strengths model" rather than from a deficit model. My teachers as well as teachers from that generation had high *expectations* of me. They taught from a caring, concerned, and committed stance—a stance I am not sure is prevalent in some of today's early education arenas. For example, if the teacher does not believe that the student is capable of learning, then he or she will tend to have low expectations of that student. If children and adolescents sense this from their parents, their teachers, and most adults in their lives, then they are less likely to excel in school, thereby not "expecting" to even be considered for college let alone prepare for the SAT or ACT tests. It is has been my experience when we have high expectations of our children, they will rise to the occasion. Perhaps we can all take lessons from our ancestors.

Another significant way in which Black students preparing to take standardized tests can use the " 'I will' is more than IQ" concept is by adopting a formalized networking and support system so that they can be supportive of each other. Forming study groups, exchanging materials related to these types of tests, and uplifting each other can go a long way to alleviate the fear Black students and most other students have regarding these tests. Also, members of this support group or someone to confer with can indeed be family members, friends, or peers, but having a mentor is particularly important.

Mentoring is critical to the " 'I will' is more than IQ" notion. Studies abound that have shown the effects of mentoring on young children, adolescents, and adults. Mentoring can serve as a preparation tool to increase the success of students taking standardized tests. We also know that developmental theorists state that zero to six years of age is a critical time in the lives of our children. It is crucial that at an early age our children be exposed to positive role models and mentors. The majority of the most successful persons I have had the opportunity to address postulate that a positive mentor contributed to their success and helped them to achieve an "I can" attitude, which in turn helped them to become successful. Often they say it is a mother, father, grandfather, or grandmother. Others have mentioned a teacher, a coach, a pastor, an aunt or uncle, a sister or brother. The bottom line is that in order to prepare our children for the new millennium, positive strokes, mentoring, and caring adults are some of the keys to successful matriculation toward higher education.

A lot of anecdotal and some research evidence indicates that Black and Latino students need more time than White students to adjust to college. But once they "get on their feet," they perform equally or better. Gretchen

Rigole calls this the "late bloomer theory" and has proposed research on that subject as well, but so far the College Board has yet to do it (Rigole cited in Chenoweth, 1997, p. 19). Interestingly, the College Board, which administers the SAT, LSAT, MCAT, and other standardized tests, claims only that the SAT correlates with first-year grades a little less than half the time (42 percent). In other words, according to Karin Chenoweth (1997),

> Students at a particular school who scored highest on the SAT wind up with the highest grades in the first year of college a little less than half the time. High school grades correlate with first year college grades a little better (48 percent). When combined, the SAT and high school grades can be used to predict freshman year grades a little more than half the time (55 percent). That's it. The College Board does not claim anything more. It has nothing to say about later college performance—not even about the likelihood of the student to graduate. (p. 19)

I believe that the SATs and ACTs fail to take into consideration two important things: student motivation and the university's ability to intervene, to teach students and to motivate them.

There are all kinds of discrepancies and limitations that have brought standardized testing under attack for decades from education reformers who say two things: first, that the SAT and the ACT are not good measures of academic aptitude and are biased against women, African Americans, Hispanic Americans, and children from poor or uneducated homes; and second, that the tests are used inappropriately, compounding the unfairness.

The most vigorous of the groups opposing the widespread use of standardized test scores is FairTest, which is funded by the Ford Foundation, the Joyce Foundation, the Rockefeller Family Fund, and others. People connected with it include Dr. Deborah Meier of the Annenberg Institute for School Reform; Chuck Stone of the University of North Carolina, Chapel Hill; Dr. Asa Hilliard of Georgia State University; and Dr. Howard Gardner of the Harvard Graduate School of Education. Despite such backing, however, FairTest has had relatively little success in denting the public perception that standardized test scores are valid measures of success.

Perhaps the most profound example of how the widespread acceptance of standardized scores is affecting educational policy is the way affirmative action is being dismantled because of them. In *Hopwood v. the State of Texas,* four White students claimed that they deserved admittance to the University of Texas at Austin law school more than Hispanic students who had been admitted. Their case rested on their slightly higher Texas Index scores, a combination of college grade point averages and scores on the LSAT, the law school version of the SAT. A panel of the Fifth U.S. Circuit Court of Appeals agreed with them in 1996 and dismantled the university's affirmative action program on that basis (Chenoweth, 1997).

In another odd twist, a different panel of the same court ruled in 1997, in *Ayers v. Fordice,* that Mississippi's use of ACT scores as the basis for scholarships was discriminatory against African Americans. But the ACT is still used as a basis for admissions in that state. Only those students with minimum scores can get into the prestigious University of Mississippi, for example, thus eliminating many of Mississippi's Black students, who score consistently lower on ACT tests than White students do (Chenoweth, 1997).

During the fall semester of 1999, Florida governor Jeb Bush announced his "Florida One Plan" for the state. His plan eliminates consideration of race, ethnicity, and gender in admissions to the state university system. In exchange, the plan offers scholarship dollars to high school students who graduate in the top 20 percent of their high school class. In my years of experience in education I have seen that few Blacks place in the top 20 percent of high school graduating classes. Obviously, the governor's plan has drawn much criticism from those in favor of affirmative action and many educators in the state (Jamilah, 1999).

Following are other key factors contributing to being successful on standardized tests and adopting an " 'I will' is more than IQ" attitude:

1. Spiritual grounding and belief in oneself and one's ability to succeed
2. Preparation, persistence, and perseverance
3. Very good study habits and skills in preparation for the test
4. Plenty of rest and a good night's sleep the night before the test
5. The motivation and inspiration to be successful
6. Willingness to ask for help when needed
7. The determination never, ever to give up on your goals, your dreams, and your aspirations

It is absolutely essential that we begin the nurturing process early in children's and adolescents' lives. I believe that this will give them a head start on exposure to the aforementioned key factors contributing to their success related to preparing for standardized testing. Graduate admissions offices around the country are vying for the candidate who does well on standardized tests; however, some graduate admissions committees have the foresight to recognize a holistic approach, which in my opinion requires us to view the candidate from a "strengths" perspective. The GRE, GMAT, LSAT, and MCAT are only one predictor, not the only predictor.

REFERENCES

Chenoweth, K. (1997, September 4). A measurement of what? Although "reliability constant," experts say standardized test scores are often misunderstood and misused. *Black Issues in Higher Education, 14*(14), 18–25.

Jamilah, E. (1999, November 25). Bush-whacked in Florida. *Black Issues in Higher Education, 16*(20), 16–19.

Jones, L. (2002). *Black in America: When a Ph.D. is still not enough.* Sterling, VA: Stylus Publications.

Stamps, S.D., & Tribble, I. (1995). *If you can walk, you can dance; If you can talk you can sing.* Silver Spring, MD: Beckham House Publishers.

Tribble, I. (1992). *Making their mark: Educating African-American children.* Silver Spring, MD: Beckham House Publishers.

CHAPTER 5

Choosing the Right Field of Study

DOROTHY V. SMITH
Conrad Hilton Professor of History, Dillard University

This chapter is a brief attempt to acquaint potential graduate and professional students with some of the complex issues they will face when they pursue graduate study. Although faculty members and administrators might find this chapter useful, it is written for Black undergraduates for the express purpose of preparing them for their graduate school adventure. The chapter is not an exhaustive probe, and it is not designed to speak only to the broad topic "Choosing the Right Field of Study." Instead, it offers a brief assessment of the graduate school experience.

This chapter includes information on education and preparation at Historically Black Colleges and Universities (HBCUs); the transition from undergraduate to graduate and professional schools; and finally, the many social, political, racial, and gender issues that students will encounter in their graduate school experiences. These issues should be given serious thought by both Black students and academicians because the problems of Black students are very real and, if not addressed, can be disastrous not only for Black students in particular but for the nation in general. We all suffer when approaches to education lack diversity.

When applying to graduate and professional schools, most undergraduates give a great deal of thought to the school's location; the availability of scholarships, fellowships, and financial aid; the diversity and gender ratio of the student body and faculty; the graduation track record of minority students at the university in the undergraduate's field; and, above all, the scholars who will be assisting them with their career choices. These are major concerns, but others of equal importance are the strength of the department to which students are applying and the productivity of faculty who will direct their research. Students need to be very clear about their area of interest because research requires a genuine commitment. If students are not committed, they can easily abandon the project and fail in their pursuit of graduate degrees.

Students must be willing to fight for the research topics they are interested in by showing the importance of the topics to their field of study. The topics that students are interested in are often different from those in which professors have expertise or, for that matter, interest. Students should choose topics they believe need to be explored rather than topics the professors want to be explored. Doing this takes courage because professors have a major impact on the completion of graduate students' research projects. It goes without saying that the writing of a dissertation is one of the most serious endeavors in which graduate students engage, if not the most serious.

Unfortunately, many students compartmentalize graduate school responsibilities, and as a result, they do not give serious thought to research topics early in their studies. They begin looking for a research adviser only after they have completed course work and the qualifying examination. Given the importance of the dissertation, however, finding an adviser should be a priority soon after students enter graduate school. Although they might not know all of the professors in the department, students should talk to other students and professors about the research topics they want to pursue. Doing so could provide students with excellent clues as to the professors' philosophy, their relationships with students, and—of major importance— their track record with minority students. The professor others suggest might not be the professor the students need, but identifying someone early on allows students an opportunity to be selective before making such a major decision. When doing research on professors, students should do their homework first in order to be clear and informed about the kinds of questions they want to raise. Students should not select an adviser based on race or gender, but rather on the professor's availability, expertise in the topic under research, and commitment to students. Students must be comfortable with and have confidence in the advisers who direct their research.

Select a topic that can be completed within a reasonable period of time: two to four years. Students have to realize that they probably will not write the final work on the topic, and if they do, it does not have to be a part of the dissertation. Research thoroughly, but know when enough research has been done. Understanding and piecing together the research is tedious. To that end, be prepared to do many drafts of the work. Students must always keep in mind the persons who will be reading the drafts by trying to satisfy as many of their concerns as possible.

Know the specific requirements of the department to which you are applying. Some general questions that may be useful are Do you need a specific number of courses to complete the program? Should the courses be in a particular area? How many fields of study are necessary? Is there a prescribed number of courses in each area? Will you be tested in all areas? Will the exams be oral, written, or both? What is the language criterion? Will you be responsible for teaching or research duties? If so, how much, and who will supervise? What is the general time frame for completing course work? How will the dissertation committee be selected? Certainly other questions will surface, but if you have some of these answers, the path will be smoother.

Once students have decided to pursue a graduate degree, they must prepare mentally, socially, and financially for the transition from the undergraduate experience to the graduate or professional experience. An important issue is how well the students know themselves. This is important because it will be essential to live virtually in solitude. Solitude is profound for the mastery of any subject. This is important also because the support contingency available at small colleges and HBCUs is rarely available at graduate or professional schools. Students coming from HBCUs must realize that they are coming to graduate school with strikes against them. Although they were aggressively recruited and can compete anywhere, they are usually considered to be less qualified than other students. This assessment is made because most Whites do not believe that real education takes place at Black schools. In fact, most recruiters believe that education at Black schools consists primarily of Black rhetoric and Black history. Of course, this is far from the truth. In most instances, Black curricula mirror that of White institutions. In fact, HBCUs do such a good job of teaching Black students about White America and its opportunities that students confront race and gender issues for the first time in a serious way only when they enter graduate school.

At some point, it is hoped in the very near future, HBCUs will realize, accept, and celebrate their uniqueness as positive features of who they are. Ironically, Black studies has never been the major emphasis of HBCUs. Furthermore, if Blacks need financial assistance, the need is immediately equated with inferiority. Black students are made to feel that they are being accepted because that particular school decided to give them a break. This is far from true, because Black students certainly qualify for general admission. However, if the idea of improper credentials takes hold, the students can be made to feel beholden for the opportunity and begin to doubt the quality of the education they received at Black schools. They often accept that their destiny is to survive and not challenge erroneous assumptions, because they have been allowed a rare providence. This is an early lesson in psychological warfare and could result in the students believing the propaganda. The tremendous amount of work required, often coupled with teaching and research assignments, leaves precious little time to do anything of a social nature. Students must, therefore, choose wisely the social activities in which they wish to engage.

There are many issues in the Black experience that need to be explored. Black students in graduate school must be ever mindful that the educational establishment and many White professors are not convinced that the topics selected by Blacks are worthy of study. Black students have to be strong and clear about the direction of their research. They have to make the best case they can for their research, but they also must understand that often they will not prevail. They cannot become so disgruntled with the process that they refuse to continue to pursue scholarship. Their goal should be to acquire the degree and position themselves to do the kind of research they feel will make a difference for the academic community in general and the Black community in particular.

Reading often becomes the outlet for survival. Sometimes it is reading trying to get caught up for class assignments. Other times it is reading just trying to maintain sanity. Most students coming from small schools and HBCUs are faced with reading lists that overwhelm them. They must learn early that they cannot read every text assigned. However, they must read enough to be familiar with the topic and know the advantages and disadvantages of the readings. Small schools and HBCUs simply cannot offer the same number of courses that larger colleges and universities can. This does not mean that the students from these schools are not prepared for graduate work. Instead, it means that they will have to fill in gaps that others may not have. Students soon find themselves competing with persons who seemingly have read everything. As a result, they must spend a tremendous amount of time understanding the new challenge, the professors, and other students.

Black students are often interested in topics about the Black experience, especially when they get very little from the courses in which they are enrolled. They see this as an opportunity for self growth. Black history tends to be presented in segments and fragments, rarely holistically, and American history is presented in chauvinist traditional ways. Despite all of our education and attempts at integration, Black students are still expected to be experts on race and poverty and women are expected to be experts on gender during class discussions. These expectations are both a burden and an opportunity for students. They present an opportunity in that others hear students' analysis of various issues. They present a burden, however, when others sometimes dismiss alternative views that do not conform to the norm. Black students are often seen as too emotional and too sensitive to racial and gender issues to be rational. This kind of debasing is often led by the professor.

Most Black students see higher education as a dual obligation and responsibility. They seek to better themselves and know that they must compete successfully with everyone in order to earn a degree. At the same time, they realize that they must gain additional insight about themselves and their communities in order to make a substantial difference for the rest of their lives. Black students do not see education as an end in itself. They are cognizant that whatever position they will attain in life, they will be expected to be the experts on race, gender, or both. They cannot pursue education solely for personal aggrandizement. They must give something back, for they have been helped by others along the way. They always have to remember that they did not get where they are because they were so smart, but rather because they were the beneficiaries of sacrifices made by others. Blacks who have attained an education must assume responsibility for the less fortunate among their people. Educated Blacks must give voice to those in the Black community and in the academic arena who have no voice. Blacks who do not go this route are often seen as having sold out by their peers and others in the community.

Many of the myths and stereotypes in society about race and gender have been perpetuated by historians. Rather than being intentional, this was probably the result of socialization, training, and the tendency of most people to go with the status quo. Knowing this to be the case, Black students have to dedicate themselves to seeking the truth, conducting research, and correcting past errors. This is not a responsibility exclusively for Black students, but often they take the lead because of the manner in which Blacks have historically been portrayed. This often means that the most blatant racist and sexist assumptions about race and gender must be confronted. However, students bold enough to confute such notions are generally prime targets for ridicule. They are labeled as racist, feminist, or sometimes antisocial and too sensitive to such issues. However, if they are serious about their education and the education of others, they must take such positions. The challenge has to be grounded in sound ideology and not in emotion and rhetoric. It is also important to realize that not all racist and sexist statements can or should be challenged, because otherwise precious little time would be left for the discussion of other topics.

Black students confront racist and sexist statements throughout their stay at graduate universities, and consequently they must choose their battles wisely. They cannot afford to become frustrated if others do not support their position. They must realize that the goal is for them to get the best education they can, thus placing themselves in a position of sharing their knowledge with others. They must be prepared to take the road less traveled without alienating themselves. Their fellow Black classmates might not support their position, but that in itself does not make the position incorrect. They might truly disagree with the position or fear that support for another Black student could jeopardize their chances for completing the program.

Black students must always be prepared to participate in study groups. They cannot be dismayed if the study group moves several times during the course of the semester and everyone else knows where the group is meeting. Study groups provide a number of invaluable experiences, such as allowing Black students to analyze important issues and to challenge themselves and their peers. Peers are often very useful because they sometimes understand the position of the Black student and during class discussion that position is rendered by the peer. Black students know and realize that the position is theirs, but at that stage, it does not matter because that peer has accepted what has been said. Often in the classroom Black students are overlooked or a White student has to articulate their position, although they have clearly stated the case. While Black students are very visible on the campus at large, somehow, in the classroom, they become invisible and without voice.

The social scene is especially difficult for single Black females. Seldom is there an opportunity for these women to get a date on campus, or even to be recognized as women. Black males in advanced degree programs are very limited, for a number of reasons, and those who are enrolled are either sought out by or in pursuit of women in other racial or ethnic groups. Black women, for the most part, are left to go it alone. The paucity of Black males and the large number of Black females in the educational market make it a challenge for Black women to engage in social conversation with Black men, not to mention going out on a date. Understandably, they use other avenues as social outlets, among them churches, recreational facilities, and theaters in the city. Negotiating the social scene becomes time-consuming and expensive as well. Some Black women start to believe that they are unattractive and can never be totally successful women and scholars. The other side of the coin is that some Black women hear that they are attractive (almost always in a sexual context) but never that they have anything to offer academically. Both scenarios leave Black women feeling inadequate and uneasy about the future. Often they form social groups in order to deal with the multiplicity of issues confronting them and to enable themselves to continue the fight.

Black males also have problems of equal concern. They are truly an endangered species. Once they get to the graduate or professional school level, they are often perceived as more of a threat to the power structure than are females. They are expected to emulate White males in dress and demeanor, but they are not expected to date White females. Since Black males are appreciated principally as jocks, they are seldom appraised as serious scholars. Many Black males see gender first and race second. Understandably, then, they see little commonality with the single Black female. Many adhere to the notion that Black females are so dominating that Black men should get as far away from them as possible. Others seek friendship but no personal relationship because they see Black women as pushy women who are obstacles to their success.

Black males and Black females have to acknowledge a common ground and support each other. Black students simply do not have the time or the numbers to be divisive. Plainly, they cannot rely on pseudo-research that indicates that a power struggle exists between them. Neither Black males nor Black females possess any real power. The disagreement, then, cannot be about power. Blacks cannot get caught up in the same gender discussions as

Whites because the issues are very different. Instead, Black students have to talk about substantive issues, discuss class assignments, and concentrate on how to get out of school. In the final analysis, their lives are intertwined.

Despite the many obstacles, Black students must continue to pursue graduate and professional degrees and at greater proportion than what is the current norm. Graduate and professional students must recognize that they cannot solve all institutional problems of race and gender. Others before them have endured to complete the programs, and they must do the same. Not all professors are racist and sexist; nevertheless, students need to be prepared for those who are. And, in the final analysis, if such students can find a comfort level, while at the same time remembering who they are and why they are in school, they can and will be successful in their fields of study and life.

CHAPTER 6

Study Habits and Techniques

When and How to Study for Maximum Effect

LISA PERTILLAR BREVARD

Dean of Humanities and Associate Professor of English
and African World Studies, Division of Humanities, Dillard University

MAKE APPOINTMENTS WITH YOURSELF

It is crucial to schedule times for research, reading, and writing. Use a standard itinerary book to note appointments for class times, meetings with professors and university administrators, and most important, the times for you to *commit* to starting and completing your research and writing. Often graduate students make time for everyone and everything but themselves. By placing your research and other educational requirements on a timetable alongside everything else, you give them the priority that they deserve and are more likely to follow through. While enrolled in courses, work on your final projects *every day*. Upon completing required course work and examinations, make regular appointments with yourself to write something related to your master's thesis or doctoral dissertation *every day* (an outline, paragraph, or even a chapter, if possible). Consistency goes a long way.

ATTEND TO ADMINISTRATIVE REALITIES

Department and graduate school secretaries are among your most important administrative allies. They can inform you of approaching deadlines affecting your time-to-graduation and also advise you on professors' work habits. Many students make the mistake of completing the final phase of academic work without regard to institutional deadlines. There is nothing worse than pushing to complete the academic work for a degree and then being forced to wait a full semester or even an academic year to graduate, simply because required paperwork has not been filed. Make sure that important papers such as your application for degree are filed on time. Department and graduate school administrative requirements and deadlines are often very different, and some forms also require professors' or deans' signatures before they can go into effect, so you will want to file your papers during the academic year whenever possible. At the beginning of every semester, meet with the department secretary to find out what paperwork, if any, must be filed. Then repeat this step at the graduate school. At the end of every semester, request an official transcript to make sure that the registrar has current information. Make and keep copies of all administrative paperwork filed in the department and graduate school.

RESEARCH AND READ EFFICIENTLY

In beginning research on any topic, ask a professor or librarian to suggest a solid scholarly book or Internet resource with substantial bibliographic or other references—these often become your starting point for investigating that topic. Often students have relatively little trouble with locating resources, but they do experience trouble in two areas: obtaining research materials and using them efficiently.

Be sure to contact the library or research facility ahead of time to find out rules and restrictions on accessibility of research materials or specialists. To obtain materials faster, one technique is to file multiple requests for the same item at different research facilities, and then utilize the material that arrives first. (To remain on good terms with the secondary research facility, be sure to cancel the unused order.) If you are investigating several resources in person but are restricted as to the number of materials you may investigate at one time, then you may wish to bring along a friend or family member who can assist you in filing requests for materials. There is nothing worse than waiting many minutes or even hours for a document, only to find that it is (a) not available or (b) not helpful to you.

One of the best techniques to utilize when trying to assess the viability of large amounts of written material—especially critical writings—is to *read the conclusion(s) first*. First, visually scan the bibliography to make sure the book or scholarly article is based on solid evidence. For published books, begin by reading the overall conclusion; then follow by reading chapter conclusions. Then read the introductory paragraphs. (A similar conclusion-first process may be used for critical essays as well.) This technique enables you to determine the overall logic of the text and the degree to which the author proves his or her point. Remember: not every written text, however well intentioned, is well written. Using this strategy, it should take you no more than fifteen to twenty minutes to assess whether a written text may be helpful to you. Many students waste a great deal of time by borrowing unhelpful materials. Evaluate the helpfulness of a resource before bringing it home.

UTILIZE SECOND-LANGUAGE SKILLS

Many African American graduate students have a tendency to ignore or delay completing foreign-language requirements until the very end of their graduate degree program. This is a major mistake, often costing many graduate students the very degrees for which they have been working. If your graduate degree program requires second-language competency, then complete that requirement during your first year of study. Many universities offer intensive language courses specifically geared toward completing foreign-language requirements, and many of these courses are offered only during the regular school year.

If your second-language skills are simply rusty and you plan to fulfill the requirement by examination, then begin a self-devised intensive review by reading books, magazines, and newspapers in that second language on a regular basis. It is often also helpful to tune in to a foreign-language radio or television show at home. Borrow foreign-language books on audiotape to listen to while exercising or driving. Campus language laboratories may also be used by individuals eager to brush up on their language skills with video- and audiocassettes—use the language laboratory on your own. Many universities also have foreign language clubs or discussion tables. It might be wise to consider joining them, or at least sitting in on a few meetings.

If translation is a problem for you, then whenever possible buy or borrow the English versions of texts alongside foreign-language ones. Then you can compare and contrast the use of language and begin to decode varying structures.

DO NOT TAKE "INCOMPLETES"

You should begin working on your final papers or projects for graduate courses as soon as classes begin. If necessary, meet with your professor during office hours or by phone to get your paper or project topic approved during the first two weeks of the course. Remember: the work for any course is best completed while the course is in session, when you can more easily consult with professors and colleagues. Submit your final project for each course on the last day of class, even if the professor provides a more generous deadline. Then, if the project requires revision, you will still have the remainder of the semester to do so. Even if the projected final grade for a course is not as high as you would like, it is best to take the lower grade and accept the credit hours. Most universities allow professors to change a grade to a higher one if a student completes additional work or revisions— often this can be done over January break or during the summer. "Incompletes" create a considerable backlog of work for both professors and students; they impede progress toward the degree and often negatively affect fellowships or scholarships. They should be used only in emergencies, such as extreme illness.

USE YOUR SUMMERS WISELY

Summertime can be the best time to get yourself ahead of the game with respect to your studies. Some graduate schools offer free or reduced tuition to full-time graduate students willing to take a summer course or two, so be sure to take advantage of that whenever possible. Even if full tuition is required, it is still advantageous to earn extra credit hours during the summer through a regular course or a directed study or independent study course under the direction of an approved faculty member. Some universities also allow students to transfer a limited number of credit hours earned at other institutions; consider taking an extra traditional class time course or distance-learning course during the summer. Even if the credit hours are not transferable, such a course may help you strengthen skills needed for comprehensive examinations.

Summer months are also prime times to investigate university research facilities, as they often go underused at that time of the year. Thus the overall time required to access and utilize materials is often greatly reduced. For example, there is usually little or no waiting time for computer terminals, photocopiers, microfilm and microfiche readers, and the like. Also, interlibrary loan requests often are granted earlier, as fewer people place requests during the summer.

If you are still taking courses, one strategy to maximize summer research time is to talk with your professors before they leave for the summer and get a sense of what topics will be discussed in the following fall or spring courses. Then come up with brief outlines of research projects that you might like to do. If your professors approve your proposals, then it makes sense to do the research over the summer, in anticipation of the course. The same holds true for master's theses and doctoral dissertations: get your topic approved by the end of the spring semester and then get busy researching during the summer.

TAKE COMPREHENSIVE EXAMINATIONS

Understandably, many graduate students are apprehensive about taking comprehensive (also known as "qualifying") examinations upon completing course work. It is best to take such examinations within one semester (twelve to fourteen weeks) after completing course requirements. The longer you wait, the more anxious you are likely to become, and the harder you will have to work to remember all that you have learned. Devise a schedule for the examinations (verbal and written) while you are taking final courses toward the degree. This gives you a chance to prepare and the committee members time to work your examination into their next semester's schedule. Plan ahead by discussing expectations and procedures with those administering the examination.

CAREFULLY CHOOSE YOUR ADVISER(S)

Some people think that a good adviser is someone who approves every course of study or academic paper project that a student thinks is interesting. Yet an adviser who simply agrees to every idea you have is not necessarily a good one. A good adviser is someone who warns you about the potential pitfalls of a particular plan of action and alerts you to options. Realize that you may not always agree with your adviser, even if he or she is working toward your best interest. You may not always be able to choose your official adviser, but there is nothing stopping you from seeking advice from others "in the know": colleagues in the graduate school, alumni, administrative staff, and other professors.

KEEP IN TOUCH WITH YOUR PROFESSORS

Many students make the mistake of actually encouraging professors to forget about them once course work is completed. "Out of sight, out of mind" unfortunately becomes a reality for many graduate students who have completed their course work and are writing theses or dissertations off campus. Keeping the lines of communication open between graduate students and professors is crucial, for it enables professors to continue to advise you or even share information about research or employment opportunities for which you may be qualified. It also makes graduate students accountable for completing writing assignments on time. Playing telephone tag is frustrating for both students and professors, although an answering machine or voice mail does help. A great way to keep in touch with professors is through e-mail; sending a postcard once a month is also a good way to update professors on your progress.

CAREFULLY CHOOSE YOUR DISSERTATION OR MASTER'S THESIS COMMITTEE MEMBERS

Nothing is worse than assembling a dissertation or master's thesis committee whose members simply do not get along, or whose schedules are so different that they can hardly meet to discuss your work. The ideal committee consists of members who are committed to the research project, who treat each other collegially, and who will take time to read your dissertation or thesis. Extremely popular professors do not necessarily make the best committee members; their time is often compromised. A less well known professor may go out of his or her way to assist you.

The process of choosing committee members should begin in the classroom: whenever possible, students should enroll in courses taught by professors under whose direction they may wish to work in the future. This gives professors a chance to know the quality of the student's work and gives students a chance to learn the professor's overall temperament and working style. The department secretary has access to the names of past committees and the records of professors whose students have successfully completed the degree. Talk to him or her and find out which professors have successfully worked together in the past. Also find out which professors are more likely to graduate students on time.

When the time comes to assemble the dissertation or master's thesis committee, approach each professor in writing and include a one- or two-page summary of your work (or a vita) as well as a prospectus of your dissertation or master's thesis. If a professor says "no," do not take it personally; count your blessings and move on. If a professor does not respond within two weeks, then it is likely that he or she is too busy. Find another candidate for the committee.

Once a preliminary group of professors has been assembled, meet with each individually to learn whether he or she is willing to work with the other proposed committee members. When all potential committee members agree to work with each other, solidify the arrangement with a brief note detailing committee members. The director of the master's thesis or dissertation is usually the highest-ranking professor on the committee.

CAREFULLY CHOOSE YOUR QUALIFYING EXAMINATION COMMITTEE MEMBERS

In some cases, the composition of the committee for the qualifying or comprehensive examination(s) differs from that of the dissertation or master's thesis committee. Follow the steps outlined above to make sure that committee members for the qualifying examination have the requisite time and willingness to cooperate in order to administer and evaluate your examination.

DEMYSTIFY THE DISSERTATION OR MASTER'S THESIS

The dissertation or master's thesis is simply a collection of essays on a particular topic. As you write, continue to see it that way. Also, using such phrases as "ABD" (all-but-dissertation) or "ABT" (all-but-thesis) to describe yourself is self-defeating; neither represents an official degree. Recognize your accomplishment, but do not rest on your laurels. It is better to describe yourself as a "master's or doctoral degree candidate" upon officially reaching that stage—and then get busy with writing the manuscript that will enable you to complete that last step toward attaining that graduate degree.

Some professors prefer to scrutinize one chapter at a time; however, this process can considerably extend the amount of time to completion. Consider drafting the entire manuscript—ask your dissertation or thesis adviser if he or she is willing to critique the whole and agree upon reasonable dates for completion and review. Whatever you write will have to undergo at least some revision, so it makes sense to revise the whole, after your adviser has been given a more complete picture of your work.

Resolve to write something germane to your thesis or dissertation *every day*. This work is best done early in the morning, before other distractions demand your energy and time. If necessary, arise an extra hour and fifteen minutes earlier each day. You will need the fifteen minutes to center your thoughts and gather any beverage or snack—then use the remaining hour to actually compose.

Compositions are most efficiently written using a word processor or computer. It is still possible to make progress by writing longhand and then transferring that information to a computer disk; however, this method will double the time needed to complete the thesis or dissertation. Be sure to save your work every fifteen minutes, print out all pages of any drafts you complete using the word processor or computer, and back up your files. There is nothing worse than composing a great deal of material and then losing it because of a computer crash, power failure, or other mishap.

On the matter of preparing the final version of the master's thesis or dissertation, be sure that you follow the guidelines of your graduate school to the letter. Graduate schools provide or direct students to the appropriate handbook for this purpose. Whenever possible, draft the final version of the document yourself—this saves both time and money. Many word processing programs allow you to quickly design or reformat your document to the specifications of your graduate school or department.

Consult a thesis or dissertation recently approved by your department in order to get a sense of how yours should appear. Also, if your project requires special materials (paper, ink, etc.), be sure to order them in advance. Do not wait until the last hour to request special materials.

As soon as professors have approved the final version of your thesis or dissertation, immediately gather their signatures to that effect. There is no point in pushing to complete the manuscript, only to find that a key professor is not available to sign off on it. Without requisite signatures from professors, a thesis or dissertation manuscript cannot be submitted to the graduate school for final approval.

TAKE CARE OF YOURSELF

Maintaining optimum physical and emotional health is paramount in making steady progress toward any graduate degree. Take care of yourself by eating and resting properly and by taking the time to rejuvenate your spirit and senses. Partaking in religious services or going for nature walks in a local park can be refreshing. Quiet meditation at home or even occasionally going to a music concert or movie theater with family or friends helps provide the balance you need to refresh yourself. Fellow graduate students often make very good companions, since they know exactly what you're going through.

If funds are tight, then screening a video at home and popping corn on the stove or in a microwave is often just as good as going to a movie theater. Playing board games like checkers or Scrabble with family and friends is both fun and educational and can provide a much-needed release for busy graduate students. The bottom line is to recognize and honor yourself.

CHAPTER 7

Toward a Paradigm Shift

Adjusting to Technology

CARLOUS CAPLE

Assistant Professor of Instructional Technology, Department of Curriculum and Instruction, North Carolina Agricultural and Technical State University

As we ease into the twenty-first century, we are granted the luxury of reflection. In our reflection, we can take notice of the past, which gives us a foundation for who we are and what we've become at present. This same foundation supports our views, expectations, and anticipations for the future. We have had the luxury of seeing the advancement of the automobile, flight, and space navigation. We have also seen the rapid change of the family structure, the workforce, communications, information, and institutions. The pace at which society operates has increased so expediently that we are faced with the task of keeping up, staying ahead, or being defeated by demands.

As students, you are faced with the unexpected task of acquiring a knowledge base that will assist you with meeting your goals or completing tasks in a timely manner. How, then, are we to keep up with every little technological change that presents itself as an obstacle? Do we progress through trial and error, or simply wait for divine intervention? How do we change our way of thinking toward technology so that we have complete control?

My experience was one of trial and error. I experienced more error than trial because there were factors that were fundamentally out of order with my way of thinking. When I entered college in 1985, technological tools were not available and accessible like they are today. My first exposure to computers was not until my junior year of high school. My school had a computer lab with IBM computers, and it was reserved for students taking accounting class. I chose not to take accounting and instead opted for home economics with Mrs. Logan and Mrs. Wilson. My rationale for this was that home economics was supposed to be easier, and the cutest girls were taking the class. I burned everything and never got a date. Upon entering college, I had no real exposure to technology other than typing with Mrs. Shirley Herbin. I can sincerely say that she sparked what is now my present career as an instructional and information technologist. The typewriters in her class were new and provoked excitement and interest. The way she taught the class was innovative. Of course, I didn't like the timed typing tests, but I learned quickly and well. The skill of typing has been with me ever since. While in college, I utilized my newfound skill with all of my assignments, yet I still had not purchased a typewriter. I would rent an IBM-Selectric typewriter for fifteen dollars a week, complete my assignment, and return it. I know you are thinking that is crazy! Well, that is what I would do, because my way of thinking was not progressive. The money I spent on rentals would have purchased a new typewriter. It wasn't until my junior year of college that I had exposure to computing. I was a psychology major and was taking a class in which I had to keep statistical data on lab rats. A computer lab had been established through a grant for that purpose. I remember hating computers because of all the c-prompts and codes for the one simple program that maintained my statistics. Stress can cause all sorts of problems, especially if you are not aware of the computing skills needed to move forward. To make matters worse, the faculty members were novices with the new technology as well. Somehow we all persevered. By 1989, I had managed to earn a bachelor's degree with minimal exposure to emerging technologies.

I wanted to go to graduate school because it was the thing to do for psychology majors. Graduate school, however, was a different ball game. Not only was I expected to use computers, but I was also expected to teach computing skills to others. It was at that point that I came to the realization that somewhere in my collegiate career I had goofed, and I had not taken advantage of a learning opportunity. Learning opportunities don't come around very often, but when they do, you should take full advantage of them. Still, without thinking, I went out and purchased an electric typewriter. I still use it to this day for things my computer cannot handle, but my teaching effectiveness was null and void because my students had been exposed to computers. I began using word processing software to complete my master's thesis. I felt so relieved and lucky to have access to the computer simply because of the ease of making revisions. I stored everything on a disk and could go back at any time and make changes. I would go into the lab at midnight and stay until four o'clock in the morning. I had found a tool that I enjoyed using, and I had access to it at any time during the day. The computer had become my best friend.

MAKING THE PARADIGM SHIFT

In 1992, upon entering graduate studies for my doctoral degree, I was forced to take inventory of my knowledge and skill with technology, and more specifically, emerging technologies. I had entered North Carolina State University, an institution noted for engineering, science, and technology. I chose to major in mathematics, science, and technology education. The program had a well-rounded curriculum, which introduced me to trial-and-error learning, problem-solving skills, drafting technology, mechanical engineering, production plant technologies, and software development. Although all of this was new; I was excited. My foundation had been laid while in high school. My past served my present and facilitated what is now my future. Graduate school was tough at first, yet I managed to persevere. That persistence paid off.

What was it that I did personally and internally? If you had asked me that five years ago, I would not have been able to tell you. In fact, I probably would have laughed and said, "I gotta graduate on time." Personally, I adjusted to change. The changes around you will shape your performance and outcomes. If I had ignored the consistent changes around me and had not adjusted to those changes, I would not be where I am professionally. It is very difficult to ignore change, especially as it relates to technology. It's a simple case of lead, follow, or get out of the way. My adjustment to change also fostered my internal thinking. I was forced to think about my consequences. If I don't learn new skills in order to teach the students, then my teaching is ineffective and my students suffer, and history repeats itself. Believe the fact that ignorance can be taught, especially to students who are not taught to think but instead to regurgitate information from text or spoken word. Internally, my thinking had to be adaptive. It had to be responsive to the change my physical world was encountering. No longer could I settle for just getting by. I had to be proactive, meaning that I had to get involved with my learning to the point that everything had to be performance-based and hands-on. My higher-order thinking skills had to be intact in order for me to be effective professionally and to achieve. I had to make a paradigm shift from reactivity to proactivity.

What is a paradigm shift? Simply put, a paradigm shift means placing yourself in a position to view something or a situation differently. It is a very difficult thing to do in some instances. I used to ask myself, how could I afford a computer? My need outweighed cost evaluations. I had to have a computer to effectively complete my dissertation in a timely manner. My first computer was financed; it was a Macintosh Performa. I have since made another adjustment, an environmental one. I needed a PC in order to be effective on my job. Paradigm shifts are made more easily when foundations are established. My foundation was my typing class. Linking the past and present is important in making a paradigm shift. You want to ask yourself, what is it that I did before that affects what I do now? This mode of thinking can only provide you with the answers that make a difference. You must come to the realization that the desired outcome can be produced only via this way of thinking.

FEAR OF CHANGE

In most schools around the country, we see minimal use of technology by teachers and students, yet most states are mandating technology competency. This to me sounds like a serious group of problems. Could it be an issue of equity? Are schools receiving funding and equipment on an equal basis? Does socioeconomic status have anything to do with it? Maybe. I truly think that progress can be made without an excess of resources. The best and the new are not always appropriate. That is not to say that basic necessary resources should not be available. In fact, they should be available and accessible on an equitable level. Skill dynamics count for a large percentage of successful attributes with regard to technology. I firmly believe that fear of change and fear of technology provide most of us with struggle and stress. Our fears have been caused by changing versions of software, business corporation involvement with education, and corporate mergers that affect us technologically. These things control how we think. The fear arises from not knowing what will happen next or not having some personal control on how it affects your world.

Fear can also come from a chaotic environment, which can result in avoidance behaviors all together. Poor establishment of policies and procedures can result in negative academic preparation. Successful human-computer interaction is dependent upon a knowledge base with appropriate and intact policies and procedures. To understand and value successful human-computer interaction and technology in general, we must examine a relatively new paradigm called chaos theory. Chaos theory was developed by scientists to study the behavior of natural systems. For the graduate student, it allows clarity of view. In order for you as a graduate student to be completely successful, you must have organization and stick-to-itiveness. As a graduate student, your goal is to earn the degree, so you have to stick to it in order to graduate, in order to get the chapters done, in order to complete those revisions. In short, you have to remove all chaotic interference and reserve time toward your goal. Having a family around was chaotic for me while in graduate school. I couldn't ignore them because they were my support system, and I do love them. However, in order for me to achieve my goal, I had to wait until everyone was asleep. I would complete all of my work overnight without disturbance. That was the time that I took to focus on my goal without chaos or interference. Your style of work ethic may be different. Sleep deprivation doesn't work for everyone. I must say that my computer worked beautifully when no one was in my way.

MAKING THE ADJUSTMENT

In life we have to make adjustments to everything, from friendships, to relationships, to work, to children, and even to the environments. With technology, we have to adjust to rapid change. Every time we turn around it seems as if a new and innovative product has been introduced to the consumer. We, the consumer, are usually caught up in the middle of advertising wars. Remember when Pepsi-Cola was at war with Coca-Cola? The marketplace became saturated with in-your-face advertising. The cola wars dominated every ounce of media, from radio, to television, to print. The cola wars controlled your thinking and spending habit behaviors. We the consumer are not new to this. When mass media began to dominate American popular culture, cigarette manufacturers utilized its every corner to promote their product. Ask yourself, how did they do that? It's easy; they focused upon the ego of the consumer. Cigarettes were marketed to and aimed at popular culture. Marlboro Man and Joe Camel come to mind. These icons promoted sex appeal and the ideal of being cool. Virginia Slims marketed toward the psyche of women with its ad "You've come a long way, baby," and rightfully so. Since the turn of the twentieth century, women have come a long way independently and professionally. Technology takes advertising a step further by marketing toward one's intellect. No one wants to be considered unintelligent. Yet technology can be tricky. Unlike cola or cigarettes, which remain constant, technology introduces new gadgetry and versions. I know that this all sounds confusing, but intellect accounts for 100 percent of how we the consumer respond to technology advertising. Our greatest asset is the ability to read, and better yet, to read thoroughly. We no longer have to know HTML code in order to produce a Web site. We can go out and purchase software that can do it for us, or even better, we can go to the Internet and locate a Web site specifically established to help one develop a home page. Reading and searching offers us the ability over the dependence of advertising to move forward in the technology and information age.

There is a multitude of information that is accessible to us by the click of a button, or by reading, more so than ever before. As a graduate student, you are given the upper hand and opportunity over any consumer. Your job as a graduate student is to seek out information and opportunities and to synthesize that data into something real that people can relate to. How then do you organize and manage those opportunities around you in order to be progressive? It's not difficult; people are making careers out of technology management. The ideal is to utilize and seize the opportunities around you in order to be successful at what you do and to achieve your goals.

AWARENESS AND IDENTITY

Awareness is the key to making an adjustment to technology. We all have to be cognizant of mass media as a tool of awareness. Every day *USA Today* or some other form of print media writes about some technological development. Every day CNN and Headline News speak about some technological advancement. We are bombarded with news and information so much that it becomes a part of our daily routine. Each morning while having breakfast, I watch ESPN, the sports network, for the latest information. I don't go into my office without *USA Today*. These habits are a part of my daily routine. They keep me current on sports, world news, stocks, and technology. The media keep me aware of my surroundings and how I can manipulate those surroundings for positive outcome. Because I like sports and information, I am given something with which I can identify, something that holds my interest. Keeping or maintaining interest is an important issue, especially as it pertains to education and children. Your identification will keep you challenged. I am a firm believer of the fact that education has to be challenging in order for learning to occur.

For me, technology is challenging. You can experience a boost to your self-esteem and self-confidence only after you have been challenged and have conquered your opponent. As a graduate student, you are faced with the challenge of meeting your desired goal. This challenge will fill you with the spirit of a fighter, much like Don Quixote, but as a winner in the end. Don Quixote battled the windmill time and time again. As a graduate student, you must persevere to completion. I consistently tell my students, "Keep your eyes on the prize," and that alone brings them back to reality when they have lost perspective and a sense of confidence and organization. Technology can only help you maintain structure with your goals. The basic technologies can assist you with the production of documents, while at the same time they can help you weed out unnecessary interference from other sources. Having basic technology competencies can also assist you. Knowing everything can sometimes cloud the achievement of your goal. For instance, word processing programs are now available in dual platforms, which make them compatible with various computer types. Spreadsheet applications are simpler than ever, providing you with ease of data migration from other sources such as the Internet; no more number crunching. Internet skills can assist you in ways once unthinkable. The data you fought so hard to find are now right at your fingertips. Software designers are now realizing their earning power by making their products hybrid, suitable for any type of computer. At some point, as a graduate student you will encounter the dreaded course Statistics 101. Your fears and your blood pressure will rise, and you will encounter your first true panic attack. Relax! The Internet now provides you access to statistics tutorials, Web sites that will conduct a chi square as well as other formulas for you, and provide you with a complete analysis of and inference on your data. Technology can make the experiences of your graduate studies less intimidating and more enlightening. The purpose of technology is to make life easier, much the same way the microwave and the washing machine changed the household.

CONCLUSION

In order to make a paradigm shift and adjust to technology and the change it brings, I urge you to focus upon your past experiences. Examine how technology affected your past. Was it positive? Was it negative? How did technology shape the person you've become? I urge you to start with the place you spent most of your time away from home, the school. Once you have examined your past, link it to your present. Ask yourself if your present-day situation is better than your past, and if not, how can technology change or enhance it? At present, you should envision your future, or the outcome you wish to achieve; taking inventory of your surroundings can do this. When I did this, I examined the pros and cons of owning a computer as opposed to owning an electric typewriter. I examined the importance of time value, as well as the value of personal time. I had to learn not to let technology control me but to utilize it within my control.

Basic technology skills are important in this changing technological world. I urge you to develop those competencies that can carry you a long way, no matter what changes occur. Basic skills transcend all new versions of software, new ways of completing documents, and all competition from your fellow classmates and even professors. When making your paradigm shift, think about the past, present, and future and how society has structured your thinking. After doing that, extract the positive ideals and utilize them to forward yourself to the completion of your goal. That is how you make the adjustment to technology.

CHAPTER 8

Establishing a Coalition
for the Utilization of Learning Skills

Black Students Using Cooperation
to Achieve Academic Excellence

WILLIAM C. COLLINS

Adjunct Associate Professor of Psychology and Director of Comprehensive Studies, The University of Michigan–Ann Arbor

In the United States, over 120,000 doctorate and professional degrees are awarded each year, but only 5 percent of them are awarded to African Americans. Moreover, among Blacks who do earn terminal degrees, almost twice as many degrees are awarded in the professions (e.g., medicine, law, dentistry) as in disciplines that award the Doctor of Philosophy (Ph.D.). College faculty, scientists, and researchers are representative of those who typically earn the Ph.D. Indeed, representation among future generations of college faculty requires diversity in graduate school enrollments today. We should all be concerned that Blacks received only about 3 percent of all doctoral degrees awarded in the United States in 1994.

The relative lack of diversity in graduate and professional programs is a long-standing problem, and clearly it is one that persists even today. The reasons behind the meager graduate enrollment of Blacks are many and well known and include limited economic resources, poor urban schools that ultimately restrict college attainment options for their graduates, and college attrition rates. But in addition, Black students interested in graduate study should seek out experiences and opportunities that serve to make them more attractive to graduate study programs. Doing so will actually serve a dual purpose: not only will it help to prepare students for the academic rigor of graduate study, but also it will acquaint them with the lifestyles, rewards, and commitment typical of research scientists and college faculty.

Testing one's interest in the often less well known academic fields may also balance the powerful and understandable attractions of professions such as law and medicine, which also require advanced degrees. The professions are well known for the security, financial rewards, and prestige they offer, even as they fill clearly identifiable needs within our communities, while the important roles played by college faculty, researchers, and entrepreneurs often are not as obvious. As a result, by focusing early on the professions, some students may actually limit themselves as they fail to explore the many career options and opportunities that accrue to those with other advanced degrees. Among the benefits of the Ph.D. may be included insights that lead to new research applications, business ventures or independent contracting, government service, or college and university professorships.

The variety of obstacles that limit Black access to graduate study and professional careers may be addressed with a comprehensive set of services and opportunities for developing interests and abilities during the undergraduate years: skill development, collaborative learning, adjustment support (no single option will do; Black students differ and may have different needs), research experience, and career exploration.

Former university presidents William Bowen and Derek Bok (1998) have discussed many of the issues involved, while also pointing out that 40 percent of Black students who graduated from selective colleges and universities went on to earn graduate or professional degrees (i.e., Ph.D., M.D., J.D., D.D.S.). The comparable figure taken from the 1990 United States census was about 8 percent. In other words, students who attended selective colleges and universities earned advanced degrees at a much higher rate than did students who did not attend selective schools. Bowen and Bok suggest a number of reasons for the relative success of these students, including the idea that students who entered selective schools had higher standardized test scores as they entered college. The ability to perform well on standardized tests is an important element in the decision to admit at graduate level. But in addition such students had strong aspirations for advanced degrees and also performed well academically as undergraduates. They also allude to a combined commitment and investment on the part of both the individual and the institution to encourage and support students through the process. This pattern is reflected in the experiences of students at the University of Michigan. A recent survey of graduates found that 40 percent of respondents were enrolled in graduate or professional study programs and that fully 86 percent of those who were not indicated that they planned to pursue an advanced degree within the next five years.

Clearly the main consideration for acceptance to graduate study is good preparation for future work as evidenced by good grades in undergraduate years. Thus it is vitally important for students to stay focused on future goals. College is different from high school, and the experience itself is often novel, even intimidating, as one strives to achieve independence. The situation is compounded by the fact that most college students were successful as high school students. They were leaders and were well-known; they were involved in school activities and community service and generally felt confident and comfortable in school. These characteristics made them attractive to colleges. But once in college, the reference points have generally shifted upward; that is, everyone admitted is talented and hardworking. It is not hard to understand that such energetic people would seek the same kinds and levels of involvement that they had in high school. But the challenges of college are different, and it is probably wise for most first-year college students to concentrate on the academic adjustment rather than to seek the level of social involvement that was typical of high school. This is not to say that you should not be involved in your campus community; on the contrary, such involvement is a major source of information, social support, and guidance about how to negotiate the college experience. Rather it is important to be selective about the kind and level of involvement one has so as to limit distractions and competition for your inherent resources of time and energy. For example, leadership roles can be very time-consuming, particularly as one has to learn the ropes about how things are done as well as organize and lead in a new environment.

The character of one's undergraduate education will be an important consideration for graduate schools as they decide whom to admit, so a balance between good grades and extracurricular activities should be sought. An applicant who has good grades but is one-dimensional is often unimpressive; similarly, a long list of extracurricular activity will not compensate for weak grades. So try to strike an effective balance between the two. But how can you know what such a balance is? One way is to discuss your goals with an academic adviser in order to settle on a plan of action for achieving them. Then you must focus your attention accordingly. It is not only effective study habits that contribute to good grades but also a good working relationship with an academic adviser who can help you to make wise course selections. In some colleges, academic advisers are professional counseling staff, whereas at other colleges faculty serve as advisers. In either case you should try to develop an ongoing relationship that will allow you not only to explore possibilities but also to place them in perspective while evaluating them as well. A faculty member can be particularly insightful about graduate study options and prospects, so it is a good idea to cultivate such a relationship with a faculty member if possible, even if that person does not serve in the formal advising role.

Scientists and professionals often work as a team, and increasingly undergraduate programs incorporate some form of group learning, often called cooperative or collaborative learning. There are numerous benefits to collaborative learning, including improved communication skills, organizational skills, and intergroup relations, as well as better grades. However, effective collaborative learning is not always easy to achieve, especially among college students who are more accustomed to succeeding on their own academically. Yet the experience of creating a successful collaborative learning effort is often representative of precisely the kind of effort that will take place in graduate school. Substantial research shows that success in college is related to the amount of interaction one has with one's peers, including opportunities for active learning with classmates outside the formal classroom setting. Collaborative learning can improve your communication skills, critical thinking abilities, and confidence about your understanding of subject matter.

In addition to having good grades, attractive candidates for graduate and professional study should broaden their academic base rather than narrow it. This may seem counterintuitive to many students. After all, if you want to go to graduate school in economics, the thinking goes, shouldn't you demonstrate your knowledge and good work in economics? Certainly you should. But you should also keep in mind that economics takes place in a social and historical context and that mathematical models may be used to explain economic behavior. And so one's knowledge about related fields is useful as well. In addition, a broad liberal arts background is generally considered essential preparation for graduate study. Rather than simply selecting a major and then taking course after course in that major, it is wise to be able to demonstrate breadth of knowledge across a variety of disciplines as well as depth in a given subject.

Good academic performance and preparation are the essential base for gaining acceptance to graduate study, but in addition it is becoming increasingly important to be able to show that you have tested your interest in the field and having done so that you remain committed to it. This has long been evident for professional study and remains so today. That is, aspiring physicians historically have been advised to volunteer in hospitals or in a doctor's office so that they can gain an appreciation for the doctor's work, including the patient's perspective. Similarly, prospective attorneys have been advised to volunteer or work in law enforcement and legislative or judicial settings so that they can understand the scope and interaction of agencies involved in the law. Such insight, gained from experience, is an increasingly important consideration for graduate study as well. Interested students should seek research opportunities with faculty or summer work in related industry settings (the latter is often harder to secure than the former). Doing so provides invaluable knowledge about working conditions, about procedures and techniques used, and about the joys and the drawbacks associated with particular kinds of research.

Students interested in graduate and professional study should work to get good grades, should demonstrate breadth as well as depth of knowledge, and should show that they have tested their interest in the field. Institutions can help the enterprise by developing opportunities for students to pursue. Opportunities are available at institutions across the country, but they might not be available at your particular school. If that is the case, you should look for related opportunities wherever you can find them. Often just asking a professor about research opportunities can produce good results.

Next to good grades, knowledge of the field gained from research work with a distinguished faculty member is a decided plus for applicants to graduate school. If you are interested in graduate study and your school has a program for facilitating connections between students who want to do research and faculty members with projects to complete, then you should be first in line to sign up. Often such programs provide structured opportunities not only for doing research but also for writing results and presenting findings in program-sponsored research symposia. If your school does not have such a program, do not be deterred from this as a goal. Many academic departments list the research interests of their faculty members, or you may discover such research interests in your own course work. If a subject interests you, consider approaching a faculty member to ask if there are opportunities for you to work on a project he or she may be doing. If not, perhaps the professor would consider sponsoring you for independent study or research on a topic of interest to you. In either case, you will have to take the initiative to define a potential research topic and to inquire about opportunities.

It is unrealistic to think that you will obtain invaluable research insights unless you take the initiative to do so. On this point, it is important to realize as well that the absence of relevant research experience often will be seen as a serious omission from your application for graduate study. Students who are serious about graduate or professional study will find a way to demonstrate that such interest is genuine and that it has been honestly tested in a relevant setting, whether academic research, volunteer service, or paid work. Another important reason for testing your interest in the field is the requirement that all applicants to such graduate programs submit letters of recommendation. The person who supervises the applicant's relevant academic research, volunteer service, or paid work is an important source for a letter of recommendation. A letter from such a person is more apt to focus on important considerations taken into account by admissions committees than would a letter from such sources as an academic adviser or general employment supervisor. Students who aspire to graduate and professional school should take the initiative to cultivate a relationship with faculty who can facilitate research or work experience related to the field of study the student wishes to enter.

Many of the articles in this volume underscore the importance of graduate and professional study, both in terms of the benefits that accrue to the individual and also in terms of the benefits to society. Those selected for graduate and professional study form the backbone of democratic leadership for the future. Thus aspirants to professional careers should understand the unique roles they will play in society as well as the place of both undergraduate and graduate and professional study in their development.

The goal of undergraduate study is to provide the common basis of knowledge and skills that allow one to contribute meaningfully as an informed member of the democracy. Such common knowledge is also the base for advanced study success in graduate and professional school. Thus undergraduates who aspire to graduate and professional study should view their undergraduate years as an opportunity to broaden their horizons even as they major in a specific discipline. Effective communication skills, facility with symbolic and quantitative manipulation, as well as an appreciation of history, science, and the arts should be fundamental components of a liberal education and the foundation for advanced study. In addition, knowledge of the contributions made to modern society by distinct cultures, as well as knowledge about the dimensions of diversity in contemporary society, serve to inform the work and the analytical and interpretive abilities of the educated person.

In contrast, graduate and professional study seeks to build upon the common knowledge base to prepare students for careers as professionals. There is a further distinction as well; professional schools, that is schools of law, medicine, or business, for example, have a decidedly applied focus. Their graduates will apply learned knowledge in the service of societal needs, such as in jurisprudence, health care, or enterprise. Professional study usually involves a clearly defined path of study, often followed by a period of internship or other supervised practicum, such as medical internships or service as a law clerk. The objective of professional study is usually a career of direct service delivery to a clientele (e.g., patients or legal clients).

Graduate study is much more devoted to the creation and furthering of knowledge per se. Its concern is with the free pursuit of scientific research. It is important in this context to emphasize that the term *scientific research* is not to be confined to the laboratory; fieldwork, historical analysis, and even the purely theoretical exploration of ideas are also encompassed by the term *scientific*. Graduate study in the arts and sciences is less clearly defined than is study in professional school. That is, in comparison with professional study, in general graduate study affords greater flexibility in course selection but also concomitantly greater responsibility on the part of the student to identify and refine an area of study and investigation. The employment objective of graduate study is usually a career as a college or university professor, a research scientist, or more rarely government service. But there is another underlying goal of graduate study and that is the opportunity to create and advance scientific knowledge.

So far I have emphasized the preparation for and the goals of graduate or professional study. But a final word is in order as well. Those who complete graduate or professional study generally lead lives as professionals. That is, they serve as doctors, lawyers, professors, and scientists, among numerous other careers, who form a highly responsible segment of society. Such people are usually bound by a set of professional ethics requiring a commitment to standards of service; often such standards may require that personal considerations be placed secondary to professional ones. This means that all clients will receive the same caliber of high-quality service. This also means that clients cannot be abandoned or their needs ignored because it is a personally inconvenient time to serve them. It means that the professional has an obligation to maintain current knowledge and even to improve skills so that clients can be served properly.

In other words, not only does the professional make a commitment to learn certain factual knowledge or to develop particular skills, but also the professional makes a lifelong lifestyle commitment to the profession. It is a commitment that should not be taken lightly.

REFERENCE

Bowen, W. G., and Bok, D. (1998). *The Shape of the River: Long-Term Consequences of Considering Race in College and University Admissions.* Princeton, NJ: Princeton University Press.

CHAPTER 9

Finding a Faculty Mentor to Help Guide You through the Doctoral Process

VERNON L. FARMER

Acting Assistant Vice President for Academic Affairs and Graduate Dean, Professor of Education, Grambling State University

> For minority students, good mentoring is a key variable for determining success or failure in completing a doctoral program. (Adams, 1992, p. 4)

> Like finding a spouse, finding a mentor can be a long process filled with disappointment or it can be a quick natural match. The course of the mentor-protegé relationship, like true love, seldom runs smooth. The key to success is not to leave things to chance. (Moore, 1985, p. 66)

INTRODUCTION

The research shows that Black doctoral students' relationships with faculty in higher education institutions tend to be regarded as the single most important aspect of their graduate experience. Meanwhile, for many Black doctoral students, their relationships with faculty are viewed as one of the most dissatisfying aspects of this experience. The research has accentuated the crucial role that faculty play in the Black students' doctoral experience; nevertheless, little empirical research has been reported showing what actually happens in these relationships that makes them so valuable to Black doctoral students' success. It is therefore evident that more attention needs to be given to the development and experiences of Black students' matriculation in doctoral programs. Such research focus should help educators identify factors that may help guide, motivate, and enhance Black doctoral students' success in America's institutions of higher learning.

SELECTING A FACULTY MEMBER AS YOUR MENTOR

This chapter explores the mentoring relationship between faculty and Black doctoral students in higher-education institutions, with emphasis on predominately White colleges and universities. This chapter focuses specifically on strategies to help Black students identify faculty mentors who can help guide them successfully through the various stages of doctoral study. Although it would not be fair to say that Black students cannot successfully complete doctoral programs in predominantly White institutions without a mentor, the quality of the experience may be compromised without an adequate mentoring experience. Finding a mentor who will be a good match for you as you matriculate through your particular doctoral program will be greatly enhanced, however, if you seek out the type of faculty mentor you need instead of waiting for a faculty member to be assigned as your mentor by the department. However, in order to facilitate the development of effective mentoring relations, you might need to take the initiative. Too often Black doctoral students place themselves in the position of waiting for some faculty member to offer to serve as their mentor. Let's face it. Faculty are busy professionals who teach classes, write funding proposals, attend meetings, preside over research groups, advise graduate students, consult, and so on. They often have very little time or inclination to seek out some student whom they do not know to volunteer their advice, counsel, and resources. To gain a commitment of time and support from busy faculty members requires that they be asked. A good way to begin the search process is to get to know all of the faculty members in your department who are eligible mentors. There are a number of things to consider when searching for a faculty member to serve as your mentor: Does the faculty member work in the area in which you are interested? Will this person be around when you need her, or is she planning a sabbatical or research leave in another country? Or worse, is she facing a tenure or promotion decision? Remember not to exclude department heads, deans, and other administrators, many of whom are former professors who still have faculty status and still teach a course periodically. These individuals can make powerful mentors.

Once you have completed evaluating and conducting some research on all of the faculty who are eligible to serve as mentors, you can then use the information gathered to develop a short list of professors that match as closely as possible your needs and personality. In order to further validate your short list, you should also talk to other doctoral students, recent doctoral graduates of the department, and individuals outside the department whom you know and whose opinion you respect. Most important, consider what you need from a faculty mentor, because you will undoubtedly need different kinds of assistance at different stages of the doctoral program. For example, if you are a new doctoral student, you will obviously need help in selecting courses; learning how the system works; perhaps obtaining a teaching, research, or administrative assistantship. On the other hand, if you are about to begin your dissertation research, you are searching for a major professor or chairperson, someone who will share interest in your research, be able to assist you in identifying and dealing with other faculty members for your dissertation committee, and be capable of helping you get the resources you need to complete your dissertation research. It is also important that the mentor you choose be the type of individual who has earned a reputation for helping Black students successfully through the doctoral process. You certainly don't want to make the mistake of getting bogged down with the type of individual who has students lingering around for a number of semesters without making steady progress. A constant consideration should also be the mentor's ability to help you secure a position in your career area when you complete the doctoral degree. Is he well known in areas in which you might want to work? Does he have a network among professionals outside academia? Does he have a reputation of helping students find employment in their career area (Moore, 1985, p. 67)?

The questions listed below are basic areas identified by Adams (1992) to help guide the investigative process for selecting a faculty mentor.

- Is the faculty member in a position to share her time and advice? Typically graduate-level faculty members are expected to accept new doctoral students as mentees. However, because of temperament, research constraints, tenure status, and so on, some faculty members might not have the time or will to take on a student, especially a Black student, in a helpful mentoring relationship.
- Does the faculty member have a reputation for producing quality research in a timely manner? A major part of the doctoral process for each student is the development and completion of an original piece of research that is of publication quality. The faculty mentor's research expertise and laboratory output will be crucial to the student's research productivity.
- Is the faculty member's current research area of interest to you and in keeping with your doctoral study goals? If your research interests are totally opposite from those of the faculty member, then this person is probably not a good choice. To form an effective relationship, there needs to be some commonality of interest.

Now that you have finalized your short list of faculty members eligible to be your mentor, you are ready to enter a mentoring relationship. Don't forget to take it upon yourself to initiate the mentoring relationship. Perhaps the best way to get to know the faculty in your department and to let them get to know you is simply to register for their courses. In this case, the situation is not threatening to either you or the instructor. It is best, if possible, to select an advanced course or seminar in which you will have a better chance to interact with the professor. If the relationship seems to have potential, it is in your best interest to go all out to produce a high-quality research paper or other class project that will impress the professor. It is also beneficial to see the professor outside of class to discuss your research interest and to be familiar with his research related to your topic. If it is not possible to register for a professor's course and it is early in the process, you should check to see if there is a job opening to work as a teaching or administrative assistant with the professor. If there is a position, do everything you can to secure it. However, before applying for the assistantship, make an appointment with the professor to explain your interest not only in the assistantship but also in the professor's area of specialty and her research in particular. Be sure to make the professor aware that you are interested in working in the area yourself. If you have a colleague or a contact who works or previously worked for the professor, be sure to ask the individual to put in a good word for you.

If an assistantship is not available with the professor, you may wish to volunteer to assist the professor with his research. But first find out what research the professor is involved with. If his research interests you, make the professor aware that you would like to assist him on the project. Volunteer to do only a discrete part of the research, which will give the professor a chance to judge your work while you get the opportunity to know the professor. Volunteering on such projects to help the professor can also lead to a paying position. Other options include having another faculty member or a colleague or contact person who knows the professor introduce you, making a point of meeting the professor at colloquia or guest lectures, or arranging to serve on a departmental committee with the professor.

One thing you don't want to do is select a professor as your mentor prior to having had the opportunity to evaluate and conduct some research on all eligible faculty mentors at your institution. The research shows that some doctoral students have utilized the tactic of simply picking a professor early in the doctoral process, making an appointment, and asking the professor straight out to be their mentor. This approach is not advised, since the professor may be ill at ease being forced to give a yes or no answer to what in academia is an intimate question. Also, by being so assertive, you may alienate a faculty member who may have been willing to enter into a mentoring relationship on a more gradual basis. Finally, this approach is also not a good one because it doesn't recognize natural gradual stages of the mentoring relationship.

You should be aware, however, that while you are taking tentative steps to get to know the faculty who are eligible mentors and test their willingness to help, they may also be testing your ability and commitment to doctoral study. Professors tend to check you out through their own grapevine of advanced doctoral students and colleagues. A professor may initiate the relationship by giving you some special attention or test you by offering you a chance to participate in some small academic assignment or project. Finally, having an awareness of how the mentoring relationship between faculty and doctoral students is initiated is simply not enough. You should also be aware of the other stages the mentoring relationship is likely to pass through.

In most departments, the range of eligible mentors is as varied as the faculty. Most faculty in doctoral programs represent the spectrum of age, gender, ethnicity, tenure status, research interest, and so on. Moreover, the experience of the faculty in mentoring doctoral students may vary widely from those with no experience to others with years of experience, including helping to matriculate Black students through the doctoral process.

As Black doctoral students you should not limit your search for a mentor to only Black faculty, because in predominantly White colleges and universities the number of Black faculty mentors are few. Ideally, it may be beneficial for Black doctoral students to have access to Black professors and other faculty with racial, ethnic, and cultural experiences that are similar and include both female and male faculty. However, given that racial, ethnic, minority, and culture makeup of the faculty in doctoral programs in predominantly White higher education institutions are Caucasian, it is simply not possible to limit your search to Black faculty. However, even if it were possible, the major criterion for choosing a mentor is which faculty member has the genuine interest and time to provide you with the guidance, support, and encouragement necessary to help you complete your respective doctoral program in a timely and productive manner.

As Black doctoral students, you must keep in the forefront of your mind that mentoring is not a panacea for solving all of the problems you may encounter as you matriculate through your doctoral program. In other words, there is no perfect blueprint from which to identify a good faculty mentor. However, the process should begin with you starting the hunt on the offense. A good faculty mentor will help you smooth out some of the "rough places," cut through some of the "red tape," serve as a comforter when the task seems impossible, and in general keep you moving forward (Holland, 1993). The most important thing for you to remember as a Black student is that much of what is required to complete the doctoral degree depends on your determination to persist because your success is predicated on your own ability.

EARLIER STAGES OF THE DOCTORAL PROCESS

The research suggests that networking and mentoring with Black students early in the doctoral process is tantamount not only to helping them successfully complete the doctoral degree but also to meeting their career goals. The research also reveals that Black students overwhelmingly assert that finding a faculty mentor early in the process helped them to complete their doctoral degree. In studies by Blackwell (1983) and Faison (1996), mentoring was found to be a significant predictor of Black doctoral students' success in higher education institutions. The mentoring relationship is so vital to completion of the doctorate that you must do all that you can, particularly at predominantly White institutions, to find a faculty mentor who will be a good match for you as you matriculate through your particular doctoral program.

RESPONSIBILITY OF FACULTY MENTORS

As a Black student pursuing a doctoral degree at an American higher education institution, you have the right to expect the same quality of mentoring from faculty in your respective departments as all other students do, which includes oversight, feedback, sympathetic consultation, and periodic evaluations of your matriculation. Genuine faculty mentors for Black doctoral students become the bridge that links students to the department, and consequently they foster a spirit of collegiality, a community of scholars. There should also be opportunities provided by the faculty mentor for Black doctoral students to present research papers, both individually and collaboratively, at major conferences and to develop manuscript and grant proposal writing skills.

An effective faculty mentor becomes a confidence booster for the doctoral student, provides opportunities to broaden the student's horizon, assists the doctoral student with finding resources (dissertation research funding, technical and computer support to statistical and writing laboratories), and assists the doctoral student in becoming a legitimate member in the department. This is extremely important because for some Black doctoral students isolation—being an outsider to the department—is a major contributing factor to them not completing their doctoral programs (Fields, 1998).

The faculty mentor and Black doctoral student's relationship can be crucial in helping the student understand the context of his or her research and the requirements of a career focused on advanced research. However, Black doctoral students must also share responsibility for making the mentoring relationship work and should also understand the multiple demands on the faculty mentor's time. Like any personal relationship, the success of mentoring depends on good will and clear communication by both parties. Many faculty mentors do an excellent job of helping with the doctoral student's professional development. However, you must be cautious, because some faculty do let their research agenda outweigh their mentoring responsibilities.

When faculty become effective mentors and assume responsibility for guiding, challenging, and championing their doctoral students, they can have a powerful and enduring effect on students' careers. At the same time, responsive doctoral students can advance their own and their faculty mentors' careers and become valued colleagues and collaborators during and after completion of the doctoral experience. Creating a productive mentoring relationship takes considerable time and effort on both sides; however, it is important for doctoral students to appreciate the significance of this unique experience.

From the doctoral students' point of view, faculty mentors can contribute to varied learning experience that comprises many kinds of skills in addition to technical ones: developing a plan of research, managing time, supervising students and technicians, overall lab management, deciding when and where to publish, creating a network of professional contacts, acquiring career skills, understanding ethical and proprietary issues, and—eventually—finding employment in their career field.

In a broader sense, faculty mentors can contribute perspectives that can be gained only from professional experience: how to avoid investigative dead ends; how to build a research project that will contribute to the doctoral student's career, the faculty mentor's agenda, and the research enterprise as a whole; and how to know when a research project is near completion. All these contributions are most rewarding when the activities of doctoral students and faculty mentors are complementary.

Faculty mentors can enhance the development of doctoral students in both explicit and implicit ways, such as modeling good practices of research, leadership, and ethical behavior. Faculty mentors who are often too busy to fulfill mentoring duties can bring in help from advanced doctoral students to help or direct the doctoral student toward other human resources.

Mentoring should be an important responsibility of the faculty. With this in mind, doctoral students should carefully choose a faculty member who has a proven record as an effective mentor. It is critical to doctoral students' success that they find a faculty mentor who is a good fit for meeting their needs.

The faculty mentor has the responsibility to provide an experience that is fundamentally educational in nature and advances the doctoral student's career. This educational experience should lead toward research independence and include the doctoral student's career goals, a coherent plan of study, teaching, internships, and other educational experiences that promote professional growth and development. However, at the onset of the mentoring relationship, the faculty mentor should discuss with doctoral students the requirements of the degree, including academic performance, the plan of study, the research plan, and the doctoral student's overall responsibility. Faculty mentors should also discuss goals with the doctoral students at the outset, so that the expectations of both are clearly delineated, and provide periodic meetings to issue status reports of their progress. Such meetings provide an assessment and reality check for both the doctoral student and the faculty mentor.

BENEFITS OF THE MENTORING RELATIONSHIP

The nature of the mentoring relationship between the faculty mentor and the doctoral student becomes coherent if one closely examines its potential benefits. Faculty mentors stand to gain from the training, energy, and enthusiasm of doctoral students, who often arrive on campus with professional experience as teachers, administrators, and faculty. Consequently, many doctoral students are employed by their respective departments as administrative, teaching, and research assistants. When the match is good, it is not uncommon for faculty mentors to involve doctoral students in their research and publishing agenda. Faculty who are good mentors can benefit by attracting the best doctoral students on the basis of their reputation as mentors. The faculty mentor also benefits since it is gratifying to teach and train doctoral students in what one has learned and to help them advance toward achieving their academic and career goals.

It is not uncommon for research topics to change for doctoral students as they mature during their matriculation through the doctoral process. Therefore, flexibility on the part of the faculty mentor often results in significant rewards in the form of the doctoral student's growth and contributions to the department and the field. Many doctoral students work most effectively when they are encouraged to pursue some of their own ideas.

Other benefits, such as gaining a supporter, advocate, and defender, can also be realized through the mentoring relationship but might not be as evident. Because of the nature of the doctoral process, Black students may experience the added stress of being given the same opportunity as the majority students. The faculty mentor as a supporter, advocate, and defender becomes the proponent who makes sure that all actions regarding the Black doctoral student are done with his or her best interests in mind.

And because such relationships have not been the norm between Black doctoral students and the faculty at higher education institutions, forming the mentoring alliance might be complicated by misgivings, apprehension, and fear.

The need for effective faculty mentoring of Black doctoral students should not end with the doctorate. Black students who move from doctoral degrees to appointments in their career fields stand to benefit greatly from the contributions and support of their faculty mentors.

LATER STAGES IN THE DOCTORAL PROCESS

Once you have reached the end of the second or third year of graduate study, you should have formulated a research topic and moved toward developing a dissertation topic. During this stage, Black students should know which faculty members' research interests are conducive to their research area. The issue of mutuality of research interest should be a key criterion for cultivating a mentoring relationship during the early stage of selecting a faculty mentor. Previous Black doctoral students have suggested that the scholarship, knowledge, and tools needed to move through this formative period of their doctoral experience tend to have been met by a faculty mentor who was genuinely interested in helping them achieve their academic and career goals. Important factors that tend to drive the mentoring dyad during this period of the doctoral experience are research interest, knowledge, and time. However, the need for a faculty mentor to spend time with them was the most important of the these factors according to Black doctoral students.

It is during the late stages of the doctoral process that Black students should increase their involvement in research and other scholarly activities. For example, you should begin to seek or maybe provide opportunities by faculty to write, copublish, and publish. Black doctoral students and their faculty mentors during this period should be engaged in conference presentations and other professional development activities. Although peer relationships tend to increase during this period, good faculty mentors continue to assume the responsibility of helping guide Black doctoral students toward their academic and career goals. The Black doctoral students reported that while the opportunities to work on a professor's research project, write and publish with a faculty member, or teach a class were very tempting, faculty mentors kept them focused and balanced on the primary goal of earning their doctoral degree.

There is no question that Black doctoral students understand that mentoring is crucial to their personal, professional, and academic well-being on predominantly White campuses. Nevertheless, they understand that their ultimate success depends on their ability and determination, which was primarily the basis for the success of their ancestors in doctoral programs. However, the range of importance given to these relationships did vary and are noteworthy. The research literature indicated that although most Black doctoral students understood mentoring as crucial, many had problems with the perception and use of the terminology—*mentoring*. The perception of empty vessels standing before full fountains was totally unacceptable among most Black doctoral students. Most Black students reported that it was essential that faculty appreciate who Black students are and respect not only what they bring to the mentoring relationship but also the experience that brings them to doctoral programs.

In my discussions with Black doctoral students of the past, they perceived the mentoring experience as being quite different from other types of faculty-student relationships. Although most Black doctoral students reported being mentored over their lifetime by more than one individual, the doctoral student-faculty mentoring relationship was seen as an exclusive one. The intensity and the amount of personal time required by both parties make this type of relationship difficult at best.

Experience has taught us that Black doctoral students, without question, recognize that successful academic and career development can be enhanced with the guidance and support of a good mentor. However, if the mentoring relationship is to work, it must be of mutual respect and reciprocity. There is little tolerance among Black doctoral students for faculty mentors in predominantly White institutions who fail to recognize the wealth of knowledge, experience, diversity, and professionalism they bring into a doctoral program. Consequently, some Black doctoral students are not comfortable with the term *mentor*. Yet without fail they tend to describe varying degrees of the positive nature of the mentoring relationship.

DISSERTATION COMMITTEE MEMBERSHIP

For Black doctoral students, one of the most important things to understand is that the makeup of your dissertation committee can determine whether you get the support and help you need to move smoothly through the dissertation process or whether you have to leap a constantly growing number of hurdles in order to achieve your goals. If you discover that you have selected a dissertation committee in which the chemistry among committee members is not good, you will have to use diplomacy to resolve the problem because your dissertation may be at stake. Therefore, you must be careful in selecting faculty members for your dissertation committee. The following criteria should be used to help guide you in making the best decision possible:

1. Select faculty who are experts in your topic and can provide you with technical help.
2. Select faculty you get along with personally. You may have to rely on the compassion of your committee at some point. If they dislike you from the start, you're in serious trouble.
3. Select faculty who get along with each other. Even if all members get along with you, if two members of your committee are feuding with each other, they will slow your progress to a halt just to prove each other wrong.
4. Select faculty who may be able to help you with your career later. Your committee will be the keystone of your network for finding jobs. Consider what network every person may help you tap before selecting them.
5. Select faculty who will be available when you need help. Faculty members have a distressing habit of disappearing at critical times. Professors go on sabbatical, fail to get tenure, or leave to conduct their own research. Before signing a faculty member to your committee, make sure that he or she will be available when you plan your examinations or need advice. Nothing is worse than facing the choice of restructuring your committee or postponing your dissertation defense a semester or two while your committee member is on sabbatical.

Although rules vary from department to department, usually your committee will have a chairperson, other members from your department, and at least one outside member from another department. In some cases, an external member from outside of the institution may also be required. The way to begin to form your dissertation committee is, of course, with a chairperson, for which your major professor may be a good choice.

The chairperson is the catalyst to a successful dissertation committee. If you have selected a strong, compassionate chair who can lend expertise and keep other committee members in line, you are ahead of the game. Finding such an individual is not necessarily a piece of cake; it can be a difficult task, as has been discussed in this chapter.

By the time you reach the dissertation stage, you should have developed a good working relationship with a faculty mentor in your department. If your faculty mentor was selected carefully, as has been suggested in this chapter, he or she is probably ready, indeed eager, to chair your dissertation committee. By this stage your faculty mentor is most likely interested in your research topic and knows how to help you find the resources to support your research.

After you have secured a chairperson, you are ready to identify other members of your committee. It is wise to recruit the other members of your committee in consortium with your chairperson. Present and discuss your short list of faculty who meet your criteria with your chairperson. You may discover that there is some hidden animosity or that you have misjudged a faculty member's expertise. Allow your chairperson to veto anyone who is totally unacceptable, but don't necessarily accept every small objection without explanation.

Once you and your chairperson have agreed on the potential committee members, you should then meet with every eligible committee member individually and ask him or her to serve on your committee. You should know as much as you can about their work related to your topic and tell them the reason for asking them to serve on your dissertation committee.

Meanwhile, if you are required to select an external committee member outside of your institution, you may want to identify someone who can bring a unique perspective to bear on your research. If this is not necessary because you have all the expertise on your committee that you need, you may just want someone who will go along with the program and not cause trouble. If the latter is the case, your chairperson may identify a colleague with whom he exchanges this type of favor.

POTENTIAL PROBLEMS WITH FACULTY MENTORS

While the mentoring relationship is critical in helping Black students to matriculate through the doctoral process, it also has potential for a number of overwhelming problems. Changing mentors can be a problem. In many ways in academia, the mentoring relationships between faculty and doctoral students are public relationships. Faculty and other students know which students are assigned to which faculty mentors. Breaking off these relationships can be compared to a divorce; although some are amicable, many are hostile. There are many reasons why you may want to change faculty mentors before one of the natural points of termination. As a doctoral student, it is possible that your interests may change. As a Black doctoral student you may find that you have a serious personality conflict with your faculty mentor that no amount of good will on your part can solve. Or you may simply wish to strike up a mentoring relationship with a different faculty member because you believe it would be more productive.

For example, if it becomes obvious that the faculty mentor you chose early in the doctoral process is not going to make a good dissertation chair, you need to think carefully about how you will resolve the situation. In the case of a dissertation chairperson, don't simply stop communicating with him or her while you look for a chairperson, because you may need the faculty mentor later. Besides, if your faculty mentor has helped you up to this stage in your doctoral studies, then she deserves to be treated with respect. Explain to your faculty mentor that your dissertation interests are leading in a new direction and that you have been talking things over with one of her colleagues in the department. When you have identified a colleague of your faculty mentor to chair your dissertation committee, make sure you discuss this with your faculty mentor before she hears it from someone else. Depending on how your relationship evolves after the change, you may want to ask your faculty mentor to serve as a member of your dissertation committee.

If your faculty mentor is unwilling to accept the break graciously, you cannot ignore the situation. If you know that your former mentor is now an enemy, the first thing to do is gently tell the new faculty mentor about it, with the warning that the new faculty mentor may also have problems with the old faculty mentor. After taking this step, it is best not to engage in either direct confrontation or a war of rumors and gossip. The best tactic is to simply downplay the conflict and hope that in time things will cool down.

While some breaks with faculty mentors are sharp and dramatic, most involve gradual shifts. If you must break up a mentoring relationship, first try to anticipate what the emotional response of your faculty mentor will be. Don't do things behind your faculty mentor's back. If you are considering taking an assistantship position with another professor, let your faculty mentor know. Discuss your reasons. If your faculty mentor is genuine and has your best interest at heart, he may accept and even encourage the change. If your academic interests have shifted, explain the shift to your faculty mentor, who may understand and even help to ease your move.

SUMMARY AND CONCLUSIONS

Finally, the research has shown that the types of relationships that Black doctoral students tend to have with their faculty mentors range on a continuum from very limited (formal academic advisement relationships) to very involved (career mentoring) interaction between Black doctoral students and their faculty mentors. The research suggests that most Black doctoral students have been dissatisfied with the formal academic advisement relationships with their faculty mentors (Holland, 1993). The study's findings also suggest that the academic guidance relationships tend to be the most prevalent and that Black doctoral students are somewhat satisfied with the academic guidance relationships they had with their faculty mentor. Meanwhile, some Black doctoral students involved in quasi apprenticeship relationships were somewhat satisfied with this relationship. Although these relationships appear to be somewhat satisfying, Black doctoral students were overall adequately satisfied with these types of involvements.

The research findings of Holland's (1993) study also showed that Black doctoral students were satisfied with the academic relationships with their faculty mentor. Respondents felt their faculty mentors went beyond the call of duty by ensuring that they were sufficiently prepared for their academic careers. Moreover, some Black doctoral students were identified as having career mentoring relationships with their faculty mentors that were very satisfying. Not only did faculty mentors purposely prepare doctoral students for careers in higher education, they also actively networked and socialized these students into particular fields of study. These relationships made it easier for Black doctoral students to get to know and communicate with other professionals in their fields of study.

The study's findings also indicate that Black doctoral students tended to have a variety of relationships and involvements with their faculty mentors in higher education institutions. In addition, the faculty mentors tend to play a significant role in the academic life, satisfaction, and career preparation of Black doctoral students. More specifically, the faculty mentors who focused on the academic and career interests of Black doctoral students were the most respected among doctoral students.

Finally, American higher education institutions can help promote better faculty mentoring practices that enhance experiences of Black doctoral students and reduce the chances of neglect or abuse because of racial and cultural differences. Simple mechanisms like mentoring awards can raise public awareness of the need for guidance. Even the signature of a department head or chair on the doctoral student's admission document symbolically raises the higher education institution's responsibility for the doctoral student. Colleges and universities can also include mentoring in their guidelines for faculty review and offer to provide training for faculty mentors in effective communication and evaluation techniques. Higher education institutions should also encourage Black doctoral students to acquire teaching and other professional skills by recognizing the development of those skills as a worthwhile use of research funds.

REFERENCES

Adams, H. G. (1992). *Mentoring: An essential factor in the doctoral process for minority students.* (Report No. HE026497). Notre Dame, IN: National Consortium for Graduate Degrees for Minorities in Engineering and Science, Inc. (ERIC Document Reproduction Service No. ED 358 769).

Blackwell, J.E. (1983). *Networking and mentoring: A study of cross-generational experiences of Blacks in graduate and professional schools.* (Report No. HE016725). Atlanta, GA: Southern Education Foundation. (ERIC Document Reproduction Service No. ED 235 745).

Faison, J.J. (1996). *The next generation: The mentoring of African American graduate students on predominantly white university campuses.* (Report No. UD031135). New York: Annual Meeting of the American Educational Research Association. (ERIC Document Reproduction Service No. ED 401 344).

Fields, C.D. (1998). Making mentorship count: Surviving Ph.D. programs requires someone who is willing to show the way. *Black Issues in Higher Education, 15*(3), 28–30.

Holland, J.W. (1993). *Relationships between African American doctoral students and their major advisors.* (Report No. HE026614). Atlanta, GA: Annual Meeting of the American Educational Research Association. (ERIC Document Reproduction Service No. ED 359 915).

Moore, R.W. (1985). *Winning the Ph.D. game.* New York: Dodd, Mead.

CHAPTER 10

Psychosocial Adjustment to the Campus Environment

KELI DREW LOCKHART
Practicing Psychologist and President of the New York Chapter
of the Association of Black Psychologists

Psychosocial adjustment refers to how you emotionally adopt and have a feel for where you are; how you make yourself comfortable on a social level, which in this case encompasses graduate peers, faculty, administrators, and staff; how you are coping in relation to other people; your sense of self and self-worth while associating in other groups and altering how you manage in those groups when you come up against challenges. Psychosocial adjustment is to know when you must alter, interpret, and understand those alterations and meanings while maintaining a solid sense of self.

Your psychosocial adjustment to graduate school began before you got there. The context that you were given about the journey you are about to embark on was a battle in your psyche before you even reached the doorsteps of your program. For many of you, the entrance into grad school will be connected with the battle between success and failure. The familial pressure for you to make it will be there. To be the first in your family to go to undergraduate school, let alone graduate school, is an immense undertaking. Most Euroamericans do not have that type of pressure. It is perceived that if you do not go to college you will be scrubbing floors for a living, so it adds an enormous amount of psychological pressure on you to achieve for your family and your culture. You must be the one to end the chain of uneducated Black folks. As well, containing the guilt of the financial pressure that your families (or yourselves) will have putting you through school is great. There is also the cultural pressure owing to internalized oppression that will come when you will undoubtedly be compared with your peers who will not be able to attend graduate school. You will be challenged academically, wondering whether you are good enough to make it, to stand up to those "overachieving Euroamericans, who are naturally gifted and don't ever have to study." Just filling out the application will be pressure!

Identity is the first requirement in the psychosocial adjustments that you will need to make it through grad school. If you have a strong self-identity, you will be able to maintain throughout. In personal communication with Baba Woza Vega (October 12, 1999), he advised, "Do not fall prey to the perceptions of 'they are better than me.' When you come up against the challenges you will face by your Euroamerican peers and faculty [and faculty of color], you must have a solid background to fight the negativity that will undoubtedly surround you." A strong self-identity will help you through.

Culture differences will permeate throughout your graduate career. Unless you attend a historically Black university, get used to being the only Black person in class. When classes are smaller and even more intense, you will find yourself forced into being the "expert" in not only Black culture but most cultures of color. Anonymity does not exist, as everyone will look to you for answers. This will often include your professors. I was blatantly told by my Euroamerican peers that I had to be a teacher or how else will "they" learn. I was really confused because I thought I paid $18,500 a year to be taught. Being in this position can weigh heavily on you. You must take care of yourself and remember that it is your choice when to be a teacher and also to choose not to be one. You do not have to represent an entire race of people.

Conversely, going to an all Black campus does not necessarily diminish some of the above experiences. You are challenged in different ways. On Black campuses the reverse may occur, where you may feel that your professors will make it almost impossible for you to graduate because many will want you to experience the hard knocks that you will experience in the "real world." So you will again be left feeling "on," like you have to represent an entire race of people by graduating.

The politics of graduate school is another area of psychosocial adjustment that must be taken into account. Politics are heavy, and often people of color are thrust into the middle of issues that are meant to cause a divergence from your studies. Pick and choose your battles. When these issues arise (and they will), make sure you have a support system in place.

Support systems are extremely important in graduate school. They are the absolute key to your making it through with some semblance of sanity! The main theme in making it is to connect with other students so you can feel empowered and propped up when needed. You will experience many feelings from day one. Even orientation can be an overwhelming experience. You will question yourself and ask, is everyone in a master's or doctorate program a genius? Can I keep up with them? Will I make it through? Financially you will feel overwhelmed: Do I have enough money? Will I be able to work with my course load? Will my course load suffer if I do have to work? It can be helpful to identify an individual or individuals whom you can bond and commiserate with. In a personal communication with Christine Healy (October 9, 1999), she found that she made it through the orientation stage by identifying with other, primarily African American students and students of color in general from the beginning. This made her transition smoother and helped ease some of the anxieties she experienced early on. You want to identify as early as possible, even before you start your program, a Black Student Union or other Students of Color organizations. If you can, find a student of color, speak to any student to learn about the positives of your program, and also to take heed of the horror stories! Being able to ask the real questions you could not ask in the interview will help you be prepared when you arrive at your program. Again, your adjustment will be much smoother if you have an idea of what to expect. Speaking of expectations, it is a misconception that all Black professors and professors of color are on your side. Seek them out and feel them out. Most of your professors will be supportive of you and have your best interests at heart. They will guide you and nourish you and will definitely push you beyond your limits. In terms of taking care of yourself psychosocially, expect a difference in Black faculty, but if you don't receive it, don't be surprised and feel let down. Everyone's agenda and goals are different. Do not let theirs hinder your progress. Your goal is to absorb as much information as you can and graduate—preferably in less than ten years!

No matter where you go, you will have to deal with "ism" and it is hoped that you will find faculty who are enlightened. These were my expectations, especially being in the field of psychology. For the most part this was factual, but you cannot afford to let naïveté cloud your reality. As in any situation, there is an assortment of flavors (or tudes, if you will) to deal with, and you must seek out supportive faculty who will be there for you in trying times.

Psychosocial adjustments will be made just because many of you will be relocating to your graduate school of choice. This journey can be exciting and lonely at the same time. I came from the east coast to a west school for my grad school studies, and in the beginning I was very homesick and lonely because I did not have the support network I had at home. This forced me to develop a new network of support. I knew a second-year student who attended Howard University for our master's program, and she helped me learn the ropes and introduced me to her peers. Being African American, we bonded on cultural familiarity and developed a relationship that has lasted to this day. Finding a core group of five women helped me adjust to being on the west coast and find comfort through some extremely trying times.

The relationships developed above allowed me to give back and make sure I mentored incoming students of color and showed them the ropes. This is also another way for you to cope psychosocially. You want to get involved in your environment, your studies, and the social aspect of your experience. It is easy to fall prey to isolation, particularly if you are a Black student in a predominantly White school.

Your support group is multi-purposed. You must have a balance between work and play. This can be done in many ways. Study groups offer a great psychosocial adjustment, particularly with guilt-driven graduate students who tend to feel that if they are not studying twenty-four hours a day, they will be doomed to hell. Studying with your peers offers you time to socialize and time to study. And don't stress yourself out if you study for one hour and talk for two. It's still one hour more than you probably would have studied alone. Dr. Healy (personal communication, October 9, 1999) offers that group study is also a time for social adjustment. You allow yourself to come down off the steady rigor of classes and definitely have time to vent about professors and get to know your peers as well.

Reaching out to peers who look like you, though they may and will have different experiences, will provide safety and security in numbers. If you are not a social person, befriending at least one person who can be your study partner or someone whom you can call when in need is an essential tool to your psychosocial adjustments. You will definitely use this number.

Support networks will come in many different forms. Outside organizations such as the Association of Black Psychologists can be a key tool in providing support throughout your graduate career. In a personal communication with Michele April West (October 12, 1999), she described the difference between graduate and undergraduate school as the ante being up in grad school and stressed the importance of seeking group support. She stated that as an undergrad you are more likely to find a group such as the Black Student Union. In grad school, you are not as likely to find a group for people of color, let alone one specifically for Black students. It is a disadvantage and a challenge to not have a peer group of color readily available, so one option is to go outside to find one. West attributes her main support to the Association of Black Psychologists.

Associations such as the Association of Black Psychologists (ABPsi) can offer you many tools. One of the association's goals is to develop concepts, theories, philosophies, principles, and programs to enhance the practice of psychology among Black psychologists and in the Black community, as well as to promote freedom of Black scientific inquiry, teaching, and professional practice. At an association such as ABPsi you will have peers who are experiencing what you are experiencing from surrounding areas and professionals who have already paid their dues, so they can offer you a wealth of information. At ABPsi you can find an abundance of resources: references, dissertation committee members, seminars and conferences to attend, job possibilities, or just knowing that once a month you can meet with professionals and peers who look like you. In whatever field you choose, there will most likely be a professional Black association for you to get support from.

If your school does not have an organization that meets your needs, do not hesitate to start one of your own. At the California School of Professional Psychology, Alameda, where I attended, the students of color started Students of Color Alliance (SOCA). While it did not meet all of my needs, it certainly was a social and political forum where I received the support that I depended on. Unfortunately, it was difficult for the members to understand that just because we are people of color does not mean that we have the same plight. There still was a necessity to have a Black students' organization or social group. Also, if you are on a large campus and cannot find a group within your own discipline, search outside and join a group in another discipline. Or, again, begin your own group with mixed disciplines. The key is to have a support network. You will find that other Black students want and need the same support that you do.

Keeping it real, you must realize that it may be difficult to connect with classmates because most likely they will all be White and will have more resources available to them. West offered an example of when she had to work in a department store as a Ph.D. candidate. She was working with brothers and sisters, many of whom could not relate to her, and some looked down on her. Because she was in a predominantly White university, she could not find peers to relate to the concerns that she was experiencing in school. She took care of herself by connecting with the students she could tolerate. Realize that you may not connect and may feel like an outsider. For example, in the study groups mentioned earlier, you may not be asked to be included in a group or you may not have the same study habits, but don't let that hinder you. Your goal is to graduate, and with connections or without, you will graduate.

Speaking of study habits, remember that many of you are now entering a system more rigorous than undergraduate or master's programs, where you may have to study ten times more depending on your background. If you were not rooted in a rigorous educational system, you will have a difficult time with some of the core concepts to make it through graduate school. You must psychologically prepare yourself for a different method of study. Gone are the days of reading the day before the test. You must begin your studies early. You must gear yourself for purchasing twenty to thirty books a semester. You must begin your dissertation or master's thesis early.

I think it is extremely important to keep yourself on a timeline, even if your school does not require one. My grad school was excellent at this. You could not apply for internships if you had not cleared your Dissertation Proposal Orals. In addition, dissertations were begun during your first year, if you were in the Psy.D. program (which I strongly recommend!). On that note, do not wait to begin your dissertation. The last minute is not the minute to start. You also do not want to choose a topic that cannot be completed. You want to graduate in four to five years, not ten! You can save the world after you take that degree!

The dissertation process (and the master's thesis to a certain degree) is yet another extremely stressful time, particularly when you begin writing your results and discussion sections. This is the part of graduate school where I believe you are challenged, mentally, physically, and emotionally, unlike any other time before. You absolutely must have a support system, preferably peers who are in the same stage of dissertation as yourself. You will question yourself, you will feel like you cannot do the work, you will cry, shout, throw disks, and maybe try to throw your computer. Be prepared for large phone bills if your support system is out of state. However, when you are done, you will be in a complete state of satisfied exhaustion.

As a psychologist, I must highly recommend another way to assist in your psychosocial adjustment through graduate school, and that is to take advantage of psychotherapy. This is another venue where you can release the anxieties you will definitely encounter. Therapy can offer one-on-one support, particularly in areas where you may not feel comfortable discussing topics with a peer or faculty member. When those "isms" arise, psychotherapy is the perfect support to have. It will be time for you to unwind about whatever may come up for you. Many therapists offer student rates, so it is an affordable and worthy option to consider.

Attending seminars and conferences is another way to meet people and network, hone your skills, and not feel guilty about not studying because you are getting hands-on experience. Other tidbits to make it through are to understand your course requirements to graduate. Do not obsess on how many of this and how many of that. Get the written requirements, the order in which they are to be taken, and take them. Although you will be assigned an adviser, it is your responsibility to know what it will take for you to graduate. Having a thorough understanding and a checklist of courses (on which you check off completed courses at the end of each semester) will help ease tensions and questions. Check in with your adviser, but don't rely on her or him. It is also good to get to know department chairs and administrative directors. The financial aid director, the internship coordinator, the secretary to the registrar, the registrar. These people are your friends! On the financial aid tip, the majority of you will make it through graduate school with student loans. Understanding your loan responsibilities, when the money will come, how much refund you will receive, will again help you with your psychosocial adjustment. You will also experience some "cultural weight" from your Euroamerican peers who will take issue if you are there on financial aid or scholarship. It will be a rough time; utilize your resources. For example, if you thought books were expensive in undergraduate school or master's level, on the doctorate level the cost is ridiculous. I remember that for one class I spent almost four hundred dollars. Let me say that again, in case you thought I said for all of my classes: that was four hundred dollars for one class. I had six classes my first semester. As graduate school is not the time to develop stubborn pride, I asked second-year students if I could borrow their books or purchase them at super discounts! Utilize your resources!

Before you know it, the time will come for you to prepare for internship. Do not wait until the last minute to research your choices. The application process is extremely lengthy and competitive. This is where the organized student has the upper hand. Information gained by keeping your relationships with your professors and advisers positive and current comes in handy for recommendations, and knowing the exact number of hours you completed for your practicums is necessary. Remember, wherever you are applying, at least fifty other students in each state are probably applying to the same internship site.

Internship will also be another adjustment period because, depending on your field, you will more than likely be relocating again. Time goes by fast in graduate school, and change is the only thing that will be constant during your year. You will definitely need to take care of yourself during this period. Like your graduate classes, you are almost guaranteed to be the only Black intern at a site. Now you will be challenged not only by your peers but by professional staff who will have preconceived notions about your abilities not only as an intern but especially as a Black intern. Internship can be extremely stressful, because you will be putting your knowledge into actions. At the same time, you probably will be working on your dissertation. It will be challenging, but it can be done. Even though many of you have probably worked, going back to a forty- to sixty-hour (that is correct, you can work up to sixty hours) workweek will take some getting used to. I recall as Christmastime was approaching, I was getting excited about the winter break when my supervisor kindly reminded me that I was no longer in school, that I had to apply for my vacation time, which was a total of three weeks that could not be taken all at once and did not begin until January, because as an employee I had a six-month probationary period. Some employee, at fifteen thousand dollars a year!!! This is also an area of adjustment because you are operating in a new arena. You are called a professional, so your forty plus hours can be justified, but you are treated like a student, so your forty plus hours can be justified! The psychosocial adjustment will come with the challenge of convincing the professional staff to take your recommendations seriously and combine it with the learning you still need to do. Again, you must take care of yourself and find a support network. Being the only Black intern will again force you into situations where you must represent an entire race. You will again be forced to pick and choose your battles. Part of making it through is to learn to take time for yourself. You must go out and socialize and network, and don't forget that the time will speed by, so do not forget your dissertation.

Last but not least, do not forget the power of prayer. Wherever your spirituality lies, do not forget to ask your creator for guidance and support every day. Take time out to pray or meditate, give thanks, and ask for strength.

Remember, to make it through graduate school with a fairly healthy psychosocial adjustment, you want to establish a support network, make connections with people who are supportive, and find a balance between education and socialization. You must have a social life. Find an organization of color, such as the Association of Black Psychologists, find a mentor in your faculty, and do not wait to start your dissertation. When you receive your doctorate degree, you will have such a feeling of completion, knowing that you and only you did all of that hard work. Good luck and take that degree!

CHAPTER 11

Maintaining Black Pride, Self-Esteem, and Self-Concept

HAKIM RASHID

Associate Professor of Education and Psychoeducational Studies,
Department of Human Development and Psychoeducational Studies,
Howard University

The road to a graduate or professional degree has many challenges for the African American student. Financial obligations, the impatience of family members who may fail to see the importance of an advanced degree, emotional fatigue at the prospect of "more school" after the rigors of one's undergraduate years—these and other factors conspire to make the prospect of graduate or professional education a daunting task. Once the decision has been made to pursue an advanced degree, however, another set of challenges faces African American graduate and professional students as they walk further down the "hallowed halls" of academia. One such challenge involves the maintenance of one's pride as an African American. Another closely related challenge involves developing and maintaining one's self-esteem as a professional in a context that can range from overtly hostile to benignly paternalistic.

ASSAULTS ON THE DIGNITY OF AFRICAN AMERICAN GRADUATE AND PROFESSIONAL STUDENTS

America is a racist society that emerges out of a racist cultural and historical context. This is an undeniable truth, and any African American graduate or professional student who denies this reality has already taken a major step toward the distorted sense of self that comes from an ignorance of both history and the current state of race relations in America.

The dignity of African American graduate and professional students is first of all assaulted by the racist cultural context in which universities are embedded. As American educational institutions, American universities serve as major vehicles for the perpetuation of American culture from one generation to the next. American culture is rooted in the ideology of White supremacy, that is, the belief and behavioral system that promotes European cultural and intellectual superiority over people of color around the world. Thus American universities overtly and covertly promote the mythology of European cultural superiority primarily through the humanities and social science curricula; they overtly and covertly promote monopoly capitalism via the prominent roles of multi-national corporations in university life; and they overtly and covertly promote American political and military superiority via direct involvement in the foreign policy and defense establishments. American universities have played major roles in the exploitation of oppressed people around the world, and it is critical that African American graduate and professional students not be misled by the illusion of liberalism that the American university would like to project.

ACQUIRING KNOWLEDGE: THE KEY TO ETHNIC CULTURAL PRIDE AND SELF-ESTEEM

In *Stolen Legacy,* George James reminds us that inscribed on the entries of the great temples in ancient Egypt (Kemit) is the command "Man know thyself." Thus it is apparent from even ancient times that self-knowledge is the foundation of all other forms of knowledge. If self-knowledge is absent, knowledge of the other dimensions of reality cannot be complete. What is self-knowledge? Self-knowledge involves the individual's understanding of the nature of self as an individual and an understanding of the nature of self as part of a cultural group. From a traditional and historically African perspective, the essence of self as individual is spirit, a nonmaterial reality connected to a higher power (e.g., Creator, God, Allah, etc.). It is this spiritual essence that must control the material body and bring it into accord with the laws of the higher power (e.g., Mystery System, Bible, Qur'an). The individual, thus comprising this spirit/body connection, is born into a cultural context designed to perpetuate the group's beliefs, values, and behaviors from one generation to the next.

Again, from the traditional African perspective, it is the group that defines the nature of the individual's relationship to it and the outside world. These dimensions of self-knowledge are an essential component of the African worldview, a worldview that must serve as a reference point and filter for the African American graduate or professional student. Self-knowledge, however, must be complemented by historical knowledge, that is, a knowledge of human history from ancient times to the present. An African American graduate or professional student must know that civilization and culture did not begin with the ancient Greeks and Romans. An African American graduate or professional student must know that by the time the Greeks and Romans achieved any semblance of civilization, ancient Egypt (Kemit) had long since reached its cultural zenith and was in a state of decline. An African American graduate or professional student must know that the people of ancient Egypt (Kemit) were not Europeans, as the purveyors of the myth of European cultural superiority would have us believe. The magnificent work of Cheikh Anta Diop has put that myth to rest in an emphatic manner. The foundation of racism and White supremacy as we know it lies in the totally erroneous belief that African peoples have contributed nothing to civilization, a belief continually perpetuated by both Hollywood and the American educational system. Thus it is ignorance, ignorance of the true history of Africa and Europe, that is the real enemy of people of African descent. Europeans, so-called White people, are not the enemy. An in-depth knowledge of history will liberate the African American graduate or professional student from the burden of self-degradation that promoted mental and cultural enslavement for four hundred years.

PICK YOUR BATTLES STRATEGICALLY AND KNOW YOUR PROFESSORS

The African American graduate or professional student must come to the classroom armed with (1) a strong knowledge base, (2) a confident attitude, and (3) the wisdom to use both strategically. First of all, it is important to remember that what your great-grandparents, your grandparents, and your parents said is true—you do have to be better than your White counterparts. Your knowledge base must be both deeper and wider than that of your Caucasian classmates. You must certainly master the discipline as it is presented to you in a particular academic program. There can be no doubt about your knowledge of the subject matter. It is essential, however, that you look at this subject matter from the perspective of the African worldview and the growing knowledge base that is emanating from it. Let the African worldview serve as a filter for the paradigms, theories, assumptions, and empirical data presented within the context of your discipline. This is vital if you hope ultimately to have some relevance to the African American community and not simply be a Black reflection of Eurocentric thought.

The personalities of your professors in graduate or professional school are likely to be as varied as those in any other segment of the population. Get to know them! Stop by their offices. Have a conversation about something other than school. Ask them questions about their lives and perspectives. Are you sucking up? Of course not!

Some of your professors will welcome your input in class; others won't. It won't take you long to decide who is open to sharing and interaction and who simply enjoys the sound of his or her own voice, or the voices of those like him or her. Remember—you are not White, and it is possible that your input will not be interpreted in the same way as that of "Barbie" or "Ken." Make your judgment on the basis of your knowledge of the professor, not someone else's. Keep in mind that you don't have to fight a battle every day in class to maintain your dignity and self-respect. Of course you will want to correct blatant inaccuracies that may be stated in class by professors or students. You will want to challenge assumptions rooted in the racism and cultural imperialism that is usually ignored. Know in advance, however, that in some situations you may have to pay a price for your assertiveness (aggressiveness to some). You may be willing to accept a lower grade in a class if speaking your mind contributes to your overall sense of well-being and self-esteem. Be strategic, however; the integrity of your grade point average must be maintained! If you do decide to speak your mind, do it in a way that does not allow *how you said it* to become the issue rather than *what you said*. I'm sure this needs no elaboration! I can remember, for example, asking a particularly racist and arrogant professor what made certain people continually need to compare themselves with other people. This was done within the context of his presentation of some data showing lower African American scores on some personality dimension. He was clearly surprised by the question and sheepishly responded that he had "never thought about that question." That was exactly my point, and of course I thought I won that battle. I also thought that I should have gotten a higher grade for the course, but my self-esteem had received a needed boost!

JOIN AFRICAN AMERICAN PROFESSIONAL ASSOCIATIONS

One of the best ways of maintaining your dignity and self-esteem as an African American graduate student is to join African American professional associations. This includes not only African American organizations but also the Black caucuses of predominantly Caucasian organizations. Activities such as attending conferences with hundreds of other African Americans in your field and networking with Black caucus members at your discipline's major national or regional conferences can only serve to connect you in a positive way to those who are engaging in a struggle similar to your own. The value of meeting and engaging in dialogue with the top African American scholars in your field cannot be overstated. You will quickly learn that you are not the only one who has experienced racism, discrimination, and paternalism while pursuing your graduate degree. You will also learn that the activities of African American professionals must be primarily proactive rather than reactive. Of course the battle against racism must be continually fought, but we must continue to draw upon our worldview and cultural assets in creative ways as we seek to develop the African American community.

NETWORK WITH OTHER AFRICAN AMERICAN GRADUATE AND PROFESSIONAL STUDENTS IN YOUR FIELD AND RELATED AREAS

Your primary support group in graduate or professional school will be other African American students in your department or program. Get to know one another, socialize with one another, travel with one another, collaborate with one another on research projects. In the final year of my doctoral program, I worked with three other doctoral students on a research project that we designed in a way that allowed each of us to obtain our dissertation data. We collectively selected the instruments, gathered the data, and ultimately produced four dissertations from the data set. Over the previous three years we had been in classes together, had socialized together on a regular basis, had argued with one another, and felt that we trusted each other enough to embark upon the final task of our graduate school careers together.

This kind of group will function as your family as you matriculate through your program. As "family," however, members of this group will sometimes anger you, annoy you, and make you wish that they would go away! You won't mean it though, any more than you would wish ill upon your blood brother or sister. The combination of stress, honesty, and personality differences tests our patience in some strange ways. Therefore it is extremely important to broaden your support group in some creative ways. Getting to know African American graduate and professional students in related disciplines is one way. You will likely have a similar disciplinary language and related research interests. African American graduate and professional students in disciplines not directly related to your own can also be a source of considerable social support. Often a common interest in serving the African American community or the African diaspora can serve as a means of forging a long-lasting social and professional relationship.

READ! READ! READ!

As an African American graduate or professional student, you will certainly be inundated with a considerable amount of reading material from your discipline and related areas. There are, however, a number of books that won't be seen as required reading by your professors, yet they are in fact required reading for any African American who seeks to develop a positive sense of self and cultural identity in America. The following represents my own personal "top ten" in that they represent works that have contributed greatly to my self-esteem and cultural identity both as a graduate student and as a professional:

1. *Stolen Legacy*—George James
2. *Black Athena*—Martin Bernal

3. *African Origins of Civilization: Myth or Reality*—Cheikh Anta Diop
4. *They Came Before Columbus*—Ivan Van Sertima
5. *Blacks in Science*—Ivan Van Sertima
6. *The Miseducation of the Negro*—Carter G. Woodson
7. *The Souls of Black Folk*—W. E. B. Du Bois
8. *The Wretched of the Earth*—Frantz Fanon
9. *Black Skin/White Masks*—Frantz Fanon
10. *Neocolonialism: The Last Stage of Imperialism*—Kwame Nkrumah

These are ten of my favorites, books that I think have had the greatest impact on me as an African American and as an African American social scientist. Develop your own top ten, twenty, or thirty, and let these books influence how you view the world.

DIVERSIFY YOUR CULTURAL INTERESTS

In addition to establishing some required reading, African American graduate and professional students must seek national and international experiences that serve to build self-esteem and cultural identity. Travel is one major way to strengthen your connectedness to your brothers and sisters in the diaspora—assuming, of course, that there is no "Ugly American" baggage hanging around your neck! Instead of that spring break trip to Las Vegas, why not travel to Jamaica or Trinidad-Tobago? Why Hawaii, when you can travel to Ghana or Senegal for the same price? Be careful, however, not to travel with your "Black Skin" covered with a "White Mask," that is, a European American frame of reference for judging all things African. During my first days of a trip to Khartoum, Sudan, I took a bus ride into the central city area. As I got off the bus, I noticed a large group of young men congregating near a corner. My American sensibilities were immediately activated and I thought "Young Black Men plus darkness plus street corner equals trouble." It didn't take me long to find out that they were waiting to enter a mosque for the Muslims' evening prayer. As I joined them in prayer, I couldn't help but feel embarrassed by my initial apprehension. This and other lessons showed me that traveling to various parts of the African world can be a true test of whether the African worldview is real for you or simply a "phase" that you are passing through on your way to greater feats of "competitiveness," "rugged individualism," or "conspicuous consumption."

Other ways of enhancing your cultural identity and self-esteem include theater and fiction. Joining a group of your fellow students at an African or African American–oriented theater production can provide a thought-provoking and rewarding evening. Issues related to identity, gender, racism, economics, and family life are often presented in ways that force audience members to critically assess their own values. Getting together over dinner or coffee afterward can result in discussion and dialogue that will likely be remembered well beyond graduate or professional school.

The works of fiction writers from throughout the African diaspora can also serve as vehicles for the enhancement of cultural identity and self-esteem. Aime Cesaire, Ralph Ellison, Jean Toomer, Chinua Achebe, Toni Morrison, and Alice Walker are just a few of the fiction writers who have skillfully woven cultural themes into their fiction. Whether you agree with their perspective or not is irrelevant; they are among those writers whose works will force you to think.

ENGAGE IN RELEVANT WRITING AND RESEARCH

A few years ago, I heard a noted African American scholar say that he had asked a noted European American scholar if he could write an article without referencing any White authors. The European American scholar winced, took a few seconds to think about it, and ultimately said "no." The point being made by the African American scholar was that there are perspectives, bodies of knowledge, and ways of analyzing information that do not have a European reference point. While it is essential for you as an African American graduate or professional student to understand this reality, it is not necessary to actualize it while still a student. Just knowing that you have the ability to write a paper without a White reference will empower you tremendously. That ability cannot be realized, however, without a thorough study of African and African American scholars over time. As you choose paper topics, research and thesis topics, or dissertation topics, don't be afraid to choose topics that are directly relevant to the condition and struggle of African and American people. Seek out perspectives on this topic from a variety of cultural points of view, but make especially sure that you have clearly presented an African American perspective. Engaging in this process in a variety of contexts over time will solidify a feeling of empowerment in you that cannot come from a constant diet of "other" perspectives.

CONCLUSION

To conclude, the period of one's graduate or professional education *can* be time in which cultural identity is strengthened and a strong professional self-esteem is developed. On the other hand, it can be a time when these dimensions of self are weakened and redirected into a perpetual state of inferiority and cultural confusion. This period of time will be what *you* make of it. You may not want to take every bit of advice offered here and act on it, but you should at least consider whether it makes sense for you. Ultimately you will have to chart a course of action with which you feel comfortable. I can only hope and pray that this course of action will result in you becoming an African American graduate or professional student who feels good about yourself as an African American and that you feel you have something positive to offer our community as we enter the twenty-first century.

CHAPTER 12

Developing a Global Identity among Black American, Black African, and Black Caribbean Students

WILTON A. BARHAM

Professor and Head of the Department of Educational Leadership,
Grambling State University

In introducing Black Americans, Black Africans, and Caribbean Blacks to strategies for creating successful careers at the graduate and professional school level, it is important to explore some of the cultural, political, educational, and economic factors that will determine the level of success. It will undoubtedly require the development of a global identity among these groups of individuals in order to ensure successful experiences in graduate and professional schools.

What do I mean by a global identity? By this I mean the incorporation of cultural, political, educational, and economic experiences that transcend national, regional, and international boundaries that compel individuals to create support groups for survival and success. Identity is necessary for the level of organization needed for success in graduate and professional schools. That is, for Black Americans, Black Africans, and Caribbean Blacks to experience high levels of success in graduate and professional schools, they must be willing to embrace effective techniques and strategies of a cultural, political, educational, and economic nature that are developed from a common identity—a global one.

In this chapter, I present the rationale and evidence that the development of a global identity among Black Americans, Black Africans, and Caribbean Blacks is a necessary and sufficient prerequisite for achieving success in graduate and professional schools. This presentation embraces the similarities of cultural, political, educational, and economic experiences of the three groups. The chapter concludes with the presentation of techniques and strategies that flow from these experiences to form a global identity that will enhance these graduate students' success in the pursuit of a graduate and professional education and career. It also discusses the need for students to utilize other organizational resources for the promotion of survival and success.

CULTURAL EXPERIENCES

Black Americans, Black Africans, and Black Caribbean students share similar cultural experiences. The infamous slave trade brought Africans from West Africa to the New World. The infamous "slave triangle" established the physical link between Western Africa, the Caribbean, and the North American continent. The societies that emerged from this economic and personal exploitation have demonstrated similar cultural manifestations. These manifestations include the language, arts, music, and social institutions.

Although many Black Africans speak many different languages, they share the language of a common colonial master with Black Americans and Black Caribbean students. That common language is English. The British colonizers of West Africa, the Caribbean, and the United States of America forced the slaves to learn the language of their masters at the demise of their native tongues. It is this acquired language that these students must use to help forge this global identity. This common language fosters better communication and understanding among and between these groups. It makes it easier for these students to overcome other cultural differences in creating a global identity that will enhance academic survival and success.

The different languages and dialects spoken by these students have negative educational manifestations. The natural predisposition to the speaking of native languages and dialects prevents members of these groups from mastering the English language, the language of instruction and communication in graduate and professional schools. Therefore they enter the arena of learning at a disadvantage. However, their unique cultural heritage provides them with the tools for success in a very competitive learning environment. These tools must be put to use individually and collectively for survival and success.

According to Bullivant (1993), culture is a group's program for survival in and adaptation to its environment, and Banks and Banks (1997) indicated that it is also shared beliefs, symbols, and interpretations within a human group. This program that Bullivant mentioned "consists of knowledge, concepts, and values shared by group members through systems of communication" (Banks & Banks, 1997, p. 8). There are many beliefs, symbols, and interpretations that are common to these groups that can form the basis for a global identity. These common cultural manifestations can be seen in the groups' art forms, music, and religion.

POLITICAL AND ECONOMIC EXPERIENCES

Black Africans from English-speaking Africa, Black Americans, and Black English-speaking Caribbean students are from emerging political and economic democracies. The legacies of British colonial rule in Africa and the Caribbean are political and social institutions that promote democratic principles. Parliamentary democracies with the British monarchy as symbolic head of state have been developing in these independent states. Students from these countries recognize that an educated citizenry is necessary for the successful development and maintenance of democratic principles and institutions.

On the other hand, Black Americans have experienced another form of democratic system where the president (executive) shares governance of the country with the legislative and judicial branches. The president is also the ceremonial head of state. The cultural principles of equality, individualism, and individual opportunity are components of the core culture of the United States (Banks & Banks, 1997) to which Black Americans subscribe. These principles are in conflict with traditional African values of collective engagement, but students from Africa who experience these phenomena of modern political and economic institutions have adapted to the demands of this foreign system. A global identity will counteract this individualism that often threatens collaborative strategies for survival.

As the modern political and economic systems developed, students within these groups have experienced discriminations and other manifestations of institutional racism that impacted their educational, political, social, and economic development negatively. Despite the promises of democratic political institutions, these students represent a generation that has not escaped the detrimental effect of racism, social stratification, and sexism within their countries. It is this common awareness and desire to break out of the stranglehold that must become positive forces for change and success.

EDUCATIONAL EXPERIENCES

The elitist societies that were established by the British in the Caribbean and Africa relegated a large number of citizens to an educational system that did not and cannot meet the needs of this vast lower class. However, the talent and motivation of some of the students from this lower class result in academic successes in elementary, secondary, and postsecondary institutions. These students now seek educational advancement in a country—the United States of America—that also relegated its Black American citizens to substandard education in elementary, secondary, and postsecondary institutions. Thus they experience barriers to educational advancement in their respective countries. Despite these obstacles, there is a burning desire to beat the odds and succeed in higher education.

DEVELOPMENT OF A GLOBAL IDENTITY

There is a small proportion of graduate and professional school students who are Black Americans, Black Africans, and Black Caribbeans. In order for them to survive and succeed, they must rely strongly on the development of collaborative relationships that can foster success. The individualism that is so strongly espoused in the American culture cannot propel these students to successful heights. They must utilize their common heritage to build interrelationships that promote academic and social development.

How can this be done? It can be done through the development of student support organizations. In organizations, clear identity is a certain goal. Identity, and in this case global identity, is at the core of every organization, and this fuels its creation.

Black American, Black African, and Black Caribbean students should bring together their common experiences to support each other in their common goal to achieve academically. They need to explore why they have come together. By organizing themselves into a collective force, does this connect to their individual hopes and desires? Is the purpose big enough to welcome the contributions of all?

The desire to succeed in graduate and professional schools is big enough for these students. They have the capacity to create a support organization among themselves because there is coherence among their needs and expectations. This type of organization can be effective because it supports the students' abilities to organize themselves into a cohesive group. Through this cohesive organization, these groups of students can begin to develop connections. This is how an organization develops in all living systems (Wheatley & Keller-Rogers, 1996). Within the organization are many simultaneous connections, and individual contributions evolve too rapidly into group effects.

Molefi Kete Asante's framework of intercultural communication can greatly assist in the development of this global identity among Black American, Black African, and Black Caribbean students. Intercultural communication is a complex type of communication that emphasizes the personal (affective) and academic (cognitive) development of individuals (Vora, 1995). Asante urges that different cultural systems must learn from one another. This is exactly the same idea that I am promoting with the development of a global identity. Further, he indicated that it is essential to view concepts, events, and situations from diverse cultural perspectives so that we can obtain an unlimited view of social reality and a complete understanding of the human experience (Asante & Vora, 1978). Black African,

Black American, and Black Caribbean students must utilize their concepts and their knowledge of events and situations to forge this global identity so that they can use their better understanding of the human experience to their advantage. These students' view of reality is based upon their history, culture, and philosophic perception, which is different from the predominant European perspective encountered in America. They must also be willing to listen to another's perspective with an open mind so that effective intercultural communication can take place (Vora, 1995, p. 73).

UTILIZING OTHER ORGANIZATIONAL RESOURCES

In addition to the development of a global identity, Black American, Black African, and Black Caribbean students must seek out other established institutional support systems to aid in the development of needed skills such as writing, reading, speaking, and computational skills, among others.

Black African and Black Caribbean students are also known as international students, and even though they may develop this global identity discussed earlier, they bring many challenges to instructors in the many classes in which they are enrolled. These students have to be integrated into regular university classes, and having international students in our classes and communities can be both challenging and rewarding (Parker, 1999).

Initially, the most frustrating challenge for both faculty and these two specific groups of international students is a sense of "culture shock," which can lead to feelings of confusion, anger, and even despair (Parker, 1999; Schnell, 1990). Their academic and social expectations may differ, and although they want to be successful, they may not initially be able to adjust to the setting. This is the case, despite their knowledge and experience gained from being part of the organization that is fueled by building a global identity. Misunderstanding of cultural background and prior academic experience may lead to role confusion and frustration (Parker, 1999). However, the development of a global identity, along with an organizational structure, is expected to reduce this role confusion and frustration.

In addition, Black African and Black Caribbean students often have difficulty adjusting to the academic environment of American institutions of higher education (Robinson, 1992). Black American students have difficulty to a lesser degree.

Instructors who teach international students and researchers have identified some areas of concern: (a) Success may be motivated through individualism or competition. As indicated, the development of a global identity is intended to foster cooperative activities in which students rely less on the results of individualism. Nevertheless, students' orientation to one area or another (individualism versus competition) can be a challenge for instructors. (b) The academic setting may be one of equality versus informality. (c) Some students may be pragmatists, or some may develop alternate reasoning styles. (d) Students may be confused in settings where process is valued as much, or more, than actual product (time versus process orientation). (e) Instructors have to deal with the concept of plagiarism and knowledge ownership (Parker, 1999).

Many Black Africans, Black Americans, and Black Caribbean students need guided and consistent help in developing academic writing skills and in the writing process (Reid, 1997). This is precisely where these students must utilize available resources to assist them in developing these academic writing skills. Other areas of needed development are reading, speaking, and computer literacy.

What are some of these institutional resources? Some institutions have organized many different types of assistance for all students. The more successful programs are those that are comprehensive, which address the personal (affective) and academic (cognitive) development of all students. Components of the comprehensive models include advising, academic assistance, and personal support. Many of these programs are developed for undergraduates, but many graduate and professional students can benefit from them. In some cases, specific programs are developed for graduate and professional students and are separate from those of undergraduates.

Whatever the structure of these programs, Black African, Black American, and Black Caribbean students must seek out and use these resources for their benefit. Many of these support models are effective (Collins, 2000), and I am confident that many students will benefit from some or all aspects of them. The message is this: if all Black African, Black American, and Black Caribbean students develop a global identity and also utilize all available affective and cognitive support programs, they will have a very good chance of succeeding and surviving in graduate and professional schools. The result will be achievements that will have positive local, national, and international consequences.

REFERENCES

Asante, M.K., & Vora, E. (1978, February). *Intercultural versus interracial communication: Differences in perception.* Paper presented at the Society for Intercultural Education, Training, and Research annual conference, Phoenix, Arizona.

Banks, J.A., & Banks, C.A.M. (Eds.). (1997). *Multicultural education: Issues and perspectives* (3rd ed.). Needham Heights, MA: Allyn & Bacon.

Bullivant, B. (1993). Culture: Its nature and meaning for educators. In J.A. Banks and C.A.M. Banks (Eds.), *Multicultural education: Issues and perspectives* (2nd ed., pp. 29–47). Boston: Allyn & Bacon.

Collins, W. (2000). A comprehensive model of affective and cognitive support services for developmental college students. In Vernon L. Farmer and Wilton A. Barham (Eds.), *Selected models of developmental education programs in postsecondary institutions* (pp. 91–105). Lanham, MD: University Press of America.

Parker, R. (1999, March 5). *The challenges and rewards of working with international students.* A paper presented at the annual meeting of the Louisiana Education Research Association. New Orleans, LA.

Reid, J.M. (1997). Which non-native speaker? Differences between international students and U.S. students. *New Directions for Teaching and Learning, 70,* 17–27.

Robinson, J. (1992). *International students and American university culture: Adjustment issues.* (ERIC Document Reproduction Service No. ED350968).

Schnell, J.A. (1990). *The multicultural classroom: Working to create opportunities out of possible obstacles.* (ERIC Document Reproduction Service No. ED 320175).

Vora, E. (1995). Asante's contributions to intercultural communication. In Dhyana Ziegler (Ed.), *Molefi Kete Asante and Afrocentricity: In praise and in criticism* (pp. 71–85). Nashville, TN: James C. Winston.

Wheatley, M.J., & Keller-Rogers, M. (1996). *A simpler way.* San Francisco: Berrett-Koehler.

CHAPTER 13

Competencies for Developing an African American Scholar

The Community of Scholars Model

LEE JONES

Associate Dean of the College of Education and Associate Professor of Educational Leadership, Department of Educational Leadership, Florida State University

> An African American Scholar is one who contributes original ideas, new insights and information to the existing fund of knowledge—whether or not he/she has a string of academic degrees or executes scholarly activities in a manner appropriate to the traditional and conventions of the existing world of scholarship. (Nathan Hare)

A HOLISTIC APPROACH TO SCHOLARSHIP

Despite the challenges that are before us, we know from American history that our plight on the soils of this land has been consistently difficult. We have always had to justify our existence and clarify why we do what we do. It does not matter whether we are talking about sports, education, science, research, or any other profession. We also know from history that we were left a legacy to push forward despite the odds. People like Shem Hotep, John Henry Clark, Harriet Tubman, Fannie Lou Hamer, and others have paved the way for every African American and other underrepresented groups to achieve personal and collective goals. There will be academicians who will read this book and perhaps feel that it is not scholarly enough. I would argue that higher education, more than any other profession, ought to expand from a linear and monolithic view of scholarship. If we are ever going to move from a place of global acknowledgment of diversity to manifesting this commitment through accepting the unique contributions that ethnic and racial scholarship bring, we will need to begin to transform the academic enterprise. This paradigm shift will offer quite a challenge to those who have spent a lifetime in perpetuating the status quo. My guess is that we will need to continue with our plight. I purport that those who are aspiring to higher levels of educational attainment will need to adopt a model of scholarship development that will continue supporting our research interest while continuing to add to the array of research that is conducted. I would also offer that we have to begin to develop not only a community of scholars who will broaden higher education's definition of scholarship but a group who will increase the number of African Americans pursuing terminal degrees.

High attrition rates and overall underrepresentation of African Americans in higher education graduate programs is an issue of critical concern. Therefore the primary focus of the Community of Scholars (COS) model is to produce African American scholars who will succeed in doctoral studies and within the academy. Previous research has provided linear approaches to examining persistence issues for African American scholars in doctoral programs. One such approach includes simply providing access, recruitment, and retention initiatives within the academy. What is needed is a comprehensive model that supports, nurtures, and develops African Americans as scholars within the academy. Critical focus is necessary during the doctoral process—a time in which most students are developing their perceptions and beliefs about scholarship.

The COS model proposes a society of scholars who will work collaboratively within the academy and beyond. Aside from incentives that assist in student persistence (i.e., financial assistance and mentoring), the COS model will influence the academic, social, professional, spiritual, and emotional development of scholars. Scholars would then be educated in synthetic thinking, which means thinking from within and from without various systems while maintaining perspective on all paradigms. The Community of Scholars seeks to fully utilize and actualize the advantage of the diverse perspectives and approaches of educators. Members literally challenge, encourage, and educate each other to achieve advanced paradigms. Members also incorporate community service and leadership within the academy and greater community. In so doing, members will create a perpetual framework for future generations to achieve excellence in scholarship, community, and humanity.

THE VISION

The primary outcomes of the COS model are African American scholars who will revitalize and reshape scholarship and research as they relate to the

African American community. This is not the vision itself but a single component. An African American with a degree is not sufficient in light of the quality of life African Americans currently experience. Previous scholarship that has sought to explain African American life has tended to examine it as a negative experience in itself. What we need are scholars who will counteract this trend with the intention of elevating the community. The COS vision is a society of African American professionals who nurture subsequent generations of scholars to levels of accomplishment greater than one individual.

Furthermore, the structure of American education does little to include the contributions of all of its constituents. Hence another component of the COS vision is a relationship among the scholars that fosters, in the African tradition, synthetic thinking. Specifically, this means thinking within and without the system(s) and maintaining the perspective of each item and its relevance to the whole. Members literally challenge, encourage, and educate each other to achieve more advanced paradigms. In so doing, members develop a framework for future generations to have an understanding of scholarship, community, and humanity that is applicable to their time and space.

The vision of the COS also implies a community of scholars who work with the African American community. Woodson (1990) provides an explanation of the afflictions of African American professionals and the implications of a miseducated and unnurturing population. The COS vision requires that all scholars maintain and strengthen their relationships with the African American community and utilize the advantages of beginning an ascent of the socioeconomic ladder from the bottom rung. The COS vision recognizes that one of our most debilitating characteristics is poor solidarity, as evidenced by our political and economic behavior (Kotkin, 1993).

Scholars who participate in the COS model will depart from their degree programs understanding their relative position in society. They will receive an academic degree, possess a holistic paradigm, work with the African American community, and create scholarship that is central to highlighting and improving the African American community.

PSYCHOLOGICAL HEALTH DEVELOPMENT

African Americans who enter the American educational structure face a system that was not originally designed for inclusive practices. In its evolution, all efforts to accommodate the expanding diversity of the populace have confounded its ability to accomplish the espoused goal of providing all students with the necessary education for a quality life. Though the immediate concern of the COS is higher education completion, the cumulative effects of K–12 education must not be ignored.

When a student arrives at the college and the community, there is some healing that must be done. Matriculation to the collegiate level is not without psychological influences that may result from experiences such as suppression of identity, education without practical relevance, and saturation of negative images of African Americans. There are also established societal norms, particularly in advanced degree programs, that are culturally different from what many African American students are accustomed to.

The Community of Scholars model has three primary components (the self, the community, and outcomes), and a fourth component (Maat) that is its structural component.

The Self

The self component of the COS model deals primarily with what each individual member brings to the graduate school and scholarly experience. This includes readiness for scholarship, readiness for collaborative learning, adjustment issues, individual purpose, and expectations and perceptions of the graduate experience and of the community of scholars. As the self begins to better understand its principal concerns for scholarship, it should open the possibilities for synergistic developments within the community.

Below are the competencies of a developing African American Scholar:

1. Commitment to a spiritual force higher than life
2. The development of a personal vision statement outlining the multiple steps and strategies needed to accomplish your ultimate vision
3. A thorough assessment of the technical skills needed to excel in your academic discipline
4. An understanding of the social, political, intellectual, academic, and psychological realities of African Americans in America
5. The development of a personal conceptual framework that facilitates the actualization of spiritual balance, mental stability, physical conditioning, and internal peace
6. A personal discipline audit aimed at establishing a proactive teaching, research, and/or administrative commitment to quality
7. A thorough understanding of group dynamics, which leads to meaningful interpersonal communications across ethnic and gender lines
8. A passion and desire to always be willing to "take somebody with you" to the top

The Community

The development of a paradigm that is more suitable to African American intellectual expression and affirmation is a primary concern for the Community of Scholars. Carter G. Woodson's alert recognition, more than fifty years ago, that something is severely wrong with the way African Americans are educated, provides the principal impetus for the development of a paradigm that is most suitable for our training and development. The community consists of the coming together of young scholars and mentors from the academic community, the larger community, or both. The community should initially set forth a vision and purpose for the group. Many of the core activities that will occur within this scholarly community will consist of mentoring, scholarly identity development, support and motivation, and professional, personal, and social development.

The critical place of community for self-realization, the centrality of an ethics that reaches beyond individual satisfaction, and the encompassing framework of a relational worldview are all aspects of the community that will resonate as the community develops.

The Outcomes

The primary outcomes of the community of scholars will be degreed professionals that will effectively use applied and theoretical scholarship for progress. Other primary results should include a well-formed scholarly identity, focused research interest and community interest, a feeling of responsibility to humanity, an established nurturing cycle to perpetuate the growth of the Community of Scholars. Ultimately, the Community of Scholars will provide a holistic approach to scholarship, which will lead to Ph.D. completion for more African Americans.

REFERENCES

Kotkin, J. (1993). *How race, religion, and identity determine success in the new global economy.* New York: Random House.

Woodson, C. G. (1990). *The miseducation of the Negro.* Lawrenceville, NJ: Africa World Press.

CHAPTER 14

Utilizing Internships and Teaching and Research Assistantships to Enhance Learning

ERNESTA P. PENDLETON

Program Analyst, Office of Academic Affairs, Division of Academic Programs and Research, University of the District of Columbia

One of the greatest deterrents to higher education at the graduate level is the cost factor. Because of the negative lore of burdensome loan repayments, many students fail to explore or overlook the many other opportunities that exist in the academy to continue their education. It is difficult to convince some students that higher education is not only available but affordable as well. Through the years higher education institutions have assumed the responsibility for presenting students with options to enhance their learning experiences. By following these established pathways to success, savvy students are able to complete master's and doctoral degrees by channeling what may have started as volunteer service during the undergraduate years into financial packages for graduate-level higher education. Through careful financial, academic, and vocational planning, you too can carve out a niche for your life's work.

Institutions of higher education have long recognized the gold mine of talent and capability that their students represent. Now more students are beginning to appreciate the level of support institutions can provide in helping to meet their career goals. They are seeing that when preparation meets opportunity great things can happen. Internships and graduate assistantships are plentiful. I know of no better way to "get a foot in the door," to "climb the corporate ladder," or to gain relevant work experience than to embark on an on-the-job learning experience as a complement to a degree program of study. Major corporations (Sony, NBA, the *Washington Post*, Procter and Gamble), government agencies (the U.S. Department of State, the White House, the CIA), and private businesses and foundations (Kennedy Center, Hewlett-Packard, Mellon) work in partnership with colleges and universities to solicit potential employees through various incentive programs. These are win-win situations for all involved; the students get the job experience, the companies get enthusiastic workers and good public relations, and the institutions produce employable graduates.

I would encourage minority students to take advantage of opportunities to participate in these learning-enhancement experiences beginning with the sophomore year of their undergraduate education on through graduate school. The benefits of such programs are well worth the time spent applying. They enable students to

1. Earn income, credit, or tuition waivers to further their educational pursuits
2. Get exposure to professionals in the field who might not be accessible otherwise
3. Experience an actual job environment in a field of professional interest
4. Network in the field as a prelude to a full-time job offer
5. Check out a potential employer, company, or educational area of interest
6. Gain confidence in the ability to handle professional working relationships
7. Graduate with solid work experiences on the resume

APPLICATION PROCEDURES

To apply for the more popular and competitive internships and graduate assistantships, the following are usually required: a cover letter, a statement (about three hundred words) of your personal objectives, a resume, two or three letters of recommendation, and a transcript of college courses. A sample portfolio or video may be requested in some fields (e.g., television, graphic arts). The most important requirement is often the cover letter, which should be well written and should express knowledge, enthusiasm, and interest in the company and the field in general. Have in mind what your strengths are and browse the company's Web site to learn enough background history of the organization to know where your talents could best be used for the benefit of the company and your own personal interests.

A subliminal message results from a sloppy application, just as it does from a well-written one. Ask yourself, what message does my application send? Typographical and grammatical errors are definite turnoffs to reviewers of your material. Promising applications may be followed up with a telephone or in-person interview before the final selection is made, so practice presentation skills and wear proper attire at the interview. Most important, since these opportunities are competitive, adherence to deadlines is essential; usually all material must be on file at the stated time. The reason most often cited for not favorably considering an application is that all requested documentation was not received in a timely manner. Late deadlines are usually March to April 1 for summer positions, June to August 1 for fall, and October to January 1 for spring. Some applications are due six months prior to the starting date, so careful planning and follow-through are essential.

Some companies' application procedures may be less formal and less competitive than others owing to a lack of applicants; the ratio of applicants to selectees varies according to type and within programs. Generally speaking, though, internships are granted on an average to 5 to 20 percent of those sought. Administrative and teaching assistantships are restricted and easier to obtain, at a rate of about 70 percent, while research assistantships with even less competition are usually easier to get, at an 80 percent rate.

INTERNSHIPS

Internship opportunities are everywhere. They have become fashionable among young adults looking for work experience. Oldman and Hamadeh (1999b) agree that "as common as internships were a generation ago, these days have seen an explosion among students and employers alike, in the popularity and perceived importance of internship programs" (p. xiii). Internships, which may be full-time for a short period or part-time for a longer period, are supervised work experiences related to an undergraduate or graduate field of study and carried out for a business, government agency, nonprofit organization, or professor. Orientation and training are provided by the company, and for the period of the internship (usually about eight weeks) you will be accepted and treated as an employee. Parrish (1999) advises, "Prior to accepting the internship, there should be an understanding between the student and the employer as to the type of training the student will receive and whether he or she will be compensated" (p. 45).

The internship program is usually overseen by a coordinator, who reviews applications, interviews and selects the interns, and is responsible for the overall coordination of the intern experience. Moreover, the coordinator is usually the individual who provides the intern with the confirmation letter designating the placement site. This regular, full-time staff person is often a member of the personnel or human resources unit of the organization. While many internships will specify a minimum grade point average, coordinators have some discretion in making their selections. The internship coordinator is a good person to know, since his or her recommendation will carry great weight with the person making the final selection.

Most internships are designed to provide students with in-depth exposure to professional-level techniques and practices. This degree of responsibility involves both challenges and benefits. Though some interns are assigned administrative and production duties, because of collective bargaining agreements within a company, some internships may not provide interns with hands-on experience in the sensitive areas of operation they would prefer (e.g., television). Companies like to have interns who are enthusiastic but professional and mature as well. For someone with limited work experience, an internship may involve a stressful adjustment in time management. It may even challenge one's fear of travel if it entails relocation to a new area.

But the perks alone of an internship are inviting. Some perks include free entertainment passes, daily interaction with company bigwigs, acknowledgment in company publications, access to recreation and sports facilities, discounts, permanent jobs, superb working environments, breakfast and lunch meetings. Moreover, "For some students, an internship ... gives them the opportunity to travel and explore other cities and cultures" (Cates-McIver, 1998, p. 72). The range of incentives and opportunities afforded interns are broad and varied.

An internship may be academic or nonacademic, paid or voluntary. Stipends, if offered, are usually paid half at the midpoint of the internship and half upon the intern's successful completion of the program (applicable payroll deductions are taken from payments). Sometimes an intern is given the option to receive three or six hours of college credit in lieu of the stipend, in which case it is an academic internship. The applicant and the appropriate college official must sign an internship agreement form prior to the assignment. After successful completion of the internship, the intern submits a final report and the company submits an evaluation of the intern. Upon approval, a credit notation is entered on the college transcript as for any other course. Just as common and desirable, however, is the unpaid internship, which yields no monetary or academic reward. Such internships may be more valuable, however, than a paid assignment. Some of the most prestigious internships offer no compensation (e.g., the White House, C-SPAN, the Smithsonian Institution) but are very impressive on a resume and may result in priceless contacts for later full-time job references. In fact, some corporations such as the Federal Reserve Bank provide higher education grants as incentives to remain with the company.

My own unpaid four-month internship was completed at the headquarters of the National Association for Educational Opportunity (NAFEO), the umbrella organization for the nation's historically black colleges and universities in Washington, D.C. It was a rewarding experience, and I was able to fit in and accomplish some things I might not have done otherwise. I was assigned primarily to work in the office of *Black Excellence* magazine, where I was able to publish an article, assemble the annual conference summary, edit presentations, and perform other duties as assigned for professionals with whom I maintain contact today. For this internship, I earned six graduate credits toward my doctoral degree from Grambling State University in Grambling, Louisiana.

Some famous people and their internships include the following:

Patrick Ewing—Capitol Hill
Bill Gates—congressional page
Spike Lee—Columbia Pictures Studios
William J. Clinton—Capitol Hill
Jodie Foster—*Esquire Magazine*
Monica Lewinsky—the White House

While some internship sources (such as the Academy of Television Arts and Sciences) reimburse students for their travel expenses, interns are usually responsible for their own housing, food, and other expenses. Foreign students in U.S. schools already possess the necessary visa to accept an American-based internship, but an Employment Authorization Document (EAD) must be secured through the Immigration and Naturalization Service (Oldman & Hamadeh, 1999b, p. 121). Overseas internships usually require vaccinations, a passport, and a visa or work permit, the paperwork for which often takes two to four months to process. For these reasons, early identification and application are a must for international internships.

GRADUATE ASSISTANTSHIPS

Graduate assistantships, funded by private foundations or the budget of the applicant's major department, may be teaching- or research-oriented. In addition, some institutions make available administrative assistantships, which are earmarked for graduate students but may not come under the jurisdiction of the graduate school dean. To apply for these opportunities, students must be enrolled full-time as master's or doctoral students. A suitable undergraduate grade point average (3.2 or above) is critical for receiving initial financial assistance in graduate school, but once admitted, assistantships and other programs become available upon demonstration of satisfactory progress. One-on-one tutoring and internship experiences are valuable preludes to graduate assistantships. Students who accept these institutional positions are paid for services rendered in addition to receiving remitted tuition. Assignments are usually related to the area of specialization. These offers are dependent upon satisfactory academic progress, which may be determined quantitatively (based on number of class completions) or qualitatively (based on acceptable grade point average).

TEACHING ASSISTANTSHIPS

Teaching assistantships are academic appointments awarded to graduate students; they do not involve academic tenure. Teaching assistants, or TAs, work under the general guidance of a senior faculty member in their major department. These opportunities provide experience in planning and implementing instruction with a minimum of supervision. Recommendations from faculty members, good oral and written communication skills, computer proficiency, and completed relevant course work, as well as the ability to work independently, are required of applicants. Applicants must be perceived to be making satisfactory progress toward the degree. Attention to detail, strong organizational skills, and reliability are essential qualities in a successful teaching assistant. TA training provides the experience required to pursue a tenure-track position in the professorate, the full-time college faculty, at a future date. In fact, "Traditionally, the *college* teaching path has begun in graduate school, where graduate students begin the training and socialization that allow them to follow a well-trod path into their first job as an assistant professor, through promotion, tenure, and retirement" ("Pathways," p. 7).

Other benefits of a teaching assistantship include tuition remission and a stipend, dependent upon an applicant's qualifications and the number of hours worked per week. For a typical twenty-hour per week assignment, the stipend may be about ten to fifteen thousand dollars plus health insurance. Most appointments may be extended up to about four years. Undergraduates often don't appreciate the difference between a TA and a professor except for age and may address the TA (erroneously, of course) as "Doctor so-and-so." While clearly this is an ego booster, the real benefit lies in the fact that teaching is arguably the best way to learn a subject. Both the TA and the student, therefore, benefit from the experience.

Furthermore, TAs have become essential to the personnel structure of higher education institutions today. A recent study of who teaches undergraduates at Yale University indicates that 70 percent of class instruction is performed by graduate students and adjunct instructors (Wilson 1999). TAs teach undergraduate classes, lead discussion groups, advise students, attend faculty meetings, oversee laboratory work, and grade examinations and lab reports. These activities require that they be able to communicate effectively with faculty, staff, administrators, and students. Most TAs hold weekly office hours.

RESEARCH ASSISTANTSHIPS

Research assistantships offer stipends to students to assist a professor on an experiment or research project. These awards afford academically talented students a unique opportunity to acquire valuable hands-on research training, study, and experience useful toward careers in their chosen fields. Research assistantships require analytical skills, experience working with questionnaires and statistical data, survey technology, and outcomes assessment. Writing skills are essential as well as the ability to work well with faculty, staff, and administrators with a minimum of supervision to prepare and analyze reports, charts, and graphs. Personal qualities required are curiosity, dedication, and compatibility. Some research assistantships are renewable annually for up to four years or for the life of the project. There are two types of research options: as the primary investigator and as support to a primary investigator.

Key to research opportunities of the first type is the development of a proposal. Each applicant must independently prepare a proposal based on his or her research plans. Proposals must conform in format to the guidelines specified by the solicitor. A basic well-organized proposal will contain a cover letter, a three-hundred-word executive summary, statement of the problem, objective, background, statement of work to be performed (with timeline), description of facilities, estimated budget, bibliography, and personnel. Section titles should be bold for quick identification, and the entire document should be double spaced with pages numbered. It is important to convince the reader of your proposal that you are capable of handling the project in the time allotted. Prior courses taken or papers written on the subject can therefore be used as evidence and reasons for accepting your request for funding. Such internal proposals can vary in length, should express interest and enthusiasm in the subject, and should convince the reader that you are the person who can best carry out the project.

The second type of research assistant is selected to assist with an ongoing experiment or research project under the direction of a major professor or group of professors who function as mentor(s). A major responsibility of these types of research assistants is to be of support to the project director. For this reason, "They may risk losing their assistantship if their work is not compatible with that of their mentor, if it deviates from the overall research design, or if the research grant supporting the work is not renewed" (*Graduate Student*, 1990). Research assistantships may be funded by a philanthropic foundation or the major department's or project's budget. Consequently, there is a significant cost-benefit analysis that undergirds such work.

In all, graduate students, both TAs and researchers, are encouraged to publish and present their research findings as a prelude to professional careers as professors, project directors, policy analysts, senior researchers, and so forth. Graduate assistantships, therefore, may involve surveying a field of literature, writing articles, and attending various meetings, conferences, and related workshops as a part of the students' professional development. Increasingly, similar research opportunities are being extended to the undergraduate level through such programs as Honors and the Department of Education's Ronald McNair Post-Baccalaureate Achievement Program. If these programs are available on your campus, seek to become affiliated with them as early as possible in your undergraduate career.

ADMINISTRATIVE ASSISTANTSHIPS

Administrative assistantships provide graduate student support to administrative units of the institution. Most of the nation's large institutions provide these positions, which involve extensive student contact through advising, transcript evaluations, graduation audits, and recruitment and retention efforts. Data entry skills, weekly staff meetings, and good organizational skills are some of the requirements and expectations of these positions.

The availability of administrative assistantships may be overlooked, since they may not originate in the student's department. Because these positions may be publicized selectively, it is wise to inquire and to self-promote in the area of interest. Some positions, by default, may get filled by less experienced undergraduates, so it is important to get the word out on campus that you are available and in need of financial assistance.

CONCLUSION

Internships and graduate assistantships are excellent and beneficial supplements to a college education today. Most institutions feature their use. Many of these opportunities are designed to solicit participation at the graduate level by members of underrepresented groups in the field. Minorities, therefore, are encouraged to apply. Not only may they be of monetary benefit, but more important, they provide students with additional knowledge and competence to set realistic goals and pursue related careers. And it is always good to approach a potential full-time employer with quality work experiences.

You should think of these exploratory opportunities as real jobs, because they are connections to the real world. Employers look for the same qualities in the intern or researcher as they look for in regular employees: a positive attitude, strong communication skills, favorable recommendations, relevant courses taken, good grades, and high interest (*EQW Survey,* 1995). Once you get the opportunity to work, make a success of your efforts, because a good impression just might lead to a senior-level position once the degrees are completed. Maintain good attendance, dress professionally, and establish good and positive relations with other workers. Keep a daily log of activities and a file of telephone numbers of your professional contacts. Extended appointments, though common, are not automatic; they are contingent upon a performance review and satisfactory progress toward the degree.

Finally, make the most of the resources at your disposal. While the foregoing information is applicable to full-time students, part-time student assistance is also available. The graduate school and other campus offices are sources of brochures, applications, and other information that will assist your search efforts. In addition, INROADS, Inc., an Atlanta-based company, recruits participants for internships offered by companies in this country and abroad. Visit its Web site at www.internships.com to order national listings of internships available by city.

See the references below for more resources available to help you in your search for the opportunity that's right for you. Good luck!

REFERENCES

Cates-McIver, L. (1998). The value of internships and co-op opportunities for college students. *The Black Collegian, 29*(1), 72, 74, 163.

EQW National Employer Survey. (1995, February). National Center on the Educational Quality of the Workforce, U.S. Department of Education.

Graduate Student Financial Support. (1990). Washington, DC: Council of Graduate Schools.

Kaplan, R.K. (1999). Interns: Know your legal rights. *Careers and the College Grad, 13*(1), 44–45.

Oldman, M., & Hamadeh, S. (1999a). *America's Top Internships.* New York: Princeton Review Publishing.

Oldman, M., & Hamadeh, S. (1999b). *The Internship Bible.* New York: Princeton Review Publishing.

Parrish, R. (1999). Making the most of the perfect internship. *Careers and the College Grad,* 13(1), 43.

Pathways through the field of higher education. (1999). *Academic Leader, 15*(6), 1–8.

Wilson, R. (1999, April). Who teaches at Yale? *Chronicle of Higher Education,* A15.

CHAPTER 15

Promoting Scholarly Writing and Publishing to Enhance the Scholarship of Black Graduate Students

EVELYN SHEPHERD-WYNN

Assistant Professor of English, Department of English,
Grambling State University

I became involved in publishing when I chose Vernon L. Farmer, a professor of educational leadership at Grambling State University (GSU), for my adviser. He had an established track record for publishing and a no-nonsense attitude about it. He believes that publishing is the paramount of scholarship and that graduate students should be serious about developing an agenda to enhance their personal scholarship. It did not take long for me to become acclimated to this way of thinking, so I became immersed in the scholarly, hard-working, and driven environment that he created for his students. I was ready to enhance my scholarship, but the opportunity came sooner than I had imagined. Dr. Farmer and Dr. Wilton A. Barham, his colleague and protégé as well as a professor of educational leadership at GSU, were invited to serve as guest editors for the *Journal of Research in Developmental Education,* one of the leading periodicals in the field of developmental education. It was at this time that Dr. Farmer offered me the opportunity to publish. Because this would be my first time writing an article for publication, he suggested that I consider coauthoring it with an individual who already had her doctorate and who had similar career interests. After months of endless research hours, sleepless nights, heated debates, and rigorous rewrites, our article was finally in print. By no means am I oversimplifying or implying that the publication process is a glamorous one, but it would take too long to explain every setback we experienced in getting the article accepted for publication. In fact, this was one of the most stressful, grueling experiences I have ever encountered in writing for publication, and at the same time, it was one of the most enriching.

Although publishing offers many rewarding experiences for graduate students, many of them do not attempt to publish. The literature reveals that graduate students without a publication record will have a difficult time in the job market. It is foremost then that you publish while attending graduate or professional school to build a strong publication portfolio, making yourself more marketable. Many graduate and professional schools provide opportunities for students to develop their writing skills within a discipline; nevertheless, some institutions do not have programs structured to help students enhance their scholarly writing and publishing. Because some institutions do not provide an infrastructure for strengthening graduate students' writing skills, this chapter presents information, suggestions, and strategies for Black graduate students who wish to develop a personal program of productive publishing and who wish to increase the chances of having their articles accepted for publication.

MAKE TIME OUT OF NO TIME

While pursuing your graduate degree, there will never be enough time to publish. Or so you think! My major adviser constantly reminded me that there will always be some event impacting or distracting my graduate study. Some will be more detrimental than others. So whenever I complained about not having enough time to publish because of my busy agenda, he would always respond emphatically, "Make time out of no time!" He was right; I always found a way to publish even when there seemed to be no way. There are some simple strategies that you can employ to develop a productive publishing program. First, collect data prior to beginning to write; it hinders your productivity when you have to conceptualize, write, and collect data simultaneously. Also, prior to your writing sessions, you can list both short- and long-term goals along with attainable deadline dates. It might be helpful to go a step further by breaking the list of short-term goals down on a weekly or daily basis. This list should be visible, placed in key locations such as on your computer, desk, or refrigerator as a reminder. Once you decide upon the best time for composing, make sure that you maximize your time by having all materials ready and organized. In other words, don't spend your writing time looking for paper, pens, cartridges, toner. For those who prefer to use tape recorders, use a small, compact, easy-to-carry tape recorder to record your writing ideas. There will never be enough time; you simply have to make time.

WORK CLOSELY WITH PROFESSORS WHO PUBLISH

Often graduate students shy away from publishing because many professional journals call for a different kind of writing, and they are afraid that their chances of getting published are extremely slim. You can diminish the shyness or fear concerning scholarly writing and publishing by working closely with professors who publish. Identify professors who have an excellent track record for publishing and who also encourage students to publish. Published professors can offer valuable suggestions and strategies to graduate students desiring to publish. Moreover, professors who are willing to spend extra time sharing their publishing experiences and critiquing papers for students can help remove the fear of publishing. You should also seek assistance from professors who serve on editorial boards. The advice and suggestions from this kind of professional support can help you improve your manuscripts, thereby enhancing your publication efforts. Finally, published professors can serve as mentors and at the same time help to demystify some of the anxiety and fear concerning writing for publication.

COLLABORATE WITH PEERS

Collaboration has grown tremendously over the past decades. The image of graduate students conducting research and writing papers in isolation no longer exists. Many choose to work in concert with peers because collaboration increases productivity, maintains motivation, and stimulates creativity. Working closely in collaborative groups will help you to critically review writing projects in progress, conference papers, or journal articles before they are submitted to faculty and journals. This will also help you discuss and transform your ideas. Therefore, I urge you to become actively involved in brainstorming sessions with faculty and peers.

EXPLORE RESEARCH AREAS EARLY IN YOUR DEGREE PROGRAM

Graduate students' research efforts typically focus on their thesis or dissertation. Therefore, Black graduate students should explore research areas of interest early in their degree program. When deciding on your thesis or dissertation topic, you should make sure that you discover the links between your academic interests, prior experience, and career goals. One of the first things my adviser did was to query me about my career goals and experiences. He stressed the importance of students selecting a research area they enjoy, one that can enhance their career and that can contribute to the body of literature in their related research area. The sooner you decide upon your dissertation focus, the sooner you can begin writing about and researching the topic(s) in your courses. Graduate students who write papers on topics relating to the dissertation can receive critical feedback from professors. For example, every time you take a course and the opportunity presents itself, you should write papers updating and expanding the research topic(s). One strategy I used was to keep notebooks containing research articles, book chapters, any literature relating to my dissertation topic. I further organized the information according to variables, which was extremely helpful when I wrote chapter 2 of my dissertation. After each paper has been critiqued, you should make revisions in preparation for publication. The more you research and write about the same area, the more likely it is that you will become an expert in your chosen profession. Professional critiques from professors, published or unpublished, are the next best thing to having editorial comments.

COAUTHOR WITH PEERS AND PROFESSORS

Coauthoring is a joint effort that involves common goals and outcomes for which the authors share responsibility and credit. Consequently, it is one of the best ways to publish for novice writers. Teaming up with peers or professors can increase your publication productivity. Since no two people write or think alike, this can help to ensure that the article will be globally written, increasing the chances for acceptance. Because of these divergent and global perspectives, it is important that you carefully examine the following prior to committing to coauthorship: the purpose of the article, the best person with whom to share this coauthorship, the possibilities of being lead author, the divisions of labor, and the guidelines or parameters to follow. Moreover, you should consider your ability to take constructive criticism about your writing from a peer. These are some of the key issues that should be considered openly and honestly during the initial stages of the writing process, because they will help determine whether you should consider coauthoring. Some of these issues can be easily addressed. For example, if you coauthor with your professor, he or she will more than likely serve as the lead author. Professors may ask you to conduct computer and manual literature searches, collect and analyze data, follow up on correspondences, and other logistical tasks. On the other hand, if you are coauthoring with a peer, whoever contributes the most to the article should be the lead author. Another factor that helps determine who should be the lead author is who is the individual responsible for conceptualizing the idea(s) for the article and for conducting the research.

Moreover, after your dissertation has been completed, you may publish sections of the document with minor modifications. At this time, you can and should be the lead author; however, because your professor may proofread, edit, and make suggestions for publications, he or she may serve as a coauthor. You cannot afford to be a selfish author, because a selfish author ends up being an unpublished author. The most important thing is that you will be breaking into print.

PARTICIPATE IN WRITING PROGRAMS

As mentioned earlier, many graduate and professional schools offer programs structured to help develop Black graduate students' writing for publication. In some cases, graduate-level writing courses are included in the curriculum to help students move their writing to a more advanced level for publishing. Professors should guide and encourage their students to write for publication, thereby empowering them as professional practitioners and reformers in their fields. Professors can take steps to create an environment of professional scholarship within their courses. Demystifying writing for publication reinforces class content and gives students a view of writing as part of their scholarly dialogue. In addition to these courses, many graduate and professional schools provide graduate writing labs where students can seek editorial and technical assistance. Taking advantage of such programs is a strategy that you can employ to achieve your publication goals.

DEVELOP PAPERS AND PRESENT AT CONFERENCES

Another way to enhance your publication agenda is to write papers to present at local, state, national, and international conferences. Submitting papers to conferences provides another opportunity for your papers to be critiqued and judged by peers. Moreover, you will have a chance to share papers with an audience with similar academic and research interests; therefore the feedback can be very valuable in preparing papers for publication. For novice presenters, it is recommended that you begin presenting at local conferences and later at national and international conferences. Receiving feedback on conference papers is an excellent strategy for Black graduate students working toward a journal publication. You will benefit from the conference experiences while developing a professional network that will help you in pursuing your publishing goals.

BECOME FAMILIAR WITH RELATED JOURNALS

If you want to be successful at publishing, review journals related to your research interest(s). One of the best ways to increase the chances of having your article accepted for publication is to submit the article to the right journal. Having a well-written, polished article means nothing if it is submitted to the wrong journal. Therefore you should identify and survey related journals, examining them to find out more about their mission and other specifications including the following:

- The type of audience
- Whether they have themed or unthemed issues
- What is their track record for accepting articles for publication, particularly from novice writers
- Whether the journal is considered prestigious
- The status of the journal's readership
- Whether the journal is refereed
- Whether the journal accepts research articles
- Whether electronic submissions are acceptable
- What style manual is acceptable
- Whether charts, graphs, tables are acceptable
- Whether there are photo requirements
- Whether there are publishing expenses or reading fees

As you do for conferences, you should begin submitting manuscripts to related publication journals on the state level.

MODEL WRITING STYLE OF ARTICLES PUBLISHED IN RELATED JOURNALS

Once you have identified publication journals related to your research topic, you should observe the structure and organization of the journal, noting different sections and requirements concerning submission of your manuscript. In fact, I recommend subscribing to the journal(s) so you can keep abreast of the type of material, issues, audience, and specific guidelines for publication. You should model the writing styles of articles, following the conventional style of other articles published in the journals. The writing styles of journals, however, can vary immensely. For example, some journals accept only research articles that call for a more rigid and formal style of writing, while other journals accept practical types of articles sharing classroom strategies and techniques. Moreover, some journals accept book reviews and editorials, which also require a different style of writing. Because different journals utilize different writing styles to fit their scope and mission, you should make a concerted effort to follow the journal's distinctive writing style when submitting your manuscript for publication.

PAY SPECIAL ATTENTION TO EDITORS' SPECIFICATIONS FOR SUBMITTING PUBLICATIONS

Often the poor quality of papers submitted for publication is the cause for rejection. Therefore you should pay a great deal of attention to the editors' specifications when submitting publications. Many editors report that half the manuscripts they receive ignore at least one of the guidelines specified by the journal. In most cases, the editors' specifications are located in the front of the journal. The following specifications are generally covered: length of article or number of words, line spacing, margins, type size, number of duplicate copies, diskette, photo, disks, graphs, tables, figures, references (in the text or at the end), subheadings, contact information (mail, phone, fax, e-mail), biographical information, and self-addressed envelopes. Other specifications involve contractual statements concerning whether the article has been published or whether it is being considered for publication by another journal. Because many students do not study and follow the editors' specifications, their articles are rejected. For example, you may have a well-written article, but it may be too long or have too many references for the journal you submitted it to. It is your responsibility to make sure that the editors' specifications have been met. This increases the chances for your article to be accepted.

EXPLORE OTHER FORMS OF PUBLISHING

In addition to preparing articles for scholarly publications, you should become proficient in all aspects of publishing. You should consider other forms of publishing, including reviewing books, CD-ROMs, Web sites, and other materials, along with responding to previous publications and writing letters to the editor. Moreover, writing technical reports and grant proposals are great opportunities for publishing. If you want to prepare yourself for the realities of professional existence in the academy, you should develop a meta-awareness of your writing skills and practices. Prolific scholars should diversify their writing to enhance their publication productivity. This simply means that you should prepare yourself for the rigors of professional survival. Therefore, you should pay more attention to developing succinct and appropriate writing skills for publishing not only research articles but also grant applications. Many institutions do not prepare their graduates for the realities of such professional existence. One of the best ways to learn how to write grant proposals is to work with professors who are known for writing grant proposals and who have a high acceptance rate. Again, grant proposal writing is a different type of writing, which can be learned from working with others. Because you will be considered a neophyte, and you are, you may be asked to do only technical services such as word processing. This is great because you have an opportunity to read the document as you type it, observing the various components and writing style of a document of this nature. Typing the grant also broadens your knowledge base concerning the particular topic. You might be asked to do only the research or simply the leg work. But what is important is that you are exposed to grant proposal writing. Learning how to write grant proposals while in graduate or professional school can accelerate your publishing agenda and can prove to be very lucrative and rewarding for you and your institution in years to come.

PREPARE FOR ELECTRONIC PUBLISHING

Electronic publishing has become increasingly successful since the 1990s. Students who submit articles to electronic journals increase their opportunity for wider dissemination of knowledge than through print publishers. In addition, electronic journals can enhance your article by adding features such as hyperlinks, audio and video, and graphics, going far beyond what the traditional print publications can offer. You should remember, however, that writing for an electronic journal is still writing text. Therefore the same careful attention should be placed on editing and proofreading for an electronic journal as for a print publication. If you are interested in submitting articles for publication to an electronic journal, you may refer to *The Directory of Electronic Journals, Newsletters, and Academic Discussion Lists,* a publication by the Association of Research Libraries (ARL). Publishing in electronic journals can greatly enhance the readership of your articles because it makes them more accessible for the reader. A reader no longer has to visit the library or worry about library schedules.

CONSULT WRITING GUIDES, STYLE GUIDES AND HANDBOOKS

Below is a list of writing and style guides and handbooks to assist you in writing at and beyond the graduate level:

Alred, G. J., Brusaw, C. T., & Oliu, W. E. (2000). *Handbook of technical writing* (6th ed.). New York: St. Martin's Press.

Anderson, D., Bret, B., & Paredes-Holt, B. (1998). *Connections: A guide to on-line writing.* Boston: Allyn & Bacon.

Bell, J. (1993). *Doing your research project: A guide for first-time researchers in education and social science* (2nd ed.). Buckingham, England: Open University Press.

Booth, W. C., Colomb, G. G., & Williams, J. M. (1995). *The craft of research.* Chicago, IL: University of Chicago Press.

Cook, M. (1992). *Freeing your creativity: A writer's guide.* Cincinnati, OH: Writer's Digest.

Cooper, H. M. (1989). *Integrating research: A guide for literature reviews* (2nd ed.). Newbury Park, CA: Sage Publications.

Forbes, M. (1993). *Writing technical articles, speeches, and manuals.* Malabar, FL: Krieger Publishing.

The Chicago manual of style (14th ed.). (1993). Chicago: University of Chicago Press.

Gibaldi, J. (1999). *MLA handbook for writers of research papers* (5th ed.).New York: Modern Language Association.

Henson, K.T. (1999). *Writing for professional publication: Keys to academic and business success.* Boston: Allyn & Bacon.

Herman, J. (1998). *Writer's guide to book editors publishers, and literary agents 1999–2000.* Rocklin, CA: Prima Publishing.

Hiemstra, R., & Brier, E.M. (1994). *Professional writing processes, strategies, and tips for publishing in educational journals.* Malabar, FL: Krieger Publishing.

Kirkman, J. (1999). *Full marks: Advice on punctuation for scientific and technical writing* (3rd ed.). Wiltshire, England: Ramsbury.

Madsen, D. (1983). *Successful dissertations and theses: A guide to graduate student research from proposal to completion.* San Francisco: Jossey-Bass.

Matthews, J.R., Bowen, J.M., & Matthews, R.W. (1996). *Successful scientific writing: A step-by-step guide for the biological and medical sciences.* New York: Cambridge University Press.

Merriam-Webster's Manual for Writers and Editors. (1998). Springfield, MA: Merriam-Webster.

Merriam-Webster's Standard American Style Manual. (1985). Springfield, MA: Merriam-Webster.

MHRA style book: Notes for authors, editors, and writers of theses (5th ed.). (1996). London: Modern Humanities Research Association.

Polking, K. (Ed.). (1993). *Beginning writer's answer book.* Cincinnati, OH: Writer's Digest Books.

Publication Manual of the American Psychological Association (4th ed.). (1994). Washington, DC: American Psychological Association.

Pyrczak, F., & Bruce, R.R. (1992). *Writing empirical research reports: A basic guide for students of the social and behavioral sciences.* Los Angeles: Pyrczak Publishing.

Rudestam, K.E., & Newton, R.R. (1992). *Surviving your dissertation: A comprehensive guide to content and process.* Newbury Park, CA: Sage Publications.

CONSULT BOOKS ON PUBLISHING

You should also consult other references on publishing. Below is a list of suggested books specifically written to help writers publish:

Breedon, L., & Heinmiller, J. (1979). *Writing for education journals.* Bloomington, IN: Phi Delta Kappa Educational Foundation.

Day, R.A. (1983). *How to write and publish a scientific paper* (2nd ed.) Philadelphia: ISI Press.

Debakey, L. (1976). *The scientific journal: Editorial policies and practices: Guidelines for editors, reviewers, and authors.* St. Louis, MO: Mosby, Directory of Publishing Opportunities.

Harman, E., & Montagnes, I. (Eds.). (1976). *The thesis and the book.* Toronto, Canada: University of Toronto Press.

Huth, E. (1982). *How to write and publish papers in the medical sciences.* Philadelphia: ISI Press.

Literary market place: The directory of the American book publishing industry. (2002). http://www.literarymarketplace.com.

Michaelson, Herbert B. (1982). *How to write and publish engineering papers and reports.* Philadelphia: ISI Press.

Mitchell, J.H. (1968). *Writing for professional and technical journals.* New York: Wiley.

Silverman, R.J. (1982). *Getting published in education journals.* Springfield, IL: Thomas.

Van til, W. (1981). *Writing for professional publication.* Boston: Allyn & Bacon.

Finally, publishing can call for a very aggressive agenda, which can cause your writing to become dysfunctional. Therefore if you adhere to the aforementioned suggestions and strategies, your publication program will be greatly enhanced. When your articles are carefully prepared and the right journal carefully selected, you will find the publishing process rewarding and professionally satisfying.

CHAPTER 16

Preparing for a Career after Professional Sports: Pursuing a Graduate Degree

C. KEITH HARRISON

Associate Professor of Sports Management and Communications,
Department of Sports Management and Communications,
The University of Michigan–Ann Arbor

> I thought I would be seven feet forever, so I decided to prepare for other things. (David Robinson, quoted during NBC halftime report interview)

> The truth of the matter was and is simply this: I am an African-American male who had a special talent to play sports, in my case football. As long as I was on the field of play I was treated and viewed differently than most African-American men in this country. Because of my physical abilities, society accepted and even catered to me. Race was not an issue. Then reality came calling. After a nine-year career in the National Football League filled with honors and praises, I stepped into the real world and realized, in the words of Muhammad Ali, that I was "just another nigger." (Kellen Winslow, cited in Shropshire, 1996, p. xi)

Often television informs society of the contemporary status of athletes and their success while active in sports. In terms of black athletes, the high visibility of black masculinity in advertising and promotion might lead one to think that life is a sport "and the rest is just details" (Advertisement, 1997). In reality, the average football, basketball, or baseball career lasts for less than five years (Edwards, 1984). Black men need to be informed of cogent strategies and have intelligent mechanisms for making a smooth transition "from the field to the forest" (Harrison, 1997). The purpose of this chapter is to synthesize the academic literature on the career transitions of athletic individuals, identify the cultural context of African American male student-athletes, examine potential scholarly disciplines that athletes can engage in, and empower professional and collegiate athletes that their sporting experience has allowed them to develop many characteristics and traits that can be transferred from the sporting context to any graduate or professional opportunity after the air goes out of the ball (Lapchick, 1991).

LIFE AFTER SPORTS

In the literature on coping with losses and the grieving process, the work of Kübler-Ross (1969) identified the stages of adjustment to retirement as being shock/numbness, denial, anger/depression, and understanding/acceptance. Kübler-Ross suggests that there is no set schedule for these reactions, nor is there a one-way direction through these stages. There is little doubt that losses experienced in retirement force athletes to make psychosocial adjustments in their lives. The adjustments required relate to how athletes, once retired, will (a) resolve their loss; (b) identify and evaluate who they are; and (c) replace their involvement (physically and mentally) in the athletic role. However, the extent to which these adjustments will lead to problems appears to be largely dependent on each athlete's emotional and physical commitment to sport.

Furthermore, while extreme cases involving suicide and crime receive the most publicity, the majority of athletes appear to exhibit adjustment problems in the form of short-term denial, outbursts of anger, overindulgence in drugs or alcohol, or immobilizing depression (Ogilvie & Howe, 1986). Thus athletes' responses to retirement vary. These factors, which play a part in both the decision to retire and in each individual's ability to cope with and accept that decision, make it difficult to generalize about retirement.

Nevertheless, while athlete retirement literature does not clearly define or measure factors related to psychosocial adjustment, Ballie (1985) believes it is possible to identify several factors that appear to be related to athletes' success in adjusting to retirement, including (a) anticipatory socialization; (b) identity and self-esteem; (c) personal management skills; (d) social support systems; and (e) degree attainment. An athlete will move through these stages of adjustment at his or her own pace. For some athletes, the transition is smoother and quicker than for others, but for those who perceive retirement as a complete barrier to their goals (a reaction that is more common among athletes who are forced to retire because of injury or managerial decisions), denial ("I can still play"), anger ("What a stupid coaching decision!"), bargaining ("Give me one more chance to play"), and depression ("I can't do anything anymore") are the more prevalent responses (Ballie, 1985).

In addition to the personal and intrinsic losses that an athlete may experience after retirement from sports, certain external losses are also important. For example, the most important is the loss of the traditional social support network that exists within sports. Among the athletes who participated in the research by Ballie (1985), friends and teammates were seen as being "very important" by 56 percent of the respondents and as either "very important" or somewhat important" by 82 percent of each of the athlete groups, both professional and elite.

Hundreds of thousands of athletes, from high school teams to professional leagues, at some point in their sports career have to face retirement from competition. For some, the transition will be smooth and adjustable. For others, it may be seen as an off-time event that seriously disrupts the plans, values, and expectations of the individual. Not making the team is the most frequent reason for retirement from sports and also one of the most difficult for many athletes to accept. Distress may therefore occur at any level of competition.

Ballie (1985) argues that "the retirement of athletes exists because of the intensity of involvement and commitment which athletes often make to achieve success in their sports" (p. 77). Failure to prepare for life after sports arises for a variety of reasons. In our society, there is a reluctance to discuss this topic while athletes are actively competing. Coaches in particular are resistant to athlete involvement in other career-related areas, fearing that it will detract from their concentration on sports (Hill & Lowe, 1974). Athletes themselves may also avoid thinking about life after sports, considering that such thoughts would take away from their ability to focus totally on their sport. For individuals who have spent the majority of their lives as athletes in a sport environment, they enter unprepared into the real world, where their athletic talents will be of little use. Reluctance to anticipate and plan for life after sports is exaggerated further by the singular commitment required in sports (McLaughlin, 1986).

McLaughlin suggests that the commitment in time and energy that sport requires makes it difficult not to neglect other aspects of life. This emphasis on sport is often at the expense of education and career preparation. Thus athletes are often inadequately prepared for a post-playing career. McLaughlin believes athletes who have few career options, lack of direction, and few goals are forced to start at the bottom of a field years behind their peers.

GRADUATE TRANSITION FOR BLACK MALES

The emphasis on the graduation rates of college student-athletes is relatively new. It was not until 1974 that an association of academic advisers for athletes was established. This concern has been so intense, however, that the

NCAA regulations regarding academic requirements for scholarship athletes have required colleges to provide their graduation rates to all prospective scholarship athletes. Attention is focused primarily on the large number of African American athletes who play for four years but do not earn degrees.

Those promoting the interests of the African American community cried "exploitation," and the data supported the claim. Black student-athletes in college are graduating at a rate far behind their White counterparts, according to one NCAA survey (NCAA, 1998). Ironically, the survey also revealed that the statistical average of graduating African American student-athletes is higher than African American students who did not participate in athletics. Student-athletes of both sexes, White and Black, who entered Division I universities and colleges in the early 1980s were tracked by the NCAA over a six-year period. The findings indicate overall that only 35 percent of Black student-athletes graduated within six years, compared with 58 percent for their White counterparts.

A study by the NCAA (1998) found that Black college athletes are lagging far behind White athletes in academic performance. The study found that 52.3 percent of White athletes who entered school in 1984 and 1985 graduated, compared with 26.6 percent of Black athletes in 1984 and 1985. Nearly 62 percent of Black college athletes accepted by colleges did not achieve a 2.5 grade point average in high school, compared with only 25 percent of White athletes. The study also found that more than 42 percent of Black athletes leave school in less than good standing and that almost as many Blacks leave in their fourth or fifth years (38.3 percent) as in their first or second years. Richard Lapchick, director of Northeastern University's Center for the Study of Sport in Society, states that these percentages show that Black athletes are allowed to remain in school to perform in the sports arena rather than to post academic achievements.

Similarly, an article presented in *Black Issues in Higher Education* viewed graduation rates of Division I scholarship athletes who entered college in 1983 or 1984. The majority of the 290 Division I institutions had overall graduation rates for athletes under 50 percent, with Black males the most detrimental. Several institutions reported that no Black male athletes had graduated. For example, Georgia State University, which had an overall graduation rate for athletes of 24 percent, reported no African American male graduates. Athletic director Orby Moss said the dilemma was "one of the major challenges and concerns of the president when he took the job" in 1990. Moss said that prior to 1990 the Georgia State athletic program "just existed, with nobody caring really too much if it was successful. But when a new president, now departed, came in, he decided to raise the expectations, image and recognition for athletics. Along with that was the knowledge that additional scrutiny would also come, and there was concern that poor graduation rates would generate negative publicity." Anderson and South (1993) believe among the rationales for intercollegiate sports is the belief that participation will provide individuals with educational and status enhancement opportunities. Over the past fifteen years, sociology and sport literature has documented racial differences in educational outcomes for college athletes. In fact, recent NCAA (1998) disclosures of graduation rates revealed that nearly twice the percentage of White athletes compared with the African American athletes graduated from college over the past year. This work focuses on some of the circumstances that have not been favorable for the purpose of education for African American athletes.

African American athletes at predominantly White institutions continue to be faced with a particular set of problems. One of these problems is overcoming the stereotype of being intellectually inferior while possessing innate athletic superiority. Often the message given to African American athletes is, "You are inferior intellectually, and we do not expect you to achieve success academically. You are here because of your athletic ability" (Anderson & South, 1993, p. 91). In a study by Kiger and Lorentzen (1987), it was found that the type of sport and race were negatively related to university academic performance for males.

Minority male athletes participating in revenue-producing sports tend not to do as well academically. Adler and Adler (1989) found that student-athletes enter college with high expectations, and then over the course of their college careers make a major adjustment and resign themselves to inferior academic performance. This adjustment on the part of the student-athlete was due to time demands of sport and the coaches steering them to manageable athletic-related majors such as physical education and recreation. The athletes received greater reinforcement for athletics than for academics. This has caused many African American student-athletes to focus on their athletic prowess, leaving academics in the background.

SHINING STAR: MAKING A DIFFERENCE

Black male student-athletes should realize the uniqueness of their opportunity to participate in both academics and athletics and receive an athletic scholarship, thus moving on with their lives to engage in other challenging activities. Only one in a thousand student-athletes receive a Division II scholarship, and at the Division I level the odds are even less—only one in three thousand will receive athletic aid.

While often not articulated in public discourse, it takes dedication, persistence, commitment, faith, diligence, and courage to participate in athletics, to name only a few of the potential outcomes of sport. These traits are necessary and required for graduate and professional school, but from a student-athlete's perspective they have been mastered during an intense period. Athletes at both the college and professional level are asked to balance and juggle several areas of their lives at once (education, sport, family, friends, community).

More important, athletes bring a unique perspective to the graduate and professional school context. Institutions of law, medicine, and education need the perspective of athletes in the curricula and courses. Athletes must internalize that graduate and professional schools need the next Michael Jordan and that they can succeed parallel to their dreams as a professional athlete. Specifically, the professorial world is in desperate need of the participant and observer perspective in terms of research and the investigation of race and sport issues. These can be examined from several graduate disciplines, which include education, sociology, psychology, history, anthropology, science, art, communications, sport management, kinesiology, and physical education. Without the perspective of athletes on athletic issues, rigid quantitative designs overlook deeper and more qualitative issues that need to illuminate in the literature in the twenty-first century. Black athletes are prime candidates to research these issues as graduate students.

A MILLENNIUM MODEL

My influence as a scholar has been significantly impacted by three individuals, all of them individuals who have successfully made the transition from sports to life. Robert Sellers (Michigan), Bernard Oliver (Missouri–Kansas City), and Harry Edwards (California–Berkeley). Sellers played football at Howard University and was an All-American. Since his athletic days, Sellers has earned two graduate degrees from the University of Michigan and presently is an associate professor in psychology after several years as an assistant professor at the University of Virginia. Bernard Oliver is a professor and dean of the College of Education and has held administrative positions at the University of Texas–Austin, St. Cloud State (Minnesota), Syracuse University, and Washington State University. Oliver played football at California State University–Hayward, majoring in history with a minor in physical education. Oliver also received his terminal degree from Stanford University and is one of fewer than twenty African Americans at the head of a school or college of education in America. Harry Edwards has received tremendous attention over the years for his scholarly activism, but often his personal transformation is neglected. Edwards played basketball and track and field at San Jose State University before receiving a Woodrow Wilson Fellowship for the Ph.D. program at Cornell University. These three individuals are what I call "scholar-ballers." In other words, these are individuals who have used sports intelligently and as a means to an end, rather than an end in itself. These three have "kept it real" and are images that I aspire to be: cool, smart, and athletic.

Young brothers today are often not exposed to images in power that can relate to the student-athlete experience, and the academy is in desperate need of former student-athletes in disciplines throughout the curriculum. There are many former student-athletes holding faculty and administrative positions in academe, including Kofi Lomotey (Medgar Evans College), Tyrone Howard (Ohio State University), and Gary Sailes (Indiana University). We can transgress the limited imagery of the athlete, entertainer, and drug dealer by continuing to access higher education after earning an athletic scholarship. Nearly half of Division I scholarships are possessed by African American males, especially in the sports of football and basketball. If half (if not more) of these same individuals will engage in the graduate and Ph.D. process, strides can be made to shatter the silences and stretch the boundaries of scholarship at the Ivory Tower.

CONCLUSION

I work with student-athletes at the Paul Robeson Research Center for Academic and Athletic Prowess at the University of Michigan. Some of my graduate students are African American males and former student-athletes. As their mentor, I talk about career transition and life after sport. We collaborate on research projects, conference presentations, and youth intervention programs that emphasize education.

Graduate students Jarrett Irons and Eric Mayes are former elite athletes and team captains. Jarrett (an All-American linebacker in college) captures the issues well by saying, "When you try to play professional football, you put yourself in a situation where others dictate how you feel. My education allows me to dictate how I feel." Eric adds, "I didn't want to try out for any professional teams. That part of my life is over. It's time to move on and get my master's degree and possibly my doctorate."

When student-athletes begin to work with me, they say that they are motivated by images of professional male athletes, yet they struggle with the reality that these same "role models" are often corrosive (in jail, suffering from drug and alcohol abuse, preaching one thing and doing another). My advisees want to convey that you can be cool—and an athlete—and still be involved in school.

In the final analysis, African American male athletes must invest the same time and faith into the second half of their lives as they did in the first half. Possible roadblocks may be the Graduate Record Examination, the application process in general, and a time period when identity outside of athletics seems foreign and empty. Finding a mentor who believes in individual research interest areas, as well as graduate student strengths as a former athlete and well-rounded person, enhances the possibilities of life after sports!

REFERENCES

Adler, P., & Adler, P. A. (1989). From idealism to pragmatic detachment: The academic performance of college athletes. In D. S. Eitzen (Ed.), *Sports in con-*

temporary society: An anthology (pp. 142–157). New York: St. Martin's Press

Advertisement. (1997). Basketball is life, the rest is just details. *Slam magazine.*

American Institutes for Research. (1987). Report no. 5: Analysis of academic transcripts of intercollegiate athletics at NCAA division I institutions. Washington, DC: author.

Anderson, A., & South, D. (1993). Racial differences in collegiate recruiting, retention, and graduation rates. In D.D. Brooks & R.C. Althouse (Eds.), *Racism in college athletics: The African American athlete's experience* (pp. 70–100). Morgantown, WV: Fitness Information Technology.

Ballie, F.W. (1985). Intercollegiate athletic competition and students' educational and career plans. *Journal of College Student Personnel, 26,* 115–116.

Edwards, H. (1984). The black "dumb jock": An American sports tragedy. *College Board Review, 131,* 8–13.

Harrison, C.K. (1997). *Transcending the field (sport) to the forest (life).* Lecture given at the University of Oregon, Ebony Man program.

Hill, P., & Lowe, B. (1974). The inevitable metathesis of the retiring athlete. *International Review of Sport Sociology, 4,* 5–29.

Kiger, G., & Lorentzen, D. (1987). Gender, academic performance, and university athletics. *Sociological Spectrum, 7,* 209–222.

Kübler-Ross, E. (1969). *On death and dying.* New York: Macmillan.

Lapchick, R. (1991). *Five minutes to midnight: Race and sport in the 1990s.* Lanham, MD: Madison Books.

McLaughlin, B. (1986). Advising college athletes in the 1980's: A higher education abstracts review. *NACADA Journal, 6,* 31–38.

NCAA. (1998). *The status of minority participation in intercollegiate athletics.* Washington, DC: American Institute of Research.

Ogilvie, B.C., & Howe, M. (1986). The trauma of termination from athletics. In J.M. Williams (Ed.), *Applied sport psychology: Personal growth to peak performance* (pp. 365–382). Palo Alto, CA: Mayfield Publishing.

Robinson, D. (1999). Interview during NBC halftime report, NBA finals.

Shropshire, K. (1996). *In Black and White.* New York: New York University Press.

CHAPTER 17

The Career Hunt

Putting It All Together and Marketing Yourself for a Major Role in the Workforce

BARBARA J. HOLMES

Associate Professor of Communication, Department of Communication, University of Colorado–Denver

The remarks that follow are based on the assumption that you have pursued a graduate or professional degree in a discipline or field in which you are interested and to which you are willing to make a commitment. However, getting situated or entering your field can present some challenges. This brief chapter offers broad suggestions that may be helpful and provides insights into some of the real life challenges in the workforce.

As you prepare to enter the workforce, it is important to realize that the American workplace has undergone tremendous change over the immediate past twenty-five years, not just from the beginning of the century to its end. This means that you need to carefully analyze as many variables as you can see presently and assess your goals and objectives in light of your analysis. That analysis should include information about the location you would like—at home or abroad (maybe you would like to move around), the burgeoning diversity in the population, and the continuing disparities in opportunities—both in education and employment.

Consider your career hunt in light of major changes in the nation and the world. You do not have to confine yourself to the United States. Many nations welcome Black Americans. People in some other countries want to learn about Black Americans and create alliances with us. Remember, the picture others have formed of Black Americans is drawn by an often biased media. You can pursue a position with a multinational corporation (many of the high-tech companies have operations abroad), and you can consider a foreign service or diplomatic position with the U.S. State Department or the Peace Corps.

Obviously one major and very significant change is the proliferation of technology in all sectors and types of workplaces, from very small operations out of the home to massive multinational corporations in every industry from food production to the manufacture of cars and heavy equipment to the making of space satellites.

The impact of the technological revolution continues to astound us and is ongoing. For example, technological change has created a work environment wherein the average individual will no longer be employed for twenty to thirty years in the same company, gradually working "up the ladder." Now that average individual will more than likely have three to four significant changes in the type of workplace, level of work, and—most important—the requirements and qualifications for securing work. The technological revolution has stimulated change in organizational structure, in management behavior and strategies, and in virtually every aspect of working. For example, middle management has all but disappeared. Consider the new vocabulary of the workplace: teaming, outsourcing, downsizing.

Another area of significant change in the workplace targets "how work is done." Increasingly employers, whether in academia, assembly lines, or information services, view the capacity to work in small groups as one of the most valuable skills an employee can have, even if the company itself employs thousands. The process of securing the degree has credentialed you. Now it is up to you to prove that it was worth it. Application is now the important goal.

MARKETING YOURSELF

What will you offer to your area of work? I am going to assume that you have engaged in some selection of whether you desire to join the academic community; enter the corporate world; become engaged with nonprofit, service, or research organizations (some of which are sponsored by your discipline); or become part of various nonprofit, service, community-based organizations. While each sector will allow you to utilize your discipline knowledge, each requires you to tailor your particular package of skills, competencies, and interests because of the organizational setting, its structure, and how it chooses to function in a very competitive environment. Think about the following items as a type of general guide whether you want to join the private or public sector or whether you want to join the profit or nonprofit sector.

ASSESS YOUR SKILLS AND COMPETENCIES

Do you have a unique vision, a set of insights and skills to offer the profession? Difficult as it appears, think of yourself twenty-five years from the present and what you want to be doing in your profession. Remember that the average worker no longer works in a single organization or corporation for his or her entire career. Even top CEOs are switching companies. This does not mean that you will be required to make radical shifts by changing your core profession. It does mean that you will continually need to adapt your knowledge, your continuing learning opportunities, and your actual application of that knowledge. Develop a "backward mapping" exercise for yourself wherein you write down the destination goal (e.g., Director of Everything!) and begin a process of working backward through each phased goal that leads to the destination goal. Next, list the accompanying tasks and levels of skills and competencies you have to achieve before you can become the Director of Everything! Achieving phased goals acknowledges that one needs both a short-term and a long-term plan with fairly well-defined goals along the pathway.

BE FLEXIBLE

Learn that the destination goal may not be in the location, the organization, or the sector you thought it would be in. Accept that there are variations of the destination goal. The important point is that you are using the skills, competencies, and insights that you have developed during the graduate school stage and while in the workplace. Don't be locked into one style of working or presenting yourself: be versatile and flexible!

RECOGNIZE THE SIGNIFICANCE OF PLANNING

Comprehend when to develop Plan A, Plan B, and an additional contingency plan. The concept of careful planning undergirds your personal exercise in backward mapping as well as having significant applications once you begin working.

ACQUIRE KNOWLEDGE AND INFORMATION ABOUT THE VARIOUS TYPES OF ORGANIZATIONAL STRUCTURE AND FUNCTIONING

Do not assume that you automatically comprehend what is going on or that what is occurring now is what you may have observed in the past. Learn how the structure has evolved and why.

ACQUIRE INFORMATION ABOUT THE ENTITY
IN WHICH YOU ARE SEEKING A POSITION

Learn as much as you can about the mission of the organization—its history, its policies, and its procedures and practices—and think about how you can enable the organization to live up to its mission: can you support the mission? The Internet may be helpful in your research efforts.

RECOGNIZE THAT THE WORKFORCE IS DIVERSE
AT THIS TIME

The workforce is becoming increasingly diverse. Therefore it is essential that you learn some of the social graces of greetings and leave-taking, personal distance, eye contact, touching, appropriate relationship, and content of conversations, including work-related and personal conversations. People in the workforce may not practice the norms and values of traditional America at this time. They may not view competition, confidentiality, loyalty, or sharing of ideas as you may have been taught. Attempt to learn about some of these categories of norms and values before you make incorrect assumptions.

ALIGN YOURSELF WITH OTHERS OF SIMILAR
RESEARCH AND PROFESSIONAL INTERESTS

If possible, become part of a small group of persons like yourself professionally with whom you can discuss and dissect new ideas, concepts, and policies.

BE ETHICAL IN YOUR INTERPERSONAL
AND PROFESSIONAL INTERACTIONS

Keep your word. When you have responsibility, meet it with dispatch and thoroughness. Although these pointers are not confined to a particular field or discipline, I believe they have application in many, many situations. A review of the U.S. Bureau of Census data reveals that in many professions and occupations, the number of Black Americans is minuscule (i.e., it doesn't even amount to a percentage number of the total).

PROFESSIONAL ASSOCIATIONS AND NETWORKING

A great deal of the networking you will be required to engage in once in the workforce was begun while you were matriculating in graduate or professional school. The major avenues for networking run through the discipline's professional associations and organizations. The major research emphases tend to emerge over time at this level. Also, the policy directions and standards of the discipline are assessed and communicated from this level of the discipline. Therefore it is time to selectively and carefully align yourself with the major content streams or foci of the discipline presently. These do change with time as the organization keeps abreast of and responds to societal pressures. The general professional associations of the workforce in that field (e.g., if you have decided to become an elementary or secondary teacher in public or private schools, you will want to become affiliated with the discipline organizations such as the National Council of Teachers of Mathematics, the International Reading Association, or the National Association of Secondary School Principals).

If you are planning to join the academic community at the higher education level, it could also be very helpful to become affiliated with the large umbrella organizations such as the American Association of Higher Education (AAHE) and the American Council on Education (ACE). If you are in a medical, legal, business, engineering, or technology profession, you will want to affiliate with the comparable organization for those professions. If you are planning a career in higher education, then it is essential to subscribe to the primary research periodical of your discipline or profession. Additionally the bimonthly publications *Black Issues in Higher Education* and the *Chronicle of Higher Education* are essential periodicals for staying abreast of national as well as international trends in higher education.

GAINING PERSPECTIVE: TRANSFORMING EXPERIENCES

Earlier in this article I mentioned the prospect of living and working abroad. Allow me to share a personal recollection. My perspective was altered as a result of living abroad in five different countries from 1964 to 1969. During this period each of the countries my family and I resided in experienced a major coup d'état, wherein one governmental party or interest was overcome and ousted by another party or set of interests. In some instances the coup d'état triggered a major civil war. (According to Conflicts Reports Archive, 1998, there are more than thirty civil wars presently fought on every continent except Antarctica.)

The Biafran War in Nigeria is an example. I did not comprehend what forces were generating the intergroup conflict within the country. It was difficult to distinguish between the "patriots" and the "rebels" because we were ignorant of the country's history. (Interestingly, during the 1970s, Marvin Gay penned a powerful popular song that posed this very question, "What's going on"?). I realized that I knew very little about the histories and political pasts of the countries we were in.

Later I realized that Americans generally know little of the past, neither the history of this country and how it came to be a nation nor the history of any group outside of Europe, including Egypt, Sumaria, and Mesopotamia. Indeed, the recognition that Egypt is on the African continent is nearly nonexistent. Moreover, too many Americans are not aware of how this continent was wrestled away from the indigenous Native Americans and how West Africans were imported as slaves to build the country.

Too many of our population are also unaware of the dynamics generated by subsequent waves of immigrants and the various social revitalization movements that have resulted in what we today smugly believe to be our unique reality. We tend to tell the back story of America selectively, failing to acknowledge many issues and events. This failure makes reconciliation and harmony difficult.

My overseas experience was so transforming that I returned to school and did not stop until I had earned a doctorate degree. While matriculating in the academy I became aware that American scholars were calling what my family and I had experienced cultural shock, with an emphasis on the perception of "cultural differences." Within the discipline of communication, the study of intercultural communication began to emerge as a major focus, but the underlying theoretical components of this focus were inevitably based upon the perception of difference. There are at least two problems with underscoring cultural differences. First, emphasis on the perception of differences as a potential barrier to effective intercultural communication suggests that one will automatically experience difficulty in the encounter. Second, underscoring the perception of differences tends to lead to the view that the other culture is somehow deficient to one's own culture. This in turn promotes the simplistic interpretations of situational dynamics and promotes the continuation of inaccurate information about a group's history and social organization.

People from different continents and countries are communicating with one another constantly. They are not necessarily experiencing communication problems—even when they do not speak the same language. Indeed, in the United States, where there is probably more diversity or heterogeneity of groups than almost anywhere else in the world, people are not really experiencing "communication" problems per se. People are experiencing problems having to do with group histories in this country, and role and status disparities, installed by public policy positions.

CONCLUSION

Although you have become credentialed, keep in mind that practical application is the primary goal of what you have learned. Be creative and open to change—in yourself and others—and willing to continue changing.

CHAPTER 18

Learn to Learn the Joy of Work

The Dignity of Honest Work ... Honorably Done!

LAWRENCE F. DAVENPORT

Deputy Chief Administrative Officer,
United States House of Representatives, Washington, D.C.

Lansing, Michigan: middle class ... middle America ... middle sixties; a blue-collar working families' neighborhood; my neighborhood, full of everyday folks, like my parents. It was a good place to be, a good place to grow up. We had a strong sense of community, of family, of self. You were a Davenport ... you were just expected to do it. Don't mess up; don't make excuses. Don't let your family, your neighbors, yourself down.

My grandmother expected me to be one of the first of her grandkids to get an education. In our family, my mother was strong. She set the rules. My father enforced them. We were a family of twelve kids. From early on, my mother impressed upon us the need, the importance, the seriousness of an education. With her it was simple logic. School was our job, just like the assembly line at Fisher Body was my dad's job, and cleaning buildings at night was hers. By the third or fourth grade, I knew that going to school was my job.

As I grew older, my interest in school and in my education was expected—by family, friends, and teachers. I was always a "jock," but I knew right from the start that I had to take an active role in learning if I wanted to be involved in sports. In those early years, my fantasy was to play for the Detroit Lions, but I knew, even then, that if I didn't do the school ... I couldn't do the sports.

That was the right thing for my parents to do. They knew then what I know now and what many young people have to learn the hard way: there are thousands of young athletes, perhaps like many of you reading this guide, with tremendous talent who are never going to play "big time" college ball, who are never going to run track at the college level, who are never going to graduate from college. My folks knew that if you lose focus, if you neglect your academic program, you are never going to get there.

It's great to have those sports heroes. We all do ... and why not? They can be fantastic to watch ... to look up to ... to pattern ourselves after when it's a Michael Jordan ... a Sammy Sosa ... a Barry Sanders. The fact is, though, that the real heroes in your life are often found in your own home, your own neighborhood, your own school or community, not in the NBA scoring thirty points a game or in the NFL averaging a hundred yards a week.

Your true role model must be someone who is helping you to live the day. It's easy to be a role model when you're on national television, like Oprah Winfrey or Bill "the Cos" Cosby. Truth is, not many of us are going to have that opportunity. Not many of us will ever know those types of role models up close and personally either. So it's really important to look for your role models where you live.

Back home in Lansing we found such role models all around us. They were working people who knew, who understood, esteem and respect had to be earned. One of our neighbors was a janitor. He always went to work in a suit and tie. Another neighbor was a bartender who also wore a suit and tie to work. Not to say that dress alone creates respect or esteem. They dressed as they did out of self-respect and out of the dignity of honest work, honorably done. My own mother, who went to work late at night cleaning office buildings after we were in bed so she could be there for us during the family dinner hour and our study time, knew the dignity, the honor of such work. From them, we came to know the importance of that dignity and self-worth. These were our neighborhood role models.

In my life especially two people were to transform my own vision of who I was and where I was going. It was about the sixth grade when the first one made her lasting imprint upon my life. She was a favorite aunt of my friend Willie, Dr. Brunson. She was a psychiatric social worker. She was passionate, committed, outstanding at her job, but certainly a far distance from the glamour of playing for the Detroit Lions I dreamed about. So how did she change my life? By her example, I discovered that service to humanity can be the best work of life. I got excited, because she was excited, about reaching out and touching the lives of others. From that time forward, I've never lost that excitement, that passion that her work ignited in my soul. Would I have enjoyed that career in pro football? You bet! Have I enjoyed a life of service instead? Absolutely!

The second profound impact made on my life came in my senior year of high school from a teacher who "took no prisoners;" who was practicing "tough love" before it was fashionable. She was a Catholic nun, Sister Anita. She came into my life at a time when I had begun to realize the true importance of a quality education. She helped me focus my energies, clarify my career goals, set my college priorities, and apply myself diligently to making that senior year a real launching pad to college.

Besides these two life-altering role models, many others guided my development. Caring individuals like Morrison Ryder, a musician and the director of our community center, who fueled my interest in reading. He provided me with books of merit that were being discarded by the center library. Then there was Milton Bloomquist, a customer on my paper route, who awarded me a dollar for every A or B I got in school. He also encouraged me to become involved in public speaking, getting me into the Elk's Club speech contests. Later, Perry Bailey became a tremendous inspiration and role model to me as a college teacher.

All of these outstanding individuals, and so many more, contributed to my early development and success in life. They inspired, encouraged, motivated, and energized me to be the best that I could be. They set the bar very high and challenged me to vault beyond it. That's the way it was in our neighborhood, our community, our schools.

Almost everyone around me went on to earn a college degree. We may have been from a modest working-class neighborhood, but that didn't put any limits on where we wanted to go. It was just expected that we would be high achievers. We decided early in life not to let others define or determine who we were. Few of us knew or cared what our dream jobs paid. We just knew what they were. We had those high expectations, and we had a strong bond of group values, of the work ethic, and of positive groupthink. It worked.

The girl next door grew up to become the top news anchor in New York City, the Big Apple! Irving, the young boy next door on the other side of us, grew up to be "Magic" ... as in Irving "Magic" Johnson. So it went, as one after another we saw our dreams become reality.

As you read this, it is important for you to realize that you can fulfill your dreams just as we did. Maybe you're already there ... or well on your way. If so, great. If not, why not? You can do it. It's never too late to get a running start on tomorrow. Whether you're in high school on your way to college or in college headed for graduate school, professional study, or the job market, you must become master of your own fate, chief architect of your own career. If you are fortunate enough to have the kind of family-centered, community-based, goals-oriented support system most of us enjoyed back there in my Lansing neighborhood, you are miles ahead in the game. If you don't, you better start now, today, to build your own support system. There are caring individuals out there, willing to guide, direct, assist you. You must be bold enough to reach out, take hold, ask honestly for their help. More important, when they give it, you must accept it, value it, use it for all it's worth.

If those around you are not setting the highest standards for your performance, you better be setting the standards yourself … and finding the right mentors and role models to get you where you want to go. By making careful choices, by planning every detail, by taking positive action, you can measure up to the toughest standards. No matter what your personal situation is at present, you have the opportunity, the responsibility, and the power to control your own future. You can be the person you want to be. You can reach the goals you set. You can succeed in life. If you are ready to commit to what you want to be in life, what you want to accomplish, where you want to go, you can make it happen. Just as I did. Just as that girl next door did. Just as "Magic" Johnson did!

Maybe that idea surprises you; maybe not. Maybe you're saying to yourself that this guy is really out to lunch … or he just doesn't understand the situation. Because maybe you don't see how you're ever going to realize your goals, live your dreams. You don't have the money to finish college. You're not smart enough to get into that graduate school. You're not pretty enough for the on-air job. You're grades aren't high enough for medical school. How can you ever possibly make it? Well, besides those of us growing up in Lansing during the sixties, recent history is filled with examples of those who did make it against all odds.

Just within our own Black heritage, we can point to many remarkable men and women who have conquered great obstacles to achieve equally great accomplishments. Consider the lives of such global and national figures as President Nelson Mandela, Bishop Desmond Tutu, General Colin Powell, and of course the late Dr. Martin Luther King Jr. Or, for that matter, you can observe the remarkable accomplishments of such talented authors, artists, and entertainers as Alex Haley, Maya Angelou, Whitney Houston, Duke Ellington, Denyce Graves, and Bill Cosby. Then there are the blockbuster superstars such as Oprah Winfrey, Denzel Washington, Michael Jordan, and the ageless Harry Belafonte.

Each of these larger-than-life figures has had to overcome enormous personal and professional challenges to reach the pinnacle of their success, from racial discrimination to abusive childhood, from financial hardships to injustice and imprisonment. Yet without exception each of them has triumphed against all odds.

How, you may ask, did they all do it? Quite simply, they all learned to employ the basic rules of human enterprise and success, which modern motivational experts tell us are essential to a winning attitude. First, they had a dream … a goal … a burning desire to win, to succeed in achieving that goal. Second, they were willing to work hard … to apply themselves diligently … to strive constantly … to commit themselves totally to reaching that goal. Third, they believed in themselves … they believed in their dream … they believed in their ability to reach their goal … to attain that dream … and they believed that others would join with them in achieving that goal

... realizing that dream. Finally, they kept going ... kept trying ... kept believing. Even when things went wrong ... the going got tough ... the goal seemed out of reach. They did this because deep inside they knew they had the "right stuff" to make it.

It's really simple, isn't it, the secret of success? Believe in your dreams, your goals. Believe in yourself. Believe in others. Give them the opportunity to believe in you. Believe in what, together, you can accomplish. And, above all else, believe it can be done!

This guide is directed toward helping you to succeed in your pursuit of advanced education through graduate school or professional studies. If you are reading it to help you in achieving that goal, then you are already moving in the right direction for a productive life and a successful career. Will further studies in graduate or professional school assure you of the success you seek? Not necessarily! Is such graduate or professional school absolutely critical to your success? No, not really!

Much depends upon your ultimate goals and career choices. Clearly, for many professions and occupations you will need the highest level of formal education obtainable. For other life choices, you may be better off pursuing specialized training, practical on-the-job apprenticeships, or alternative learning pathways. The critical factor you must understand and accept, if you are to compete successfully in today's world, is that you must be committed to a course of constant, lifelong learning, both formal and informal.

You can never afford to stop learning. Looking ahead to your life beyond college, beyond graduate or professional study, into the workplace and your career, you should be prepared for continuously upgrading your knowledge base, specialized skills, and general capabilities. In today's fiercely competitive corporate world, for example, the leading organizations are all in quest of key team members who bring "value-added" qualities to the table.

What are these value-added qualities? They are the acquired skill sets that turn a competent technician into a star performer: people skills, management talent, communications savvy, entrepreneurial leadership, innovative problem solving, effective cost containment, as well as strategic thinking, creative project management, and adaptive organizational skills, to name but a few of the many possibilities. All of these areas, and more, are potential venues for establishing your own unique version of a value-added persona as you pursue a successful career.

When does that successful career pursuit begin? Yesterday was too late! For many of us, the decision point came and went in the primary years of grade school. For the budding classical pianist, the hopeful star athlete, the prima ballerina, the triumphant Olympic figure skater, childhood never existed. Fortunately, for most of the rest of us, if we can get it together by high school or college, the future is still ours.

Wherever, whenever you get started, realize this: your first and most important job, as you leave your formal education behind, is managing your own career, plotting the course for your own future. No one else can or will invest as much energy, time, or thought in that job as you must. As early as possible, but certainly by your junior year of college, you should be well launched in that job of career management.

STEP ONE

Begin to build a strong, enduring network of mentors, colleagues, and professional contacts, which will form the core of a lifetime support system. As you advance through your college and graduate studies, identify, befriend, and form alliances with those members of the faculty and those classmates with whom you can build productive, lifelong relationships. Schedule regular appointments with key professors to get acquainted ... build a rapport ... develop a lasting and collaborative relationship. Seek out leading faculty and administration figures from other disciplines and other programs on campus to be a part of your growing resource bank. Look for opportunities in the broader community to associate with business and institutional leaders who share your interests, your subject areas.

STEP TWO

Begin to build your resume. Associate yourself with activities on and off campus that showcase your talents, interests, abilities, and experience. Look for part-time jobs that allow you to build credentials and produce results in your chosen field. Engage in independent research or advanced study projects and get the results published somewhere, anywhere with credibility. Look for internships in your field with organizations you find attractive for future job possibilities. Volunteer your services in your future profession to worthwhile community service organizations in return for references and letters of recommendation.

Seek out opportunities to compete for recognition and honors in your field. Apply for suitable fellowships and academic awards recognizing your collegiate accomplishments. Engage in cocurricular and extracurricular activities that permit you to assume leadership roles that will broaden your management skills and experience while demonstrating your capabilities as a leader.

Above all, stand out in a positive way. Everything you do should be focused on that task of making you a standout individual. The best way to do that is to set a standard of personal excellence that makes you truly outstanding in the classroom, among your peer group, in your chosen activities on and off the campus.

STEP THREE

Begin an intensive and extensive effort to professionalize your personal habits, to polish your communications skills, and to project your most compelling image. This means taking a tough, objective, rigorous inventory of your own personality, habits, character traits, and style. Be strict with yourself but fair. If possible, get an honest, savvy, objective, mature mentor to help you through this exercise. Identify those areas of your personal life that require improvement. Pay close attention to your work habits, your personal appearance, your social and communications skills.

Are you punctual, well dressed, well read on current events? Can you carry on a casual conversation regarding general topics of interest such as sports, entertainment, public affairs? Have you practiced your interviewing skills until you feel ready for the toughest job interview? When the answer to all of these questions is yes, you are on your way to a successful professional image.

STEP FOUR

Plan and launch your job search campaign. This is the most crucial step you will take. It requires all of your energy, talent, creative enterprise, and fully focused attention. It should be a full-time endeavor. You need to plan carefully, execute boldly, act decisively as you set this campaign in motion. It is a marketing challenge. It is a management challenge. It is an exercise in leadership ability and communication skills. For the marketing challenge, you must package yourself effectively. That means distilling all you are, all you have done, into a clearly written, precisely formatted, concisely worded resume that provides a composite picture of who you are, what you know; what you've accomplished, and why that makes you of value to a prospective employer. All in one or two pages of an attractive, well-designed, polished presentation, suitable for mailing, faxing, or sending by e-mail. To complete that package, you will need a zinger of a cover letter that brings your resume to life and frames it uniquely for each prospective employer.

Once packaged, your resume kit needs to find its way to the right people. This is where your network kicks in. By mail, by phone, by fax, by Internet, by word of mouth, it's time to broadcast your search to your universe of interest. Today, that means special attention to the World Wide Web. Among those skill sets you must have are a well-developed range of computer skills, including the ability to surf the net effectively for efficient, productive business communications and connectivity.

STEP FIVE

As the job opportunities begin to come in, you must be prepared to do your homework on each one. Review all offers for interviews carefully in priority order. Rank them by your own interests. Understand clearly what job is under consideration. Know all you can about the interested company: what they do ... their products and services ... annual sales and revenues ... significant developments ... key management ... leading competitors. On and on, until you have a clear understanding of what the possibilities are. How would you fit in? What could you bring to the table? Why should they want you? All are critical to preparing for that most important moment: the interview. Who will do the interview? What is that person's role in the hiring process? What is his or her background, history with the company, in your professional field? You need to know as much as possible about all these things before the interview. Get plenty of rest the night before. Be well groomed and well dressed in conservative business attire. Arrive early. Have a copy of your resume kit, work samples, and key references with you, along with a notebook and writing instruments. Carry it all in a professional-looking briefcase.

Once the interview is under way, be respectful, truthful, positive, and energetic. Take the initiative to offer ideas, suggestions, examples of how you could make a productive, effective difference in this job. Say why you like the company, why you want the job, and why you are the best person for that job. Answer all questions carefully, thoughtfully, fully.

Ask any questions you may have that would clarify your understanding of the job and help you reach a prompt decision if the job is offered. In conclusion, lay out clearly the terms and expectations you would require to accept an offer, as well as any lingering concerns that could delay or derail your acceptance. When it is clear the interview is over, thank everyone cordially and make a prompt exit. Follow up quickly with a letter expressing your appreciation and recapping your interest and requirements for accepting an offer. Be sure, also, to get back promptly to anyone who may have been helpful to getting you the interview, both to thank them for their help and to report how it turned out. This may also be the time to solicit any further assistance or support you may need in getting a firm offer.

STEP SIX

Be prepared to act swiftly, decisively if the offer you want is extended. Be reasonable in your expectations and demands. Be flexible in the final negotiations. You may not ... probably will not ... get everything you ask for. Just remember that this is but one stepping stone to a long and promising career. If this job offers you a good launch into that career, go for it, even if you have to give up something to land it!

Once the deal is sealed and you're on board, be profuse in your thanks to all who helped you get there. Be sure to get the word out to your network that you've scored the big one, that you're on your way! Be sure also to get as much mileage as you can out of the trade press announcements of your appointment. Put the notice out wherever you can—alumni news, hometown papers, industry trade journals, local business journals—anywhere that will raise your professional profile in a positive, effective way.

STEP SEVEN

Now that you've launched your career, don't let up for a moment. Start immediately to plot and plan your next career move. Find an inside, senior-level mentor. Start building a network of colleagues and professional associates within your new organization and its sphere of influence. Learn who the movers and shakers are inside and outside your company. Get to know them. Cultivate them.

Most important, throw yourself into your work, total immersion style. Pretend you're going for the Olympic gold ... or a Super Bowl ring. Get to work early. Stay late. Work smart. Do your homework. Always do everything you should ... and then some! Take initiative. Exercise decisive action. Innovate. Don't be afraid of an occasional mistake. Strive to improve yourself ... to learn ... to grow and expand your range of skills, of practical experience. Visualize your next job. See yourself in it. Make it happen!

Finally, learn the joy of work, the deep satisfaction of a job well done. Remember your roots, your heritage. Appreciate, as those who have gone before us, the dignity of honest work, honorably done!

CHAPTER 19

From Dissertation to Dollars

Successful Grant-Seeking Techniques

GLENDA J. ISLAND

Coordinator for Grant Development, Grambling State University

Congratulations! You have just received your graduate degree! I am sure the words of your president or chancellor are still ringing in your ears: "by the authority invested in me as president [or chancellor] of this university, I now bestow upon you the degree of ... ." All of the long hours of studying and sacrifice have paid off, and now you can turn that thesis or dissertation into dollars. I will discuss with you methods you can use to develop your thesis or dissertation into a funded grant project that can be used as a possible means of employment after graduation. For example, you may serve as director of a center for battered women that is funded as a result of your soliciting the thesis or dissertation you wrote on the topic of spouse abuse as a grant proposal. In addition, I will address suggestions for (1) developing your thesis or dissertation as a grant proposal, (2) using databases, electronic retrieval, and search engines to identify prospective grant-funding sources, and (3) steps in obtaining funding from the funding agency.

James Moore wrote that your attitude is your paintbrush; it colors every situation. As you begin to paint your road to success via your thesis or dissertation, remember to keep positive, maintain determined effort, equip yourself, be enthusiastic, and give sail to your ability. You have your brush, you have your color palette, now let's go and paint the paradise of your future—from dissertation to dollar.

DEVELOPING THE DISSERTATION
AS A RESEARCH PROPOSAL

Now that you have met all of the requirements of your committee, your thesis or dissertation has been approved, and you have received your graduate degree, you must redefine your research document. Begin thinking of it as a grant proposal that will be used to appeal to numerous funding agencies for financial support of your research idea. It is important that you think of your thesis or dissertation as a grant proposal and analyze it from a broader perspective. Create an idea that will distinguish your proposal from others. Develop a proposal that is unique, that stands out above others, and that is so impressive that it is difficult for the reader to put it down. In the words of Katherine Whitehorn, "find out what you like doing best and get someone to pay you for doing it." It is certain that you already possess everything you need to be successful.

Begin by examining your thesis or dissertation topic. Make a list of subject categories that your research project title relates to as a grant proposal. Identify a target group or agency that could benefit from your research project as a grant proposal based on the subject categories. For each of these categories decide on the type of grant proposal that would be most suitable for your research project. Examples of grant proposal subject categories include education, humanities, health, science and technology, social science, business, product development, community and economic development, and employment training. Examples of target groups include minorities (African American, Asian American, Hispanic, Native American, and women), elderly, youth, children, teens, gangs, disabled or physically challenged persons.. Environmental and housing concerns are also marketable research issues. When selecting your grant proposal type, you must carefully decide whether your project will be considered as a (1) pilot project, (2) model or demonstration project, (3) research project, (4) needs-assessment project, (5) planning grant, (6) training grant, (7) equipment grant, or (8) construction grant. In order to succeed, it is imperative that you know what you want to do. You must have a clear understanding of the direction that you want to take your project. Using the philosophy of Ralph Waldo Emerson, let your thoughts be your blossom, your language be your bud, and your actions the fruit behind it.

Once you have completed the process of examining your thesis or dissertation topic, consider ways you can revise your grant proposal to make it relate to other subject categories. Identify the geographic boundaries of your grant proposal and decide how it can be expanded to attract additional funding sources. Funding agencies often decide to fund a project based on how it affects a geographic area that is of concern to them. You must decide the type of population that your grant proposal will have a significant impact on: community, town, city, state, region, nation, or international area.

Carefully examine the diversity of your grant proposal as it relates to other ethnic groups and decide how it can be expanded to be more inclusive to serve the needs of these groups. There is an Ethiopian proverb that says when spiders unite they can tie down a lion. Remember that collaboration is the strength of any proposal. Funding agencies are very receptive to grant proposals that emphasize collaboration and that are designed to allow their funds to be distributed over a broad geographic area and serve a diverse group of cultures. The results of this exercise will be useful in your search for potential funding sources using electronic databases and grants research directories.

Getting started can be one of the most difficult tasks of proposal writing. Develop an order and plan for your writing, set priorities, schedule your work, and commit to following your schedule. At this point it is extremely important that you increase your awareness of the project that you are developing in every area. Your project should become a part of your every thought process. Once you have accomplished this, you must pay attention to those thoughts and adjust your thinking accordingly. Just like with your dissertation, you must eat, drink, and breathe your project.

As you develop your grant proposal, it is important that you avoid writing only from your perspective. You must carefully research and become familiar with and sensitive to the research priorities and values of each prospective funding agency. If a funding agency's values and priorities are different from the goals of your grant proposal, you should consider another source of funding. As the creator and developer of the project, in preparing your grant proposal, you must meet the goals and needs of the funding agency, as well as your own. Most of all, remember that proposal development is an ongoing process that requires time for you to research the funding agencies, develop the preproposal idea, and construct a tailored proposal. Effective use of this process should take from six to twelve months, as opposed to six or seven days of a last-minute proposal writing effort. An example of a proposal development timetable is listed below.

- Month 1: Define need, draft concept statement, conduct preliminary research, conduct peer consultation.
- Month 2: Write formal concept statement, conduct inquiry of funding agency.
- Month 3: Write proposal draft.
- Month 4: Conduct peer consultation.
- Month 5: Complete proposal revisions, type proposal, secure institutional approvals if applicable.
- Month 6: Submit proposal.
- Month 7: Receive acknowledgment of proposal receipt from funding agency; a preliminary review of the proposal is conducted by the funding agency; the proposal is mailed to reviewers.
- Month 8: Reviewers' comments are submitted to the funding agency.

- Month 9: The review panel evaluates and scores the proposal.
- Month 10: Program recommendations are prepared.
- Month 11: The funding agency reviews the results and makes funding decision of grant award.
- Month 12: The funding agency notifies you of its decision to award the grant.

As you develop this process, remember the words of Lafcadio Hearn, that all good work is done the way ants do things, little by little. If you let your minutes become your opportunities, you will find that you have a day full of opportunities to write a great proposal.

USING ELECTRONIC RETRIEVAL OF DATA AND OTHER RESEARCH SOURCES TO IDENTIFY PROSPECTIVE FUNDING AGENCIES

Identifying funding sources is always a challenge in writing proposals. When searching for funding sources, remember to anticipate alternatives and be prepared to adjust to some changes. Be flexible and open-minded in your search, and when your search progress turns to dust, vacuum and start again.

Federal, state, and private funding program directories; newsletters; computerized databases; and CD-ROMs are examples of resources that are generally used to identify funding sources. When conducting your research for funding sources, be sure to identify several possible funding options. You will be more successful when your search includes a variety of potential funding sources. Do not approach all of them at the same time. Remember, there may be state, local, or community funding sources that are more appropriate and attractive for your grant proposal than large national agencies or foundations. National funding sources tend to support projects that have a broad impact, while state, corporate, and private funding sources generally support those that affect their own state, community, certain geographic area, or specialized research initiative.

When selecting a prospective funding agency be certain (1) that your project goals and the funds you request for the grant are compatible with the research initiatives the funding agency supports; (2) that the location of your project is the same as the desired geographic preference of the funding agency; and (3) that the money you request or need is within the amount the agency is willing to award. It is important that you obtain (and carefully read) information on submission requirements from the funding agency before you write your grant proposal.

Electronic retrieval of data is one of the most popular means of identifying prospective funding sources. Listed below are Web site addresses that I personally recommend to assist you in selecting funding agencies when developing the grant proposal:

The Society of Research Administrators (SRA) Grantsweb: http://www.sra.rams.com

National Council of University Research Administrators (NCURA): http://www.ncura.edu

National Sponsored Programs Administrators Alliance (NSPAA): http://www.nspaa.umes.edu

Official Federal Government Web site (a Library of Congress Internet resource page): http://lcweb.loc.gov

Program Support Center (PSC) Forms Download Site: http://www.forms.psc.dhhs.gov

The Foundation Center: http://www.fdncenter.org

GEPPS Consortium: http://www.gepps.org

InfoEd International—SPIN Links: http://www.infoed.org

Electronic Research Administration (ERA): http://web.fie.com

TRAM Research Funding Opportunities: http://tram.east.asu.edu

National Institutes of Health (NIH) Office of Extramural Research: http://grants.nih.gov

National Science Foundation (NSF) FastLane: http://www.fastlane.nsf.gov

U.S. Department of Education Funding Opportunities: www.ed.gov/funding.html

What I Should Know about Ed Grants? http://www.ed.gov/pubs/KnowAbtGrants/

NASA Minority University Research and Education Program: http://www.hq.nasa.gov

National Library of Medicine: http://www.nlm.nih.gov

Health Resources and Services Administration (HRSA): http://www.hrsa.gov

The following recommended Web sites are listed by categories:

- U.S. Federal Agencies
    CFDA (Catalog of Federal Domestic Assistance): http://www.gsa.gov/fdac/queryfdac.html
    U.S. Federal Government Agencies: http://www.lib.lsu.edu/gov/fedgov.html
    FEDIX (multiple agency listings): http://www.fie.com/
    SPIN WWW (Sponsored Programs Information Network): http://spin.infoed.org/
    Community of Science (COS) Web Server: http://cos.gdb.org
    Federal Web Locator: http://www.law.vill.edu/Fed-Agency/fedweb.exec.html
    Fed World Information Network: http://www.fedworld.gov/
    Centers for Disease Control (CDC): http://www.cdc.gov
    National Institutes of Health (NIH): http://www.nih.gov
    National Science Foundation (NSF): http://www.nsf.gov
    Environmental Protection Agency (EPA): http://www.epa.gov
    National Oceanic & Atmospheric Administration (NOAA): http://www.noaa.gov
    National Endowment for the Humanities (NEH): http://www.neh.fed.us./
    U.S. Department of Agriculture (USDA): http://www.usda.gov

Department of Commerce: http://www.doc.gov/

Department of Education: http://www.ed.gov/

Department of Transportation: http://www.dot.gov

Department of Health & Human Services (National Institutes of Health, Centers for Disease Control, etc.): http://www.os.dhhs.gov

Department of Energy: http://www.doe.gov

- Regulatory Information

  Code of Federal Regulations: http://www.access.gpo.gov/nara/cfr/cfr-table-search.html

  Federal Register: http://www.access.gpo.gov/su_docs/aces/aces140.html

  Legislative Updates: http://www.thomas.loc.gov/

  PHS Grants Policy Statement: http://www.nih.gov/grants/policy/revision_to_gps.html

  OMB Circulars: http://www.whitehouse.gov/WH/EOP/omb#docs

- General Federal Government Information

  Library of Congress: http://www.marvel.loc.gov/

  NTS (Government documents): http://www.fedworld.gov/

- Agency Application Kits

  AFOSR, ARO, DOE, NASA, PHS, NSF, ONR, & Standard Forms: http://www.engineer.tamu.edu/tees/trs/forms.html#nih

  TRAM Electronic Forms: http://www.tram.rice.edu/TRAM/sponsored.html

- Nongovernment Sites

  Foundations On-Line: http://www.foundations.org/

  Foundation Center: http://www.fdcenter.org

  American Cancer Society: http://www.cancer.org/

  American Heart Association: http://www.amhrt.org/

  YAHOO (Internet search service): http://www.yahoo.com

There are several publications that serve as valuable resources when you are searching for funding sources and developing your grant proposal. Some of these publications are also available electronically.

Most federal, state, and private sponsors provide printed information regarding programs and deadlines. They also provide detailed application materials. You should request information and application forms directly from the sponsoring agency. These materials are usually available at no cost; however, federal agencies often charge a fee for additional copies. When a fee is charged for federal government publications, you must purchase them from the Superintendent of Documents, U.S. Government Printing Office, Washington, DC 20402, phone (202)512-1800. The following publications are recommended to assist you:

- Catalog of Federal Domestic Assistance, available in hard copy, CD-ROM, or online at www.gsa.gov/fdac/queryfdac.html

- Federal Register, available in hard copy or on-line at www.access.gpo.gov/ su_docs/aces/aces140.html
- Commerce Business Daily, available in hard copy or on-line at www.cbdnet. access.gpo.gov/search2.html
- National Science Foundation, Guide to Programs, available in hard copy and on the NSF electronic network.
- Public Health Service, Grants Policy Statement, available in hard copy.
- National Institutes of Health Guide for Grants and Contracts, published weekly at http://www.nih.gov/grants/guide/index.html
- Humanities, available in hard copy from the Superintendent of Documents
- Federal Acquisition Regulation and Supplements, available in hard copy and electronically at http://www.arnet.gov/far/
- U.S. Government Manual, available from the Superintendent of Documents.
- Science and Government Report, available in hard copy from Science and Government Report, Box 6226A, Northwest Station, Washington, DC 20015

Following is a list of general directories that are highly recommended for use during your search for funding support:

- **Annual Register of Grant Support**—gives details of the grant support programs of government agencies, public and private foundations, corporations, community trusts, unions, educational and professional associations and special interest organizations. Available in hard copy from Order Department, Reed Reference Publishing, P.O. Box 31, New Providence, NJ 07974.
- **ARIS (Academic Research Information System) Funding Reports**—gives information about government and nongovernment funding sources via listing of the address and phone number, description of the program, and application deadline of the sponsoring organization. Available in hard copy or diskette at ARIS (Academic Research Information System; 2940 Sixteenth Street, #314, San Francisco, CA 94103; (415)558-8133.
- **Federal Research Report**—gives information on research opportunities available from federal agencies and some private organizations. It also includes a list of recent awards and a column on federal contract tips. Available in hard copy from Business Publishers, 951 Pershing Drive, Silver Spring, MD 20910; (800)274-6737.
- **Federal Grants and Contracts Weekly**—gives project opportunities in research, training, and service. There is a section on news, grants alert, RFPs available, and RFPs calendar. Available in hard copy from Capitol Publications, P.O. Box 1453, 1101 King Street, Alexandria, VA 22314; (800)655-5597.
- **The Foundation Center Publications**—available on-line at http://fdncenter.org/book/contents.html.
- **The Foundation Directory**—gives brief summary of most private foundations (large and small) alphabetically by state. Entries for more than seventy-five hundred foundations accounting for approximately $10 billion in annual giving are included.
- **Foundation Grants to Individuals**—gives information on more than twenty-six hundred foundations that award grants to individuals, including grants for edu-

cational support, general welfare, awards and prizes, international applicants, company employees, arts and cultural support, and *students and graduates of specific schools.*

- **Taft Group Publications: (1) Taft Corporate Giving Directory**—gives information on more than five hundred corporate giving programs, including contacts, giving priorities, typical recipients and grants, areas of operation and distribution; and **(2) Taft Foundation Reporter**—gives profiles of five hundred prominent private foundations, including background information, application procedures, grant distribution and sample grants. Both publications are available in hard copy from the Taft Group, 12300 Twinbrook Parkway, Suite 520, Rockville, MD 20852; (800)877-8238.
- **Government Contract Report**—contains Federal Acquisition Regulation (FAR) supplements and other regulations, as well as providing useful updates of current regulatory practices, policies, and decisions in the field of contracting. Available in hard copy or CD-ROM from Commerce Clearing House, P.O. Box 5490, Chicago, IL 60680-9808; (800)835-5224.
- **The Illinois Researcher Information Service (IRIS)**—a unit of the University of Illinois Library at Urbana-Champaign. The IRIS office compiles databases of funding opportunities. It maintains a library of publications (informational brochures, application guidelines, and annual reports) from more than two thousand funding agencies. Available for a subscription fee to colleges and universities. Contact the Illinois Researcher Information Service (IRIS) Director, 128 Observatory, 901 South Matthews Avenue, Urbana, IL 61801; (217)333-0284.
- **ORYX Press Directories: (1) Directory of Research Grants**—gives more than six thousand grant programs alphabetically by grant title. Each program includes a description, deadline, data, CFDA number, restrictions or requirements, address, phone number and funding amount. This directory is indexed by subject, sponsoring organization, and type of organization; and **(2) Directory of Grants in the Humanities**—gives more than 1,925 programs that support research and performance in literature, language, linguistics, history, anthropology, philosophy, ethics, religion, and the fine and performing arts. Available in hard copy from Greenwood Publishing Group, Inc., 88 Post Road West, Westport, CT 06881; (800) 225-5800.

Specialized directories and newsletters can be very helpful in identifying notices of grant proposal solicitations and funding sources. Following is a recommended list:

- **AID (U.S. Agency for International Development) Business Outlook**—lists all of the procurement notices, contract awards, and information about proposed or U.S. Agency for International Development (AID) projects. Available in hard copy from International Publications, 1321 Duke Street, Suite 200, Alexandria, VA 22314; (703)791-4255.
- **AIDS: A Status Report on Foundation Funding**—gives information on current levels and the nature of funding for AIDS research among six hundred private foundations. Available in hard copy from the Foundation Center, 79 Fifth Avenue, New York, NY 10003-3050; (800)424-9836 or on-line at: http://fdncenter.org/book/contents.html.

- **Arts and Cultures**—a monthly newsletter that highlights funding sources such as NEH, NEA, and private sources for arts and cultural activities. Available from Education Funding Research Council, 4301 North Fairfax Drive, Suite 875, Arlington, VA 22203; (703)528-1000.
- **Business and Management Education Funding Alert**—identifies opportunities for business school, research, education, and training projects. Available in hard copy from Carolyn Looff & Associates, P.O. Box 22258, Lexington, KY 40522-2258; (606)266-8274.
- **Directory of Building and Equipment Grants**—lists private and corporate sources of funding for computers, software, and training projects, in addition to sources for other high-technology equipment grants with some information on proposal preparation. Available in hard copy from Research Grant Guides, P.O. Box 1214, Loxahatchee, FL 33470; (407)795-6129.
- **Guide to Federal Funding for Social Scientists**—gives information for new scholars on the variety of federal agencies that provide funding for research and research training, and informs established scholars of alternative funding opportunities available from federal agencies. Available in hard copy from APSA Publishing, 1527 New Hampshire Avenue NW, Washington, DC 20036; (202)483-2512.
- **Health Grants and Contracts Weekly**—gives advance notice of upcoming National Institutes of Health research announcements. Contains articles on other policy issues and profiles of federal agencies and foundations. Available in hard copy from Capital Publications, P.O. Box 1453, 1101 King Street, Alexandria, VA 22314; (800)655-5597.

STEPS IN OBTAINING FUNDING
FROM THE SELECTED FUNDING AGENCY

Now that you have developed your thesis or dissertation as a marketable grant proposal and used electronic means of identifying prospective funding sources, you must understand and implement the following steps involved in obtaining funding from the funding agency you have selected: (1) develop your proposal idea for funding according to the guidelines of the agency you have selected; (2) be sure the agency you selected best fits your project implementation goals; (3) write the proposal following the guidelines of the funding agency you selected; (4) submit the proposal to the agency selected; (5) follow through with the selected agency and make revisions if requested; and (6) wait to hear the decision of the agency regarding funding of the grant award.

If you are funded by the agency, you would then (1) conduct the grant project in accordance with the guidelines of the grant and the agency, and (2) write and submit a renewal proposal.

If you are not funded by the agency, do not become discouraged; immediately implement the Three Rs: Request, Revise, Resubmit. You should (1) request a copy of the reviewers' comments from the agency, (2) implement them into your proposal revisions, and (3) resubmit the revised grant proposal to the funding agency. If there are numerous revisions needed, it may be better to start over using a different approach to your proposal concept or idea. Remember that through your proposal you are marketing your research idea by putting your words together in a readable, professional, user-friendly package. Your objective is to convince the funding agency to invest its dollars in you and your ability to implement the idea. The better you prepare and market the package, the greater your chances for funding.

In conclusion, don't forget that there are five basic functions of a grant proposal. Your proposal should (1) represent you and/or your organization; (2) request the money that you need; (3) persuade the reader; (4) present a problem-solving solution; and (5) promise to fulfill the proposal objectives.

Remember that you have the power within you to do all things, and in the words of Sally Berger, the secret of getting ahead is in getting started. Once you have begun the process; things may go wrong. If they do, "don't go with them" (Roger Babson). Keep your writing and thought process simple. After all, it was the great Leonardo da Vinci who coined the phrase that simplicity is the ultimate sophistication. Keep in mind that as you develop your proposal you are creating a project that you want to be a major part of. You are creating a project that will take you from dissertation to dollars. Be sure to check it once, check it again, and then implement it with the strength of your convictions. I wish you the best in your proposal grant-writing efforts.

CHAPTER 20

Education for Liberation

On Campus with a Purpose

MOLEFI KETE ASANTE
Professor of African American Studies,
Department of African American Studies, Temple University

The impact of race as a social construction, even in the postmodern environment of the contemporary world, has been awesome, frightening, and humbling. Nothing around us prepares us to believe that the natural state of humans is peace. Conflicts rooted in deep ethnic, racial, and religious differences carve a cleavage through the meadows of the human spirit. This is so despite our more extensive means of communication, our information abundance, and the instructive examples of the meaninglessness of cruelty based on race that we see each day. Unfortunately we are victims of our own worst scenarios of hatred, ethnic cleansing, and genocide. We are doubly beguiled by a belief that in using violence we create peace. Have we humans not learned how to live with each other without killing each other because of national origin, religion, or race? To ask the question is to answer it with the contemporary crises that engulf so much of our world. Racially, ethnically, or religiously charged issues are at the core of most of the world's present conflicts. If we look from Indonesia to Rwanda, from Russia to Mexico, and from Tibet to India, and just a rock's throw from here across the Adriatic in Kosovo, we see the worst symbols of ourselves. The most degrading actions that we can commit have turned the entire region into the many faces of evil.

Young people arrive on campus amid this atmosphere of racial animosity, inadequate recognition of justice, and unequal reactions to needs and responsibilities. They are often victims of a system of education that has not prepared them to think of the major ethical issues confronting the world. I do not seek to moralize, to assert some moral or ethical superiority. I recognize in the actions of the haters and oppressors what can occur in any nation, among any people, if power is wedded to prejudice. In our society, we wage a constant struggle against the forces of hatred, and at times, as when James Byrd was dragged behind a vehicle until his body was dismembered in a small Texas town, we wonder how permanent is our peace, how secure is our person. But we are not disheartened by the fight for justice and human decency; indeed we have joined the universal movement against the doctrine of racial exclusivity. In April 1999, in Philadelphia, an international community of decent people gathered to protest the political imprisonment of Mumia Abu Jamal, a journalist who we believe was falsely and unjustly arrested, jailed, tried, convicted, and placed on death row to await execution. Mumia was convicted of killing a policeman, even though the prosecution could not prove that he had actually fired a gun. Indeed, witnesses claimed that he did not shoot the police. But he had been politically active, an outspoken advocate for the poor and downtrodden, a former member of the Black Panthers, and a politically aware gadfly in the side of officialdom. Hundreds of lawyers and numerous leading citizens of the world have protested and demonstrated against the death sentence of Mumia. But to see so many college students at the protest was reminiscent of the 1960s, when we had ethical struggles of mammoth proportions to fight and students held in their minds the idea of education for liberation. The battle against racism is indivisible.

Students should be well aware of the dangers of racism in the United States, because racism, or more accurately, the doctrine of Western White racial supremacy, has been the core ideology of all American institutions. This doctrine has warped and distorted presidential and congressional politics, religious confraternity, class solidarity, union organizing, and education.

Of course it is also clear to us that the negative impact of racism on the society has been extremely costly. Those who could have added to the discourse on philosophy, such as Martin Luther King Jr. and Malcolm X, had to devote their lives to the security of their communities in the face of racial attacks. Those who wanted to be scientists, such as Bobby Seale and Kwame Ture, spent their youth studying ways to overcome racial discrimination. Just recently in the U.K. the authorities arrested a twenty-two-year-old man, not old enough to remember either the struggles of King or Malcolm, or their deaths, for bombings in African, Bangladeshi, and gay neighborhoods of London. What are we doing wrong that allows a twenty-two-year-old man, an alleged killer, to harbor such evil and vengeful feelings against those who are different? Where did his education fail? What was missing in the curriculum of study? Or where did we fail him? What pedagogical strategies might have been used, with what content or subject matter, to have transformed his life? This is a worldwide phenomenon, and our college students cannot avoid it even if they study abroad.

Various techniques for social change have been employed from time to time. For example, there is considerable evidence to indicate that values modification, strategies for teaching empathy, and demonstrating the ability to perceive as others perceive, that is, to see from their points of view, are useful interventions in teaching against racism. Even so, racism has continued unabated to the general detriment of democracies, social justice, and fairness. We have not discovered a panacea. Nevertheless we must retain our optimism, not that we will completely obliterate the evil of racism in democracies, but that we can put into practice the behaviors that will make racism more unacceptable to the vast populations of our countries. This is a process, but it must start somewhere and not be mired in defeatism, the lack of political will, and cynicism. It cannot begin with blaming the victims of racism for the actions of the racists. A prophet who bases his or her insights on cynicism will never see the possibilities inherent in an innovative approach to racism.

The Western democracies are experiencing the present crises in race because of conflicting ideologies and interests. In the first place, the legacy of colonization, slavery, and imperialism sticks like a fishbone in the throat of the national histories. Everything that we do and everything that is done to ameliorate the racist crisis must take into consideration this legacy. Second, and perhaps most disturbing, there remains an element of European racial superiority in most of the countries. But even in that construction there are differences made between the European peoples, some considered more worthy than others and so forth. In effect, the Europeans have their own pecking order. But our students on college campuses must bring about new approaches to human interaction. There is no reason why African American students cannot continue to lead in the struggle for liberation, human liberation anywhere.

The historical legacy is fixed; we can only interpret and reinterpret, but we must make a difference. Our students who come to campus must come to change things, not to be complacent.

I believe that we must attend to the issue of White or European racial domination. It is the area most susceptible to a resolution. I have called for anti–White supremacist organizations, believing firmly in the necessity for those who have been privileged by imperialism, colonization, slavery, and a history of discrimination to rise to the moral high ground and condemn the false doctrine of racial supremacy. It is not race relations that we must seek. I say this because neither sensitivity training nor tolerance seminars can adequately deal with the doctrine of racial superiority. If the English see themselves as of a different race than the Irish, and mark that difference with beliefs, attitudes, rules, customs, and behaviors that place the Irish in a categorically inferior position within society, then we have to deal with the root causes of this problem, not temporary solutions. We must see these constructions of hierarchical difference, because that is what they are, as artificial barriers to human interaction that must be overcome. In our case, racism is at the base of the problems we face in this society. Let our young people rise to the challenge of seeing education as a means to liberation.

As a child of twelve years of age, I got my first job in a small town in Georgia in the southern part of the United States. My town, Valdosta, was a hotbed of White racial supremacy. I asked the owner of the White barber shop if I could shine shoes in his shop. Whites had more money than Blacks in the south, and so I did not think twice about the choice of shops in which to work. The owner agreed that I could shine shoes in his shop so long as I gave him a small percentage of what I earned. My first customer, waiting to get his hair cut, was a White man in his thirties. As I bent over to shine his shoes, he spit saliva on my head and began to laugh. The other Whites laughed with him. It was as if he wanted to demonstrate to his cohorts how despicable I was, how little he thought of me, how easy it was for him to degrade me. I remember not saying a word, not protesting, but immediately getting my shoe box and polish and walking out of the shop. I cried all the way home, the cry of the helpless. The fact that he could take advantage of me, with no possibility of the law protecting me, and no possibility that the other Whites would condemn him, showed how utterly powerless I was as an African in the United States. The Whites never let us forget that a Black man had been lynched because he had dared to speak to a White man as he had spoken to Black men, looking them straight in the eye. Maintaining difference was not enough for the Whites of Georgia; they had to demonstrate their absolute control over Black people. This is the maiming of conscience, the distortion of spirit that accompanies the manifestation of racial hatred based on perceived hierarchical differences. People are different; we have different backgrounds, different combinations of genes, and we look different. But difference alone does not create racism; it is the assigning of hierarchical value to difference that marks the unique problem of racism. Even the poorest, most dispirited White thought herself or himself to be superior to us. Although this supposed superiority was rarely defined, we knew it to be a part of the racist privilege, the privilege of Whiteness in America. In other societies it may be the privilege of being German or the privilege of being Hutu or Tutsi or Serbian or Croatian.

It was Jean-Paul Sartre who said that you cannot treat a man like a dog without first seeing him as a man. This is the beginning of our education, the end point of our quest. Seeing each other as human and treating each other as we expect humans to treat one another ought to be the easiest thing in the world. But education for liberation, antiracist education, anti–White supremacist education must be a radical action, because it is a betrayal of racial hierarchy. Those who undertake such an educational project will find that racists will consider that they have put White supremacy at risk, privilege in jeopardy. A combination of students and teachers, Blacks and non-Blacks, must be engaged in this process. Suppose we are successful at some point in our educational project, and the racist lays aside privilege , ideology of supremacy, and emotional attachment to advantage. We would have achieved a tremendous victory for the human race. I urge young students to become engaged in this struggle.

Let me try to explain how I see that happening in a curriculum of change, a project of transformation. All education should leave a person better in terms of insight, knowledge, and capability in many fields, including the way humans interact.

Anti–White supremacist education can do that, but it will have to deal with three perspectives of education: (1) ways of knowing, (2) ways of relating, and (3) ways of behaving. The way of knowing is the first level of attack on the idea of superiority, because it allows the person to know that Whites represent a particular experience, but it is not the only experience in the world. Or to put it in a national sense, this idea that your cultural expressions and views must be destroyed in order for mine to be valid is part of the nonsense of racism. But an educational program that speaks to the various ways of knowing, the multiplicity of human experiences, will enlarge our ability to fight against racism. A second level is ways of relating. What is the philosophy behind the attack on the common humanity of the earth? How, for example, did the Native Americans understand a culture that did not accept the earth as they did? For the Native Americans the land was sacred and could not be bought or sold, and yet the Europeans not only bought it but stole it from the original keepers of the land. What is the problem between the Arabs and the Jews if it is not a clash of civilizations, a clash of different ways of relating? Can we teach those who have enjoyed privilege at the expense of others how to share privilege? I believe it is possible, but it will depend upon a fundamental change in the way we relate and teach others to relate. Third, we must teach ways of behaving that support positive values of community. The substance of courses, the scope of curricula will respond to our own courage to become heralds of a new society. I cannot behave in ways that I do not wish for you, and I must wish for you what I wish for myself. How is it possible in the present world for a young person to enter school, study various subjects, complete the course of study, and yet believe that racism is the proper way to act? Does not this indict the educational experience? Can it truly be meaningful if it does not teach young people how to behave in a community of diverse peoples and cultures?

In a small, upper-class community in Colorado, two students, Eric Harris and Dylan Klymond, armed like NATO commandos, walked into their high school looking for African Americans and athletes and gunned down, in cold blood, fifteen of their classmates. Of course, if there ever were a compelling reason to outlaw guns in a gun-crazy society, this experience should have some effect. I regret that it will not. The gun is as American as racism, and the combination is deadly. Only one Black student was killed; yet it is useful to remember that the killers, members of a White supremacist organization, were looking for Blacks to kill. This was so despite the fact that out of a population of eighteen hundred students in the school there were only fourteen blacks.

In all the proposals that have been made for the Columbine High School, I have heard no proposal that deals with anti–White supremacist teaching or antiracist education. This would seem to be an obvious area where education is needed, but our societies rarely seem to have the will to deal with issues that impinge upon the concrete realities of racism. White supremacist ideologies are extremely prevalent in parts of the United States. They have not escaped Europe, indeed, they may have been imported from there, given the slave trade and the colonization practices of European nations. But in the United States we have an incredible phenomenon occurring. The top ten school districts have a majority of African American or Latino pupils, the results of in-migration of Spanish-speaking students and the increasing blackness of the populations of large urban centers. Many Whites have fled to private schools to escape the presence of large numbers of black and brown people in the urban public schools. They have not escaped the hatred that comes with racism, and the children of the society are stark examples of the presence of this sickness.

Maurice Berger's new book, *White Lies: Race and the Myths of Whiteness,* has taken James Baldwin's challenge to examine in intimate detail the biography of the racial superiority self. To his credit, Berger sees that Whites are limited by embracing White supremacy myths in everything from intelligence to standards of beauty.

The problem Berger faces in the racialized context of Europe and America is that many other White-identified people do not consider Jewish people as white. Since he, as a Jew, is confessing the sins of whiteness, they are not likely to hear him as they might have heard him without the racial overtones of his own existence. The Ku Klux Klan in America was formed to attack not just Africans but Jews and Catholics. The fact that Italians and Jews have become White within the last fifty years or so in America is a result of the continuing need to expand the web of race, the club of White privilege against Blacks. In a strange sort of way, the presence of Africans in a population makes others become less threatening to the host White populations.

W. E. B. Du Bois said, "A system of human culture whose principle is the rise of one race on the ruins of another is a farce and a lie" (Aptheker, *Against Racism: Unpublished Essays 1887–1961.* Amherst: University of Massachusetts Press, 1985). No national plan can work to build mutual respect if it does not consider the rights of the smallest minority. To trample over those rights ultimately is to trample over one's own in another context. We must teach our children that we are as interconnected on this planet as the ecological environment, where the disturbance of one system affects the whole. To practice racism or ethnic cleansing or genocide against any people is a profoundly suicidal act. I think that to teach children this is not religion, but the clarification of values, the drawing of a critical outline of human possibility, and an assault on ignorance and fear.

Clearly racial attitudes and particularly the attitude that Whites are superior to other people are sustained by social and cultural phenomena. Attitudes are not transmitted in DNA; thus they are not inherent in our genetic structure and cannot be passed to future generations that way. They are communicated by human society in such a way that they are pervasive and seem to be innate. Our children learn from us how to view other people, what we think of them, their possibilities and prospects, and how we see them fitting into our societies. They learn not just what to do but how to think about those people.

Since it is the belief in the hierarchical value of humanity that upholds racism, we must undermine it for a broader, more balanced and fair world. My idea is that the battle must be launched first from the home and in the family and then in education. Our first line of defense in the colleges is the fresh attitudes and positive action values of young students.

The first teachers are parents. Children model their behaviors on those of the parents. Generally ethnic attitudes and racial dispositions of children are like the ethnic attitudes and racial dispositions of the parents. Reinforced by the media, church, and other social and cultural institutions, the attitudes are made to appear normal. Society transmits racism through all types of cultural artifacts: books, movies, music, and so forth. Books are supposed to remove ignorance, to bring us to a new awareness of what is real, but they beguile us when they are filled with racist propaganda. They are carriers of racist culture. They teach that White is good and Black is bad, that White is beautiful and Black is ugly, and so forth. In ethnic situations they teach that some groups are stingy and greedy and others are thrifty and energetic. In all of these ways human beings carry cultural messages to children.

Robinson Crusoe and *Huckleberry Finn* are two of the books that show resourceful, intelligent, and powerful Whites, even if one of them is a boy, and subservient and weak Blacks. This juxtaposition is meant to carry a message of superiority. Or take Roald Dahl's *Charlie and the Chocolate Factory*, published in 1967, in which Mr. Wonka is looking for an heir for his company. Five children are invited to the factory; none is a Black child. But the oompa loompas are workers that have been recruited from the miniature pygmies who live in the very deepest and darkest part of the African jungle where no white man had ever been before. Stories for children like this book are too numerous to mention. Titles that are full of racist nuances are *Dr. Doolittle* and *Water Babies*.

Our collective wish must be for the flourishing of a healthy multi-cultural, multi-racial, and multi-ethnic world where the blossoming of Maat, the ancient principles of justice, righteousness, fairness, order, balance, harmony, and reciprocity, is the cornerstones of our lives. In such a future time and place, there will be no need for antiracist or antisupremacist education, but in the meantime, on earth, here and now, we must busy ourselves with the preparation for such a future by educating our young to think of every other human being as themselves. With this type of prescription our young people will enter college with an eye toward personal and collective liberation; this is the real meaning of education.

CHAPTER 21

African American Parents and Student Success in Predominantly White Colleges and Universities

DELORES W. SCOTT

Vice President, Office for Student Affairs, Virginia Union University

There is a great deal of discussion in the literature regarding factors related to success of African American students in higher education. This is in part because African American students in White colleges and universities earn lower grades than White students and experience lower retention and graduation rates (Mow and Nettles, 1990).

A topic rarely considered in the discussion of African American undergraduate students is parental and family involvement and influence on academic achievement, retention, and graduation rates of African American students who matriculate at predominantly White colleges and universities. The role of parents and family is important but yet is an often overlooked variable in understanding and facilitating the progression of African American students through American higher education. While parental participation is given ample attention in the literature on elementary, middle, and high school student success, it is rarely present in discussions surrounding performance and development of college students.

Of importance to this discussion is the observation that in recent years attention to parents has become increasingly important in some areas of higher education. Nicklin (1994) notes that parents are sometimes identified as potential donors through development offices and admissions committees because of their likelihood for political influence and/or potential financial contributions. Strategies such as these often exclude African American parents. Therefore, African American perspectives are often left out of discussions and positions of influence.

Other examples of parental involvement in recent years include participation with parent advisory committees, parent weekends, and parent newsletters. The emphases of these programs vary and sometimes include dissemination of information and interaction with university officials. As in the case with fund-raising, these forums foster limited opportunities for parents of African American students.

Summer and fall orientation programs also present an opportunity for involvement and influence for parents of first-year and new transfer students. These programs are often designed to provide parents information about the first year of college. Topics discussed at these programs include registration for classes, safety, and information regarding opportunities for students to become involved in the campus community.

During summer orientation, parents often learn about legislative information that might limit their access to information about their student. This information is a result of the Family Educational Rights and Privacy Act (FERPA), also know as the Buckley Amendment. Depending on how an institution interprets this legislation, parents could be restricted from gaining information on the progress of their student toward a degree and other affairs related to their child's education. Although this is not the case for all colleges and universities, this observation is important to the discussion of parental involvement for African American students, because limited access to information can influence the extent to which a parent might intervene to assist the student.

While this trend of limited inclusion of parents appears to be aligned with the mandates of the Buckley Amendment, which legislates limited disclosure of student information to parents, it might also be a result of the current culture in higher education, which assigns adult status and responsibility to those seventeen years of age and older. This legislated absence of parental involvement, combined with the absence of en loco parentis, produces an educational system that is a mismatch for the student-parent relationship experienced in many African American families (Scott, 1995).

In recent years, some colleges and universities are increasingly encouraging parents to become more involved in their students' education. This is sometimes facilitated through the use of release forms, by which students waive the right to privacy and give the institution permission to share academic matters with designated individuals. In most instances, release forms allow a specific individual designated by the student to discuss a student's performance.

The management of information about student performance has tremendous implications for academic achievement of African American students. Likewise, the way institutions involve parents and families has a significant impact. As the enrollment patterns for African American students have changed to increased enrollment at traditionally White colleges and universities, it is important to consider familial patterns and customs to ensure that the institution is meeting the needs not just of the African American student, but also of the parents and families.

LITERATURE REVIEW

A review of the literature on African American students reveals an exhaustive list of factors that help to explain the academic performance, retention, and graduation rates of African American students. Included in this list are socioeconomic status, precollege preparation (Wolfle, 1983; Young and Sowa, 1992), student effort (Pace, 1984), involvement in and outside of the classroom (Astin, 1975; DeSousa & King, 1992), adjustment to college life (Abatso, 1987; Centra & Rock, 1971; Pounds, 1987; Stamps, 1988), participation in support programs (Kulik, Kulik, & Schwalb, 1983), institutional culture and commitment (Crosson, 1988; Tinto, 1987), student institution fit (Hall & Allen, 1989), academic and social integration (Tinto, 1987), noncognitive factors (Sedlacek, 1987), faculty-student interaction (Allen, 1992; Kobrak, 1992; Tinto, 1987), and self-esteem. While these factors add understanding to the problem, they fail to fully explain the low rate of success of African American students in predominantly White colleges and universities.

The task of helping African American students obtain academic success while enrolled at predominantly White colleges and universities is one that expands the boundaries of the classroom. This is evidenced in the findings that even when there is adequate academic preparation before college and academic support services at college African American students oftentimes fall short of academic success. The possible impact of parental influence and involvement on the academic achievement of African American students in college is a phenomenon that should be studied (Scott, 1995).

What little literature there is on parents and higher education for African American students is concerned with such factors as parental income, occupational status, and level of education attained. These variables are most often used as a means to predict performance, retention, and graduation. While important, these variables do not provide a clear or complete understanding of the potential impact of parental involvement and influence on the academic success of African American students at White colleges and universities. It is important to insert the topic of parental involvement for several reasons.

First, the culture of the predominantly White institution is one that is foreign to a large majority of African American students in higher education. Even students who attend predominantly White high schools sometimes have difficulty negotiating the predominantly White college environment. While socioeconomic status of parents might be important to performance, factors that impact performance for African American students at White institutions are most often experiences that have little to do with socioeconomic variables and other traditional measures of success. Second, while many African American students are second-generation students, and while their parents have sometimes successfully completed postsecondary education, the sociopolitical experiences of today's students are quite different from those of their parents. Therefore, attempts to draw correlations between parental educational experiences and students' educational experiences are clouded by differences in society, expectations (both self-imposed and imposed by parents), perceptions of entitlement and privilege, and reasons for accomplishing academic and professional goals.

Finally, the parenting structure in the African American family is very much an intrusive one. African American students grow up in environments where parents most often do not subscribe to a philosophy of students becoming adults when they matriculate at college. For these students, the parental intent is to continue input on decisions, to expect students to abide by their upbringing (whatever that may be), and to maintain the structure, rules, and guidelines set forth in the family unit. Therefore many African American students are not ready for the freedom and "adulthood" imposed by matriculation at many of America's White colleges and universities.

When African American students go to college, it is sometimes considered a major accomplishment. Parents are proud and have high expectations. This is especially so if the student is a first-generation college student. Students are often strongly influenced in their college choice by their parents, and if an extended family is in the picture they are also extremely influential.

Hurd, Moore, and Rogers (1995), in a study that examined strengths of African American parents, found that parents were substantially involved in the lives of African American children. Further, the parents in this study emphasized achievement and effort, acceptance of pain, coping skills, respect for others, and the importance of education, self-respect, and racial pride. Hurd, Moore, and Rogers's findings parallel those of Scott's (1995) and suggest a need for further exploration of parental involvement and influences in the affairs of African American college students at traditionally White colleges and universities.

METHODOLOGY

In spring 1996, a study was conducted at Virginia Tech to discover conditions related to the academic performance of African American students at Virginia Tech. Data were obtained by conducting focus group interviews and soliciting responses to the question "What conditions are related to your academic performance at Virginia Tech?" Three relevant themes emerged: achievement motivation, social infrastructure, and faculty issues. Of importance to this article is parental influence, which was a variable of the "social infrastructure" theme. Social infrastructure is defined as the relationship and interaction patterns that exist between students and parents, family, and peers.

FINDINGS

This study showed that for African American students at Virginia Tech, parental and family involvement had a significant impact on academic performance and how students approached their personal circumstances and their academics. The findings of this research study indicated that parental influence and involvement were of primary importance in understanding performance patterns and in assisting African American students to obtain academic success.

There were clear differences in how successful students and less successful students perceived parental involvement in their educational experiences. Parental influence emerged as "pressure" and "stressful" for the less successful students. The students in the less successful group believed their parents had high expectations and that parents did not understand when students did not rise to these expectations. Participants in this group noted that they often purposely avoided parents and made extra efforts to avoid discussing academics and Virginia Tech. These students believed that their interactions with parents were not helpful and were often discouraging and debilitating.

An important finding in this study was the large extent to which the less successful students harbored self-blame, responsibility, and guilt. This might have had an impact on their ability to interact with their parents about their academic performance.

The students in the successful group considered their parents to be extremely "supportive" and "encouraging" in their academic endeavors and believed that their parents provided guidance, yet did not apply pressure. A prevalent feeling among this group was that if they did their best this was all that was expected from their parents and families. The successful students believed that their parents and families had high expectations and that they provided both support and autonomy. A question that remains unanswered is whether parental "pressure" and "support" were the causes of or the results of high or low academic performance.

The significance of parental involvement and input was important for all students, whether perceived as negative or positive. The messages that parents communicated to students about race prior to matriculation were also found to be important in helping students to be successful.

The successful students tended to be from families where discussions of race occurred often. These students discussed and embraced a philosophy of their parents, that they had to work harder than students of the majority race to achieve equal recognition and success. Students with grades below C did not mention this perspective during the interviews. This observation suggests the need for additional research to gain a better understanding of the relationships between the "work harder" phenomenon communicated by parents, social infrastructure, and academic performance of African American students.

THE RESPONSE TO THE RESEARCH—"PARENT TALK"

The findings from this research clearly identify a role for parents of African American students to assist in facilitating academic success for their students. To respond to this need, "Parent Talk" was implemented in the spring of 1996. "Parent Talk" is a weekend intervention program designed to include parents in academic support of undergraduate students. The program involves Virginia Tech administrators and support staff visiting in small groups with parents of African American students throughout the Commonwealth of Virginia. The goal of the program is to discuss the role parents might play in helping students to be successful at Virginia Tech. This series of programs provided a forum for honest and frank discussion of academic and other issues in small group settings.

Representatives from the Office of Academic Enrichment Programs and the Dean of Students Office participated in this initiative. When the program was conceived, the intent was to conduct "Parent Talk" the first weekend after students returned for the spring semester. This time was selected in an effort to ensure that semester grades were available and to be available to address any issues or concerns that parents may have had after students returned to the university. Information was discussed on experiences of African American students, parental concerns, students' perceptions of parental involvement in their education, and university policies and procedures.

This initiative was extremely successful and resulted in (a) parents feeling a connection to the university, (b) parents requesting that such meetings be arranged at the end of each semester, (c) students of the parents in attendance contacting the Office of Academic Enrichment and the Dean of Students Office for assistance, and (d) the development of a parent network for parents of African American students. "Parent Talk" received funding through the university's Affirmative Action Grant Program for the 1996–1997 academic year. The program had a tremendous impact on parents and students of African American parents.

IMPLICATIONS

The findings regarding parental involvement and "Parent Talk" have several implications for assisting African American students to be successful at predominantly White colleges and universities. First, African American parents and family members are a tremendous resource for better understanding the needs of African American students. Colleges and universities should create opportunities to take advantage of this resource.

Second, colleges and universities should examine their procedures for disclosure to ensure that parents are aware of the processes for becoming an active player in the education of their students. And finally, colleges and universities should design intentional opportunities to facilitate interaction with African American parents in planning programs and strategies to increase success of African American students.

CONCLUSION

The inclusion of parents of African American students will have a significant impact on the ability of traditional White colleges and universities to retain and graduate African American students. This is an opportunity for improvement that must be explored if colleges and universities are interested and committed to serving the needs of African American students.

REFERENCES

Abatso, Y.R. (1987). Coping strategies: Retaining black students in college. In A.S. Pruitt (Ed.), *In pursuit of equality in higher education* (pp. 123–131). Dix Hills, NY: General Hills.

Allen, W.R. (1992). The color of success: African American college student outcomes at predominately white and historically black public colleges and universities. *Harvard Educational Review, 62*(1), 26–44.

Astin, A. (1975). *Preventing students from dropping out.* San Francisco: Jossey-Bass.

Centra, J.A., & Rock, D. (1971). College environments and student academic achievement. *American Educational Research Journal, 8,* 623–634.

Crosson, P. (1988). Four-year college and university environments for minority degree achievement. *Review of Higher Education, 11*(4), 365–382.

DeSousa, J.D., & King, P.M. (1992). Are white students really more involved in collegiate experiences than black students? *Journal of College Student Personnel, 33,* 363–369.

Hall, M., & Allen, W.R. (1989). Race consciousness among African American students. In Gordon Berry and Joy Asamen (Eds.), *Black students* (pp. 172–197). Newbury Park, CA: Sage.

Hurd, E.P., Moore, C., and Rogers, R. (1995). Quiet success: Parenting strengths among African Americans. *Families in Society, 76*(7), 434–443.

Kobrak, P. (1992). Black student retention in predominantly white regional universities: The politics of faculty involvement. *Journal of Negro Education, 61*(4), 509–530.

Kulik, C., Kulik, J.A., & Schwalb, B.J. (1983). College programs for at-risk and disadvantaged students: A meta-analysis of findings. *Review of Educational Research, 53*(3), 397–414.

Mow, S.W., & Nettles, M.T. (1990). Minority student access to, and persistence, and performance in college: A review of the trends and research literature. In

J. C. Smart (Ed.), *Higher education: Handbook of theory and research*: Vol. 6. New York: Agathon Press.

Nicklin, J. L. (1994). Cultivating Parents. *Chronicle of Higher Education, 41*(14), A35.

Pace, C. R. (1984). *Measuring the quality of student experiences*. Los Angeles: Higher Education Research Institute.

Pounds, A. (1987). Black students' needs on predominantly white campuses. *New Directions for Student Services, 38* (San Francisco: Jossey-Bass).

Scott, Delores W. (1995). *Conditions related to the academic performance of African American students at Virginia Tech*. Doctoral dissertation, Virginia Polytechnic Institute and State University.

Sedlacek, W. (1987). Black students on white campuses: Twenty years of research. *Journal of College Student Personnel, 28*(6), 484–495.

Stamps, D. B. (1988). Coping ability as a predictor of academic achievement among selected black college students. In Marvel Lang & Clinita Ford (Eds.), *Black student retention in higher education* (pp. 83–92). Springfield, IL: Thomas.

Tinto, V. (1987). *Leaving college: Rethinking the causes and cures of student attrition*. Chicago: University of Chicago Press.

Wolfle, L. (1983). Effects of higher education on achievement for blacks and whites. *Research in Higher Education, 19*, 3–9.

Young, B. D., & Sowa, C. J. (1992). Predictors of academic success for black student athletes. *Journal of College Student Development, 33*(4), 318–324.

PART II

HOW I SUCCEEDED IN GRADUATE AND PROFESSIONAL SCHOOL AND IN MY CAREER FIELD

Graduate School to a Profession

A Journey of Maturation

JAMES A. ANDERSON
Vice Provost for Undergraduate Affairs and Professor of Counselor Education, North Carolina State University

In retrospect, my years of graduate training served as an excellent blueprint and guidebook for the expectations, challenges, and adversity that I have encountered in my professional career in higher education. The lessons I've learned and the success that I've attained can be condensed under four categories or vignettes of life: (1) negotiating the landscape, (2) elevating self-worth and professionalism, (3) visioning the future, and (4) weathering the storms of adversity. I will utilize this framework as I portray my graduate and professional experiences.

NEGOTIATING THE LANDSCAPE

I entered the graduate program in psychology at Cornell University during the early 1970s. This was a time of incredible social-political change and unrest. Despite its liberal reputation Cornell University was/is, in many ways, a traditional Ivy League institution comprised of high-powered academic departments. Graduate programs reflect the values, beliefs, attitudes, and personality of their faculty. In my first year I failed to adequately assess the climate and expectations of the psychology department; moreover, I assumed they would adapt to my needs, concerns, and academic interests. This miscalculation led to an unrewarding first year.

When I assumed the position of department chair (at Xavier University in New Orleans) and later served as vice provost and dean (at North Carolina

State University), I applied the approach of assessing and completely understanding the landscape at the beginning.

ELEVATING SELF-WORTH

Graduate students of color are expected to continually justify and validate their place in the academy. The subtle and overt disparagements and devaluations of our skills and expertise often represent the norm and not the exception. I incorrectly assumed the presence of equity among graduate students in my department in the eyes of the faculty (and my graduate colleagues). I simply was not ready to be knocked from my pedestal of accomplishment.

It was the presence of a very important anchor in my life that provided a reality check and the support to reclaim my self-worth. That person was Dr. Wade Boykin, the first African American faculty member in psychology at Cornell University (he is now at Howard University).

As a result of this graduate experience, I have cultivated relationships with mentors early in each of my professional positions. One common theme in their feedback has been that it is imperative that I maintain an impeccable professional demeanor in all academic settings.

VISION THE FUTURE

One of my goals during graduate school was to identify a topic or area of specialization in psychology that would reflect my interest and my socially conscious politics. I chose to focus on how groups (racial, gender, cultural, and social) differ in terms of their learning styles. Moreover, I wanted to examine whether these disparate styles affected performance in the classroom. The selection of this topic evolved into a bane and then a blessing.

None of the faculty in my graduate program were familiar with my chosen area of emphasis, and neither was there any significant research in the literature. I would generate groundbreaking work, but the price was that I would do it alone (until my mentor arrived). I also was not sure how my dissertation topic would serve my professional career goals.

The blessing is that my professional career has blossomed around that dissertation topic. The increasing diversity of students at all educational levels has kept my work in demand and fueled my national reputation. The lesson learned is to keep an eye to the future as we currently identify goals or activities to pursue. My dissertation topic is most appropriate for the new millennium.

WEATHERING THE STORMS OF ADVERSITY

I have made reference to the difficulties that graduate students and professionals of color encounter in predominantly White settings that are associated with the meritocracy. In graduate school my initial response to adversity or a devaluing of my being was reactive. And I let things ulcerate for weeks, even months.

Toward the end of my tenure at Cornell, I learned to anticipate the occurrence of adversity and to prepare a response a priori. I practiced this skill during my professional career and learned how to disarm my critics with professionalism, dignity, and a sound knowledge base. I am actually surprised when my female colleagues and my colleagues of color express surprise at the occurrence of an "ism" towards them. I have come to expect an occasional bout with Mr./Ms. "ism." Affectively, I don't enjoy it, but intellectually and morally I find a reward in successfully confronting and defeating an opponent on the battlefield of ignorance. My training began in graduate school.

Education is Just the Beginning

Professional Relationships Are Key to Success

JOE N. BALLARD

Lieutenant General, Commander, U.S. Army Corps of Engineers, Washington, D.C.

There is no doubt that an advanced degree can increase an individual's marketability and earning potential and open a great number of professional doors. Those scholars who complete the intensive, rigorous study required for a graduate or professional school degree are highly sought for their expertise—and rightly so. However, I will assert from my personal experience that an advanced degree in and of itself is not the only key to professional success—it is merely the die in which this key is cast.

The foundations for professional success can be constructed from a variety of building blocks—formal education, professional training, on-the-job experience, imagination, determination, and simple hard work, for example. But there is a vital stepping-stone that is often overlooked—mentoring relationships between junior and senior members of a profession. Although academic credentials will get you in the door, it is your professional contacts and relationships that will give your career direction.

In the U.S. Army, we actively foster mentoring relationships at all levels of the organization, and I strongly doubt there is a single senior officer or enlisted service member who achieved his or her career goals without the support and guidance of at least one mentor.

A mentor can offer an aspiring professional unique opportunities and benefits. No one knows the challenges of a given profession better than one who has met those challenges firsthand. After all, if you are embarking on a trip to somewhere you have never been, you would certainly take along a map, and you would probably talk to someone who had made the journey if given the chance. You would ask about the best route to take to your destination, about the obstacles you might encounter, and about what might await you at the end of your journey. This is the essence of a mentoring relationship—someone who is embarking on a professional journey can learn a great deal from another who is further along on the road.

A mentor can be a young person's guide through the professional maze. Every profession has its own inherent culture, language, and unwritten rules, and you won't be successful if don't learn to navigate through this environment. A mentor can also help you make the professional contacts that will assist you in landing those important positions that will keep your career headed in the right direction. After all, it doesn't matter how much potential you have if the right people don't notice it. You can bet that if a well-respected member of an organization recommends a junior person for a job, people take notice.

Today many academic and professional organizations have formal mentoring programs that are very beneficial to participants. However, an informal mentoring relationship that grows from personal commitment between individuals can often be even more successful. When I speak to students and young professionals, I urge them to seek out their own mentors—to find someone whom they would be proud to emulate and determine how that person achieved his or her success.

Often it seems that the easiest and most comfortable mentoring relationship is one between people with similar backgrounds and views, but someone who may share your experiences isn't always the best mentor. It is not important that a mentor be the same gender or race as you, only that you share the same professional ideals. In fact, we often learn the most from those whose experience is different from us. A great benefit of a mentoring relationship is that it allows both individuals to see issues through a different frame of reference. In this way, it is possible to explore options and alternatives that might not otherwise be considered. The junior person has the benefit of mentor's experience; in turn, the mentor gains fresh insight into what young professional members are thinking.

When a student chooses a course of study, he or she becomes part of a professional community. This community will have its own unique rules and its own parameters for success, and its members will share common challenges and goals. Just as it is in a young professional's best interest to learn from the experience of seasoned professionals, it is in the best interest of the professional community to foster excellence in its junior members. It is in this shared interest that the strength of mentoring lies—by passing professional ideals from one generation to another, we ensure the strength of the professional community as a whole.

Preparing for Success in Graduate School

C.O. "BRAD" BRADFORD
Houston Police Chief

I am honored to have been considered by Grambling State University as worthy to contribute to *The Black Student's Guide to Graduate and Professional School Success*. I am also proud of my affiliation with Grambling, for it is there that I began the journey that has ultimately led me to where I am today, chief of police in Houston, Texas, the fourth largest city in the nation.

I was born in the little town of Newellton, Louisiana, and raised on my parent's farm. I am one of twelve children. At our home, education was a priority of my parents. Educational achievement was demanded and expected by my mother. Such achievement was stressed to the point that we did not celebrate birthdays in our home, but excellence in our studies was always rewarded. Mother espoused the belief that reward is attached to performance. As a result, all twelve of us are college-educated people today (five of us are proud graduates of Grambling State University). Six of us have even gone on to earn graduate degrees.

After earning a Criminal Justice degree at Grambling, I joined the Houston Police Department in 1979. Upon graduation from the academy, I worked as a police officer in various assignments before being promoted. It was always my intention to return to college, and I had also given consideration to attending graduate school. With this in mind, I began planning to continue my education from my earliest days at the department.

For several years, I set aside money from each paycheck in an education fund. I have found that education is expensive, but it is a worthwhile investment. Because of my commitment of funds to my education, I decided that until my education was complete, I would avoid buying luxury items such as the fancy automobiles that many of my friends were buying. In fact,

I drove a small Toyota. I also maintained a simple lifestyle and refrained from impulsive spending.

Having set aside the funds, I entered Texas Southern University (TSU) in Houston, where I earned a second degree in public administration. One thing that I learned quickly is that going to college while working full time is extremely difficult. In order to make the best use of my time, I prepared a schedule to which I adhered rigidly. On the schedule, I set aside time for the things that I had to do, working, shopping, housecleaning, exercise, and, of course, my studies. I have no doubt that assessing the best use of my time and creating and adhering to that schedule was a major factor in my earning magna cum laude honors at TSU.

After completing my public administration degree, I was persuaded by Lloyd Kelley, a very close friend and police academy classmate, to attend law school. He was already studying law. I entered and earned my doctor of jurisprudence degree at the University of Houston's Law Center. More than ever, the principles and discipline that I used to earn my other degrees served me well during my legal studies. The discipline that I developed also was key to my successful completion of the Federal Bureau of Investigation's National Executive Institute at the FBI Academy and the Program for Senior Executives in State and Local Government at Harvard University's John F. Kennedy School of Government.

The pursuit of my degrees, professional development programs, and other training proved to be well worth the commitment of time and money when, in June of 1991 after various assignments throughout the Houston Police Department, I was promoted to assistant chief of police. In November 1996, I was nominated as chief of police by then Mayor Bob Lanier. I have had the honor of being Houston's police chief since. I have no doubt that my unique academic accomplishments were the part of my résumé that set me apart from a field of extremely worthy candidates. Today, I lead an organization responsible for providing service to over 1.8 million people. I have over seven thousand employees and a budget of more than $400 million dollars to manage.

Preparation is perhaps the single most important thing to do before pursuing graduate studies. It is best to look ahead and try to anticipate the things that must be done to effectively pursue graduate studies. Set aside some money in anticipation of your school needs. Tuition and books are expensive. I am often frustrated when I hear of a promising student who had to drop out of grad school because of a lack of funds, especially when the situation could have been avoided with proper planning. I don't expect everyone to do exactly as I did; however, everyone hoping to attend grad school should plan their finances carefully.

Let me also stress that time management is critically important when attending school, especially if you have to work to support yourself while in school. Set aside time for the things that are important to you, but always keep in mind that your studies should be given high priority. Poor time management has caused the demise of many students who were otherwise very capable students.

As African Americans, we are not always given the same opportunities as others. That makes it vitally important that we be prepared when opportunities arise. Be prepared to make short-term sacrifices. Be disciplined in your approach to your studies. Graduate studies are an excellent way to prepare for those opportunities that arise. The long-term gain is well worth the struggle and sacrifices made to attain a graduate degree.

SUGGESTED READINGS

Gilbert, L.A., & Rossmank, L.M. (1992). Gender and the mentoring process for women: Implications for professional development. *Psychology: Research and Practice, 23*, 233–238.

Frederick D. Paterson Research Institute. (1997). *The African American Education Data Book, Volume I: Higher and Adult Education*. Frederick D. Paterson Research Institute: Fairfax, VA.

Steele, C. (1992, April). Race and Schooling of Black Americans. *Atlantic, 269*, 68–78.

Thernstrom, S., & Thernstrom, A. (1997, April 7). The consequence of colorblindness. *The Wall Street Journal*, pp. A18.

CASES

Bakke v. Regents of University of Southern California, 438 U.S. 265 (1968).

Hopwood et al v. State of Texas, 851 F. Supp 570 (1996).

"Ain't Gonna Let Nobody Turn Me Around"

The Value of the Journey

LISA PERTILLAR BREVARD

Dean of Humanities and Associate Professor of English
and African World Studies, Dillard University

On May 8, 1995, I walked across the stage during Emory University's 150th commencement and "got hooded"—received my doctoral hood, in full blue-and-gold academic regalia under a shining Atlanta sun. Extremely excited, I remained unaware of the gravity of it all. The fact of the matter was that I had worked so diligently to complete degree requirements and keep my pledge to myself to "walk across that stage" with the rest of my graduating class that I had not given myself the time to contemplate what it all meant. Now I think I know.

Obtaining the doctor of philosophy degree fulfilled a pledge that I had made to my father, an obligation to my husband, and a solemn promise that I had made to myself. On his deathbed, suffering from cancer and emphysema, my father told me in gasping whispers to "stay in school.... Go all the way." Shortly thereafter, he died. At the time I was a sophomore at Smith College, majoring in Afro-American Studies. I took "going all the way" to mean earning the doctor of philosophy degree.

Later, my fiancé suggested Emory University for graduate studies; when my application was accepted, I had his unwavering support. In 1991 we married, I graduated Smith with honors and a bachelor of arts degree, and we relocated to Georgia in preparation for my graduate studies. My husband said that he would love me always but he would never forgive me if I did not complete what I had started. There really was no excuse; Emory provided fellowships for all graduate students, so I studied full time. I loved studying African American culture and women's studies in even greater depth and began to really envision myself becoming the professor that I told Emory University I had planned to become. My Emory experience was very gratifying, overall, but beyond the academic challenges and successes were challenges of a different sort that further prepared me for aspects of the world beyond the university.

The road was not easy: As a woman, a native New Englander, and one of a minority of African American students on the Emory University campus, the depth of my pledge to myself was tested time and again. In addition to my simply being different and the social challenges that such status entailed, a small number of professors clearly preferred working with male students instead, so I studied under the wise tutelage of professors who were more interested in the work than anything else. Having gone to graduate school straight out of college, whenever I ventured outside the department or libraries, I was often mistaken for and treated as an undergraduate. When I began working as a teaching assistant at Emory College, I had an overall positive experience working with some of the best undergraduates our country has to offer, but I did run into a few smart alecks—White male undergraduates who spoke out of turn in the section of class that I taught and sometimes refused to complete course assignments. Thus began my additional education in learning to handle unfortunate situations—and theirs in learning to respect African American women. What the smart alecks did not realize was that the more they resisted my burgeoning authority, the stronger became my resolve to complete the degree.

"Ain't gonna let nobody turn me around!" I sang to myself, walking across campus with an armload of books, shuttling to and from the library and between classes and not caring that others may have thought me crazy for singing to myself. "Ride on, King Jesus ... . No man can hinder me!" I sang, sitting at my computer and waiting for the printout of yet another paper. During my last year at Emory, my confidence continued to grow when Professor Gloria Wade-Gayles told me about a one-semester teaching opportunity at Spelman College, which I fortunately obtained. This teaching experience was invaluably self-affirming and encouraged me to continue to give my best in the classroom.

Wearying at the thought of yet another river to cross—the doctoral dissertation—I forged ahead and finally crossed the finish line in record time, completing both an M.A. and Ph.D. in four years. Waiting for me at the end of that portion of the journey were some of Emory's strongest professors, my husband, our family, a few close friends, and my daddy, in spirit. The end of that road brought me to a new one which I still travel.

Having a graduate degree in hand means never having to look over my shoulder to wonder if I am qualified for a particular job in my area of specialization. It means that I will never be told by a potential employer, "Come back when you have finished the degree." It also entails a great deal of responsibility beyond the teaching and research that many graduate degree recipients do.

People with graduate degrees make and enact policies that affect local, national, and international communities in such areas as employment, education, science, and government, to name a few. People with graduate degrees also have access to funding for research and development. Graduate degree recipients occupy an important position in the power structure, often serving as liaisons between communities-at-large and the powers-that-be. Completing a graduate degree means more than simply "getting that piece of paper": it is the exciting end of one road and the powerful start of another.

Graduate Student Mentoring

WARREN W. BUCK

Chancellor, University of Washington–Bothell

Entering into graduate school is both a wonderfully exhilarating experience and a scary one all at the same time. It is exhilarating because it is a statement that you really are smart enough and that you can now rub shoulders and learn from the best minds around. It also means that you are going into territory that perhaps no one in your family has ever gone.

At the same time as this exuberance, the realization quickly takes hold that you may not know as much as you thought you did and that there are a lot of smart students who are your peers. Many of your peers appear to be having no problem navigating the graduate school world, while you struggle to keep up not only in your class/research work but also in the understanding of what the culture is and how you fit into it. You may even believe that you cannot possibly continue unless you have more funding, or you wish the physical handicap you may have were not a burden; by physical handicap, I do not mean race, ethnicity, religion, or sex. There is also the sudden awareness that one or more of your professors seems to be giving you a very hard time for whatever reason; perhaps they are tough, perhaps they are insensitive to you, perhaps they are trying to hide the fact that they know less than you. These realizations can be very scary, and having all of these feelings and realizations is a source of much frustration and anxiety in a student's life. Some say "Get used to it" as these occurrences can be found on and off campus, in your family, in your community, and worldwide. I say, "Get used to the process of addressing difficult issues."

Unfortunately, there is no chart or road map that all students have access to and that they can follow. However, each student can do a couple of very helpful things to reduce anxiety and frustration so as to be more secure in learning and navigating interpersonal relationships: (1) find a mentor and (2) find some colleagues you can work with.

A mentor is a person whom you can trust to give you straight answers and not just the answers you want to hear. A mentor is someone who has experiences that can be shared with you to help guide you in the development of your own unique experiences. I believe that having a mentor who is a respected faculty member in the department where you are enrolled is invaluable. This mentor could be your main research advisor or another faculty member you trust to give you straight answers and good advice.

Choosing a mentor is not always easy. Of course, if you have the good fortune of finding a graduate school mentor from a recommendation made to you by your undergraduate school mentor and it works, then you are fortunate indeed. On the other hand, it usually does not work that smoothly, and you will have to rely on your interpersonal skills to find a mentor you can get along with. This might mean bouncing around the department until you find such a person.

The classroom or research lab is not the only place to look for a mentor. Go to social events sponsored by the department and interact with people. Always be yourself and be open to learning more about yourself and others. I find that people receive me better when I am not defensive and closed to suggestions. You will be left alone to fend for yourself if you are defensive and closed to suggestions; however, this essay is not meant for those who need no help.

The benefits of having a department faculty mentor is that you have someone you trust, someone who gives great advice and someone who can run interference for you. The downside to this is that often having the mentor running interference for you can lead to jealousy by the other students and, in many cases, jealousy of the other faculty—but you will have a strong beacon in the form of your mentor to navigate by. Yes, you're damned if you do and damned if you don't. You must choose the lesser of the two evils and live with your decision no matter what. More often than finding a mentor, students find each other.

Finding colleagues with whom you can work is important in the short run and in the long run. In the short run, you can work with your fellow students in discussing issues of your various fields, in particular, classroom topics. These discussions get you and your fellow students in a collaborative mode that can often strengthen during your graduate school tenure. The best situations are when you actually feed off each others' energy and insights.

In the long run, these same graduate students enter the workforce and the bonding that took place in graduate school casts a larger net as your former colleagues spread out over the world. And as you keep in touch with each other, you also begin to bring others into your circle as you meet new colleagues and teach them your values, your techniques, and your mentoring experiences.

The bottom line is that to succeed in graduate school, you must be willing to learn; even more to the point, to succeed in life, you must be willing to learn. You must perform your work in the most ethical manner, and you must ask when you do not know. You never know who is watching you. It really is true that if you work hard and show good faith in your attempts to learn, you will receive help and sometimes from surprising sources. Learning humility can also be very beneficial in interpersonal interactions.

I have been very fortunate to have had several excellent mentors to help guide me throughout my career and, especially, in graduate school. I also have developed over the years many valued colleagues/friends whom I have met throughout my academic life. Any success I may have is tied to their good work with me, my trust in my judgment as well as in theirs, and my eagerness to discover resolution and new horizons. The judgment that I have developed is just that; I developed it—I learned by experience—I am still learning.

Finding a good mentor should not be taken lightly. If you cannot find one where you are, think about going to another institution that has a reputation for good mentoring. In this way, you can better optimize finding one willing to take you on. Please remember that there is more than one way to address and solve an issue. Mentors and friends can help, but you must be proactive in pursuing resolution.

Good mentors and friends are out there just waiting for you.

You Can Succeed in Mathematics

DONALD R. COLE

Associate Dean of the Graduate School and Associate
Professor of Mathematics, University of Mississippi

Mathematics is often viewed as a challenging area requiring special talents for individual success. Although this generalization can be made about any field, it quickly shadows and erodes the initial interests of those individuals anticipating pursuing mathematics. Women and minorities are particularity vulnerable to this stigmatization at a rather early age.

Mathematics, along with a few other subjects, enjoys a somewhat unique role in our educational system. It is recognized as important and is offered in the learning curriculum very early in a child's life. Moreover, the importance of the need to continually introduce students to new concepts in this area is recognized throughout the high school years. Furthermore, mathematics sits as the cornerstone from which the sciences are introduced and built. To an elementary student, the jubilation of getting that answer in the back of the book is as gratifying as catching that touchdown pass or of winning mom's approval of a job well done. How and why this joy loses its favor among women and minorities as their years progress is the subject of much academic study and debate.

My interest in mathematics made its debut at a fairly early age. Fortunately I was blessed that there were several key factors in place that nourished my enthusiasm. Many of these included elementary teachers who observed potential and decided to nourish it, middle school teachers who shared my enthusiasm for the subject, and high school teachers who took me under their arms. Although somewhat rare, it is yet not uncommon today to see a number of African Americans enter college with the desire to study mathematics. A far more rare event is their actually graduating with a mathematics degree. An African American obtains a master's degree in mathematics only twenty to thirty times a year in America, whereas an African American obtains a doctoral degree in mathematics only four to five times a year nationwide. Mathematics claims no uniqueness in its lack of support for African Americans at the terminal degree level as most of the sciences and engineering area lay claim to similar statistics. It is natural to ask why this is a problem and what mechanisms might be employed to elevate this problem. There is no shortage of questions: Why is America failing to train minority mathematicians, scientists, and engineers at the Ph.D. level? What can be done to attract African Americans to the field of mathematics? Is it simply a matter of finances? Whose responsibility is it to see that we address this problem as a nation? Are African Americans purposely being dissuaded from entering the field? Are we not properly prepared before entering graduate programs? Are we entering and not exiting? If so, why?

The research needed to address these and related questions is beyond my expertise and certainly beyond the scope of this essay. We bring these questions forth simply as a discussion mechanism to allow us to examine successful negotiation of the process through attainment of the Ph.D.

Many mathematicians describe our field as the "queen of all the sciences," whereas others refer to it as "the language of all sciences." The language analogy affords a holistic view of my training in mathematics. Language is generally not understood to be mastered until it is understood in both the written and spoken formats. Implicit in this understanding is the fact that it takes more than the single individual to substantiate the understanding. In the early years of my mathematical training, I relied too heavily on the professors to verbalize a clear, concise understanding of the material. In the middle years of my mathematical training, I relied too heavily on my personal ability to read and regurgitate from the mathematical literature. Finally, during my doctoral study, I was able to balance these two prospectives.

Philosophically, I often find the degree process of young mathematicians stifled by one of these two extremes. One of the differences between undergraduate and graduate school is often defined by one's ability to successfully perform independently. Indeed, graduate students are expected to have less reliance upon the professor to fill in details and bring forth the entire subject matter. However, it is not intended that the student should learn in isolation. Graduate students "learn the language" in terms of reliance upon library references, fellow colleagues, professors, and other innovative resources. On the other hand, the professor acts as a barometer measuring the maturity with which the student is acquiring the language. The student is expected to have read the material, performed self-tests, collaborated with others, and prepared to verbally discuss the material in terms of observations, questions, extensions, reasoning, and so on. That is to say, students are not expected to totally evaluate themselves in isolation.

While in college, it was popular to make fun of our college's teachers and to call them weird—especially those in the natural sciences. At the time, little did I realize that my progression to earning a Ph.D. would put me directly in that weird line of fire. Indeed, that progression could be indirectly measured by the number of times I held a mathematical notion in my mind without being able to sleep or dreamed about it as I slept. It could also be measured by the number of Post-It notes containing mathematical concepts that could be found in my pockets wherever I went (including the rest room!).

I was told early on that getting a doctorate in mathematics would require the help of many other individuals. It took me years to realize the profundity of this statement. Many times it is not easy to receive help, let alone to ask for it. Nevertheless, the Ph.D. is a "get help" degree! During various phases of the doctoral process, I found a need to call upon various faces for help, of which there is an endless spectrum: clergy, classmates, mentors within and outside the department, past students whom I didn't even know but who completed the process ...

A graduate degree is conferred upon satisfaction of the faculty in the discipline. The preliminary exams, qualifying exams, and comprehensive exams are designed to assess general knowledge in key areas of the discipline. Analysis (real, complex, and functional) and algebra (abstract or modern and linear) are two indispensable areas in mathematics, and generally a student is tested in at least three areas. These exams are also the proper place for the faculty to express satisfaction or dissatisfaction with the student's mastery of the subject area. Preparation for these exams begins at entry into graduate school, which signifies the importance of learning not only the content of a given class but the subject area as well. When possible, such major courses should be taken from those who will compose the exam questions. By far, group study has proven the most effective method for preparing for these exams.

No experience is more memorable than having a choice and making the wrong one! For this experience, I hold the record. One such unforgettable choice involved picking my major professor. My first choice was nontenured faculty in the discipline I loved. After two intense years of study with this professor, guess what happened? Yes, he was denied tenure and had to move on to another institution. And what about me? I was a much smarter person in several ways! At that stage in my career, little did I know to ask the right questions of a faculty member who could potentially be my major professor: Are they tenured? Have they produced other doctoral students? How many students are they currently advising? What is the average time to degree for their students? Have they ever produced a minority student? Did they extend an offer, or am I pushing myself upon them? Am I welcomed? Do I feel confident that this person would defend me when I'm not around? Does this person have the respect of the other faculty who might be needed to help me through?

The language of mathematics can be so beautiful when it is understood and so intimidating when it is not. It is impossible to understand without participating therein. Various national societies, including the Mathematical Association of America, the Society of Industrial and Applied Mathematician, and the National Association of Mathematicians, have all created special committees to increase the number of minorities entering the field. Efforts should be made to become an active part of these organizations. They afford opportunities to both hear and speak the language. In addition, they provide literature of interest to any mathematician. Along with your extensive mathematical literature, you should own *Successfully Negotiating the Graduate School Process: A Guide for Minority Students* by Howard Adams and *Graduate School and You: A Guide for Prospective Graduate Student* and *The Doctorate of Philosophy Degree,* both by The Council of Graduate Schools in Washington, D.C.

I cannot begin to articulate the joys associated with the doctoral degree, as it has been the most defining accomplishment in my life. I probably own the record for the longest time taken to attain the Ph.D. degree in mathematics. It is also a "don't give up" degree, and with it in hand, your choice of an academic, industrial, or governmental position awaits you without fail.

Graduate School Experience

Knowledge Is Our Future

WILLIE CURTIS
Associate Professor of Political Science, U.S. Naval Academy

On the wall of my office in Nimitz Hall at the U.S. Naval Academy is a large picture of an African wise man surrounded by students, and it is obvious that he is imparting knowledge to them. The caption under the picture reads *"Knowledge Is Our Future."* This is true today as in the past. I think of my graduate school experience at the University of Delaware as a period in my life when I sat eagerly at the feet of wise men and sought to obtain as much knowledge as possible. That picture reminds me each day that education remains the key to a better future.

My graduate school experience was quite challenging and enjoyable. However, to understand my experience, it is necessary to take a retrospective view of my life. My success in graduate school and my chosen profession as a university professor has been influenced by a career in the U.S. military. Indeed, if I may start from my youth, I decided very early to obtain two goals in life—to spend twenty years in the U.S. Air Force and to teach social studies as a second career. I attempted to enlist in the U.S. Air Force during seventh grade in public school. However, the recruiting sergeant insisted that I contact him in five years.

I enlisted in the U.S. Air Force upon graduating from high school in May 1957 and spent twenty-one years and seven months in a very rewarding career. I quickly learned that education was key to my success in the military. Having to compete for promotion with older military personnel with longer service, my only advantage was that the U.S. Air Force began to use a testing system and other criteria that gave a slight advantage to individuals who advanced their education. Indeed, if all other criteria were equal, the promotion system used additional education as a tiebreaker. Over an eighteen-year period (owing to overseas assignments and flying duties as an aircrew member) I obtained my undergraduate degree in secondary education–political science (with an Outstanding Student Teacher's Award) from the University of Delaware in May 1977. Upon my retirement from the U.S. Air Force in December 1978, I had obtained a position as a social studies teacher at a local high school in Dover, Delaware; however, I did not take the position because my major professor, Dr. James R. Soles, convinced me that I should attend graduate school in Political Science at the University of Delaware. Again by the grace of God, I made the correct decision and was admitted to the M.A. program in political science during the spring semester of 1979.

The intent of this retrospective review of my early period is to emphasize the influence that the military had on my perception of reality, acceptance of responsibilities. and ability to focus on obtaining a specific goal. In addition to the support of a loving wife and stable home environment. the support I received from the entire faculty and staff of the Department of Political Science was absolutely outstanding. Although the graduate program was extremely demanding, the advice and guidance I received from the faculty was essential to my success in acquiring a graduate degree.

The fact that a number of the professors had taught off-campus courses at Dover Air Force Base during my assignment there gave them a different assessment of my capabilities. I believe that they saw me as a more mature and responsible person rather than as a young, inexperienced graduate student. I was given additional responsibilities, and although the expectations were different, the opportunities to work as a teaching assistant and actually teach the class when the professor was absent increased my confidence. During the spring semester of 1980, I was approached by the faculty fellowship advisor and asked if I would agree to have the department submit me for a three-year minority fellowship to obtain a Ph.D. in political science. I agreed and received my M.A. in political science in June 1980.

By accepting the minority fellowship to study for the Ph.D., I was unable to act as a teaching assistant. Teaching was very important to me, however, so the department chairman agreed to allow me to teach a summer course on the presidency. This added a bit of income to assist me during the summer. In addition, I had my G.I. Bill, which paid enough to make my mortgage payments during the summer session.

I entered the Ph.D. program in the fall of 1980, and those same qualities and habits that had shaped my approach to education during my Air Force career—focusing on a specific goal, working long hours, managing my time, and enjoying a challenge—also shaped my approach to this endeavor, prompting me to take the maximum number of seminars each semester and spend the summer and winter semester in a reading seminar for the specific area in which I would have to take comprehensive examinations. I had to take comprehensive examinations in five areas, and by concentrating on each one during the winter and summer sessions, I completed my seminar requirements and the comprehensive examinations by the spring of 1982.

Because I had a year left on the fellowship, I was free to concentrate on researching and writing my dissertation. Again by the grace of God, Professor William Boyer submitted my name to the National Association of Schools of Public Affairs and Administration (NASPAA) and the U.S. Agency for International Development Committee (USAID) for their new NASPAA/USAID internship in Washington, D.C. This competition was on a nationwide basis, and I was selected from the University of Delaware along with another graduate student from the University of Southern California.

I spent six months (one month with NASPAA, five months with USAID) working in the Office of Rural Development. During my Air Force career I had flown to a number of countries and had some idea of the gap between the rich and the poor; however, I was not prepared for the degree of poverty that existed throughout the developing world. During my internship I worked on a Management Development Training in the Third World project for NASPAA and a number of development projects for USAID. I became keenly aware of the growing gap between the people of the developing world and the industrialized states. I developed a desire to study the role that this country played in assisting economic growth and relieving the causes of poverty.

During my internship at USAID, I accumulated documentation and policy papers and interviewed the project directors. While at USAID I had the opportunity to work for an outstanding lady who was director of the Office of Rural Development, and she offered me every opportunity to learn the complex task associated with development in the Third World. When the internship was completed in January 1983, I returned to the University of Delaware and began to write my dissertation.

My dissertation advisor, Professor James K. Oliver, was outstanding, and he insisted that I not begin to write a new chapter until he had approved the first one. He carefully read each chapter, and I made the revisions before moving to the next one. This technique was quite successful, and I had completed the dissertation and received approval from the dissertation committee by May 1983. I received my Ph.D. in June and began my second career as a university professor.

Although graduate school was very demanding, I am privileged to have been selected to complete my graduate work at the University of Delaware. If I were to select the most important factor that led to my success in graduate school, I am convinced that it was having spent most of my early adult years in the U.S. Air Force. Indeed, I would suggest that I grew up in the Air Force. At an early age I learned the importance of education; I learned to accept responsibility, to focus on obtaining a long-range goal, and to manage my time. In addition, I am married to a loving wife (we were married in 1958), and we both grew to maturity in the Air Force. I was also assisted by a group of highly professional wise men at the University of Delaware and will remain indebted to them.

And just as important is the trail blazed by those great African Americans who preceded me. They devoted their lives to obtaining equal rights and justice and paved the way for me in military and civilian life. Whatever accomplishments I achieve are due in large measure to their struggle. In the final analysis, my advice to any graduate student is to remember that a tremendous price was paid for their opportunity to attend a graduate school. Use the time wisely, for "knowledge is our future."

The "Old Man" and the Defining Moment That Changed My Life!

LAWRENCE F. DAVENPORT

Deputy Chief Administrative Officer, U.S. House of Representatives, Washington, D.C.

"Old man, I'm at the bus station. I need a ride home. Will you come and get me?"

"I'll be right there."

The "old man" was my dad. The bus station was in Lansing, Michigan. I was there because after just two weeks as a college freshman, I had been informed by my coach that to keep my athletic scholarship I would have to major in physical education. Because my goal in life was to be a social worker, I knew I couldn't do that. So I packed my belongings ... and headed for home. Trouble was, I didn't tell anyone else, especially my folks, what I was going to do. Now, suddenly, that ominous ring in the old man's voice had my full attention. I knew this was about to be a defining moment in my life.

The ride home did nothing to ease my tension. Not a word from the old man. Stone cold silence. A ride that seemed to last forever. Then it was over. We were home. Into the house we went, the old man leading the way. We made it to the living room ... still not a word. Abruptly, he wheeled around, planted his feet firmly, squared his shoulders, and looked me straight in the eye.

"Boy!" (Nobody called me that, in those days! Nobody! But he did.) "Boy! Why are you home from college?"

"My coach told me I had to major in physical education, not social work. Can't do that. So, I'm home to go to work. Tomorrow I'm going to go to

GM [General Motors] and get me a job in the assembly plant, just like you. I can make good money and buy myself a new Oldsmobile. I'll go to college next semester."

"Boy! You've got just three choices: one, you live at home and go to college; two, you get an apartment and go to college; three, you live on campus and go to college!"

The next morning I walked to the community college and signed up for late registration. I lived at home. In time, I came to realize that the old man forced me to face the most important defining moment of my life that afternoon in our living room. His firm resolve that day set me on a pathway of lifetime learning that has not only been a great adventure but has also opened the doors of opportunity to a life of successful accomplishment that I couldn't even imagine in our living room that day!

From those early days as an undergraduate, it was a logical step to graduate school, because it didn't take long for me to figure out that if I was to pursue my goals of a career in social work and education, I would need all the formal credentials I could muster. Looking back, it was the right choice. My formal education has made it possible for me to meet and exceed all of my early goals in my career.

From a college presidency before I was thirty to high-level national appointments by two U.S. presidents to my current position as a senior executive in financial management, I know that my commitment to lifelong learning has made it all possible. As much as that was true for me and my generation, it is even more important to young people today!

We are living in an age of incredible opportunity unparalleled in the history of humanity. It is also the age of fierce competition, complex global enterprise, and mind-numbing technological advancements moving with blinding speed across our nation and the world. The only ticket of admission that counts in this brave new golden age is knowledge, skill, and outstanding preparation to perform at maximum ability. The only way to obtain that ticket of admission is through rigorous, intensive, highly focused educational achievement.

Dr. Denis Waitley, a leading motivational expert, has often said, "Life is a do-it-to-yourself program." How right he is. Every young adult today should understand that from high school throughout life, they must prepare to train, equip, and market themselves. To do that, they must use every means available to them for formal and informal learning.

Starting in high school and moving on to college and graduate or professional school, they should be building not only academic credentials but also a network of support made up of teachers, professors, professional mentors, and peer-group colleagues. In my life, that process started during grade school in my Lansing neighborhood, and it has never stopped.

I would encourage young people today, more than ever, to get immersed in cocurricular activities and outside interests, not just to be well-rounded and balanced but to get a broader, more pervasive view of the world around them, and to develop the skill sets needed to assume leadership and management roles in the future. Be smart about it. Be focused in those activities. Make them count. Set realistic goals and priorities for participating. Use time carefully for what really matters most. As much as formal education matters … and it does … these are the skills that must be acquired for effective human relationships and for a satisfying quality of life. A professional career, important as it is, must be in balance with other priorities to produce real success in life.

Finally, most importantly, set goals large enough to grow into but realistic enough to attain. I was on that bus home to Lansing because after only two weeks of college, I suddenly realized that my dream of being a social worker was not going to happen if I followed my coach's mandate! In my case, the old man turned out to be reason enough … and am I ever grateful to him today for squaring off and saying, "Boy, you have three choices … !" As it turns out, the one I made has fulfilled my life beyond all expectations!

The Hardest Part of Graduate Training Is Getting In

JAMES E. DOBBINS

Professor of Psychology and Director of Postdoctoral Training, Wright State University

A common saying among members of the academy is that "the hardest part of graduate training is getting in." I have found this to be a truth considering that most students have prepared for over twenty years to simply have the opportunity to apply. Ironically, at the time an undergraduate fills out his or her applications, self-selection is the most important factor that operates in graduate school admissions, that is, researching the right school for the right reasons, taking the interview process seriously, and having your credentials in order. People who have been successful in their undergraduate studies usually know what it takes to be successful as graduate students. Such students are encouraged and supported by their faculty to apply for graduate training and advised how to develop their portfolios so that they fit the criteria expected of particular graduate programs. Actually, it is very difficult for graduate programs to select among the thousands of applicants who qualify as a result of their hard work and outstanding achievements. Because not all deserving students can be accepted, a second truism is that "if at first you don't succeed, try, try again." If you are not accepted, call the schools that turn you down to find out what you need to do to be more competitive, do what is recommended, and then reapply.

Taking risks is an essential part of getting into and through graduate school. As I think about the path of my career and the ingredients that have enabled me to withstand the slings and arrows of racism, money issues, naïveté, fear, damaged self-esteem, and gaps in my learning base, it is clear to me that I am here because of persistence and a willingness to learn from mistakes. There is no part of my life that did not suffer and benefit from those risks. I made mistakes, but I tried to follow the words of my father, Levi Edward Dobbins, who cautioned me to "avoid mistakes that cost too much." In order to actualize my father's admonition, I learned to rely on three unfailing supports: a tried and tested reliance on my intuition, a willingness to be mentored and guided by those who had already attained that which I aspired to achieve, and an immovable faith in an omnipresent, omniscient, and omnipotent God who supplies all of my needs.

Graduate school is difficult, as it should be. It is not possible to make it through without a support network. This is true not only in regard to graduate training but also in regard to postgraduate professional success. Getting the diploma is not nearly as difficult as developing a professional identity within your field, gaining colleagues who respect your work, and developing credibility in the community as a competent practitioner. It was helpful for me to begin my professional associations while in graduate school. Many of the fellow students whom I met in student organizations are still my best supports today. We have helped one another throughout our careers and are still affiliating on work projects and as members of professional organizations. It is well advised that you seek leadership roles in your student and professional organizations. It takes willingness, follow-through, and a concern for quality in order to build a positive national reputation among your peers. A little effort can pay huge dividends for your career. You cannot see all of the benefits from the outside looking in, so get involved from the start.

Seek to study under the professionals who are doing the kind of work you want to do. Practice loyalty to them throughout your career. Mention them as contributing to your successes so that people will know where your foundation began. Commit yourself to lifelong learning so that there is no question as to whether you are sincere and up-to-date in your approach to problems and issues. Maintain an ethic of service so that people know that on behalf of your profession and community you operate to see what needs to be done and meet the needs of a rapidly changing society.

People will remember you more for the one thing that hurt them than for the many things that you did to help them. There are times when your decisions hurt others; let your resolve be clearly based on matters of principle and not because you dislike a person or his position on an issue. However, it is not possible to have a professional career without standing up for your principles. Be willing to live by the consequences of your decisions and the principles upon which they stand. Those who cannot take a stand for something will fall for anything. How many people do you know who look foolish because their arguments are based on nonexistent virtues? It is easy to talk the talk, but your professional life must show that you walk the walk.

No successful professional operates without having a dream and having that dream translated into a strategic plan. The plan that I developed as a graduate student came true in every aspect, far sooner than projected. Plan your work and then work your plan. Monitor your plan routinely and revise it no less than annually. Focus your evaluation on your plan, not on yourself. If you are not having success, it's because you do not have the correct plan for you, not because you cannot succeed. If you know you have shortcomings, work on them as a part of your plan.

Never think that you are wise enough to judge your self-worth. That is something that only God is qualified to do. It is unlikely that the creator would deem you less than worthy of everything that was created for you. Develop an attitude of gratitude for everything that happens to you. Treat failures as challenges rather than moral deficiencies. Lastly, there are two common shortcomings among humans for which you should have no time. They are self-pity and grumbling. In the words of George Leonard, author of "The Modern Warrior" (unpublished), "live each day as if your hair were on fire."

Helping the African American Community through Higher Education

ANTHONY ECHOLS

Senior Statistical Analyst, General Motors Corporation

When deciding whether to pursue graduate or professional school, most African Americans will focus only on personal benefits such as better career opportunities and high salary. However, by earning graduate or professional degrees, African Americans can impact our community by showing youth more opportunities, setting expectations of achievement, and assisting others in reaching their goals. Specifically, individuals with advanced degrees can serve as role models for youth and provide mentoring and networking in the professional workplace.

Today, the African American community lacks quality role models. Relative to Whites, African Americans are more likely to come from single-parent homes where the father is not available. We are less likely to have obtained college or graduate school education or careers in lucrative professions. On the other hand, African Americans also have more negative role models, such as drug dealers or relatives and friends who have been incarcerated. Today, many African Americans make the wrong choices when they are developing their personal values and goals because they lack the guidance of a good role model.

My experience has shown me that the presence of African Americans with advanced degrees can positively influence young African Americans. I have many relatives with graduate or professional degrees who have successful careers. During my childhood I saw the affluence and respect that they were given by these careers. I also recognized that these career opportunities were made available through hard work and higher education, and therefore I knew that I was expected to do my best academically. Perhaps my most important learning was the realization that I could become a professional even though I was growing up as a minority member in America.

The presence of higher-educated African Americans can have the same affect on African American youth that it had on me. African Americans who obtain graduate or professional degrees will add positive role models to our community. Young African Americans will know that other African Americans have taken advantage of an opportunity for education and realize that they, too, can become educated. Over time, as more African Americans grow up knowing that higher education is not a remote possibility but the natural progression of their educational development, the African American community will become more educated and thereby able to enjoy the prosperity that comes from education.

Comparable to the need for African American role models in the African American community is the need for African American mentors and networking in the professional workplace. Mentors and networking are very important to career development. I do not know any successful person who has not been aided at some point by either mentoring or networking. Furthermore, mentoring by a person in a leadership position or a network that includes such a person is often more effective because leaders frequently have better information, contacts, and experience. Unfortunately, African Americans find it more difficult to advance their careers through mentors and networks than White Americans because of the disproportionately low number of African Americans leaders and peers in the professional workplace.

The need for African American mentors and networks can be addressed, in part, by African Americans working harder and longer than the typical successful White American at building their skills, credentials, and experience. By distinguishing themselves through skill building, African Americans are more equipped to overcome the barriers to success that they encounter in the workplace. Obtaining graduate or professional degrees is perhaps the best method for building skills and therefore an excellent opportunity to advance one's career in situations where mentors are scarce and networks are weak. If more African Americans are able to advance their careers by obtaining graduate and professional degrees, then more African Americans will be available for mentoring and networking. Over time, we will be able to eliminate mentors and networking from the list of obstacles that we endure in the workplace.

I can personally attest to this in my career at General Motors (GM). Here, African Americans who have reached management level have made it a priority to mentor and help the career development of other African Americans. Although much of my success at GM has been through their help, I also believe that my educational background, consisting of both an MBA and a law degree, has given me opportunities that would not have been available if I had only an MBA. There are other exceptional African Americans who have used mentoring and networking to become successful at GM. Hopefully those of us who have been successful thus far will be able to reach leadership positions in the future. This will allow us to be able to strengthen African American mentoring and networking so that it is easier for other African Americans to succeed in situations where they do not have extraordinary circumstances working in their favor.

Higher education is not the panacea for all African American problems. However, improving the overall educational level of African Americans will undoubtedly help improve the condition of the African American people as education is an essential building block in the foundation of any community. African Americans who are fortunate enough to graduate from four-year institutions will inevitably contemplate whether to pursue a higher degree. When making their decision, these individuals should consider that these higher degrees will add role models, mentors, and the ability to network to the African American community. Furthermore, they must also understand that not everyone has the opportunity to obtain graduate or professional school degrees and that an opportunity not taken may therefore be an opportunity lost.

Vision, Determination, Self-Leadership, and Time Management

Harbingers and Purveyors of Academic Success

MARTIN O. EDU

Associate Professor and Director of Graduate Program in Mass Communication, Grambling State University

> Anyone without a vision is doomed to failure.
>
> > (Dr. B. Johnson, college president)

> I press on toward the goal to win the prize for which God has called me heavenward in Christ Jesus.
>
> > (Phil. 3:14)

> The wisest of insights that can be gained by any man or woman is the realization that our world is not so much what it is but what we choose it to be.
>
> > (C.C. Manz and P.C. Neck)

> Time is life. It is irreversible and irreplaceable. To waste your time is to waste your life, but to master your time is to master your life and make the most of it.
>
> > (A. Lakein)

Different people are motivated toward excellence or success by different stimuli, but some more so than others. This statement is supported by a mass communication theoretical perspective known as *individual differ-*

ences theory, which argues that "because people vary greatly in their psychological make-up and because they have different perceptions of things, media influence differs from person to person" (Baran & Davis, 2000, p. 138). DeFleur (1970) states more specifically that "media messages contain particular stimulus attributes that have differential interaction with personality characteristics of members of the audience" (pp. 122–123). Despite the different factors that seem to interact with personality characteristics to motivate people to succeed, these quotes contain what can be described as the central elements that permeate the workings of the multiplicity of motivational factors functioning either singly or collectively. The centrality of these elements suggest that they can lead to success in academics or any other field of human endeavor if applied diligently. The elements, which form the nucleus of this essay's title, include vision, determination, self-leadership, and time management.

The term *success* is defined as the "achievement of something attempted" (*The American Heritage Dictionary,* 1987). Anyone who has accomplished success in any sphere of life would agree that it does not come easy. Some of the sports greats like Tiger Woods (golf), Michael Jordan (basketball), Mark McGuire (baseball), and Pete Sampras (lawn tennis), to list a few, did not get to the top overnight. They all began with a vision that propelled a determination to excel in their chosen sport. They then disciplined themselves and managed their time effectively. The same principles used by the successful men and women we sometimes idolize would yield similar results if applied to academics.

The American Heritage Dictionary (1987) defines the term *vision* as (1) "the faculty of sight," (2) "unusual foresight," (3) "a mental image produced by the imagination," and (4) "something as a supernatural sight, perceived through unusual means." For our purposes in this work, we will work with the definitions numbered two through four for their appropriateness. In the second definition, a vision is described as an "unusual foresight," which by implication means that something is known before it happens. Most high school graduates have a vision to go to college upon graduation, and once in college, their vision changes to graduation from college and getting a "dream" job. That foreknowledge is the unique characteristic of a vision. It is also described in the third definition as a "mental image produced by imagination" or the "supernatural sight, perceived through unusual means" in the fourth definition.

It should have been clear from the discussion of the dictionary definitions that a vision is like a journey from the present into an already accomplished future event, which is vivid to the visionary. It is like a road map that allows a traveler to visualize his or her destination long before arrival. Without a road map, a simple trip could easily turn into a nightmare of frustration and wasted time. The same is also true of the journey of life. Perhaps you know someone who at one time in his or her life showed a promise of getting to the top but did not. That illustrates how easy it is to veer off our carefully charted territory in life's journey. Sometimes the choices we make or the friends we keep can cause that to happen, but the chances can be reduced if, as Apostle Paul puts it in his letter to the Philippians, we make every effort to "press for the prize" set before us. No other individual in the New Testament comes close to Paul's experience in terms of his indefatigable persistence even in the face of extreme suffering. He stands out from others for his tenacious ability not only to stay focused on the prize but also to press persistently for it. It is little wonder that he took the gospel to places where no one else ventured.

Paul's missionary journey is, in many ways, similar to a student's quest for a college degree. Every college student has a desire to succeed; some do and some don't. Some people are quick to attribute the success of some students to their unique gift of talent, but that may not always be true. For example, a student who perceives college as a place for parties and socialization and pays little or no attention to schoolwork would never earn the good grades earned by a conscientious student who pays more attention to schoolwork than parties. This is not to ignore the fact that students are faced with a myriad of influences in their daily lives, but it takes determination to stay the desired course, which could help them overcome most of the influences.

Perhaps what is unique about every one of us is that we all possess qualities and ways of thinking that allow us to see the world in our own unique ways and deal with life's influences and experiences in different ways. We are leaders of our destiny. According to Manz and Neck (1999),

We all lead ourselves.... What we do with our lives, including where we work and for whom we work, is largely left to us.... In other words, we make our own lunch. If we need more training to obtain the kind of job we really want, it's up to us to lead ourselves to make the kinds of sacrifices necessary to achieve our ends. ... Belief in your ability to "make your own lunch"—that is, to lead yourself can be a life or death matter. (p. 4)

The point here is that you are your own leader, and you can be a good or bad one.

As a college student, can you remember how many times you caught yourself reminding yourself to go and study for that exam? How many times can you remember falsely assuring yourself that you still had a lot of time? It goes to illustrate that we all have weaknesses in our own self-leadership process. The process is dysfunctional in some people because it leads them to make poor decisions that affect their behavior toward their educational progress and ultimately their future. The truth is that our inner nature is a battleground between opposing forces. Although one part of us seems to be encouraging us to give up or take the easy way out, the other seems to be screaming that we could make our lives count for something and become all that we are capable of being. The part of us we yield to reflects the choices we make about our future. It raises a question as to how we could get ourselves back on track and keep the course.

A combination of strategies have been suggested. They include using physical reminders like writing or printing several copies of the tasks we need to accomplish on colored papers and placing each paper at a strategic point in the office or at home or both. Another method is to keep out of our way any cues that might suggest the behavior we are trying to beat and replacing them with positive cues. For example, if you are the kind of student who has many friends, you can devise a cue that reminds you to spend more time in the library at certain times of the day to avoid distraction from your friends and their telephone calls. You have to remember that a college education is a four-year journey in which every day counts because it takes you one day closer to your graduation and that first dream job. As you make the effort to stay focused, remind yourself of the relevance of the quote at the beginning of this paper: "Time is life. It is irreversible and irreplaceable. To waste your time is to waste your life, but to master your time is to master your life and make the most of it" (Lakein, 1974, p. 11). In fact, it would be a good thing to memorize all the quotes and use them to reinforce your determination.

As an effectiveness expert, Lakein argues that "there is no such thing as lack of time. We have plenty of time to do everything we want to do," but taking control of our time is the problem (12). According to him, "control starts with planning," which he defines as "bringing the future into the present so that you can do something about it now" (p. 25). For a college student, that future is the end of the semester or quarter. Bringing the end of the semester into the present means deciding your final grade at the beginning of the semester or quarter and working for it right then. Throughout my college education, I devised a strategy that worked very well for me. I would decide my final grade in every course on the first day of class. I would write the letter grade at the top center of every page of my notebook to remind me of the work required to earn that grade.

During my first semester as a freshman, I was enrolled in a study skills course that encouraged students to spend twice the length of instructional time for each class in which they were enrolled. For example, if a class meets for fifty minutes on Monday, Wednesday, and Friday, a student should spend two hours on each of those days studying for that class. I adhered strictly to the strategy and found that it was as effective as the instructor had claimed. It really allowed me more review and leisure time at weekends. One other strategy that worked very well for me was the design and use of a day clock to determine how much free time I had on a twenty-four-hour-day clock. It involved drawing two circles, with each representing the first twelve hours of the day beginning from midnight. In the circle that represented the midnight-to-noon hours, I indicated the actual activities in which

I would be engaged. I did the same for the remaining hours of the day. If you could try this strategy, you would be amazed at the amount of study and leisure time available to you. A word of advice: unless you are determined to take control of your time by adhering strictly to the schedule, this schema may not work for you.

If you have been making grades that you honestly believe do not reflect your academic ability, it would seem clear that like most college students, you probably have problems with time management. You may want to try the strategies suggested here during the coming semester or quarter. Before trying any of the suggested strategies, first take a few minutes and ask yourself the purpose for which you want a college degree and the purpose to which you plan to put that degree. Do not just brood over it; get a pen and paper and write down your answers. Based on your answers, you should be able to write down your *vision* of what your college degree would do for you. Then reassure yourself with Paul's words: "I can do all things through Christ who strengthens me." Also, say aloud that you are going to make a perfect grade point average from that semester on, for it is better to aim at the stars than anything lower. With that determination to achieve your vision, you should be able to take control of your time and lead yourself to greater levels of academic success. If you have decided to try the suggested strategies in the coming semester or quarter, I congratulate you, I believe in you, and I believe that you will make it.

REFERENCES

Baran, S. J., & Davis, D. K. (2000). *Mass communication theory: Foundations, ferment, and future* (2d ed.). Belmont, CA: Wadsworth/Thomson Learning.

DeFleur, M. L. (1970). *Theories of mass communication.* New York: David McKay.

Lakein, A. (1974). *Discover how to set your priorities, manage your life and achieve your goals: How to get control of your time and your life.* New York: Signet.

Manz, C. C., & Neck, P. C. (1999). *Mastering self-leadership: Empowering yourself for personal excellence* (2d ed.). Upper Saddle River, NJ: Prentice Hall.

The American Heritage Dictionary: Based on the second college edition. (1987). New York: Dell Publishing Company.

Using Networking, Role Models, and Mentoring En Route to Success

CHARLES J. ELMORE
Professor and Head of the Department of Mass Communications,
Savannah State University

I attended graduate school at the University of Michigan, where I received an M.A. in print and broadcast journalism (1972) and a Ph.D. in higher education administration (1979). At the University of Michigan, the journalism program prepared students for careers as professionals in print or broadcast media. During my master's program, all courses emphasized applied knowledge and hands-on training as well as theoretical approaches. To this end, we produced a weekly television news show, which entailed shooting and editing film, covering beats, serving as anchors on camera, and then rotating to roles as directors, camera operators, and script editors. In short, everyone rotated in all roles in television broadcasting. Conversely, the class also produced a daily newspaper where students shot pictures, attended city council meetings in Ann Arbor, and as reporters, covered the normal news beats of a metropolitan daily newspaper.

The various research components in the Michigan program allowed students to develop skills in professional library research to produce documentaries that necessitated extensive research of individuals and other pertinent materials. There were also courses designed to teach students how to write features, editorials, and hard news. Additionally, there were opportunities for students to serve as editors of the various professional-type journals in the School of Journalism such as *The Michigan Journalist*. I had the opportunity to serve as editor of the journal and gained valuable professional experience.

As a result of my journalism training at Michigan, I was able to secure my first job as a college professor when I was hired in 1972 as instructor in English and journalism in the fledgling mass communications program at Savannah State College. By 1974, the knowledge I gained in the journalism program at Michigan put me in position to be offered the job of director of public relations at Savannah State College. I held this position for two years before returning, in 1976, to the University of Michigan to study for my Ph.D. During my two-year tenure as director of public relations, I was able to send at least three of my journalism students to graduate programs in professional journalism because I kept in touch with students by teaching journalism courses, in addition to administrative duties, and was able to assist in their career development.

In 1994, after serving over twenty years as a university administrator, I returned as a tenured senior professor to the classroom. Recently, I was named coordinator of the mass communications program at Savannah State University. In this capacity, I have a direct impact on the students relative to their academic and professional development. The most valuable advice I give to students is to engage in professional internships at professional media outlets (newspapers, radio, and television), develop portfolios of their work, volunteer at the campus educational FM station, write for the student newspaper, and volunteer in the Office of the Vice President for Institutional Advancement in the areas of communications and publications.

Students should also develop skills in making effective oral presentations and should know how to write effectively and to utilize a library to conduct extensive and thorough research. Students should also insist that their respective universities instruct them with state-of-the-art equipment so they can be highly competitive and marketable in the job market of the twenty-first century. It is also important for young people developing a career in mass communications to understand that there will be times when they will fail. However, one should learn from failure and correct weak areas in career preparation. Students must also be willing to commit themselves to the time and effort that is necessary to be an excellent professional. My advice to aspiring media professionals is summed up in these simple words—focus, discipline mind and body to a single purpose, and never give up on the goals set for one's future career.

Some Strategies to Help You Earn a Professional Degree

BETTY J. FARMER

Associate Professor of Nursing, Grambling State University

Attending a professional school entitles one to be committed to hard work. A student should think in terms of preparing for a career rather than a job when attending a professional school. There are certain characteristics one must process or bring forward if they lie dormant in order to succeed in a professional school. The primary one is leadership ability or a "take charge" attitude. Many perceive that taking charge is necessary to succeed in professional schools. However, I would prefer "press toward the goal" or "persist" as acceptable terms. An average career is not good enough. Those who pursue nursing as a profession demonstrate an extraordinary ability to persist. In order to succeed in nursing, one must persist, and in doing so, leadership ability is developed.

Leadership is a quality one strives for, seeks, achieves, and develops. In every facet of life a leader steps forward, as early as elementary school, secondary school, and high school. It is a trait that is essential to the existence of the human race. Leadership abilities in various professions provide direction for the country in social, health, economic, and political matters.

A number of strategies may be applied in order to succeed in a professional school. A good attitude and persistence are two general categories that can be applied to maximize success in a professional school. The student's attitude toward the general learning environment, teacher, subject matter, and self is a major factor. Attitudes may be helpful or harmful. Good attitudes enable students to learn, grow, and flourish. They lead to high self-esteem, happiness, and satisfaction. However, if one has a bad attitude, one finds just the opposite. This type of matter leads to self-destruction, self-defeat, and low expectancy for success. Students can develop a good attitude by (1) establishing a good rapport with the teacher, (2) evaluating themselves, (3) looking at issues objectively, (4) valuing self, (5) rewarding self and, (6) adding humor to life.

Attitude toward a subject and/or learning situation in a classroom is either optimistic or pessimistic. The student must choose to be optimistic. The presence of some positive conditions stimulates learning that leads to success. Associate the learning activities with favorite things, good friends, and positive life experiences.

Attitude toward self is very powerful in regard to a student's success. When attitude toward self is positive, students look for ways to learn. This is known as a *success-oriented personality*. In retrospect, if students' attitudes toward learning are negative, they look for ways to fail. This is known as a *failure-oriented personality*. Nevertheless, a student should encourage him- or herself. This may be done by giving recognition for real effort, having faith, realistically examining learning mistakes, and seeking assistance (tutorial, counseling, and advisement) when needed.

The second category, persistence, should display an expectancy for success. The advantage of this strategy is that the student honestly expects to succeed, is motivated, and is willing to do what it takes to succeed. The student is aware of what is necessary in order to have a successful learning experience. Within this category the method of goal setting is highly utilized. Certain criteria must be met as well as planned. The goals will be as follows:

1. *Achievable.* Is there enough time allotted? If not, adjustments should be made. Does the student possess the skill and knowledge at hand? If not, is assistance available?

2. *Believe.* Does the student have the level of confidence needed? Does the student have a reasonable chance of doing it?

3. *Measurable.* How will the student gauge his or her progress or achievement? Feedback will be tangible material for self-evaluation.

4. *Desirable.* Does the student want to do this?

5. *Focus.* Avoid procrastination.

6. *Motivation.* The process should be stimulating, competence building, and gratifying.

7. *Committed.* Affirms student's involvement and increases self-esteem.

In the event that any elements of the goal have not been met, there is most likely a need for alteration.

While moving toward a goal, certain motions and behaviors must be analyzed according to the angles, speed, contours, and characteristics and then forced in order to accomplish the goal. One phase can be isolated when analyzing a goal. However, in a profession such as nursing, the leadership process tends to blend the phases into a whole. In reexamining the process, the student should identify resources within and outside him- or herself and remove potential obstacles to learning.

In conclusion, one should reexamine one's motives toward attending a professional school. This is the core that leads one to success to reappraise, to bring one's motives into alignment with one's capabilities and conscience. One's mind must be clear and receptive to complete the task that is at hand. In order to persist through professional school, one must have the mind-set to accomplish his or her goal and meet the challenges. The desire has to be imbedded so deeply that no substitute career or job will do.

Finally, the writer would be remiss if personal sacrifices were not mentioned. In order to achieve some goals, a price has to be paid. Sometimes this price may include some relationships and social events. One often hears a phrase in professional schools of nursing: "There is a light at the end of the tunnel." This statement is true.

ESSAY 14

Working with Cultural and Racial Groups to Develop a Global Perspective

LAWANNA GUNN-WILLIAMS

Professor of Psychology, Grambling State University

College life offers many new experiences for the incoming African American student. These experiences include new schedules, new study requirements, new teachers, new activities, new freedom, and new friends. In addition, the exposure to people from diverse ethnic, cultural, and racial groups is often a novel experience for many first-year college students. Most institutions of higher learning have culturally diverse student bodies, much unlike many American high schools. The multicultural student population becomes a center of activity and the basis upon which decisions are made and rules are established for the institution. A multicultural student population is deemed an asset to the institution, and it often helps to qualify the school for a number of state and federal funds. Therefore, increasing and maintaining a visible multicultural student population is frequently one of the institution's major goals. Hence, positive interaction with individuals from various cultural and racial groups becomes a necessary tool for successful college adjustment.

As the new student meets more and more people of differing origins and cultures, it becomes obvious that, among peoples of the world, there exists a variety of lifestyles, mannerisms, and expectations. In addition, African American students, too, display a diversity of styles, behaviors, and philosophies within their own cultural group. Within this group, there are various religious practices, food choices, and goals. Hence, the new student soon learns that differences are found not only between racial and ethnic groups but also within them. Through these awakenings, the African American student begins to alter his or her conception of "Blackness" and to reconsider his or her own ideology of life. The student will often compare presently held philosophies with the philosophies of others and begin to question an existing personal belief system.

The student's continued association with culturally and racially different individuals will begin to break down a sense of ethnocentrism that often accompanies little or no exposure to persons from diverse groups. Ethnocentrism is a general lack of acceptance of cultural diversity and the viewing of one's own culture or race as superior to that of others. However, positive interaction with people of other groups and cultures tends to dispel the ethnocentric tendencies that many Americans possess. Such will be true for the college student. As one begins to encounter and positively interact with others of diverse cultures, races, and ethnicities, one develops an appreciation for and acceptance of differences in others as well as one's own unique characteristics. Thus, a greater sense of self-esteem often develops through this process of interaction.

There are a number of tools for successful interaction. Using the following guidelines in interacting with culturally or racially diverse students will facilitate positive communication and promote self-growth:

CONFIDENCE

Having confidence dictates that one has faith in self, trusting in one's own capabilities. To feel self-confident, the African American student must first love and accept self. This acceptance comes through the evaluation of existing values and beliefs with those of others and the alignment of one's own beliefs with one's ideal values and beliefs. Upon this alignment, the individual may give a "stamp of approval" to self. The individual then feels a greater appreciation for and understanding of self.

With these positive feelings come self-confidence. It has been said that if you don't believe in yourself, then nobody will believe in you. Confidence implies believing in one's own self-worth, feeling competent in life endeavors, and locking out self-doubt. The confident student is one who feels that she has something desirable to bring into relationships with others and that something positive can be gained through this interaction. This student then enters into relationships with other students of various cultural and racial groups knowing that they will lead her towards greater maturity and growth as a productive citizen in a multicultural society.

WISE SELECTION OF FRIENDS

It is extremely important that the African American college student chooses friends wisely. Those who have similar values and goals will greatly enhance the benefits of friendships. Associate with those who can help you achieve your goals. Seek friends who are positive in their interactions and responsible in their behaviors. The racial or cultural origin of a friend is of little importance when true friendship exists. Friends can be a great source of pleasure, strength, and direction. Just remember that in order to reap the benefits of the relationship, you must put your best foot forward. Having a friend dictates that one has to be a friend.

The African American student who chooses to befriend students from other cultural and racial groups should simply employ the same discretion in the selection of friends as when selecting friends within the African American culture. Important considerations in choosing friends are integrity, vision, commitment, and acceptance.

Integrity refers to moral strength, honesty, and uprightness. Honest people tend to attract honest people. Look for friendship in those who display signs of integrity. Seek acquaintances with others who have admirable qualities—those persons who help to build your character rather than tear it down.

Vision is a mental anticipation of some particular life achievement. The friend who has vision strives towards the achievement of it through direction, dedication, and hard work.

Commitment refers to wholly and earnestly placing oneself in the friendship. To be committed means caring about the other person and being willing to sacrifice personal desires for those of the friend. Committed friends understand that true friendship is a reciprocal relationship. The value of the friendship depends on the commitment of the persons within it.

Choose friends who accept you. All students will probably not want to befriend you as a person or as an African American, but do not be hurt or surprised by this fact. Many people have their preferences regarding the type friends they desire, and they have various reasons for these preferences. Just remember that their choices say nothing about your worth or desirability to others. Simply look for signs of acceptance and act upon them. Those who desire to be your friends will often make this desire known in either subtle or less subtle ways. Acceptance is the act of being received with pleasure. Look for favorable signs of acceptance in your associations.

SET AND PURSUE GOALS

As one becomes more knowledgeable of college life and its expectations, is helpful to map out a plan for continuance. Start setting immediate and long-range goals. Pursuing goals gives life direction. Pursuing goals often places one in strategic positions to become acquainted with and interact with students from diverse groups. Your own perseverance will often influence friends towards greater devotion in reaching their individual goals.

DEVELOP A LOVE FOR PEOPLE

As you grow older, you will find that much of life's success is not the result of what one knows or how skilled one may be but of how one relates to others. Sincerely loving others means caring, giving, respecting, and accepting. When a student has these qualities, love will breed love. Loving individuals have few problems interacting with others. When in situations where you are not sure of what you should do, just show love. Love promotes positive interaction with all people.

Should a student interact with other races and cultures? If the student wants a well-rounded college education, positive interaction with others is essential. School books and classes can teach many terms, theories, philosophies, laws, and principles, but positive campus interaction can foster an understanding of this knowledge and enhance one's ability to successfully maneuver in life.

SEIZE OPPORTUNITIES FOR INTERACTION

It is true that students from certain groups tend to associate with those from their own groups, but this does not mean that they have no desire to associate with others outside of their groups. Relationships within one's racial or ethnic group carry with them a psychological "comfort zone," a system of social support. Yet most of these students are eager to broaden their horizons and learn more about others of diverse origins.

The perfect place to seize an opportunity for multicultural interaction is in the classroom. When volunteering for group projects or assignments, select groups with culturally diverse members. Working with these students will afford the African American student the opportunity to converse with and engage in discussion and the exchange of ideas with others while working towards a mutual goal. Planning, preparing, and presenting projects will help students learn more about each other. Studying together will foster a greater understanding and acceptance of each other.

Social activities on campus are a major part of college life. These activities are often designed to include all factions of the institution; however, many students fail to attend activities that feature attractions mostly appealing to other cultural groups. Participating in such activities can open a new dimension to one's appreciation for cultural differences. Learning more about other groups through attending special programs and functions will encourage positive interaction.

Perhaps no measure of interacting with diverse racial and cultural groups is more effective than a genuine one-on-one interaction. Through a love for humanity and an honest concern for the welfare of others, the wise African American college student will make friends across cultural, racial, and ethnic lines. Friendship is an assurance of understanding, harmony, and cooperation. Through friendship, individuals will engage in the reciprocal exchange of ideas, goals, knowledge, and dreams. Through this means, the African American student will make the needed personal adjustments to live successfully and prosper in a multicultural society.

The Art of the Vita

A Success-Building Strategy

PAMELA V. HAMMOND

Dean and Professor of Nursing, Hampton University

My road to success has not been an easy one, but it has been an exciting journey. Being the first in my family to graduate with a baccalaureate degree was an event, but the crowning moment came when I was "hooded" and received my doctor of philosophy degree in 1992. I was surrounded by a family that was in awe that there was a "doctor" among us. Obtaining the degrees is sometimes the easy part. For many of us, if we persevere and put in the time, the degrees will come. It's what you do with the degree once you get it, however. Do you plan out your future or let it just happen to you? Do you know what experiences you need to get an edge over your competitors? Do you know how to document your experiences so that you can position yourself for success?

There are many people who graduate each year with no goals, no direction, and no preparation for a career. Do not get me wrong: I believe that colleges and universities do a great job in preparing you with skills, both intellectual and psychomotor. Those skills, though, are only a piece of what you need to succeed. You have to be in control of your own dreams and goals. You are responsible for where your career trajectory leads you. That is why the art of creating an outstanding vita is so important.

The curriculum vitae, or vita for short, is usually used by individuals in academe to provide a picture of their accomplishments. The vita may be used to provide documentation for tenure dossiers or promotion through the academic ranks. Whether your career goals include an academic appointment or not, you need to create a vita. You probably had the résumé detailed to you during your undergraduate experience, but the résumé by its very nature is too brief to adequately chronicle your life adventures. How well do you even keep up with your résumé? Have you done anything with it since your undergraduate days? Did you review it as you prepared for graduate or professional school?

I suggest that you have both a résumé and a vita regardless of your career path. The résumé is a very selective document that introduces you and your professional experiences to a potential employer. The vita is much more comprehensive and can be viewed as a filing cabinet of sorts that holds all of your professional events and from which you may extract details at any time to revise your résumé in order for it to be appropriate for the position that you are seeking.

Utilizing a vita has helped me to note all educational accomplishments achieved, positions held, conferences attended, and grants written and funded as well as to list all awards, honors, service experiences, presentations, publications, and research activities. Additionally, I can clearly note deficit areas. For example, if I do not reach my publication goal for any one year, I can review the vita to see where I actually spent my energies. I can evaluate whether it was worth sacrificing a publication one year to participate in a research project that may yield additional publications in the future.

Having a vita will also give you a great picture as to whether or not you meet the qualifications of a vacant position. The vita will provide you with a handy checklist when you are competing for a job. As you inquire about the responsibilities and qualifications for the position, you are able to check off specific experiences that you have had that match what the interviewer wants. Further, if you decide to accept the position, your decision can be based on the fact that a quick review of your vita indicates a need to get additional experiences that would complement your career goals.

A vita can take a variety of forms but usually will have the following categories of information:

1. *Personal data.* Name, permanent address, telephone and fax numbers
2. *Educational history.* All degrees and certifications, institutions, dates
3. *Employment history.* All employers, addresses, positions, dates
4. *Professional activities and community service.* All organizational memberships, consultant positions, board memberships, volunteer service (separate into national, state, and local)
5. *Awards and honors.* List all awards, traineeships, and certificates of appreciation
6. *Publications.* Book chapters, articles, editorials, proceedings (separate into peer reviewed and non–peer reviewed)
7. *Research.* Indicate whether you were a principal investigator or research assistant and whether the research was funded

8. *Grantsmanship.* Indicate whether the grant was funded
9. *Presentations.* Titles of oral and poster presentations, dates, name of group
10. *Workshops and conferences attended.* Dates, location, continuing education units
11. *Other categories, as appropriate for your discipline.*

You can succeed by having an excellent vita and taking advantage of opportunities that come your way in different forms. Listen when others are talking about promotions and available positions. Check your vita and make notes of the experiences that you are lacking that would have made you eligible for those positions. I suggest that you find a mentor and have your mentor review your vita occasionally.

If an opportunity presents itself, you should review your vita and make a determination as to how that position will impact on your future goals and directions. No, I do not want you to think that great paperwork alone will get you ahead. To become a dean, I had several interviews and made presentations to different groups in my quest for a position that had a national pool of competitors. I had to have an outstanding cover letter that stood out from the other competitors' and write a vision statement that reflected my knowledge of nursing and education. A vision that would carry this premier school of nursing into and beyond the dawn of the new millennium was essential. Further, to compete with others successfully, you must have an excellent command of language skills, be able to make serious eye contact, and project a confidence that provides you with an unforgettable presence. A well-done and up-to-date vita helps you to develop the confidence to know that you can compete with the best opponents and secure the position of your dreams.

The Significance of Obtaining a Graduate or Professional School Degree

Becoming Part of the Solution ...
to an Academia Problem

S. KEITH HARGROVE

Associate Professor of Mechanical Engineering, Tuskegee University

The beginning of the academic year and semester provides another opportunity as an professor to impart knowledge to eager African American students willing to learn more about the discipline of "designing products with available resources for the benefit of mankind," loosely defined as "engineering." These students are sometimes perplexed by the absence or low numbers of engineering professors who look like them, irrespective of the type of institution they attend. Yet when asked by students about the reason why the university won't hire more faculty that look like them, my response is "because you and those before you have decided it is not important enough to obtain a doctorate and teach." In other words, African American graduates who make the decision not to choose a career in academia are the reason there are no African American professors, and they are in fact responsible for their absence and low numbers. Of course, not all graduates should decide to pursue a career in academia, but I say that to let them recognize that the low representation of African American professors in engineering is partly their fault. This presents an interesting situation for undergraduate students in science and engineering; it's just like the old adage: "You're either part of the problem ... or part of the solution."

This is all to say that there is a tremendous need for doctorates in the sciences and engineering, and certainly among underrepresented groups. As our economy changes from one based on the industrial worker to one driven by the knowledge-based/information employee and as it becomes characterized by its fast pace of technology and innovation, the changing workplace of America will demand occupations with skills in mathematics and computers. And those with advanced degrees will lead the change in designing and developing the technology to fuel a knowledge economy. Doctoral recipients in science and engineering are and will be needed in industry, government, and definitely in academia, well beyond the twenty-first century. However, of the over six thousand doctorates received in engineering in 1997, less than 3 percent were received by African Americans.

The desire and motivation to obtain an advanced degree are many. According to the 1997 *GEM* (National Consortium for Graduate Degrees for Minorities in Engineering and Science, Inc.) *Career Guidebook,* when advanced degree holders were asked what they considered the advantages of attending graduate school, they most commonly described their satisfaction with the type of work and personal accomplishments as well as the increased earning power over a lifetime in terms of career advancement and financial rewards. Opportunities are available in industry, corporate and government labs, entrepreneurship, and education. But the advanced degree, more than anything, provides formal educational accomplishment that validates technical qualifications to pursue any career endeavor a person chooses.

Upon entry to graduate school, the journey begins with selecting an adviser, choosing a research topic, conducting independent research, and presenting your research findings to a committee for evaluation of its worthiness. As a graduate student, you become an expert in your chosen area, and you contribute to its knowledge base. The journey usually results in your ability to do further research, increased self-esteem, and a desire for continuous learning. The process takes discipline, determination, and the strong desire to succeed. Several engineering graduate students suggested that having a good working relationship with your adviser and a strong support group (usually consisting of other graduate students) are key elements to success.

If you decide to pursue a career in academia, the opportunity to continue your research or pursue other areas are abundant. In the sciences and engineering, it was estimated that at least half of the present faculty will retire during the 1990s and early twenty-first century. This presents an outstanding career opportunity for those willing to stay in an academic environment, deliver new knowledge, and continue research. As a faculty member at a university, you can deliver new knowledge to students in engineering programs. This learning process can be reinforced and enhanced by your independent research. You will also serve the university by helping it carry out its mission to the internal and external community. The flexibility to do these three activities (teaching, research, and service) in a learning environment with excellent financial rewards can lead to a great career as an engineering professor.

The need for underrepresented groups to pursue graduate degrees in the sciences and engineering is extraordinary. Career opportunities exist within industry and academia. However, obtaining the doctoral degree and choosing to teach in academia will provide the qualifications to continue to promote diversity in research and be a role model for students. This, in essence, is the solution to the absence of African Americans in the academy.

Beginning Graduate School with the Right Mind-Set

ADA HARRINGTON-BELTON

Assistant Professor of Curriculum and Instruction,
University of Southern Mississippi–Hattisburg

Whatever your mind conceives and believes, you can achieve! My journey to success in graduate school and my career field began with this mind-set. This is a mind-set that everyone can possess regardless of their circumstances in life. Success in graduate/professional school and your career, like success in most endeavors, requires you to focus on your goals and work twice as hard as you do on regular tasks. Too often, I find that there is a tendency to go nowhere fast, as if you are on a treadmill, with no direction. Getting an advanced degree has to first be an achievement that you want for yourself; you must visualize yourself walking across the commencement stage receiving the degree. I was very privileged during my childhood and youth to grow up in an educational environment that facilitated my seeing and believing what I would accomplish. In this environment it was expected that I would achieve academically and professionally. My mother was employed as a public school teacher, and my father, an ordained United Methodist minister, also served as president of a historically Black college for four years. During my father's tenure as a college president, I had the wonderful experience as a little girl of interacting with erudite college professors and talented visiting dignitaries such as Benjamin Mayes. The memories of these inspiring African American scholars who made it in spite of societal racism are indelibly printed on my mind.

This background of pride in my family and racial heritage set the stage for my academic journey; however, I could not rely solely on these attributes. I soon discovered that in order to survive in the world of academe, several other intrinsic strategies were necessary: (1) setting personal goals, (2) preparing academically, and (3) persevering in spite of obstacles.

There were several steps involved in my setting personal goals. I began to set goals for my academic and career journey while in college. I knew that one day I would attend a graduate school, and I had to adequately prepare with the required courses and grades. At that time, I wanted to be an elementary school teacher and ultimately teach others how to become teachers, so to achieve this goal, I needed to attain a doctoral degree in the field of education. After the years of receiving my B.A. and M.Ed. degrees, and teaching at all levels, elementary to college, I was able to continue my journey to the Ph.D. degree while teaching seventh grade reading in New York City.

As I gained more experience teaching, I discovered that more students were in dire need of reading instruction and/or remediation, so I became interested in reading education. I continued my personal goal setting by choosing a university that was located in the area where my husband and I resided while he was pursuing his doctorate. This university offered a program in reading education in curriculum and instruction and provided a supportive academic environment in terms of the faculty and students. So I chose Fordham University, located in New York City with a diverse student body, including a significant number of qualified African Americans who graduated from its rigorous Ph.D. program from which I felt I would ultimately receive mine. Finding additional financial assistance was another consideration for my attending Fordham University. My employer gave flexibility and financial assistance, such as faculty development funds, to encourage and support professors to work on their doctorates. These funds assisted me with the tuition payments.

You must select an adviser who is willing to guide you from the beginning of your coursework to the completion of your dissertation and is genuinely interested in your success. Discuss your graduate and professional goals with your mentor. My mentor encouraged me to acquire administrative certification with the area of language, literacy, and learning, which would enable me to become a principal or director/chair of reading education at the college level or pursue other administrative possibilities. My mentor and I continue to collaborate about issues related to reading education, and she has followed my career path. We also keep in touch as friends. Fourth, study with a compatible group that has the same goals that you do. My study group shared substantive ideas, critically analyzed problematic assignments, and prepared for exams. This cohesiveness and support enabled us to tackle the rigors of the doctoral program with success. Finally, engage in a periodic self-analysis that enables you to probe into areas that need strengthening. Ask your mentor and professors questions about anything that is unclear. Statistics was not one of my strong areas, so I sought tutelage in this subject at another university. I waited until the summer to take courses in statistics so that it would be my only focus, and as a result I succeeded in receiving a grade of B, which I gladly accepted because my other grades were As.

The next intrinsic strategy to take into consideration is to be academically prepared, so in order to maintain an A average, I organized a study schedule. The scheduled time was divided into three categories: study time, work time, and quality time with my husband. The study time was devoted to reading, writing, and library research. It was very important to plan to complete assignments for courses before the due date to allow time for revisions. After acceptance of the proposal by the dissertation committee, it became vital to devise a schedule to follow for the discipline. Otherwise the human elements of internal and external distractions, such as personal problems or noise from the telephone or television, occur and deter you from completing your tasks.

I finished my coursework for my doctorate while employed at one of the public schools in New York and completed my administrative certification and dissertation in Scranton, Pennsylvania, where my husband and I moved to accept faculty positions. I then adapted to a different work schedule as director of the Freshman Reading Program at Keystone College in LaPlume, Pennsylvania, and teaching full time. My scheduled quality time worked well for me, for my husband was a professor in the Graduate School of Social Work at Marywood College in Scranton, and he was most supportive and understanding of my schedule. It is very important for your family to understand how much time such an undertaking demands. Once a schedule is devised, it is easier to stay focused and to stay on target. The most challenging strategy was how to persevere in spite of the struggles. The dissertation stage can be the most difficult stage, even in the best of situations. It appeared that the constant revisions would never end, but I consistently and immediately responded to them, adhering to the schedule that I devised. Choosing a mentor/friend is crucial because a team of other professors must analyze your paper. Pursuing a doctorate is not only an academic journey but a political challenge as well. During my tenure in the Ph.D. program, graduate students did not select their dissertation committee, so maintaining a good relationship with all of the faculty was crucial. Our inner resources of strength must be realized. Meeting this challenge is also spiritual, which is our heritage and legacy as African Americans. Ephraim David Tyler, a relatively unknown African American poet, encouraged Black people in many of his poems to rise to their perspective positions in society and to carry on in spite of racism.

As I have sought to carry on, academically equipped with a Ph.D. in Language, Literacy and Learning since 1984, my career experiences have been quite diverse. I have taught graduate courses in reading education and served as director of the English as a Second Language Program at the Mississippi Department of Education. As a result of my leadership in developmental education in Pennsylvania, I ultimately became president of the

National Association for Developmental Education. I have presented workshops nationally, internationally, regionally, and locally on college reading strategies and multicultural education. Currently a professor in the Curriculum and Instruction and Special Education Department at the University of Southern Mississippi, I am teaching preservice teachers how to teach reading in the public schools, which was my goal while in college, and also teaching Foundations of Multicultural Education, which hopefully will expose preservice teachers to the importance of equity in education. One of the highlights of my career has been mentoring minority students in the McNair Scholarship Program, which prepares them for doctoral studies, as they will indeed carry on.

Coming Home to Success

WHITNEY G. HARRIS

Director, Office of Diversity and Affirmative Action,
Eastern Michigan University

A few weeks after returning from a five-year stay in Ebolowa, Cameroon, I returned to my undergraduate university to visit with a friend. As I left her office, I met one of my former professors. After assuring him that I had completed the doctorate, he encouraged me to apply for a teaching position in the department of teacher education. Hastily, I prepared an application dossier and submitted it an hour or two before I left for Africa. Upon my return to the city, I was invited by the search committee for an interview. Most of the persons on the committee were my former professors who were aware of my work as an undergraduate. Three weeks later, I began my career as a college professor.

Thus began my current career. Within seven years, I was promoted to tenured full professor. In this position I have not only found personal satisfaction but I have also, in some small way, contributed to the formation and education of hundreds of classroom teachers and school administrators and leaders. However, this is just the beginning of the story. Exactly one year after being hired at the institution, the position of Equal Employment Opportunities Officer/Minority Affairs became available. Because of my degrees in special education and educational leadership as well as my study and work in various cultural settings including Canada and Cameroon, I was offered this position. It is in this function that I feel that I have made the greatest contribution to the university and to the community. Over the years this position has moved up the organizational chart and become executive level. As such, I serve on the president's cabinet. This means that I help to formulate university policy and to shape the institution's budget. Without the appropriate graduate degrees, this would not be possible. In addition to my own campus, I have been asked to serve on numerous system-wide committees regarding persons of color and persons with disabilities. Again, my postsecondary education serves me well in these activities. In fact, without the appropriate educational credentials, it is doubtful that I would have been chosen to serve on these commissions and committees. However, more important than the credentials is the education that I received as I pursued the degrees. It is this knowledge that allows me to participate, in a meaningful manner, in the work of the numerous local, state, national, and international commissions and committees.

Years ago I almost did not finish my graduate degree in special education because I had decided to make a career change. Fortunately, my major professor insisted that because I could not predict the future, I should complete the degree. Today, that degree not only serves me in my full-time job but because of my education and experience in special education, I also served as an impartial hearing officer for the Louisiana Department of Rehabilitation Services. Currently, I am one of two African Americans in the entire state holding such a position. Not only do we adjudicate cases, but we also help to interpret and shape policies that affect the lives of many more persons with disabilities than those who appear before us. In addition, I feel that I bring an African American perspective that would otherwise be absent to this work.

The other half of my professional life involves serving as a Roman Catholic priest. I feel that my graduate training in theology in no small way distinguishes my ministry from those of many of my colleagues. I not only completed the required sequence of courses, but I sought out other educational opportunities. For example, I had the unique privilege of studying Black liberation theology with James Cones. I often "hear" Cone in my sermons—proving once again the power of education. A solid theological education has allowed me to bring both form and substance to the ministry. Although churchgoers may well be entertained by form for a season, they expect sermons and teachings that are as intellectually stimulating as they are spiritually fulfilling. Without a solid education not only in theology but also in the humanities, one cannot approach this task in a meaningful manner. My education and training have proven to be as important as was my calling.

Finally, having grown up in a poor neighborhood in the segregated South, I could never have imagined that I would have the quality of life that I now have. Of course, it would be fraudulent not to mention the level of material comfort that I currently enjoy. I have more creature comforts than I will ever need or use.

However, life has much more to offer than homes, cars, and clothes. My education has given me a sense of value and self-worth that guides and supports me as I live a life worth living. It is my education that allows me to appreciate various cultures and their offerings. The critical thinking skills that I was taught challenge me to think out of the box and to seek questions as well as answers. It is the enlightenment that comes from years of study and reflection that empowers me to distinguish between what is and what ought to be. My lifelong quest for education is a by-product of the quest for knowledge that was kindled in me by many of my graduate school professors. In a word, my education, particularly my graduate education, made my homecoming a fantastic success.

Make a Place for Yourself Now That You Have Obtained a Graduate Degree

BARBARA J. HOLMES

Associate Professor of Communication, University of Colorado–Denver

Congratulations! You have achieved your goal. There are many good reasons for your decision to pursue a graduate or professional degree, not the least of which is the desire to prepare to earn as much as possible so that you can be assured of self-sufficiency. And, of course, you decided to pursue a graduate or professional degree because there is information and knowledge you seriously desire to attain.

As you no doubt have observed, one of the most important experiences of graduate school is the deepening awareness of what and how much you do not know! There were lots of moments when a light was turned on in your mind and you realized suddenly that supposedly new information you acquired fit with something you had learned previously.

Graduate schooling has helped you fine-tune your capacity to make connections between present events and those of the past. Unfortunately, our past educational experiences (undergraduate or what we metaphorically call the K–12 pipeline) may not have made explicit the connections between events of the immediate past and the present. At a time when the population of the United States is becoming increasing diverse, many of our citizens have insufficient information about our own past and know very little of the historical events that have spawned our country's present diversity. Look at the country and world as realistically as you can. For example, the "age of imperialism," which some texts refer to as the "age of discovery and exploration," is characterized by the twin evils of slavery and colonization, the aftermath of which continues to reverberate throughout the world. Yet much of the present population of this country is not aware of the connections between the immediate past four hundred years and the present geopolitical/socioeconomic relationships and the continuing revolutions of the twentieth and twenty-first centuries.

My purpose is to signal to you that you need some degree of perspective and context as you go forth to make a contribution in your world. I am concerned that we sometimes are not sufficiently aware of the big picture of which we are a part. If we do not see the big picture, it can be difficult to recognize the various intergroup dynamics that are arising among the diverse populations in the country. In an opinion editorial, "On the Backs of Blacks," published by Time Magazine (1993), Toni Morrison called attention to the tendency among new immigrant groups to join the Americanizing club by putting down Black people. There is a shuffling and jousting for position, actually for status or place within the whole. There are opportunities for cooperation and new alliances among groups, but will cooperation and harmony prevail, or will competition override the need for establishing a common cause?

PROFESSIONAL PARTICIPATION IN YOUR DISCIPLINE

One of the most significant attributes you now possess as a result of obtaining a graduate degree is the ability and the capacity to apply the skills of analysis, synthesis, and evaluation. Allow me to share an experience from my career that illustrates the point.

After completing the masters and doctoral programs at my institution, I obtained a position as a writer/researcher in the largest educational assessment organization. My advisers and other departmental faculty were a bit surprised that I had been able to obtain this position in an organization they did not know about. I was able to obtain and perform in the position because of my strong background in the quantitative and qualitative research methodologies of my discipline: communication.

Allow me to share some information about the discipline of communication which made it possible for me to have a fairly broad worldview. Many students major in communication because they wish to enter the world of electronic media—broadcast and television production. However, there are several foci within the communication discipline:

Classical rhetoric emanates from Isocrates, Socrates, Plato, and Aristotle and includes the major tenets of modern persuasion and argumentation.

Interpersonal describes the discipline's seminal process models of sending and receiving messages and the major categories of variables that impact this process.

Group dynamics embraces aspects of leadership in various group settings and includes problem solving and conflict resolution.

Organizational includes the structural and functional properties of complex organizations such as corporations and details insights about effective management of individuals and teams.

Intercultural involves the dynamics of interpersonal and group interaction among and between persons of diverse cultures.

Public Speaking, Speech, and Drama remain in many communication programs around the country. Often public speaking or speech making is included as a skills component of a university's core curriculum when there is one.

There is a tendency in some communication departments around the country to have a truncated curriculum (often due to limited resources) that does not include the foci mentioned here. Presently, there appears to be an emphasis on mass communication, where media, broadcast, television production, and public relations and marketing may be grouped. But as you can see from the listing just given, the discipline allows for the acquisition of critical thinking skills and competencies that are applicable across many professions and occupations. For example, one may employ the skills of criticism acquired in classical rhetoric to cultural studies, including feminism and a variety of other current topics. Or one may employ competencies acquired in organizational communications, group dynamics, and intercultural communication to employment in complex organizations. Many communication majors are securing employment in nonprofit, service organizations such as education and health professional organizations and associations.

One of the most satisfying benefits of completing graduate school is realized through your participation in and contributions to the professional life of your discipline. There is nothing more exhilarating than entering a room full of conference participants, looking around, and recognizing and being recognized by others in your field: your colleagues!

There is probably an area within your discipline to which you feel you can make a contribution. Ideally, the graduate experience provided an early opportunity to become acquainted with the people in the discipline, students, and faculty from other institutions. While you were matriculating graduate school, you began to subscribe to and read the professional publications of your discipline. Obviously, you will continue to stay abreast of people and new developments in the field.

Again, congratulations. Remember to stay alert.

Achieving Academic Success in Graduate School

FREEMAN A. HRABOWSKI III

President and Professor of Education,
University of Maryland–Baltimore County

As one might expect, graduating at the age of nineteen from Hampton University and entering graduate school in mathematics at the University of Illinois at Urbana-Champaign was a major transition for me. The Hampton experience, involving a predominantly Black student population and an integrated faculty, had allowed me to get to know well my professors from various racial and ethnic backgrounds in a setting that strongly encouraged personal interaction among students and faculty. Studying at Hampton taught me (1) to believe in myself, (2) that my classmates and I had a special mission to become leaders in our chosen fields, and (3) that even though I was different from others, those differences could be important strengths.

Dr. Geraldine Darden, my major faculty adviser at Hampton, was also a Hampton graduate and had attended graduate school at both the University of Illinois and Syracuse University. She and several other Hampton faculty did an excellent job of preparing me academically for graduate work in mathematics. When I arrived in Urbana-Champaign, however, I discovered that it may be easier academically than socially to prepare for the experiences of being, in most cases, the only African American or minority student in a classroom and of almost never seeing a professor who looks like you. Although others can tell you what those situations are like, they are difficult to envision accurately until you experience them firsthand. My graduate work, first in mathematics and later in higher education administration and statistics, taught me some important lessons that may be helpful to others whose backgrounds are similar to mine.

First, in any university setting, graduate students can find professors and staff members from various racial and ethnic backgrounds who are willing to be supportive. The challenge each graduate student faces is to identify those individuals. One approach is to ask other graduate students about faculty members' reputations. Another approach involves simply going around to introduce yourself and talking to a variety of faculty about their research. In this way, you can determine whether you are interested in their particular specialties and observe how each faculty member interacts with you as a new student. I found that professors tend to interact more favorably when they see that students have a keen interest in their fields. Also, it is important to avoid being overly sensitive and assuming that faculty and staff do not have time for you. Equally important, though you may encounter situations in which others actually behave in a racist manner, you must not allow yourself to feel victimized but work instead to feel, and believe, that you can control your own destiny. You can best exercise control by continuing to act in ways that empower you. When something happens, for example, that affects you negatively, it is important to talk about it with others in order to put it in the proper perspective.

Based largely on my graduate experience at the University of Illinois in the early 1970s, I have worked with colleagues over the years to develop the Meyerhoff Scholars Program, designed to prepare undergraduates in science and engineering to succeed at that level and to go on to successful graduate work. Those efforts have led to the development of several programmatic components that have proven to be helpful to students. Even though you may not find a graduate program with components exactly like those that provide the framework for the Meyerhoff Program, I encourage you to look for graduate programs with similar characteristics or for activities at the graduate institution you select that resemble the following key components of the Meyerhoff Program:

1. Comprehensive, merit-based fellowship support
2. Strong programmatic values that emphasize outstanding academic achievement, group study, and collegiality
3. Faculty and staff who are dedicated to the success of minority students and who are actively involved in recruitment, teaching, and research mentoring
4. Availability of substantive, year-round research experiences
5. Personal advising and counseling
6. Active administrative involvement and support
7. An evaluation component documenting the program's outcomes

In summary, successful graduate students, whether minority or not, are those who (1) are passionate about their discipline, showing enthusiasm and a keen interest in their work; (2) understand the importance of hard work and truly believe they will work as hard as necessary to succeed; (3) interact with fellow graduate students and faculty for purposes of collaboration; and (4) most important, believe in themselves and know, deep down, that they will succeed.

Mentoring in the Advising Process

MARILYN M. IRVING

Associate Professor and Chairperson of the Department of Curriculum
and Instruction, Howard University

The best advice that I can give on how to succeed in graduate and professional school and in your career field is to recommend that the graduate student find a mentor. First-time graduate students entering the academic
environment are much like freshmen entering college for the first time: hesitant, skeptical, and in need of someone to guide them through the rigors of
academic work. Whether the student is studying for faculty positions, professional endeavors, or simply to better his or her educational framework,
the common needs held by all graduate students include a mentor for guidance through difficult stages and academic challenges.

The concept of mentoring has found application in essentially every forum
of learning. In academics, mentoring is a personal as well as professional relationship. Mentors are advisers, people with career experiences willing to
share their knowledge and specific feedback on the graduate student's performance. Good mentors are able to share life experiences and wisdom as
well as technical expertise. They are good listeners, good observers, and good
problem solvers. They make an effort to know, accept, and respect the goals
and interests of the graduate student. A good mentor is a good role model
through both words and actions. They can discuss with students the special
features and satisfactions of their own position, being frank about its advantages and drawbacks. They can be constructive and provide critical feedback,
which is essential to stimulate improvement and praise when deserved.

Mentoring and networking provide the support system and environment,
which help graduate students to develop and grow professionally and personally. A mentor is someone who has had personal success in that role and

whose experience in given areas or disciplines allows them to offer insights, guidance, and assistance within the institution. The mentor can be instrumental in providing guidance to the graduate student in career aspirations and educational objectives as well as personal guidance.

Mentoring relationships are important for all individuals pursuing a degree or a career. Particularly for graduate students, positive mentoring relationships can set up a path of success. Although there is not a defined method of pairing a graduate student with a mentor who will guide and mold the student in different areas, there is at least agreement that the relationship is significant and important. Aside from providing the opportunity to share talents, the relationship also provides mentors with a sense of usefulness and importance.

Graduate students entering the world of academia, no matter how long or for what purpose, can use assistance and guidance from a seasoned professional. As students, they must maintain the energy and motivation to excel; being associated with a mentor can enhance their chances to rise to prominence. I strongly suggest that all graduate students find a mentor since he or she can have a powerful impact on one's success in school and in one's career.

Mentors can inform about and recommend activities in which graduate students should become involved. Mentors will enthusiastically write recommendation letters for them and continue to follow them throughout their career. The guidance, direction, and tutelage that mentors can provide can lead to success in graduate school and in the student's professional life. They can encourage students to explore many options. In addition, mentors can introduce students to members of their own network of contacts, recommend search aids, including Internet sources; professional societies; and ads in journals and major newspapers. Mentors can also help graduate students prepare for jobs by helping them to sharpen the skills needed, design a good curriculum vitae, rehearse interviews, learn about the current job market, and advise students to join and take a leadership role in disciplinary societies and journal clubs.

Having a comfortable relationship with a mentor allows graduate students to be able to discuss the long-term benefits of their work, proper course sequencing, available job identification services, and conferences and seminars they should attend. A mentor can be instrumental in introducing them to proposal writing, to subscribing to journals in their area, and to getting them excited about attending conferences in their field of study.

Mentors can have high expectations for graduate students that can inspire them to overcome their struggles and achieve their goals. They can challenge students and stimulate them to learn their subject well enough to successfully compete in their chosen professional area. When mentors appropriately congratulate graduate students for worthwhile accomplishments or model behavior, it does make a difference. Positive reinforcement, when given, is a significant component for graduate students on their "road to success" agenda.

A Whole Lot of Others

PATRICK O. JEFFERSON
Attorney-at-Law and Former Dean of Student Affairs, Dillard University

Graduate or professional school can be an individual's worst nightmare, or it can be the beginning of a fulfilling and rewarding life. I can well remember my vast experiences at the Ohio State University College of Law. Feelings of fear and trepidation were rampant. I was also excited as I was about to begin to realize one of my dreams of graduating from law school and becoming an attorney.

When I first arrived in Columbus, I was in awe. I was amazed at the opportunity that I had been given. I just could not believe it! After all, no one in my family had ever had this chance to earn a professional degree. College graduates were not too common in our family. Notwithstanding, I did not realize in all of my excitement that a multitude of challenges lay in store for me. I was taught, and I strongly believe, that everything happens for a reason. My experiences at law school helped prepare me for other trying moments that I have had to tackle. Furthermore, I realize that if I continue to walk and breathe, there will be other difficult situations I will encounter, other mountains to climb over, and additional problems to solve. The opulent university of life is truly an educational adventure and a worthy and exemplary teacher.

After I settled into my new environment, I attempted to gain some level of familiarity with the enormous Ohio State campus and community. I finally made my way to the law school, and I was captivated with all that I saw; from my perspective, OSU was large, impressive, and towering. This new community was quite different from the small, elegant space I had been a part of at Dillard University in New Orleans. Nevertheless, OSU was what I was looking for to strengthen and hone my academic skills. It was the place where I would have the opportunity to advance, learn, and fulfill my dream of becoming an attorney.

Although OSU afforded me a wonderful opportunity, the physical nature of the place was overwhelming. There were people everywhere. High Street at times resembled Canal Street in the familiar New Orleans. But the law school was different. The classes were not too large except for the first year, and students and faculty were basically friendly. I almost felt at home. In spite of the warm atmosphere, however, law school itself was not easy. Times got hard. I spent hours upon hours reading and studying, trying to comprehend the idea, the argument, the ruling. I was sometimes intimidated by my classmates who could uncover an issue of a case that was tucked away behind a series of seemingly irrelevant facts. It was mind-boggling to me that someone could grasp in an hour readings that took me a full four. I was cradled in a corner of the library well into the night when others had already ended their day.

I was able to survive the sometimes nightmarish experiences of law school because I found the strength within myself, and I also utilized the support of others. More specifically, I made it because I befriended classmates who had similar experiences and who were graduates of other historically Black colleges. We encouraged each other; we studied, laughed, and sometimes cried together. We built a solid community that was determined to succeed. I also had the good fortune of finding a wonderful church, and its members embraced, accepted, and loved me as one of their own. I was able to talk candidly with my professors about study habits and writing techniques. I had a strong, supportive, loving, and understanding mother who never gave up on me and encouraged me at every turn despite my doubt and fear. My mentors, people I truly respected and admired at Dillard, received and returned my calls with words expressing confidence and faith in my abilities. These individuals were often my sounding board for those problems I did not understand or accept at OSU. All of the people who were my support group pushed me to recommit myself to the task of completing my degree.

Law school was a tremendous time in my life. My years in Columbus helped me to become the person I am today. It was a humbling journey for me as I had always been at the top or near the top of the class, but in law school, I was cast in a very ubiquitous sea with individuals who had credentials just as impressive as mine and, in some cases, more so. I had to come down from the heights of a very successful undergraduate career and survive in the midst of an environment where I was just another student, but one with a dream in his heart. That in itself was an educational experience that I now am able to cherish.

Overall, law school was a challenge, a fulfilling ride on a sometimes bumpy and uncertain road. The experiences from my days at Ohio State that I now reflect upon from my first impression to the challenges in the class and sitting through those agonizing and long exams taught me a lot about life. In addition, they taught me a lot about myself. One does not necessarily have to be the brightest or the fastest to succeed. Success requires a great deal from within and from others. Today, I remain thankful that I had a whole lot of others—God, mother, friends, church family, classmates, professors, and mentors. Because of them and that which came from within, I made it. Thank God, I made it.

Mentors, Peers, and Advisers

Key Players in Making Decisions

DAVID A. JETT

Assistant Professor of Toxicology, The Johns Hopkins Medical School

I am a university professor and a scientific researcher. The experiences that led to this career choice began when I was a college freshman at a historically Black college. I knew early on that I had an affinity for the sciences, but it was my mentor in college who gave me the encouragement and exposure to science (and a job!) that made this choice easier.

Mentoring. I believe that it is the single most important advice I can offer—find, and hold on to, a good mentor during school.

Now, my choice upon exiting undergraduate school was clear: medical school or graduate school. Most of us are attracted to the many obvious rewards of being a physician, but for me, I've always found it much more interesting to go down the less-traveled path. So I chose to enter a master of science program in zoology at a large university. My first day was overwhelming—some of the classes had as many folks as I was used to seeing at a football game in college! As daunting a task as I perceived lie ahead, I still knew I could get through the program as long as I could maintain a high level of motivation. This was not easy, and it may have been impossible if I hadn't become part of a study group that shared many of the same background and interests as I. Most happened to also be African American. We became much more than a study group; we did our share of partying and carrying on. In fact, several marriages and many long-lasting friendships started in this group and remain decades later.

Peers. An essential component of a successful graduate school experience is to find and nurture relationships with peers.

I finished my research project after several years of hard work, and I received my master's degree in zoology. The project was extensive, so much so that my peers suggested I continue for a Ph.D. This made good sense, to keep pushing forward while I was young and used to living in "graduate school poverty." (Make a note to yourself—you will not get rich while in graduate or professional school.) But I was told that I did not possess the skills or have the research priorities necessary to complete a Ph.D. This was a devastating blow to my ego, and I began questioning my career choice. Then I was reminded by my peers that I shouldn't be too discouraged by the comments of one or two professors at that university. After a few years working as a biologist, these earlier conversations with my peers and my own desire to advance as a researcher led me to apply to, and be immediately accepted to, a Ph.D. program at a prestigious medical school.

Perseverance. Set your goals and do not be deterred easily. Gather as much information as you can from more than one source before you make a decision to give up on that goal.

Conducting high-powered research towards my doctorate was challenging but also exhilarating and fun. I became part of a small group of students in a new program in the toxicological sciences. This was an emerging field of study at the time, and we were very excited about our prospects after graduation. Initially I seemed lost, especially because the Ph.D. usually requires considerably more independent thinking and creativity than a master's degree. Again, what saved me was the mentorship of my adviser. She was able to guide my research with just the right amount of control such that I also was able to develop a research project that I could call my own.

The right adviser. Choose your graduate school adviser carefully. Make sure this person cares about your goal—to conduct research for your degree and graduate in a reasonable time period.

Upon receiving my Ph.D., I was once again faced with making a choice: more training as a postdoctoral fellow or jump right into the job market? This is a difficult decision, and it will depend on several factors, including the urgency to make a high salary (postdocs' earnings range from meager to decent), the type of career (a postdoc experience is almost always required for an academic position), and your desire to publish research and become known in the scientific community (most of your time as postdoc will be doing just this). I chose to accept a postdoctoral position. This led to many opportunities to conduct cutting-edge research under the appropriate "loose" guidance of my postdoc adviser, and eventually I was offered a faculty position at the same institution based on my successes. My experiences since then have been interesting. As a university professor and researcher, I have seen days where I would have never guessed that life could be so hectic and require so much multitasking effort. But I have also seen times where I could not dream of a better job. The joys of this profession can be seen on a student's face when a concept you are trying to convey is first understood and in the discovery of a scientific breakthrough in the most unlikely place. Finally, I make it a priority to take time to help others using the tools I have acquired through my experiences. By getting involved in the community and in educational programs for minorities at secondary schools and universities, I have been able to come full circle and be the mentor to someone else.

Give back by helping others; you honor those who have helped you.

Mentoring Strategies

A Report Card for Faculty

IRENE H. JOHNSON
Interim Dean of the School of Graduate Studies and Professor of Counseling,
Alcorn State University

Cusanovich and Gilliland (1991) state that "a mentoring relationship involves professors acting as close, trusted, and experienced colleagues and guides.... It is recognized that part of what is learned in graduate school is not cognitive, it is socialization to the values, practices, and attitudes of a discipline and university, it transforms the student into a colleague" (p. 1).

Mentoring programs are being implemented in many colleges and universities in order to attract graduate students of color and to retain them until graduation. Without effective mentoring, many students of color are unable to cope with the demands of the graduate school environment. Thus, the primary goal of the mentoring program should be to enhance the educational experiences of graduate students and facilitate their successful adjustment to living and working in a campus setting. Many students of color attending postsecondary educational institutions are the first members of their family to attend college. In many instances, they are unfamiliar with the written (and unwritten) guidelines and policies. Typically, they are "uneducated consumers" who depend on faculty and staff to teach them the necessary survival skills (Basti, Johnson, & Basti 1994).

Faculty mentoring is a vital link in this survival process. Without it, loneliness, poor self-esteem, and value conflicts often influence students' decisions to separate from the institution. At the graduate level, mentors are needed to offer advice and guidance in academic matters. In addition, the mentor becomes a valuable support person for the mentee. He or she can assist the mentee in finding university resources such as funding or research support, and the mentor can help the mentee in becoming a legitimate member of the department. On the importance of faculty advising and mentoring in graduate school, the graduate deans of the Association of American Universities and the Council of Graduate Schools (1990) issued the following statement:

Advice and support from mentors are among the most important factors in determining the success of students' doctoral education. Faculty advisors must assist students in choosing course work that meets their needs and interests without unnecessarily extending their programs. They should also encourage students to move on to seminars and laboratory work that will lead to dissertation topics, and define dissertation topics that are realistic in scope. Good advisors already do these things; to make sure that they happen more routinely, departments should establish explicit requirements for all faculty advising. (p. 2)

The actual role of the faculty or staff mentor is one of nurturing and providing support for a student during the difficult transitional period. The mentor must also serve as a resource who will answer many questions, trivial or complex, that the student might pose. Most important, the mentor must serve as a positive role model. Graduate students typically mimic the behaviors of a composite of professional models and individuals, both positive and negative (Bucker & Stelling, 1997). For this reason, all faculty must engage in formal and informal interaction with minority graduate students. The quality and frequency of faculty–student interaction and of graduate–peer socializing are important predictors of graduate student success (Hartnett, 1976; Nettles, 1990).

Mentoring is a significant aid in development, particularly among African American graduate students (Phillips, Smith, & Davidson, 1992). Minority graduate students are likely to receive unequal or substandard graduate education experiences, especially in the area of mentoring (Blackwell, 1983; Cusanovich & Gilliland, 1991). These students often have more difficulty than nonminority students in finding mentors (Gilbert & Rossman, 1992).

Positive mentoring relationships increase the chance that students will remain active, engaged scholars after graduation (Willie, Grady, & Hope, 1991). Mentors advance their protégés' careers in several ways: they provide them with opportunities to test new hypotheses and research plans; they can lead a protégé to sources of academic support, including colleagues, and to literature relevant to the student's research interest. In addition, a mentor relationship can provide opportunities for participation in publishing and professional conference presentation and can impart "trade secrets" (Cheatham & Phelps, 1995).

A need for mentoring programs at colleges and universities is well documented in the literature (Adams, 1992; Bedient, Snyder, & Simon, 1992; Cusanovich & Gilliland, 1991; Galo, 1988; Moses, 1989; Wagener, 1991). Unfortunately, many mentoring programs are mediocre at best and are often quite ineffective, thus leading to a high rate of program dropouts. One of the major reasons why some programs fail is that faculty who become mentors often lack the basic understanding of what the mentoring process actually entails. Many understand it to be counseling or advisement, which it is in part, but mentoring goes beyond advisement. Adams (1992) recommended very specific guidelines, which he called "Effective Mentoring Techniques: A Report Card for Faculty Mentors" (p. 6). What follows are some useful mentoring strategies, including some of the techniques proposed by Adams. These are described across three categories: college, institutional, and departmental; personal issues; and career development issues (Johnson, pp. 64–65).

MENTORING STRATEGIES

College, Institutional, and Departmental Strategies

- Expanding the working dynamics of both formal and informal systems within the institution.
- Scheduling meetings, student receptions, or appointments with faculty and key administrators.
- Informing the mentee of perceptions about departmental culture and its evolution.
- Advising the mentee of departmental and college politics and what pitfalls to steer clear of.
- Providing opportunities for informal discussions with department faculty.
- Explaining the roles of the support staff. Do not assume that mentees understand office procedures and protocol.

Personal Issue Strategies

- Serving as an advocate for the mentee, especially in resolving any difficulties or conflicts that may arise.
- Providing an empathic ear to professional and/or personal problems and being ready with referrals to professional counselors, if needed.
- Devising methods to sharpen the mentee's intellectual skills.
- Discussing issues related to students' thesis or dissertation topics.
- Providing guidance, coaching, direction, and encouragement during the research process.

Career Development Strategies

- Helping students articulate and develop true career goals.
- Providing feedback to the mentee regarding her or his self-assessment and longer-range career goals as well immediate needs and responsibilities.

- Explaining the necessity for attending professional meetings and conferences, and explaining the advantages of membership in professional organizations.
- Recommending that the student attend seminars emphasizing writing and "how to publish" skills. It is necessary to emphasize that good writing skills are essential for actualizing career goals.
- Inviting the mentee to observe your classroom pedagogy and instructional processes if he or she is not taking your class.
- Advising the mentee on which jobs might be most advantageous to apply for, how to properly apply for jobs, and proper behavior during interviews.

Building upon Zelditch's (1990) definition of mentors as advisers, supporters, tutors, and models, the graduate dean and the Graduate Council at the University of Arizona endorsed a new graduate school policy that encouraged academic departments to assign, or let the students select, mentors upon their arrival to campus. The council noted that students may have multiple mentors and that the role of the mentors may change over time. In addition, they noted the special significance of the mentoring process for underrepresented students. The council summarized its expectations by stating, "All departments have in place definable mentoring programs and that they have developed the appropriate infrastructure (courses, practices, procedures, etc.) to integrate students into the discipline fully. The depth and breadth of the mentoring program in any given department or program certainly will have an impact on students' ability to compete for resources within the Graduate College and the University" (Cusanovich & Gilliland, 1991, p. 3).

EFFECTIVE MENTORING TECHNIQUES: A REPORT CARD FOR FACULTY MENTORS

Grade yourself with an A, B, C, D, or F as a mentor to minority graduate students. An A means excellent for that area; an F means that you have a lot of work to do.

Do I:

_____ Introduce protégé to faculty in the department.

_____ Introduce protégé to key administrators within the college/school.

_____ Teach protégé survival skills helpful to masters/doctoral students.

_____ Provide feedback on protégé's self-assessment and targeted career goals.

_____ Protect protégé from the pitfalls of departmental politics.

_____ Suggest opportunities for relevant research and training experiences.

_____ Share information about the dynamics of formal and informal systems within the institution.

_____ Share perceptions about departmental culture and its evolution.

_____ Suggest articles, authors, or titles designed to broaden experience base.

_____ Share relevant aspects of personal career and resulting lessons learned.

_____ Provide coaching on behavior and skills that can facilitate career progress.

_____ Make myself available for counseling on professional and personal problems.

_____ Share information about how to get things done within the departments.

_____ Help establish protégé's scholarly reputation.

_____ Provide guidance, coaching, and direction during the thesis/dissertation research process.

_____ Help to prepare students for the milestones that must be met.

_____ Help launch protégé's professional career.

Developed by Howard G. Adams, Ph.D. ©1990

REFERENCES

Adams, H. G. (1992). *Mentoring: An essential factor in the process for minority students.* Notre Dame, IN: National Center for Graduate Education for Minorities.

Association of American Universities and the Association of Graduate Schools. (1990). *Institutional policies to improve doctoral education: A policy statement of the Association of American Universities and the Association of Graduate Schools.* Washington, D.C.: Association of American Universities and the Association of Graduate Schools.

Basti, C. F., Johnson, I. H., & Basti, A. Z. (1994). *Successful faculty mentoring in higher education.* Proceedings of the Midwest Business Administration Association. Chicago: Chicago State University.

Bedient, D., Snyder, V., & Simon, M. C. (1992). Retirees mentoring at-risk college students. *Phi Delta Kappan, 76*(6), 462–466.

Blackwell, J. E. (1983). *Networking and mentoring: A study of cross-generational experiences of blacks in graduate and professional schools.* Atlanta: Southern Education Foundation.

Bucker, R., & Stelling, J. G. (1977). *Becoming professional.* Newbury Park, CA: Sage.

Cheatham, H. E. & Phelps, C. E. (1995). Promoting the development of graduate students of color. In A. S. Pruitt-Logan & P. D. Isaac (Eds.), *Student services for the changing graduate student population.* San Francisco: Jossey-Bass.

Cusanovich, M., & Gilliland, M. (1991). Mentoring: The faculty-graduate student relationship. *Communicator, 24,* 5–6, 1–2.

Galo, M. T. (1988). Mentoring: Critical guide for graduate retention. *Black Issues in Higher Education 5*(17), 23–24.

Hartnett, R. T. (1976). Environments for advance learning. In J. Katz and R. T. Hartnett (Eds.), *Scholars in the making: The development of graduate and professional students.* Cambridge, MA: Ballinger.

Johnson, I. H. (1996). Access and retention: Support programs for graduate and professional students. In I. H. Johnson & A. J. Ottens (Eds.), *Leveling the playing field: Promoting academic success for students of color.* San Francisco: Jossey-Bass.

Moses, Y. T. (1989). *Black women in academe*. Washington, D.C.: Project on the Status and Education of Women, Association of American Colleges.

Nettles, M. (1990). Success in doctoral programs: Experiences of minority and white students. *American Journal of Education, 98,* 494–522.

Phillips, Smith, E., & Davidson, W. S. (1992). Mentoring and the development of African American graduate students. *Journal of College Student Development, 33,* 531–539.

Wagener, U. (1991). How to increase the number of minority Ph.D.'s. *Planning for Higher Education, 19,* 1–7.

Willie, C. V., Grady, M. K., & Hope, R. O. (1991). Campus experiences of faculty scholars. *African Americans and the Doctoral Experience: Implication for Policy.* New York: Teachers College Press.

Zelditch, M. (1990). *Mentor roles.* Tempe, AZ: Western Association of Graduate Schools.

Graduate School Literacy and Academic Success

JOHNNYE JONES
Vice President of the Office for Academic Affairs and Professor of Biology,
Jarvis Christian College

Preparing for graduate school is an exciting and challenging undertaking. Graduate school represents more formal and tailored training in a specific discipline for the areas of research, teaching, and scholarship. It is my hope that your decision to attend means that you are looking at no less than a terminal degree. Completing the requirements for a terminal degree is a major undertaking. The accomplishment offers the potential for participation and contribution to a professional area, including published articles and books, professional meetings, service on boards, and collaborations. These endeavors promote effective participation in an arena for academicians. Furthermore, it is most important that participation comes from all ethnic and cultural backgrounds as the need to prepare for the challenges of the "2000 and Beyond Workforce" will require participation from the total human resource pool. The entire ethnic spectrum must correlate with the composition of the workforce if it is to effectively support the national agenda to improve and increase the participation of underrepresented groups in specific careers and areas of need. Of personal significance, there is the satisfaction of having made such an achievement, as the attitude of "I can really be what I want to be if I put my mind to it" prevails.

There are a number of issues that must be considered after having made the decision to pursue a graduate or professional career. These may include financing, program types, locations, and even which field of study. The recommendations here are to foster success upon entry at a particular school and/or program. The assumption here is that you have already been selected, the financial package has been offered, and awards have been made. So now that you are set, what is the next step? This endeavor should have a plan of action and preparation. The plan should outline every critical and essential step in designing a pathway that will not only guarantee a successful venture during your period of matriculation but will also offer a rewarding future as well. Becoming "graduate school literate" requires developing strategies to gain access to appropriate opportunities and resources that will impact your success and future career. The most important ingredient of your plan is to begin with a positive attitude. This will allow you to accomplish the hardest tasks and gain access to information and opportunities you never anticipated. Two other important considerations must be seriously incorporated in the graduate student's plan. First, make every attempt to understand the environment in which you have chosen to place yourself. A thorough understanding of the community, the climate, and the way of life will help to facilitate academic success. Secondly, gain additional knowledge and develop a profound appreciation for your field of study as a potential lifestyle that will remain with you forever. You must love and enjoy the world you have chosen, not only to be successful as a graduate student but also to continue success as a professional and as a contributor to your area. As you learn, you must also become a part of the network that creates a community of understanding, participating beyond the social agendas set to distract you.

Two skills, how to gain and apply information and how to manipulate information, are paramount for a successful strategy. Always remember that knowledge is power and power inspires respect. Learning how to apply information gained makes you an asset to any organization. You must be able to manipulate information. This promotes your stardom in a particular area, for one who distinguishes himself will also bring distinction to the area of study or to the training institution. The ability to manipulate information for the purpose of problem solving is a unique attribute that is fostered by a strong foundation and is individually driven.

The most important thing to remember is that your success is dependent primarily upon you. Everyone is born with a gift. You must understand yourself and how to use your gift to achieve your ambition. There is always a solution that will direct you toward the joys and rewards of accomplishing the tasks you set out to do. Although some training issues to ensure success are primarily the responsibility of the institution, other issues are individual and the responsibility resides with you. Let us now explore some of these. Try to implement the following strategies: (1) First, seek out a mentor who is willing to work and assist you with questions and problems that may arise. This is someone who can provide clear and meaningful answers to many of the problems that you will face—and you will have them, that's life. You may begin by talking to individuals in your own department, but you should not be limited to that small segment. (2) Be a reader, a contributor. (3) Make connections with other individuals who have similar interests at all gatherings including seminars, workshops, and professional meetings. (4) Take advantage of every opportunity. Finally, (5) place a high value on your education.

Sometimes the best plans may require some changes, so you must be willing to make the appropriate adjustments in order to continue to ensure your own success. These life interludes, though not what you anticipated, must be handled. Sometimes it is hard to know the best way, especially when you are a student. You must then rely on the recommendations of someone else. However, in the beginning, in the interim, and in the end, hope, determination, persistence, optimism, and knowledge will usually guarantee success. Follow the paths that have been provided by others before you, but explore and become the creative trailblazer who will impact the future of others. Be well prepared to take on new and challenging problems. Taking some risks is what life is all about. As you become successful, be a hero and a mentor to someone else by finding ways to help others. Every generation must contribute to the success of the next. That is life. Keep in mind that you have a gift that, in my mind, should be cultivated to its potential for whatever career; as a scientist, lawyer, doctor, or educator. Accept these words as useful and provided with love and high expectations to ensure success at the graduate level, no matter what the discipline is. Remember that your thoughts, your words, your actions, your habits, and your character will dictate your destiny. Go, my young intellectuals, and take advantage of every opportunity, for the world belongs to you.

Pursuing an Urban Planning Degree in Graduate School

LINDA LACEY

Associate Dean of the Graduate School and Professor of City and Regional Planning, University of North Carolina

The purpose of this essay is to expose students to the field of city and regional planning and discuss ways students can successfully complete master's and doctoral degrees in this field of study. I begin with an overview of the field of planning. Next I discuss strategies that I used to survive and excel in graduate school.

THE FIELD OF CITY AND REGIONAL PLANNING

Most students who select the field of urban planning for graduate education have a love for cities and a burning desire to facilitate change. They are concerned about a number of problems and issues that face cities, including economic decline, the physical decay of inner cities, high unemployment rates within poor minority communities, and traffic congestion on roads and freeways. Other students study planning to develop skills to protect the natural environment, preserve the history of cities, promote community development, provide for the homeless, and/or help poor families obtain affordable housing. The majority of students who pursue degrees in urban planning obtain a professional master's degree in either city or regional planning. There are slight differences in the degrees. A master's in regional planning indicates that students come from a program that focuses on both city planning and regional economic development. Those programs that offer a master's degree in city or urban planning tend to emphasize urban problems and solutions. Both types of degrees require two years of course work and a master's thesis or a master's project paper.

Most graduate programs accept students from a wide range of under-graduate programs including the social sciences, math, science, engineering, architecture, arts, and the humanities. Selection committees are looking for students with a strong interest in improving communities and students with a strong grade point average. Some programs also want students with expe-rience in working on city or community problems. Students can obtain ex-perience as a volunteer, an intern, or through employment in a planning agency or nonprofit community organization. It is best to speak directly to institutions to understand their particular requirements for their program.

Once students complete their degree programs, most obtain positions in city planning agencies. Within a large city planning office, they obtain posi-tions as housing planners, economic development planners, neighborhood planners, environmental planners, zoning planners, historic preservation planners, and land use planners, to name a few. Some also obtain positions within county and regional planning agencies where emphasis is placed on coordinating and guiding regional growth. To a limited extent, planners also work for state and federal planning agencies such as the Environmental Protection Agency, the Department of Transportation, and the Department of Housing and Urban Development. Planners also obtain positions in the private nonprofit sector. Many work for grassroots community agencies such as economic development corporations, housing agencies, community development centers, and homeless shelters. Students also obtain positions in private firms, in particular, architecture and planning firms and real estate development companies. Some also work for private utility companies and shopping mall developers. A few students, those who specialized in interna-tional development, also work for agencies within the international donor community including the United Nations, the World Bank, and the U.S. Agency for International Development.

For information on graduate programs in planning as well as detailed in-formation on the field of planning, please visit the Web site of the American Planning Association http://www.planning.org/educ/educatio.html. The Web site provides detailed information on the field of planning, colleges and uni-versities that have master's and doctoral degrees in planning, information on scholarship and internship opportunities, salary levels of planners, and career opportunities.

WHY I CHOSE CITY AND REGIONAL PLANNING AS A FIELD OF STUDY

I selected the field of city and regional planning for graduate study for a number of reasons. First, I wanted a program of study that would allow me to gain skills to improve a variety of aspects of community life, including the health status of residents, their employment base, and their physical environment. I also wanted a degree that I could apply in a variety of settings including health planning, housing, and community development. I also liked the flexibility of working in a public agency, a nonprofit organization, a for-profit firm, or an international donor agency.

I applied to the master's program in regional planning at Cornell University during my senior year as an undergraduate student. I selected this institution because it offered opportunities to learn in my areas of interest including international development, community development, and health planning. My undergraduate degree was ideal for planning school. I graduated from the University of California–Berkeley with a social science field major degree that consisted of course work in sociology, economics, political science, and statistics. I had also been an exchange student at the University of Ghana, where I obtained insights on urban issues in West Africa. I entered the program with a strong grade point average and a wealth of community service. I started doing volunteer community work at the age of twelve and had worked on political campaigns and with health care clinics, drug abuse programs, and shelter programs for the disabled.

The master's degree program consisted of sixty credit hours and took two years to complete. My course work included analysis courses where I obtained skills in math, statistics, demography, computer science, and cost-benefit analysis. The program also included a number of theory courses that focused on economic development, spatial geography, and community development. I took a number of health care courses outside of the department.

On completing my master's degree, I decided to pursue a doctoral degree. My decision to obtain a Ph.D. was research driven. I had gained insights in a number of areas that were exciting to me. I was interested in migration research, in particular, the spatial mobility of people and its impact on urban and regional development. The rise and fall of cities worldwide also fascinated me. I wanted to understand how one could revitalize or give life to decaying cities. After I was accepted into the Ph.D. program, I took a two-year leave of absence to work in Nigeria on a migration study. When I returned to Cornell, I used the data set for my dissertation. I also enrolled in courses that helped me become a researcher, scholar, and teacher.

SURVIVAL STRATEGIES FOR GRADUATE SCHOOL

Graduate school required a lot more time and energy than my undergraduate program. To survive and excel in graduate school, studying became my primary focus, and all other activities came second. I now provide some tips on how to obtain a degree in any graduate field of study including city and regional planning.

Study Groups

Courses at the graduate level are highly compact with information. The speed with which the materials are presented in class is much more accelerated than in an undergraduate course. Some courses, especially quantitative courses, are best completed while working in study groups. For just about all of my quantitative courses, I worked in study groups. A key benefit of study groups is that they helped me fill in gaps in my lecture notes. I also learned that when I explained my notes to another student, it helped reinforce my knowledge of the materials. From my experience in teaching statistics courses, I've noted that those students who study alone receive lower grades than those who choose to study in a group. I never waited to be invited to join a group. In some cases, I formed my own.

Network with Everyone

It's important to get to know your professors and classmates well! Scholarships for the following year and internships during the summer months will require that you build strong relationships within your faculty. I spoke to my professors on a regular basis in graduate school. I always came to class prepared, engaged in class discussions, and raised questions about aspects of the lecture that were unclear. I visited my professors during their office hours to discuss the class as well as for opportunities to work on their research projects. Once faculty got to know me, they shared information on fellowships and internship opportunities. My classmates were helpful as well. Many of my classmates shared scholarship and internship information with me. I obtained a two-year position on a research project at the University of Ibadan, Nigeria, through information that I received from my classmates.

Seek Meaningful Internship and Research Experiences

You need to find internship and/or research opportunities that will help you develop professional skills. For students seeking a master's degree, the internship experience will play a major role in obtaining that first planning job. I obtained a variety of internships as a master's degree student that helped me develop written and oral communication skills. As a Ph.D. student I worked on research projects with the faculty.

Time Management

Time management skills are critical in surviving graduate school. To stay on top of my course work, I structured my time to study *five hours every day.* Studying was my first priority. On a given day, I went to classes, reviewed my notes immediately after class, and then read the assignments for the next class period. I also developed a list of questions to raise in class about the readings. I set aside one day a week for family activities and household chores, usually Saturdays.

Seek Top Grades

You must continue to seek top grades as a graduate student. Faculty recommend their best students for jobs, fellowships, and internships. If your grades are declining because of the rigor of the program, seek support services on campus such as study workshops, computer services, and writing centers. I worked hard at maintaining a strong grade point average throughout the M.A. and Ph.D. programs. My grades helped me obtain fellowships, internship opportunities. and my current position as professor of City and Regional Planning at the University of North Carolina at Chapel Hill.

SUMMARY

If you have a love for the urban environment and wish to creatively explore ways to improve poor minority communities, a graduate degree in urban planning will be highly rewarding. I encourage you to research a number of different planning programs and apply to accredited programs that match your interests.

Graduate and Professional School Success

The S.I.M.P.L.E. Approach

OCTAVIA MADISON-COLMORE

Assistant Professor of Counselor Education,
Virginia Polytechnic Institute and State University

Keeping it simple is perhaps the best approach to my success in graduate school and in my profession. Using each of the letters in the word *simple*, I developed a strategy that became the foundation to my success in graduate school and in my profession. The S.I.M.P.L.E. approach (spirituality, identity, management, persistence, love, and enjoyment) is as follows:

SPIRITUALITY

Spirituality, to me, is the most important tool to have to survive the challenges of graduate school. Unfortunately, it was not until I entered graduate school at a predominantly White institution after graduating from a historically Black university that I relied so heavily on the importance of having a spiritual foundation. This need, of course, for spiritual gratification could have been attributed to a number of factors such as maturity, the need to fill an empty void, or to just maintain family values. In any event, the emotional support that seems to be so readily available at a predominantly Black institution was not available to me at a predominantly White one. When I speak about emotional support, I am referring to the brothers and sisters on campus who soon become your extended family or your family away from home. And, like most African American families, regardless of what you do, they are always there to support you.

Unfortunately, the predominantly White institutions that I attended did not lend themselves to that friendly, family, emotionally supportive atmosphere. Hence, the harder I worked at trying to create such an atmosphere, the more I lost sight of the one person who could help me conquer the challenges and demands of graduate school.

At that point I began to put my priorities in order and rebuild my spiritual foundation. This foundation provided me not only with the proper gear or armor, if you will, to conquer the challenges but also with a reminder of who I am.

IDENTITY

Identity is also an important tool to have to succeed in graduate and professional school. Knowing who I am and what my values and morals are helps to build self-confidence. Although I thought after graduating from a historically Black university that I had confidence in myself to tackle any problem head-on, I began losing part of that confidence when I entered graduate school at a predominantly White institution. I found myself either remaining silent or agreeing with issues of the dominant culture that I probably would have disagreed with had the environment or atmosphere been different. I felt that it was important to maintain peace rather than rock the boat. Although my thoughts are different today and I am confident in who I am, sometimes it is easier to remain silent until you get what you want.

MANAGEMENT

Management is perhaps equally important as spirituality and identity. All too often I found myself becoming overly involved in various community organizations, which consumed too much of my time. Quite simply, I had a hard time saying "no" to people. As a result, my grades began to plunge as my coursework was often put on the back burner. I soon had to make a decision regarding my purpose for entering graduate school; do I want to really get involved in all of these organizations or do I really want to learn and move on? The answer, of course, was the latter. Hence, this is not to say that one should not get involved in various organizations, it simply means that one must evaluate one's goals and determine whether or not these goals are, in fact, manageable.

PERSISTENCE

Persistence is definitely a key to success. In light of the demands and challenges, never give up. I do not know how many times, particularly during my doctoral studies, that I simply wanted to give up. I observed the painful experiences some of my colleagues had in attempting to pass certain examinations or "jump through the hoops," as it is often referred to, that led to my not wanting to finish my program. I remember, after witnessing one particular experience that continues to be a vivid image in my mind, going to my adviser and asking her, "What do I need to do to get out of this program?" My adviser responded by stating, "You will not go into an examination unprepared as this particular student was." Although I was a bit relieved by the response, I was still fearful of the experience. Needless to say, I was persistent and I did not give up.

LOVE YOURSELF

Love yourself and, more importantly, share a little of that love with others. I found it quite easy to get so involved in my schoolwork that I simply forgot not only about myself but also about my friends. Prior to entering the doctoral program, I went to the health spa three, sometimes four times per week; shopped with friends on the weekends; visited the beauty salon every week; watched my favorite television shows; and just simply relaxed. My life was undoubtedly stress free. Unfortunately, my stress-free lifestyle changed when I entered the doctoral program. Time did not permit me to go to the health spa, shop with friends, visit the beauty salon, or watch television. In fact, nothing was more important to me than completing my program. Hence, the lack of these pleasurable events led to an abundance of stress in my life. I soon began incorporating these events back into my life. I found the health spa a good place to read while I peddled the bike. I also found the beauty salon a good place to just gossip and be with friends. Thus, the point I am trying to make here is that you can succeed in graduate school while loving yourself and sharing a little of that love with others.

ENJOY THE BENEFITS

Following the S.I.M.P.L.E. approach will definitely lead to success. I completed my master's program in fourteen months while working a full-time job and attending school full time at Lynchburg College. I completed my doctoral program in three years while working as a graduate assistant for Virginia Polytechnic Institute and State University and attending school full time. Currently I am employed as an assistant professor in the counselor education program at Virginia Polytechnic Institute and State University, Northern Virginia Campus. I am also a licensed professional counselor, a licensed marriage and family therapist, and a certified substance abuse counselor in private practice in Vienna, Virginia.

Overall, having a spiritual foundation; knowing who I am; managing my time wisely; being persistent; loving myself; having the unconditional love and support from my husband, family, and friends; and enjoying the benefits have definitely led to my success in graduate school and in my profession. I truly enjoy what I do and, more importantly, I enjoy being the product of a historically Black Hampton University, where the foundation of my career first began: helping the African American community through higher education.

Reflection and Introspection

Black Graduate Students at a Predominantly White Institution

PAULINE E. "POLLY" MCLEAN

Associate Professor of Media Studies, University of Colorado–Boulder

There was complete bewilderment and disbelief on the face of the graduate secretary. I was an anomaly. Black, nontraditional, a single mom of two, who showed up at her office (baby in hand) with an acceptance letter to enroll for classes in the doctoral program. I had more than a couple of things going against me, in a part of America that I had never ventured into. Suddenly I began to ponder, "Why am I where I am? Why am I doing what I am doing? Why was I pushing myself in this direction? Why am I with these people in this environment?" These questions are common and recurrent in graduate school, but they mean something different when you're Black. That is because many Black students come to graduate school with a different set of baggage and sometimes a different set of expectations and experiences from those who will teach them and from their fellow students.

This essay on reflection and introspection is based on my graduate experiences at two predominantly white institutions, one Ivy League school in New York City, the other a state university in Texas. It is also based on my many years of being a faculty member at a predominantly white Colorado university and research institution. Although this essay is tailored to the Black doctoral student, the lessons from my blueprint for academic survival can equally apply to masters' students.

LESSON ONE

Pick the faculty and not the institution. Sometimes we have no choice where we pursue graduate work. But if possible, select the institution based on what the faculty is engaged in, whose work you admire and would want to work with and not because the institution is in a particular location. There must be a match between your interest and the faculty interest. If not, you can become resident expert, and that is a lonely road.

LESSON TWO

Get a feel for the cultural landscape. As a graduate student, you have now entered a completely different environment in which the culture of the professorate rules supreme. This is place where professional attitudes and values are solidly shaped. Although there are fundamental changes and challenges occurring in academia, there is still a very traditional mold from which faculty members are cast. At a predominantly white institution, faculty demographics still correspond to most of the graduate students whom you will encounter: white, male, and largely middle class. What does a Black student do in this milieu? Begin by studying the written rules of the graduate school and those of your particular department.

As an undergraduate, you were more than likely not exposed to the range of activities that faculty engages in. As a graduate student, get to know what faculty does in the university because this is where you will ultimately hang your career hat. Simply put, faculty teaches, prepares exams, grades papers, engages in research, publishes in peer-refereed journals, writes books that hopefully get good reviews, sits on countless committees, guides theses and dissertations, makes hiring decisions, presents research to colleagues at professional conferences, stays in touch with the developments in their field, sometimes does a good job in mentoring students, and provides some kind of service to the community (the latter being the least valued).

I mention the latter because many Black students come to graduate school with a desire to use the opportunity to apply gained knowledge to problems within the Black community. Yet application is not considered serious scholarship, particularly on the doctoral level. As a Black student, you can end in a quagmire on what you value on one hand and the expectations of the professorate on the other. When doctoral students come with a service mission, I remind them that although I may be sympathetic, the majority faculty will not be. It's not part of the academic culture. My advice is to get through the program on their rules.

After reviewing the written rules, begin to tackle the unwritten ones. This is a murky territory that is not laid out neat and clear. Here the rules are guarded and protected. Faculty members are not often willing to share them because they can become vulnerable. And although faculty members in media studies are staunch defenders of freedom of information, free speech, and so on, they are still products of a closed culture. Nonetheless, observe, listen, and ask questions. The graduate secretary provides one perspective; so do students who are in the program. If there is a multicultural or diversity office that addresses the needs of graduate students of color, go and talk to them. Become familiar with those who will be teaching you by reading what they have published. This helps in two ways: First, it gives you some direction about whom you might want to eventually work with. Second, let's face it: faculty ego gets in the way here, and they are most impressed if you have taken time to read their work.

LESSON THREE

Get situated with a mentor/adviser with whom you are comfortable. All graduate students get faculty advisers who review their course work and make sure that they are generally on track. Sometimes an adviser can also be a mentor. In either case, this should be someone with whom you are comfortable, who listens and will have time for you. The first bit of advice is to learn the rules about how advisers are appointed, whether you can change an adviser and at what step of the process. The graduate secretary should be helpful here. On the doctoral level, an adviser must also be a mentor. This faculty has a dual role. Besides the advising aspect, mentors play a pivotal role in getting a student access to the culture of the professorate. They can help fill you in with the unwritten rules; they can advocate for you and help make your graduate experience rewarding. Doctoral students who are finding it difficult to make the mentor connection in the department should not be afraid to look elsewhere on the campus.

LESSON FOUR

Take the initiative to reach out to people. In a predominantly White research institution, you can get marginalized very easily. There is no doubt some of that marginalization can be attributed to race. White academic institutions are still hostile and insensitive to Black students. But faculty members at research institutions are also preoccupied with their own work and career. They can be so self-consumed that you may get cut out of the picture. I learned the latter as a student. What I've learned as faculty member is that graduate students count. In all institutions there are yearly reporting procedures where faculty report the classes they teach, the research they are doing with graduate students, the advising they provide them, the theses/dissertations they are directing, and/or the committees they serve on with graduate students. Also realize that shaping the next generation of scholars begins with mentorship and collegiality. As a result, some faculty do relish the opportunity to shape the student into the disciplinary paradigms by instilling into the student their own academic interest. This can become a source of tension for the Black graduate student. The bottom line is to hold faculty accountable for what they are supposed to do by reaching out to them if they don't reach out to you. For me, given my particular baggage, reaching out to people also meant building a personal support network and not being afraid at any moment to say, "I need help."

LESSON FIVE

Get focused early. Faculty members at research institutions tend to shy away from graduate students who seem to not be sure of why they are there or what they want to do. This is particularly true on the doctoral level. If you are taking too much time getting focused, get out and do something else and then reenter.

LESSON SIX

Join the professional organizations in your field. Professional organizations help you gain visibility and ultimately job placement. Find out from faculty members the major organizations (professional and scholarly) in the discipline and join them at the discounted student price. Attend the annual conferences and get a feel for who's doing what and network. Doctoral students should take the initiative and write research papers and enter student competitions. The downside is that these organizations are predominantly White, elitist, and cold. Find out whether there is an African American or minority interest group within the major body. They are valuable and provide good support. In media and communication studies, interest groups exist in organizations such as the American Culture Association, the Association for Education in Journalism and Mass Communication, and the National Communication Association. An organization such as the National Association of Black Journalists provides a professional focus but can also spur on thesis or dissertation ideas.

LESSON SEVEN

Take advantage of all opportunities on campus. Look around the campus, find out what special programs (e.g., teaching resource centers) or funding the institution has for graduate students. Black students have to be aggressive and creative when seeking funds. Money is available in all sorts of places if you know where to look. If you have to deliver a paper at a conference, your department or graduate school may have travel money. Finally, if you get an assistantship, don't get saddled with research only and not teach or vice versa. Talk to your adviser and see how you can integrate both.

LESSON EIGHT

Don't get sidetracked. It is one thing getting sidetracked with issues outside the academic institution and those we have no control over; getting sidetracked by institutional issues is quite another. You are a temporary resident in a community. If it's a predominantly White institution, you won't influence the racism or injustice that's ingrained. If you take these issues on as a student, there is a risk. You can also get sidetracked by the demands that may be placed on you as the race spokesperson. Even your fellow graduate students will ask you to come to their classes and talk as an informant of the Black experience. This insider role will only be bestowed on you if you toe a line that is acceptable to the white majority. Perceived radicalized views from Black students whether in the classroom or on the university speaking circuit are quickly severed.

LESSON NINE

Think of graduate school as a type of initiation. You come to graduate school to jump through certain hoops to gain entry into an academic fraternity/sorority—a place where certain values and attitudes are instilled and shaped. The rules are laid out. You must demonstrate the ability to understand and master a body of literature within the confines of a chosen field, to be able to do original research, to be able to build and give meaning to knowledge. Think of your thesis or dissertation as the last initiation hurdle in which you bring together everything you have learned. Although it is your piece of work, faculty members must stamp their approval on it. Don't be rigid if they suggest changes. A student has little recourse, and there is little to be gained from a recalcitrant faculty.

LESSON TEN

Black graduate students at predominately White institutions frequently have to demonstrate their legitimacy with fellow students and with faculty. It's amazing how often Black students are looked upon as not arriving at the institution on their own merit. As you move through the institution, you may find yourself engaging continuously in a process of clarifying for others and for yourself just who you are and why your interests lie in a particular area. Although this essay provides lessons on navigating the system, the most important lesson comes from inside, and this begins with self-confirmation. Remember the personal motives for undertaking graduate work in the first place and have faith in yourself.

Implicit throughout this essay is the need to do groundwork, to learn how others have succeeded in their endeavors, to network—professionally and personally—to gain the cooperation of those whom you will need to succeed in your undertaking, to plan wisely, and to compromise to get what you need because this, too, shall pass.

God Should Be the Architect as You Pursue Your Academic Goals

SAMUEL E. MIMS

Colonel, U.S. Army, retired

I am deeply gratified to have this opportunity to share my experiences as contributing elements to this guide for Black students seeking graduate and professional degrees. Although I believe that personal beliefs and attitudes play a significant role in what we ultimately become, I sincerely believe that what really sustains us is a belief in God as creator and his son Jesus as Lord. No one, Black, White, or any other color or race, can experience all that life has to offer without the realization that God is the architect of all and that Jesus is the master builder.

My story is really no different than that of most of my generation. I grew up poor and Black but lived in the Deep South in northern Louisiana. As a little boy molded by the hatred and bigotry of the South during my youth, I knew that education was a way out, so no one had to tell me to study or do well in school. I just knew that I had to overachieve to overcome. I believed that the only thing I had to fear was the yoke of racial oppression that my family had grown accustomed to. They managed to cope with it, even though it required enormous swallowing of pride and the resultant lowering of individual self-esteem. No one could have made me then believe that the race that produced Martin Luther King Jr. would today be where I sense we are, a people seemingly at war with ourselves and without God.

During the educational journey that took me from high school to college and graduate school with thirty years of military service thrown in, I learned that education is never finished. Education is an evolutionary process, and true scholars never stop learning. To be pitied is the man or woman who feels that learning can cease. For as God says in His Bible, "My people perish for lack of knowledge." I have a B.S. in microbiology from Southern University in Baton Rouge, Louisiana, and an M.A. in public administration from Shippensburg University in Shippensburg, Pennsylvania. I am also a graduate of the U.S. Army War College. Although all this is a record of some pride, it does not compare with when God pulled me to him and I became his pupil. Degrees alone cannot compensate for the void within man that only God can fill.

As I alluded to earlier, I felt that education could deliver me from hatred and bigotry. I don't know that it did that all by itself, but coupled with my experiences, I learned that we are all God's people made from one blood. I learned that all Whites are not evil, and neither are all Blacks good. So get all the education you can and then use it to do whatever God has called you to do. In case you did not know this, one of these days you are going to give up this present earthly trip and all that will matter is what you did or did not do for God while you were here. As you pursue your educational advancement, find out who God is and ascertain for yourself who Jesus Christ is. Do not accept my belief without getting educated on the subject. So if you decide to go to hell regardless, at least you will have made an ill-advised but informed decision. Go get that advanced degree and then use it for God's purpose.

While you are being educated and subsequently receiving the worldly compensation that generally benefits an enlightened mind, do not forget where you came from or how you reached the educational plateau that you ultimately reside on. So what am I saying? Education is a good thing—a very good thing. But education all by itself will not solve our problems. If you think that is not true, look at the world around you; some of the best minds in the world have combined to create this sorry mess of a society in which we live. The attainment of the advanced degree and God's purpose should mesh. What you *do* with the advanced degree that I sincerely hope you pursue may positively impact this society and the world to such a degree that God Himself will be pleased. Doing with the degree is infinitely more important than the getting. Education is indeed a good thing, especially when used to promote and edify the advancement of mankind as directed by the wisdom of God. So go get God's guidance and your advanced degree and go to work!

Self-Awareness

An Important Attribute for Graduate School Success

CLIFTON A. POODRY

Director of Minority Opportunities in Research,
Department of Health and Human Resources, National Institutes of Health

I am pleased to be asked for advice. Although I am not a Black scholar, I am an American Indian who grew up on a reservation in the late 1940s and 1950s; at least some of our experiences and struggles surely overlap. I was for twenty-two years on the faculty at the University of California, Santa Cruz, as a professor of biology. I served in administrative positions as department chair, acting dean, and acting associate vice chancellor. I take pride in my research accomplishments and in the students from my lab, Black, White, Hispanic, and American Indian, who have gone on to earn doctoral degrees. My current position as director of the Minority Opportunities in Research Division at the National Institute of General Medical Sciences, National Institutes of Health, takes advantage of many years of experience working with minority programs. Because many other terrific writers in this volume will no doubt address critical points on mentoring, on networking, and on key issues for professional development, I would like to address some personal attributes that helped me along the way.

SELF-AWARENESS

What skill is needed by those who thrive in graduate school and as young faculty? Understanding oneself. Discussion of this answer can easily wax philosophical; but I am interested in a practical awareness of oneself that, if you don't have it, can be developed and is a powerful tool of successful people. Books have been written on the topic, for example, Steven Covey's *The Seven Habits of Highly Effective People* (Jossey-Bass, 1996). (I encourage you to read his works.) One of the important skills that little children learn is about learning itself. They learn that some things require memorization and that some things can be figured out. They learn that examining things in a certain ways yields solutions. Being aware of how we think and how we solve problems for ourselves is a powerful and necessary tool for improving our thinking and problem-solving skills. As young adults an advantage of being self-aware is that we can have better focus on what is important to ourselves and also how to direct our energies better.

I'll share a few personal examples that are very simplistic but will hopefully illustrate my point. The first concerns basic physiology. Some people are night people and some are morning people. I learned early on that I could work late into the night on routine or even finely detailed activities for electron microscopy but that my clearest thinking took place in the morning. I believe that some of the most creative thinking of my career took place while bicycling to work in the morning. Afternoons, in contrast, were no time for me to be trying to concentrate on esoteric, abstract journal articles, but they were good times to do microsurgery. Later in the afternoon was a good time to do the chores that required little or no brainpower. The fact that my brainpower varied during the day was further dramatically emphasized in an embarrassing way during a lecture. One day, part way through a lecture in introductory biology, I found myself putting material on the board and showing my slides but without any understanding of the big picture or what I was really trying to convey. I had drawn a complete blank. How mortifying! How could I go blank right in the middle of a lecture? Did it have anything to do with the cup of coffee and glazed donut that I had just before the class? You bet it did. Although that was the most dramatic example of non-alcohol-induced loss of brain power I experienced, I have since learned that daily ups and downs in blood sugar level (modifiable by coffee and sugar intake) make a huge difference in my ability to think. Thus, if you are aware of your basic physiology, you can make the optimum use of the brainpower you have. The real point of this example is that awareness of how you are doing, how you are feeling, of what works for you, is necessary if you want to play to your strengths and strengthen your weaknesses.

My second point is that there are only so many hours in a day! You should be aware of your priorities and be prepared to act accordingly. My Hopi friend, Frank Dukepoo, asks children in his honor society, "What will you give up?" You say you want to accomplish something such as writing that paper, mastering that new methodology, learning a new pedagogy, writing that research proposal, getting your files organized, or losing fifteen pounds. We have all heard children wish for some accomplishment. " I wish I could play piano like Johnny." "I wish I could get straight As like Maya."

But does it really mean, "I wish I could play piano without the hours of practice"? Or "I wish I could get straight As without having to study"?

As adults, we recognize that we have to pay the price for accomplishment; but we often fail to recognize that we are already using every hour in the day. There are no more. So it boils down to making priorities that match what we really want and then deciding what we will give up. Successful people make conscious decisions about their time and their priorities rather than leave their schedule to chance and incur feelings of guilt for tasks left undone. In judging my own career, I'd only give myself barely passing marks in time management and prioritizing. If I had it to do over, I'd make much better use of my time.

For me, graduate school (after qualifying exams), my postdoc, and my time as an assistant professor were wonderful, rewarding periods of my life. Although many of my peers worried about whether they would get jobs or, once employed, whether they would get tenure, I concentrated on improving and enjoying my work. I figured that if the department didn't want me, I didn't want to be there. It would be their loss, and there would be many other things I could do for a living. Luckily, they did want me, and I hadn't burned energy needlessly worrying. Judgment never ends. I had tenure but was again reviewed for promotion to full professor. My grant applications were judged. My manuscripts were judged. I was judged again when I applied for this job. My final point of self-awareness, therefore, is to be true to yourself. Work to your own standards so you can take pride in your accomplishments. You will no doubt work better and you will enjoy life more.

In closing, let me encourage you to benefit from the collected wisdom of the authors of this series. As you look outward to learn from the experience of others, don't forget to look inward; be self-aware so that you can apply that wisdom uniquely to yourself.

The Experimental Student

ALVIN F. POUSSAINT

Faculty Associate Dean for Student Affairs
and Clinical Professor of Psychiatry, Harvard Medical School

In the early 1970s, when Harvard Medical School was embarking on a program to admit more minorities, the admissions committee was challenged by an exceptional Black applicant who didn't fit the traditional profile of the students we accepted then. This student was from the rural South, the first member of a poor farm family to attend college. In his favor, he was a campus leader who had been active in extracurricular and community activities, and he had spent a summer engaged in research at a prominent science center in the North. But his A-minus average had been earned at a public, historically Black college in the deep South, a school that was not known for academic excellence. And his Medical College Admission Test scores (MCATs) were only in the middle range.

At first, most admissions committee members felt that this student probably wouldn't be able to handle the demanding Harvard curriculum. Although positive points were given for such things as community service and demonstrated leadership ability, Harvard Medical School's admissions criteria focused on grades and test scores. Some committee members did acknowledge that White students with low MCATs had been admitted in the past, but they also pointed out that those students had earned high grades at colleges with high academic standards, and this Black student's A-minus average might be equivalent to a C average earned at a more demanding school.

I argued that given his background, MCAT scores might not be a valid predictor of this student's ability to handle the basic science and clinical curricula and that he might have undemonstrated academic potential. Some of the other committee members agreed. Like me, they saw his participation in the summer research as evidence of his intellectual talent; like me, they looked at the way he had overcome significant obstacles in order to get a college education as testimony to his strong drive and motivation.

After much discussion, the committee members who opposed this student's admission yielded, but they suggested that we follow his career as an experiment in admitting a student who appeared to pose an academic risk.

What happened? The "experimental" student had no academic difficulty and did outstanding clinical work. He also took on a long-term research project and spent an extra year to earn an M.A. in public health in addition to an M.D. He graduated with honors, was accepted into a leading hospital's residency program, and went on to a successful career in medicine.

Our experience with this nontraditional medical student led us to reexamine the Medical School's basic admissions criteria and give more weight to a quality we call "distance traveled," which refers to the barriers an applicant has surmounted to reach his or her present level of performance. We've always known that there's no foolproof way to determine which students will succeed in medical school and become good physicians; research conducted in recent decades indicates that predicting who will become a successful physician cannot be determined solely by preadmission GPAs and MCAT scores, and experts in the field now recommend that admissions committees give more weight to relevant personal characteristics when selecting students for a helping profession such as medicine.

In the thirty years since the matriculation of that first nontraditional Black applicant, Harvard Medical School has admitted many minority students who did not fit the traditional profile. And it's been my observation that despite the pressures of being minorities in a predominantly White environment, almost all of Harvard Medical School's minority students—even those from nontraditional academic backgrounds—have mastered the basic sciences, performed at a very high level during their clinical years and in their residencies, and made significant contributions to their communities as physicians. Moreover, these minority students have demonstrated, on the whole, a heightened sensitivity to patients from cultures other than their own, and they have proved more likely to care for patients who are indigent or very sick: the populations who are most in need of good medical care but least likely to get it.

Black students, even when they have strong undergraduate records, often hesitate to apply to top medical schools, fearing that they won't be accepted because their academic background isn't strong enough or that they won't have the necessary skills to succeed once they're accepted, perhaps because no one else in their family has gone to graduate school. But Black students should pursue their dreams. I believe that a student's personal strengths are critical to academic and clinical success. And a graduate degree in medicine can create real opportunities to improve the lives of people in our communities.

Developing a Mentor-Mentee Relationship during Your Doctoral Studies

EVELYN SHEPHERD-WYNN

Assistant Professor of English, Grambling State University

During your pursuit of the doctoral degree, many decisions concerning your plan of study, research interests, and dissertation topic will be made under the supervision of your adviser, major professor, and dissertation chairperson. All of these decisions and experiences will in the long run enhance your career choices. At many higher education institutions, the roles of these individuals vary; however, they may be the same at other institutions. This short essay shares my graduate experiences concerning the mentor-mentee relationship with my adviser, major professor, and dissertation chairperson. It will in retrospect show how my mentor guided my graduate experiences concerning the values, standards, and practices of my chosen profession and how he helped me develop the skills, tools, and habits of inquiry within this profession. As a graduate student, you will need professional guidance to help monitor your progress and to encourage and motivate you during stagnant periods throughout your program of study; therefore, it is important that you select a mentor early in pursuit of the doctoral degree. You can learn a great deal from a mentor in all capacities. The mentor, for example, can advise you on how to successfully overcome certain hurdles throughout your course work: exams, residency, internship, conference participation, oral defense, and the dissertation. A good mentor can also teach you how to write grant proposals, improve teaching techniques, make spending decisions, create budgets, make career decisions, and publish articles, to name a few. When you acquire these skills, you will be better equipped to contribute to the program and to compete for future positions.

Advisers, major professors, and dissertation chairpersons may serve under the umbrella of mentors. As mentioned earlier, a professor may often serve in all three positions, or a different professor may serve in each position. In my case, my mentor served as my adviser, major professor, and dissertation chairperson. When I began my doctoral studies in 1994, I chose Vernon L. Farmer as my mentor during the early stages of my course work, and he later served as my adviser, major professor, and dissertation chairperson. He was consistent and persistent, and he was persnickety. This was fine with me because I wanted to become a scholar; the rigor was good. Because we established a good mentor-mentee relationship, I always sought his advice when confronted with an obstacle. He advised me on how to approach certain seminars as well as what approach to take in dealing with certain professors. As a mentor, he always looked out for our overall well being. He never advised us unless he understood all the dynamics involved.

An adviser typically monitors whether a student is following his or her plan of study; however, a conscientious adviser plays a more significant role in a doctoral student's matriculation. Dr. Farmer was indeed a conscientious adviser. He was not merely concerned about my following the plan of study but with my exam preparation, research activities, residency, conference attendance and presentations, publishing agenda, personal obligations, and my long-range career plans. Obviously, Dr. Farmer's advising sessions always went beyond the surface of "What courses do you plan to take?" or "What is your area of concentration?" Instead, he asked pertinent questions such as "What do you plan on doing careerwise ten years from now?" "How do you think this degree will enhance your career?" "What research areas are you really interested in?" As he did with all his advisees, he asked the same probing questions. We never left his office without experiencing his piercing brainstorming sessions. This type of probing, along with his open door policy, made it easy for us to develop a rewarding professional relationship with him.

While serving as my adviser early in the doctoral process, I had an opportunity to observe Dr. Farmer interact with more advanced doctoral students. It was his supportive, concerned attitude that led me to later ask him to serve as my major professor. I believe that one of the best strategies he used was having his advisees periodically meet to share common concerns and problems as well as hear about the research of others. In these group activities, students came to know their uniqueness and their value during the collaboration. There were times when we realized that our problems, professional or personal, could be solved based upon others' experiences. Again, this helped to strengthen our mentor-mentee relationship.

Dr. Farmer was also very involved in research and publishing—something that I longed to do. Consequently, he obtained for me a research assistantship that allowed me to participate with him on a number of research projects. Although I understood his policy on publishing, I had no idea that he would encourage me to conduct more research and to begin publishing so early in my studies. Of course, I thought I needed more time and experience. He gave me a persuasive talk about how research accomplishments usually occur in small steps, and how my career would become stagnated unless I presented my work in a public forum where it could be read, reviewed, and evaluated by my peers. Because Dr. Farmer had a rigorous research agenda, he expected his advisees to do the same. The first article I wrote was in collaboration with one of my peers. It was perhaps one of the most grueling experiences I have ever encountered, yet it was one of the most learned and rewarding experiences. Sleepless nights, endless rewrites, and heated debates are memories that I fondly remember, but that of which I am most proud is an article that represents the beginning of my scholarly work. As he fondly reminds his advisees, the dissertation is merely the beginning of our scholarly work. "You don't have time to relax; your scholarly work has just begun," he always added. In fact, he urged all doctoral students to publish; it did not matter whether he was their major professor or not.

In addition to his research agenda, Dr. Farmer always made sure that his mentees presented at key conferences in their research area. Even when we were not presenting, he insisted that we attend professional conferences. Therefore, he encouraged me to attend a minimum of one professional conference a semester, preferably two. I quickly learned that attending professional conferences was an avenue that I could use to gain confidence and enhance my professional visibility. Dr. Farmer was often able to obtain financial support from his department, college, or grants to support mentees' travel. I soon found that presenting at professional conferences was an opportunity for me to present the bits and pieces of my research and to gain experience in and from the larger research community. One of the major points that I learned from making presentations at professional conferences was that feedback from colleagues strengthened my research efforts. Professional conferences also provide excellent opportunities to meet faculty from other higher education institutions and to build a network of colleagues. Research communities are relatively small, and meeting one's peers can have lasting importance in finding collaborators for joint projects and contacts who may lead to rewarding employment. More importantly, you can find jobs through networking.

One of the most important contributions that a dissertation chairperson can make is to help you select manageable topics and to discourage you from undertaking topics that are too broad in scope to complete in a reasonable and timely fashion. This will help to reduce the time spent in the process and to facilitate completion of the dissertation. Typically, you should identify possibilities for a dissertation topic and select a dissertation chairperson no later than the end of the second year of study. As mentioned earlier, I was very fortunate to have my mentor serve as adviser, major professor, and dissertation chairperson. Consequently, I identified my research topic early during my studies. Dr. Farmer was very instrumental in helping me select a manageable research topic. His primary questions were "Will this research add to the knowledge base in your field of study?" "Will this research topic help to enhance your career?" "Is this a researchable topic?" "What does the literature say about the topic?" and "Can this research be done in two years?" Selecting a dissertation topic early in the graduate program reduced a great deal of anxiety and gave me an opportunity to become immersed in the literature. In addition, I wrote about some facet of my research topic in every course when I had an opportunity to do so. Because of this encouragement from the onset, I was able to make tremendous progress. Therefore, when it was time to write the prospectus, much of the literature had been reviewed, and the data-gathering process had already occurred.

Barriers to timely completion of the dissertation are myriad, but one that faculty and students tend to recognize is students' lack of adequate financial assistance during the dissertation phase. Upon my dissertation chairperson's advice, whenever I had time in the beginning stages of my studies, he encouraged me to do word processing for doctoral students who were writing their dissertations. This provided me an opportunity to learn the various sections of the dissertation, to read committee members' comments, to become more familiar with the required handbooks and manuals, to observe the feedback and improved revisions, and to see finished products. Though sometimes taxing, this was an invaluable experience that helped me tremendously during my dissertation process.

The dissertation chairperson can serve as a liaison between the doctoral student and committee members. In this role, Dr. Farmer encouraged me to work slowly and methodologically while working on my dissertation. He made sure that all committee members were informed, meeting on a regular basis. In regards to my external committee member, we had numerous telecommunications that expedited the dissertation process. Finally, it is important that you select a mentor who is actively involved in advanced research, publishing, and scholarship in the graduate programs of his institution. You will indeed benefit from working with a mentor, someone to whom you can turn for advice, someone with a listening ear and a critical eye. As my mentor, Dr. Farmer worked at trying to provide opportunities that would enhance my career and to make certain that doors were unlocked. Once he understood my career interests and goals, he worked to make sure that I was prepared when the opportunity presented itself. It is not uncommon for the mentor-mentee professional relationship to continue long after the doctoral student has graduated. Now that I have received my degree and found a promising new direction in my career, the timing for increasing my publishing agenda is critical. One of the things that I learned under Dr. Farmer's guidance is that research is becoming more collaborative. In other words, successful research depends heavily on interacting with others. As I aim for professorship, I am confronted with the familiar "publish or perish" syndrome. Therefore, continuing my research career with a supporting cast, such as that of my mentor, is a plus. Had it not been for the valuable experiences I had during the pursuit of my doctorate, my career would not be where it is today—on the verge of pursing another one, a Ph.D. in English.

How to Be Successful in Graduate School

SANDRA L. TERRELL

Associate Dean of Robert B. Toulouse School of Graduate Studies
and Professor of Speech and Hearing Sciences, University of North Texas

The work ethic and philosophy that were the cornerstone for my success in graduate school, especially in a large, urban, majority-White institution, were established when I was a little girl in Pittsburgh, Pennsylvania. For you see, as far back as I can remember, I knew I was going to college. Of course, being only four years old and not yet in kindergarten during the early 1950s, I didn't know what college was. I only knew that I was going because my father said I would.

I was the oldest of three children in a loving extended family. My immediate family included my father, whom we all called "Daddy"(George Bennie Thomas Sr.); my mother, whom we all called "Mommy" (Margaret Thomas); my little brother, affectionately called "Snooky" (George Bennie Thomas Jr.); my father's mother and her husband, the grandparents we all called "Mom" (Sallie Mae Rucker) and "Pop" (Claude Rucker); and Mom and Pop's late-in-life surprise, their little girl named Runetta but whom we all called "Sugie." Thus, I had an aunt who was a year younger than I was. Additionally, with my mother being one of eighteen children, there was a very large quantity of aunts, uncles, cousins, in-laws, and assorted "outlaws" (as my mother called common-law spouses) who came and visited, some visiting longer than others depending on their current financial status.

My father was the first generation of his family to graduate from high school. His mother finished grade school and his stepfather finished eighth grade. Daddy and Pop worked in the steel mills of Pittsburgh. Daddy was very intelligent and wanted to learn masonry. However, I remember him saying that after he outscored White applicants on the various admission tests, he was asked to repeat the same tests and take more of them than the White applicants. Finally, after completing everything he was told to do, the boss told my father that he would not be accepted for masonry training because he was "colored." I remember the hushed but animated discussions among the adults about "colored only" places, schools, buses, and so on in the South and the problems that colored people had. But I vividly recall that it was to these persons, whether in a group or on an individual basis, that my father would also proudly announce that I would be going to college one day. And when anyone asked me what I was going to be when I grew up, I told them that when I grew up, I would be going to college.

I do not have empirical evidence to support this theory, but I do believe that each person of color has an experience that causes them to realize that the color of their skin makes a difference in the way they are treated. Further, I believe that the response that children receive as a result of this experience shapes the pattern of their lives. For me, this realization came in second grade. There was another Sandra in the classroom; she had honey blonde hair that came to her shoulders, and she wore a different, pretty dress each day of the school week. My mother expertly braided my hair in large cornrows onto which she tied ribbons. I had two school dresses, wearing one dress each day for two or three days before changing into the other for the rest of the school week. One morning, as we were marching in single file to the other side of the classroom for reading "Dick and Jane," my teacher said, "Sandra, I really like your hair." (It is strange that I can remember this White teacher's name and what she looked like to this day.) I said, as I had been taught to do after receiving a compliment, "Thank you." Then she replied, "I didn't mean you." I felt the sting of tears and barely got through the rest of the day. I ran home and told my mother. My dear Mommy told me that I was just as pretty and probably even more smart than the other kids in the class and that it didn't matter whether the teacher liked my hair or anything else about me. What mattered, she said, was the opportunity that I had to learn. Many would not like me, but they did not have to. As long as I was within earshot of what was being taught, whether the information was directed toward me or not, I could still learn it. What I had to do, she said, was to work twice as hard, study twice as much, do more than what I was asked, and strive to do a better job than everyone else just so that others, such as this second grade teacher, would have no choice but to acknowledge that I was "just as good." I believed my mother. Because she said I could, from that day forward, I set out on a pathway to excellence. I made the best grades in second grade and continued to outrank every student through elementary school. I received honors in high school, pursuing college preparation courses. Because my mother said I could, my father's announcement that I would attend college became reality. I not only went to college but finished my doctoral degree.

There is more to the story concerning my mother. Shortly after the birth of my third child in 1980, my mother and I began talking about that "I didn't mean you" incident in second grade. Much to my surprise, she said that she clearly remembered going to the school and "blessing out" the teacher, principal, and everyone else in charge that she could find, telling them they had better not "mess" with me anymore. I found it quite interesting that my mother gave me words that would guide me through life but that she never told me that she simultaneously had words with the teacher and school officials about how I was being treated. I did not know about her school visit until I was an adult holding my third baby. And the school never knew about the words of affirmation that she had spoken to me. I still follow my mother's wisdom in mentoring students, especially those of color. I try to give them words and guidance that will see them through the barriers of their education and life while, unknown to them, I confront the issues within the institution that pose barriers to my students.

The road through graduate school and my career until the present has not been easy. Indeed, the paths have not been without a various assortment of subtle and not-too-subtle racial and gender barriers. However, the words that both of my parents pronounced to me as a child, my motivation to be the best, a keen sense of God's love for me and my love for Him, and the people (White, Black, and otherwise) that He has placed along the road to assist me have carried me through.

Graduate Education Is the Road to Excellence

MARGARET DANIELS TYLER
Chief of Staff, Norfolk State University

There is always a desire to know the future, to see around the corner of the days and the years. Even when we say we do not concern ourselves about what will happen next month or next year, the nagging insistence still remains—we want to know.

This normal feeling is a part of the anxiety that we face on the threshold of any new adventure. If we could be sure that all will be well—if we could have some guarantee that our present hopes would not fail us—then we would find peace. We say to ourselves, "When my ship comes in, I will ... " or "When I get a certain job, I could ... " or "If I had a graduate degree, I would. ... " When we are young, we are inclined to think that our youth is a prelude to the real business of living. But life is not like that. The future is never separate from all that has gone before. We bring into the present baggage from the past, and that is with us as we take the unknown road. All that we have learned, felt, and thought; all of our experiences from birth to now; all the love that nourished us—all these are with us as we walk on the unknown road toward the future.

And then, there is the witness of others who have gone along the road we take. The road will mean something different for us, but it is not altogether unique. There are many roads that go in many directions. There is the high road and the path of least resistance. I challenge you to take the high road to excellence, in this case, the road to graduate school.

As we travel the road to excellence, there are basic truths that we must recognize. The graduate degree will provide access to tremendous opportunities. It will also position you to exercise the power to influence the direction and practice of your discipline. However, I humbly submit the following for your consideration: we must face the possibility of failure and acknowledge the fact that we will not escape struggle and conflict. Yet we must persist.

Let us first consider the possibility of failure. We have all experienced feelings of frustration at points in our lives. The fact is, we may not pass the test. We are frequently tested—tested in academic classes, tested in our relationships with people, tested in our commitment to an organization or a principle. Therefore, we unavoidably experience feelings of failure from time to time. We may even consider giving up, but remember, you cannot fail unless you quit.

Let us also consider the fact that we will not escape struggle and conflict on this road. It is true that some individuals seem to have a natural ability to excel in a particular field or endeavor. But these are rare people. Most of us acquire competence and excellence the long, hard way. Only clear thoughts and purposeful actions will determine if we will take the right road. We must take on the lifetime responsibility for reaching our fullest potential—intellectually, spiritually, and physically. The important thing to hold in mind is that all of our energies must not be consumed in merely getting through the day or the week. Our living must be structured by what it is we are trying to achieve with our lives. We must have a plan.

You would not take a trip, stage a wedding, or add an addition to your home without a plan. Yet pursuing a graduate degree is usually far more expensive than any of these, so you certainly want to do at least as much planning.

To succeed, you must do those things known to cause success: evaluate your strengths, weaknesses, opportunities, and threats; set objectives; choose a strategy; and most importantly, develop a plan. Your success as a graduate student has a great deal to do with you as a person—your skills, habits, background, thoughts, and ideas. Answer these questions honestly. If you know your weak points, you can protect yourself more effectively. Why are you pursuing a graduate degree? to escape a treadmill grind? to prove something to yourself? to prove something to others? to live up to people's expectations? to gain excitement? desperation—no job? because it is easier than a job? to control your life? to make more money? to earn by filling a known need? because you respond well to challenges? The first seven reasons are not compelling. The last four reasons may point to success. Proving something is fine, but not by itself. There are far cheaper, quicker, and easier ways to gain excitement. Above all, remember that pursuing the degree is very hard work.

Those who succeed can usually answer these questions in the affirmative: Do you have an attitude of success? Do you have a plan? Are you willing to act and put your plan into effect? Are you disciplined? Do people call you determined? Do you schedule and manage time well? Do you enjoy working with others? Do others enjoy working with you? Are you accustomed to a sixty-hour workweek? Can you handle emotional stress? Have you a list of abilities required? Do you have all or most of these? Have you worked in this field? Do you know your total living needs? Do you have a budget to meet these needs?

Once you are admitted to a program and decide to matriculate, then the major question you must answer is this: How well do you know your adviser/research group? Are you familiar with your adviser's body of research? Are you familiar with your adviser's current research projects? Do you know the history of your adviser's research group—how and when it started, how it grew, and what it is like today? Have you discussed your ideas with your adviser? If so, did your adviser give you feedback? Did your adviser make suggestions? Did you act on these suggestions? Do you have a plan prepared? If you have answered even a few of the previous questions unfavorably, correct those items or protect yourself from them so that you will not be taken by surprise. Then set your goals.

Goals are almost the heart of your entire effort. Goals let you manage by objective, which means that you aim all of your efforts at your main purpose. If the action doesn't help you reach your goal, then you don't do it. Make your goals both short range (this year) and long range (the next few years), both quantitative and qualitative, clear (put them in writing), measurable, and challenging yet attainable.

A plan is a blueprint and a picture of your success. A person with a careful plan often has a certain attraction and influence. A planner anticipates problems and takes positive steps to prevent them. A good plan sets priorities and will apply your unique talents in constructive ways to generate the most results.

With a good plan in place, there is nothing left to do but dig in; do first things first, one thing at a time. Most people have trouble deciding what is really important. One easy way is to assess two factors: (1) the value of the project to your adviser and (2) the lead time involved. Projects with high value and short lead times should be done first.

In closing, always remember that for some of us, the job of pursuing a graduate degree has been—or will be—very difficult. Perhaps not as difficult as the jobs faced by our forefathers, but difficult nonetheless. You may feel a deep sense of uncertainty as to the immediate future. For others, a door that has long been closed to us may open. I say to you, in either case, be encouraged. Continue on the road to excellence. Your success is in your hands and within your grasp.

The exhilarating task before us is the task of facing this struggle with the joy of our ancestors, who couldn't be stopped or destroyed by anything. They came down the same road we are traveling when the road was harder and the mountains taller and the ditches deeper, and they did not turn back.

People of African descent are at the crossroads. No matter where Africans are—in America, on the continent, or in the diaspora—our condition is the same. We are in peril. As we read thoughtful books about the future by renowned authors like Thoreau, Kotkin, and Huntington, it becomes apparent that either African people are not mentioned at all, we are noticed with pity, or we are noticed in terms of whether or not we contribute to the agenda of others. As you forge ahead, securing higher levels of education and greater amounts of knowledge that can be used to lift our people to greatness, consider the words of that magnificent spirit, Nelson Mandela. In his autobiography, Mr. Mandela wrote:

I have walked the long road. I have tried not to falter; I have made missteps along the way. But I have discovered the secret that after climbing a great hill, one only finds that there are many more hills to climb. I have taken a moment here to rest, to steal a view of the glorious vista that surrounds me, to look back on the distance I have come. But I can rest only for a moment ... and I dare not linger, for my long walk (along the road) is not yet ended. (p. 625)

REFERENCE

Mandela, N. (1994). *A long walk to freedom*. Randburg, South Africa: Macdonald Purnell, Ltd.

Being Persistent Helped Me to Achieve My Wings as a Navy Aviator

DIALLO SIKOU WALLACE
Lieutenant Junior Grade, U.S. Navy

Born in Oakland, California, I am currently a twenty-six-year-old lieutenant junior in the U.S. Navy. I received my wings as a naval aviator on October 15, 1999. It was a glorious and significant achievement for me that represented an undertaking of seventeen years of dreaming, studying, and hard work. This is just the beginning of my achievements that I have planned for myself and with God's help and grace. I try not to use the terms *want* or *hope* but rather *will*. It is a state of mind. I tell the young children to whom I teach aerodynamics and astronomy that they can want something all their life, but when they say they are going to do or achieve it, they must be 100 percent diligent about getting it. I know this sounds idealistic, but it has helped me thus far in life. I strongly feel that my few achievements have come from my many failures. The irony in that is comical, but it is also true. I tell my wife that I have failed at many things, but it was from those failures that I found the strength to continue.

I know exactly when it all began for me. The date was April 11, 1981, and I was eight years old. I watched two men take a wonderful gossamer into the sky. It was the Space Shuttle *Columbia* of 1981, with John Young, an Apollo veteran who has walked on the moon as commander, and Robert Crippen as the pilot. When I saw the two solid rocket boosters, I knew exactly what I was going to do in life. And I turned to my mother at that young age and told her. The funny thing is that I still tell her I know what I want to be now that I am twenty-six. I began learning and studying the art, science, and beauty of the space program. Sure, I played sports and had childish hobbies, but my joy was sitting down and reading books on space by people like Jim Oberg and learning space facts. The more I learned about the space program, the more I learned about how the space project had influenced so many other subjects of science that I loved. Growing up, I did not have much, but somehow holding onto my dream through the books I read seemed to help me and even gave me some purpose to life. Accordingly, my father took a strong stand in teaching my brother and me about Black history. I guess in a way it gave me an accountability to those who made it possible for me to have the opportunities that could be mine as long as I worked for them.

I learned of people such as Benjamin Banneker, Crispus Attucks, Elijah McCoy, Buffalo Soldiers, the Fifty-Fourth Regiment of the Civil War, and many other people. It may also sound idealistic, but I felt ashamed if I did not try to go as far as I possibly could for these people. I think one problem with our youth today across all color and ethnic backgrounds is that there is no accountability for them. If they truly understood the sacrifices their parents, forefathers, and foremothers made in order to put them where they are, there would not be some of the problems in our society that are running rampant. However, that is an entirely different subject.

As I began to learn about the space program, my eyes opened to so many other subjects, such as astronomy, physics, history, and literature. I just cannot get enough of any of these. One thing I began to notice was that there were no Blacks to emulate at that time. They were in training, but I did not see them. I figured that if there were not any, maybe it was time there were, and if so, why couldn't I be the first Black man to go into space?

After changing this goal a few times once it had been met by others (Guy Blufored, Charlie Bolden), I came to my final goal, one that hopefully I can achieve: to accomplish as much as I can in my lifetime. I decided that my series of goals was to get my degree in engineering, join the military and get my "Wings of Gold" from the Navy, go back to school and hopefully get a degree in either physics or astrophysics, and then apply to the space program.

Just to give you an idea of what happened with me over the past five years, I graduated from high school in 1991. I wanted to get into aerospace engineering and was doing a type of mentorship program with Hughes Aircraft. It was just after the Gulf War, and the person who was helping me said, "I realize that you know more about the space program and aviation than anyone, but in four years you want to have a job." So he directed me into electronics so that I could still be in the aviation and space industry. But there came a time when the industry was on the tough side of the wave. I could branch into other related industries such as communications. After seeing the engineers getting their pink slips at so many aerospace companies, I thought this to be sound advice. I then went to school for electronics engineering technology. It was extremely difficult for me because of my interest.

My passion was to learn about rocket engines, orbital mechanics, and aircraft, so it was very hard to be excited about IC chips and oscilloscopes.

I had the good fortune of meeting a hero of mine and becoming friends with him. He was astronaut Jim Irwin, who had been the lunar module pilot on the Apollo XV mission. He had helped me to go to Space Camp on a scholarship in Huntsville, Alabama. He died a year after we became friends and before I was able to thank him for his help in getting me to space camp. I thought of no better way to honor his memory than to do my best while I was there. The result was that I won some awards and medals for my accomplishments at Space Camp. After returning from that week and not really enjoying what I was studying, I vowed to get into aerospace engineering no matter what the cost. I was also opened up to the idea and beauty of the subject of astrophysics.

I finished school and had three options that were equally important. I had the opportunity to go back to Officer Candidate School for the Marines, to try to start a masters in astrophysics at San Diego State University, or to try to work on a second bachelor's degree in aerospace engineering at Embry-Riddle Aeronautical University. I decided to go for my first love, flying, and the Marines gave me a shot. That didn't work, however, because I was injured, and I could not complete the training. So I returned home after being there for the initial stages.

I then thought, "If I had two degrees, it would really help in the future when it came time to submit a package to NASA." I then went to Arizona to attempt to complete the aerospace engineering courses, and after a year I returned to San Diego owing to lack of finances. I was working so hard there because I could not qualify for financial aid, and thus I did not have time to study. It really hurt me to have to leave . If ever there was a place for me to be, it was there. The school curriculum and people were just incredible. What hurt the most was the fact that I let something that I wanted very much slip away. That was another disappointment. While I was in Arizona, I learned so many new skills. I learned to build computers at my place of employment, and I also learned to build telescopes from a friend. It was a gain in the end, any way I looked at it. I came away with a skill and a new trade.

When I returned to San Diego, I was working for a company and thinking that if the other two options did not work out, maybe I could try the master's program in astrophysics at San Diego State University. I was already spending a great deal of time there taking pictures of the lunar surface through their telescope.

The subjects were another matter that needed more time than I was able to spend. These were the three things that I cared very much about, and I was unable to do them. I was very frustrated and felt very beaten down to be honest. Undaunted, I decided to check back with the military to see if I could try out with the navy. I then went to Officer Candidate School for the navy in the summer of 1997. I needed the feeling of accomplishing this big challenge. I received my commission on a day that was probably just a normal day to anyone else. But to me, it was a day that was more incredibly beautiful than any other in a long time.

I then started aviation preflight training in Pensacola, Florida, for six weeks of water survival and basic ground school instruction in subjects such as engines, aerodynamics, and others. I then went to Corpus Christi, Texas, to begin primary flight training. I was selected for helicopters after completing primary training and went back to Florida to learn to fly them.

Now that I have my wings, that is one goal that I can check off. Hopefully it will be the first of the many I intend to accomplish. Right now I have other things that I hope to achieve. I plan to go to the Naval Post graduate school in Monterey for aerospace engineering. I am also working to create a scholarship program in Jim Irwin's name at Space Camp, building more telescopes, and talking with and inspiring young people.

As I stated before, the reason for my success is twofold: first, being accountable to the people who made it possible for me to have the options I had and second, learning through the hard letdowns and failures. How you look at each depends on your frame of mind. I chose to take the failures and learn from them. This decision helped me to continue to grow.

A Gift to Yourself

The Doctorate Degree

NEARI F. WARNER
Acting President and Provost, Professor of Education,
Grambling State University

The greatest professionally rewarding and personally fulfilling gift you can give to yourself is the attainment of the doctoral degree. I use *gift* as a symbolic term because everyone loves gifts, enjoys getting things, and delights in receiving presents. Gifts bring about joy, happiness, excitement, surprise, anxiety, and anticipation.

Some gifts are for private use, whereas others are for public display. Some gifts have adorning qualities that attract, whereas others have utility purposes only. Still, some gifts are practical, and some are not so practical. Regardless of what the gift may be, it will have special meaning and will make some kind of difference in the life of the recipient. In like manner, the doctoral degree has many characteristics and will provide its recipients with a variety of ways in which it may be used. In order to give this wonderful gift to yourself, several important issues must be considered.

MAKING THE DECISION

Making the decision is first and foremost to successful matriculation and attainment. Although this sounds simplistic and easy, it is actually difficult and complex. Therefore, careful, deliberate thought must be given before entering a doctoral program. Paramount among your deliberations should be the issue of financial resources. You must make sure that you have the financial base to achieve the goal. Your first inclination should be to seek external assistance and funding. The ideal place to begin is the university of choice. It is not merely enough to investigate the university catalog, but it is also smart to personally speak with the head of the department in which you will matriculate. Special departmental initiatives and program incentives may not be widely publicized. Additionally, you should contact the traditional foundations as well as seek fellowships through government agencies and philanthropic groups. If none of those sources provide the funds needed, you should consider getting a personal loan. This will be an investment you will never regret.

Equally important in the process is developing the mind-set for school and study. For those who have had a breach in their school days, it will be imperative to recall the seriousness, rigor, discipline, and commitment needed to achieve and excel in educational settings. If you are ready and willing to employ and to magnify the traits that brought you through the undergraduate and masters years, your decision will be easy.

STAYING THE COURSE

Staying the course is another consideration that will surface throughout your matriculation. There will be times when you want to give up. (Do not!) There will be times when you wonder if it is worth it. (It is!) There will be times when you wonder if it will ever be over. (It will!) There will be times when you wonder if you can do it. (You can!) There will be times when you wonder if you made the right decision. (You did!)

Synonymous with perseverance and patience, staying the course means that you will have to make sacrifices. It means that you may not be able to do all of the things you like to do. It means that you must engage family and friends for their support and understanding. It means that you must be willing, for just a few years, to live a life that revolves around attaining this wonderful gift.

USING YOUR EXPERIENCES

Using your experiences is a strategy that you should employ. You bring valuable resources to this venture and should use them to your advantage. You have much to offer to your course of study. Your practical experiences will be able to correlate with the literature and can make the research real. It will be up to you to demonstrate the relevancy and make the compelling connections. Specifically, the experiences that you take for granted and the daily routines that are so familiar to you can serve as points for written assignments and as springboards for classroom discussion. In either situation, they will provide you with a comfort zone from which you can move confidently into larger research projects in preparation for the dissertation.

COMPLETING THE PROCESS

Completing the process is as fascinating as enduring it. Once you have received your degree, you will initially discover that you have an abundance of free time. However, that will change very soon. Also, you will be pleasantly surprised at how this credential (this gift) validates your knowledge, skills, and professionalism. Your colleagues without the degree will look to you as a role model. You will very likely and unknowingly be a motivating force that inspires someone else to seek the gift. Your colleagues who hold the doctorate will look at you with admiration and respect. Knowing the trials and travails you encountered, these colleagues will embrace you and celebrate your accomplishment.

In terms of your career, it can grow and prosper as much as you want it to. You will be a much-sought-after professional. You will have to decide the path that you will pursue. You will also want to extend your affiliations and may even consider leadership positions in the professional organizations and the learned societies of your discipline.

In the final analysis, the doctoral experience is comparable to no other experience. In order to successfully negotiate the process, you must want the degree passionately, believe in yourself and be prepared to accept the challenges inherent in achieving it. Without a doubt, it is truly a worthwhile undertaking and will ultimately be the greatest personal and professional gift you can give to yourself.

A Producer versus Consumer Consciousness

HOMER B. WARREN

Associate Professor of Marketing, Youngstown State University

What helped me to succeed in my masters and doctoral work and in my present career as a marketing professor was how I changed my consciousness. In the middle of my masters degree, I came to view everything from a producer's consciousness (as distinct from a consumer's consciousness). America is the great consumer culture of all time. The vast majority of Americans (of all ethnic groups) are consumption oriented. Indeed, for all products (to include all tangible goods, all types of services, and all types of entertainment) the consumption mentality is quite omnipresent. Much of our time is spent either contemplating (and dreaming about) the purchase of some product, actually in the marketplace actively involved in the purchase process, using products previously purchased, and in conversation with others about products. We've become a culture of need satisfaction through products. If we like something (and can afford it), we buy it; if the product doesn't do anything for us, we simply leave it on the rack or shelf and ignore it.

As a consequence of this omnipresent consumption mentality, the average person has come to view everything in his or her life from the perspective of a consumer (in many cases, this behavior is subconscious). Even personal relationships have come to be predicated on the notion of "if it doesn't fit in the least bit, put it back on the shelf and move on." Our approach to politics has been shaped into a simple like/don't like proposition (which has led to the thinking of "because I don't like what's going on in politics, I'll just ignore it").

Unfortunately, many Black college students sit in class with this same consumer consciousness. The college classroom is filled with students who have the attitude of "if I like it, I'll deal with it; if I don't, I'll just go through the motions." The worst of it is that knowledge, information, and intellectual skills are being purchased like food only to be eaten for momentary pleasure and nutritional requirements and then moved through the body to be disposed (the metaphor here is simply that students forget much of the information learned once the class is over).

In graduate school for my masters in economics, I recognized that I couldn't have a consumer mentality and fully appreciate the importance of education to my professional and personal life. I came to realize that a consumer mentality (even when consumers are making intelligent decisions) places the individual in the position of a receiver, taker, disposer, and, for the most part, the passive partner in the exchange dynamics of the market economy. Although consumers are pleasure seekers and need satisfiers, producers are planners, implementers, and doers—pleasure and need providers. I knew that I had to begin seeing myself as a producer (and not a consumer) in all things that I did! I especially had to have a producer's consciousness about everything regarding my education.

But how was I a producer? And what was I producing? In short, I am a producer of the financial and emotional security for my family. As a member of my community, I am a producer of effective and productive contributions to social and civic organizations to which I am a member. I am a producer of a positive identification for younger Blacks. I am a producer of rational (meaning uncorrupted, un-ego-filled) analyses of the political, economic, and social issues that affect my community. I am a producer of how well I am aware of myself and others around me. I am a producer of a loyal friend to my friends. I am a producer of my spiritual being. I am a producer of love, affection, trust, hope, peacefulness, and kindness. Obviously, as each of you can see, my product list can be very long. I offer that you can reflect on this idea and come up with a long list of specific products that you are presently producing and would like to produce in the future.

Thinking of myself as a producer led me to the obvious conclusion that in order to produce the best products that I could, I needed the proper resources and raw materials. Clearly, I needed to possess knowledge, information, and critical thinking skills. I recognized that the college experience was the best systematic way to attain these raw materials for my products. Hence, each class, each textbook, each teacher became far more than just a class to take, a book to read, a teacher to listen to. A class, a textbook, a teacher was now a factor of production, a resource that would allow me to effectively and efficiently produce my products. With this change in consciousness (from consumer to producer), no class was a drudgery, no textbook was an unwanted task, no teacher was a bore.

Since my college days, I am still viewing the world through producer's eyes. This philosophy certainly won't protect me from the trials and tribulations ushered in by the complexities of relationships, the surprises of health, and unanticipated crises. Maintaining a producer's consciousness, however, has made me come to terms with the fact that I am responsible for creating how I deal with my world. If I want good personal and professional relationships with others, I have to produce the products of love, affection, trust, hope, peacefulness, and kindness. And to produce these products, I need the resources and raw materials of the knowledge and skills of awareness, understanding, and listening.

The producer versus consumer consciousness is a metaphorical exercise that some may consider a bit dehumanizing. Arguably, corporate America and the methods of capitalism have a few distasteful historical realities, and to propose the usage of a production metaphor for individual behavior is an insult to the sensibilities of those who see the corporate world as exploitative and corrupt. I won't argue that point. And if I had more space, I would propose that the productive processes long predate capitalism and mass production. In this essay to the future Black intelligentsia, I simply offer one person's consciousness for success. Who knows but there may be a few who may find the producer's consciousness equally helpful to their successes.

Setting the Agenda for Success

ELVIRA M. WHITE

Assistant Professor of Criminal Justice, Grambling State University

The road to success for me was paved with many obstacles, curves, mountains, and valleys. I actually lived the words of that great African American poet Langston Hughes, who wrote, "Life for me ain't been no crystal stair." Despite and in spite of my humble beginnings, I believe that success is achieving the dreams that you have set for yourself. In order to achieve your dreams, you must set clearly definable goals and priorities. This involves planning an agenda early and executing the plan with meticulous precision. If you encounter delays, detours, curves, and mountains on your road, go around the road until you approach the sign that reads *solution.*

As the eighth of eleven children raised in a segregated northeastern town, there were few material pleasures with the exception of one black-and-white television, a radio for my mom's spirituals, and every book and newspaper my parents could sacrifice to purchase. At the age of seven, I developed an interest in law by watching *Perry Mason* on Saturday evenings with my father. My late father relived the moment time and time again when I looked into his eyes and said, "I am going to be a lawyer." Though we personally knew of no Black lawyers and had never met one, he told me I could be anything that I wanted to be. I began the dream at that time and perhaps without realizing it, *I set the agenda.*

I read everything that I was given in school from secondhand books sent to our Black school from the White school. By the time I was ten years old, the public library permitted Blacks to check out books in limited quantity. I read every mystery book that I could get my hands on. Through reading I increased my written and oral communication skills. *I was following the agenda.*

Upon reaching high school, my dream of becoming a lawyer was as great as it was at seven. Our Black teachers reminded us daily that "we had to be twice as good to be thought half as good" as they continued to teach us with those secondhand books. The source of the books did not concern me as much as the information that could be obtained from them. I had no mentor who could tell me what courses to concentrate on and how to academically prepare myself for the lawyer dream. The lack of information was really a blessing in disguise because my ignorance of the requirements caused me to excel in every course. I was following the agenda and then the detour came.

In the middle of my tenth grade year I met a college guy who was handsome, charismatic, and very popular. My instant infatuation resulted in my making one life-altering decision. Shortly thereafter this fifteen-year-old virgin was pregnant. The disappointment expressed by the looks and tears of my parents could not have been any worse if I had physically stabbed them in the heart. The stares from the teachers and community members were unbearable because I was one of the "good girls." My relationship with God became even stronger. My parents, my church, and the minister became my rock. They assured me that even with this valley detour, I could still achieve the goals that I had set. I missed one month of school, completed all of my assignments, and had them delivered to school by a very dear friend. In October 1968, I gave birth to a beautiful baby boy and returned to school for my eleventh grade year two weeks later. It was fortunate for me to have supportive parents and friends who assisted with my son. *I was on a detour but the agenda was the same,* to earn a law degree.

With a combination of loans, grants, scholarships, and prayers, I entered North Carolina A&T State University. As an out-of-state student and a teenage parent, I knew that the graduation plan had to be expedited. Taking extra credits each semester; I graduated three years later magna cum laude with a bachelor's degree in political science.

A decision was made to obtain a master's degree prior to law school in order to work and have my son live with me. I had no money and limited access to other resources. A graduate teaching fellowship and a midnight waitressing job supported my son and myself. Bartering for babysitting was the order of the day. Two years later, I was teaching part time at a university and ready to enter law school. *A detour had taken place, but the agenda remained intact.*

Law school was a total surprise. By the second year, I learned by accident that after going through this grueling three-year ordeal, I was going to have to sit for an examination in order to be licensed when I graduated. This may sound strange to today's student, but I was a country girl from the sticks who had never met a lawyer until law school. Even though I was a full-time mom, full-time student, and part-time instructor, I managed to graduate and ultimately pass the bar examination. Finally my agenda had been met, or so I thought.

I practiced criminal and civil law for over twenty years, trying well over a thousand cases ranging from parking tickets to death penalty defenses. The blessings from these experiences allowed me to be the first African American woman to achieve many milestones within the profession. It opened doors for those coming through the ranks behind me. Just as I became comfortable with my successes, new doors opened for challenge and opportunity. I am now able to combine the best of both worlds, my love for the law with my love for the student in all of us. *The original agenda had been broadened.* Teaching at Grambling State University has allowed me to share the knowledge and skills that I learned with the future leaders of America.

In order to achieve your own agenda, you must possess perseverance, dedication, and a willingness to work hard. If the road has a detour sign that says *finances, academics,* or *personal problems,* go around the road to the sign that says *solution.* Once you demonstrate the willingness to work hard, there will be people on the solution road who will assist and guide you in achieving your dreams.

As a college student today, the rules for success have not changed, but responsibility for the rules do. Instead of your parents telling you to get up and go to class, you now make that decision. Your agenda must be to attend class as a responsible adult and to soak up every morsel of knowledge put out by your professors. When you fail to attend class and fail to perform to your full capacity, you are cheating yourself, and ultimately you will pay. The costs of an A and an F are the same tuition amount.

The purpose of this writing is not to extol the virtues of teenage and single parentage; it is just the opposite. If you are already a young single parent, you can still achieve your dreams. If you have not traveled down this road, think carefully about the mountains. If I could achieve success with the adversity that confronted me on a daily basis, then you can, too. Though my dream and agenda was set at age seven, age is limitless. *Begin today to set your own agenda, and success will be yours.*

How to Be Successful as a Full-Time Law Student While Working Full Time as a Police Officer

BRUCE D. WILLIAMS

Attorney-at-Law and Houston Police Lieutenant

On numerous occasions, prospective and current graduate students, police officers, and others have approached me with one question: "How did you complete law school while working full time and carrying a full academic load?" My response has always been tailored to the individual asking the question and is always prefaced with a number of my own questions, such as "Are you currently a graduate/professional student?" "Are you planning on becoming a graduate/professional student?" Many of my cohorts and colleagues in the police department ask the question about educational pursuits out of mere curiosity, with no intent of pursuing such a path for themselves. My response to the curious is markedly different than the response to those conducting research for their own journey. I always praise the inquirer who wants to pursue an education and extol the phenomenal benefits that can be derived from a professional/graduate degree. In order to accomplish the goal of tweaking their interest even more, I inquire as to what type of degree they are seeking and for what purpose are they going to use it.

Once some rapport has been established with the inquirer, I attempt to tactfully identify the obstacles that "all" professional/graduate students face, for example, financial concerns, choice of schools, and so on. I then attempt to determine any unique indicators of success or failure. After weaving a sort of mosaic about this serious inquirer, I tell them a story about my successes and failures, always keeping in mind their particular perspective.

In this way, it is easier to connect familiar obstacles and strengths and better understand the options available to them in their unique circumstance. Even though I have had inquiries about other graduate programs, this essay will focus on my experiences in law school. The following is a capsule outline of how I was able to successfully complete law school while being a full-time employee and how I currently enjoy both a successful private law practice and a fulfilling career as one of only a few Black male police lieutenants with the City of Houston. Following the outline, I will explain each item in greater detail: time management, finding a mentor, academic ability, employer management ("the boss"), cutting out the fat/avoiding acts of futility, remarks from a mentee (Alaina King Benford), and success in practice/mission statement.

TIME MANAGEMENT

Time management is absolutely essential for success. If a candidate knows going in that he or she is deficient in the area of time management, I advise them to take a course, read a book, or otherwise give up the idea of successfully completing a program in graduate/professional school. This is particularly true for individuals with such demands as work, children, mortgage/rent, and household management, factors many Black students pursuing postgraduate degrees must contend with. I advise inquirers to map out the day, the month, and the semester, actually writing down such things as (1) time physically on campus; (2) time spent studying per course; (3) sleep/rest time; (4) personal fun time; (5) family and friends time; (6) do nothing time; and (7) nondiscretionary time, that is, employment. If after mapping out the day hour by hour there still exist free hours in a twenty-four-hour period, one of two things is true. You have miscalculated your day, or you are not spending enough time in one or more areas. The thing to realize is that you will not have enough time to do it all, so you must carefully craft a plan of success. The prospective student should create success icons and enjoy small increments of success to achieve the stated goal(s). Reducing to writing what you expect to accomplish that day is one way to create a success icon and an important first step to succeeding on any particular day. Success should be measured in the smallest increment possible in order to reap the "good feeling" benefits of a job well done. These feelings will become invaluable when inevitably the bottom falls out from under you and stress and fear of failure encroaches. I'll revisit this issue in the "Cutting out the Fat" section.

FINDING A MENTOR

The proverb "seek and ye shall find" should be the guiding principle here because it is the rare mentor indeed who will go out on a pilgrimage to find a mentee. There is no better teacher than experience, and a strong surety of success is imitating the success of others that have gone before you. Therefore, having a mentor is crucial to the Black graduate student. You should try to find a mentor with similar circumstances as your own, one who faced the same or similar obstacles, one willing to share the incremental successes with you, and most importantly, one you can count on during the inevitable crisis.

ACADEMIC ABILITY

Know your own personal skills and abilities. Your area of study may not be tailored to your true desires. In my law school class, there was a fellow from Florida who left medical school to pursue a law degree. He was cut after the first year. He went back to Florida to complete medical school and his residency. I spoke with him before he left, and he said he wanted to do something different because his father is a doctor and he has a sibling who is a physician. In the end, he stated that law was just not his cup of tea. Our academic success is tied to our interests in a particular area. If you don't have at least a smoldering interest in the area you have chosen to study, consider getting out or not pursuing it at all.

EMPLOYER MANAGEMENT ("THE BOSS")

If you work while attending school, this area is crucial; know your boss. If the boss is an impediment to success, then you will likely fail in school, at work, or both. If you are a boss as well, your subordinates must be supportive in order for you to be successful. During my first year of law school, my boss and I had a parting of the ways to such an extent that I nearly dropped out. It took a frantic all-out effort on my part to mend the relationship and gain his support or I was sure to flounder. Luckily during this time, my subordinates were supportive. Make no mistake, if I had failed in mending the relationship between my boss and me, law school would still be a dream. Meet with your employer and/or subordinates and have an open dialogue about what you are trying to accomplish. They should be your allies, and you should point out ways that your education will assist the unit, the individuals assigned to it, and ultimately the entire organization.

CUTTING OUT THE FAT/AVOIDING ACTS OF FUTILITY

This is really a subsection on time management, but it is placed in a separate category because I believe it is uniquely important. In law school, it seems that each class is structured as if it is the only class you have. The assignments are voluminous, and you begin to feel that the professors forget that you have four or five other courses to prepare for. The successful candidate must realize what is important and what isn't. We fondly referred to it in my graduating class as where to take an "L" (loss) in order to get the JD. The law school I attended has a very high first-year attrition rate for sub-par academic performance. To avoid the first year "harpoon," students had to become adept at cutting out the fat. Part of completing any rigorous academic program requires not only academic skill but the ability to get through the maze as well. The successful candidate must get to know the professors, the political workings of the school, and so on. I'll sum this up with an example. I challenged a grade I'd received on a quarterly exam, and during the course of our conversation the professor became agitated and proceeded to berate and curse me in front of other students and faculty. Later that day, I requested a meeting with the professor and advised him of his violation of the law and that repeated violation would result in my filing charges for disorderly conduct/abusive language—not a smart maneuver! Up to this point in time, only a close group of friends even knew that I was a police officer. After this incident more people knew, and I could not afford to take an "L" in this class. This occurred during what was for me the most rigorous academic semester in law school. Well, to say the least, the professor by the stroke of the pen established where the power was. Again, I went on a frantic crusade to mend the relationship; by second semester we were playing golf together. It is not enough to be academically gifted; you must visit the school and do some reconnaissance on the professors and their inner workings. Adapt your approach to success to include the loss of little battles to get to the ultimate prize: matriculation. Above all, don't get caught up in "acts of futility," the busy, mundane kind of stuff that yields little or no real benefit in the end. Success should always be measured in increments and according to the stated goals. Acts of futility, although different for each individual, drain precious time and resources. For example, joining an organization on campus may be a blessing if it moves you toward your goal(s) via networking, mentoring, and the like; it may be a curse if it requires too many social or organization-centered activities. To illustrate this point, I'll refer to one final example for this category. A fellow law student wanted desperately to graduate on law review, a law school honors program with two methods of acceptance: (1) academically, with grades dictating acceptance, and (2) scholarly excellence, with written articles dictating acceptance. As a 1-L (first year law student) he spent substantial and crucial first-year time developing an article for publication and succeeded in gaining acceptance to law review. He was cut after the second year; he could not recover from the first-year academic sacrifices made to do a great article, one of only two such souls. What good will a label of scholarly excellence do you if you never matriculate? Do not engage in acts of futility!

REMARKS FROM A MENTEE (ALAINA KING BENFORD)

The following are remarks from a successful mentee of mine. Alaina King Benford, my cousin, is a Black female law student who will matriculate in May of 2000.

Commitment. Hard work. Discipline. Sacrifice. Focus. Those words became my mantra during my first year of law school. Consequently, I excelled academically as a result of applying those words to my daily living. It has not been easy.

Graduate and professional schools attract the best of the best. I, like so many other students pursuing a graduate or professional degree, enrolled in law school with the hopes of expanding my personal and professional horizons. I knew obtaining success at this level would require a lot more than a half-hearted effort. So, from the first day of classes, I began running the "learning" marathon and in the process, my life has completely changed.

First, I made a personal commitment to do my best. I then shared that commitment with my family and close friends so that they would not only respect my commitment but would also cheer me on from the sidelines when I became distracted, frustrated, and doubtful of my ability to carry on.

Next, I decided to work harder than I had ever worked before. I was determined to not only learn the material but to "own" it as well. In order to do that, I would need to be disciplined and make sacrifices. So, I turned off the television and turned on my mind. I hung up the telephone and picked up the books. I missed the parties but I hit the mark.

Finally, I focused on the finish line. Keeping my eye on the prize helped to filter out all of the distractions that had the potential to break my stride.

SUCCESS IN PRACTICE/MISSION STATEMENT

Several professors have told me that preparing for law school admission and the LSAT is one thing, succeeding in law school another, passing the bar still another, and finally the practice of law yet another; and none is related. How can this be? Having done all of these, I can affirm that those professors were right. My modest goal was to hang out my shingle, open a practice, and simply have it sustain itself until I retired from the police department in a few years. Modest to say the least; any entrepreneurial endeavor should be so fortunate. Thanks in part to the same principles I utilized in law school, my practice is thriving; I am actually trying to cut back on my caseload. It is with great pride that I'm able to say that I completed the final pages of this essay at my private retreat in East Texas, bought and paid for solely with law practice proceeds. It was by no means easy to get started; I didn't turn a dollar for the first eight months my doors were open. If there is one thing to which I attribute the success of my practice, it is this one guiding principle, "Do unto others as they would have you do unto them." Give your clients what they want within the confines of professionalism and the law. Sit on the other side of your desk during downtime and try to see things from your client's perspective. Treating your clients the way you would want to be treated does not take into consideration your client's uniqueness; they may not want to be treated like you at all. Be fair, honest, and dedicated from the heart, and prospective clients will see it and they will come. In addition, every worthwhile endeavor should have a purpose and/or mission. Finally, and most importantly, run all that you do by the universal boss for approval; give deference to God the Almighty.

ESSAY 40

Achieving Your Professional and Career Goals against the Odds

MARGARET WILSON
Major, U.S. Army Reserve

My desire to always learn and "be the best that I can be" started long before I realized that the previous quote is often used by the U.S. Army. After finally deciding on a career in nursing, which made me feel excited, I applied to one of the vocational schools in my area and took the entrance examination.

The first time that I took the examination, I was informed that I had not passed for entrance. When I called the school to inquire about the passing score and my individual score, I was told that scores could not be given out. Determined not to let an examination determine my fate, I waited until the next year and reapplied for the course. I passed the second examination and enrolled in school. It was later into the year when I learned that I had passed the original examination but the school had already reached its quota of students for admission.

The course lasted almost two years. I spent many hours up late at night reviewing patient conditions, preparing care plans, writing medication cards, and also writing three copies of homework assignment. There were approximately ten to fifteen students who started in my class and only seven who graduated. I took state boards in New Orleans and became a licensed practical nurse.

I worked in this position for approximately eight years, being open and receptive to every opportunity made available for me to learn in the field of nursing. During those eight years, I became very aware of the fact that I was outgrowing my level of educational training. I wanted to do more and felt capable and challenged to do more. However, in order to perform more complicated nursing skills and treatments, I needed a higher degree of nursing education.

By this time I had a family with two children. Although the thought of returning to school was exciting, finances and the possibility of having to leave home for school were a concern. I had two coworkers who were single and had returned to school, starting at the community college. For me, this was ideal in that I wouldn't have to leave home. However, it meant that I would be working and going to school along with my duties as a wife and mother. My children were very active in school and extracurricular activities, and I felt that I could not expect them to give up opportunities of their childhood for things that I could and should have done prior to giving birth to them. So after talking more with my coworkers, who advised me to attend the community college for academics, I requested and received a catalog from the university that had a nursing program nearest my home. After receiving the catalog, I enrolled in the community college. Of course, there were entrance examinations and counseling. I knew what courses I needed, so I declined counseling and took the required academic courses, as I felt I was able to handle them because I was working full time. I enrolled for six hours the first semester and gradually increased to nine hours. I attended the community college until I had taken all of the courses that the nursing school would allow to be taken without enrolling into their program. At that time, there were no limitations on academics taken at another college or university prior to enrolling for a degree. So I completed all academics except orientation, which I would have to take at the university where I planned to receive my degree.

By the end of my academic courses, I was divorced with no support. It became necessary for me to work full time to provide for my children and myself. So my goals were revised. I felt that I could graduate with a degree, start working to improve my financial status, and do more in the nursing field while working on higher degrees. I applied for a grant and enrolled in the nursing school to complete academics for the associate degree nursing program.

On receiving the grant, I found out that I needed to be a full-time student in order to receive the full benefits of the grant. Now, because I had enrolled in the nursing school, I needed to have a counselor even though I had already planned courses for the semester. The counselor assisted me with scheduling academics that could lead toward an advanced degree while performing my clinical nursing requirements in the associate degree program. This satisfied my full-time student status and gave me an advantage when I returned to school for the bachelor's degree.

For three years, I worked full time on the 11–7 shift and went to school full time during the day and evening. I also attended school and extracurricular events with my children. When I graduated with my associate's degree in nursing, I didn't know what to do with all of the spare time.

Again while working, I took every advantage to learn as much as possible about new treatments, procedures, and advances in nursing. So I joined the U.S. Army Reserve as a second lieutenant. I was an army nurse assigned to a field hospital called an evacuation hospital. The military has since revised its medical section, and there are no "evac hospitals" now. However, along with the lasting comrade, the advantages afforded me in the army for nursing heightened my desire to learn and do more.

In the reserves, I worked in the examination area of the evac hospital. I also volunteered to assist other military units with procedures such as drawing blood, physical examinations, and other medical duties.

As a young military officer, I also served as a platoon leader. This position started me in the right direction for military leadership training. I also spent time in the field in tentage with my reserve unit. We were required to go out in the field at least once a quarter and also spend two weeks in medical training. Many times those two weeks of medical training were in the field also. Having made the decision on my own, without coercion, to join the army, I took my obligation seriously. I set out again to learn as much as I could in the event that our training became a real-world situation. If I had any doubt about what I was doing and why I was doing it, my chief nurse reinforced my desire with a compliment that she gave me during one of our field duties. She told me that I reminded her of a young officer years ago, always adventurous and seeking information about what's going on in camp. When I asked the chief nurse what happened to the young officer, she smiled and replied, "Oh, she became a colonel and a chief nurse."

Those words of encouragement helped me make up my mind to make a career in the army. I enrolled in the required military leadership classes, which allowed me to qualify for promotion to first lieutenant and to captain. The military offers educational opportunities to its members that are not available to civilians. So after obtaining three letters of recommendation and a letter from my immediate supervisor in the military, I applied for and was granted the opportunity to further my education through the army's Approved Systems Training Plan (STRAP) Program for nurses seeking to further their education. In return, I agreed to give the army two years of service for every year that it provided financial support for my education. Because I had been in the military for about twelve years and I planned to make a twenty-year career of the army, it was not hard for me to agree to this contract. I knew that if I went to school two years and gave the army four years, I would have accomplished two things. I would be closer to my military career goal, and I would have received an educational opportunity that would last me a lifetime, even after I retired from the army.

During the time I was taking courses for my bachelor's degree, I was promoted to major. I also took courses in foreign languages, Spanish in particular, and sign language. Then I sat for the examination and became certified as a medical case manager. Oh, yes, I also took many business courses because at one time business was to be my minor.

The desire that I spoke of at the beginning of this essay has resulted in the following accomplishments. I am a major in the U.S. Army Nurse Corp serving as an army nurse and as an army instructor. I have taught young service members courses that will enable them to qualify and recertify as army medics, and I am currently teaching courses that will allow soldiers to sit for practical nurse board examinations. I have satisfied my obligation to the army for my own personal advanced training and will be eligible for military retirement in a year. However, I am up for promotion to lieutenant colonel, and if I am successful, I will put retirement on hold.

I am also a certified case manager, and I have held the positions of program case manager/coordinator, physician liaison nurse, and assistant clinical director of a rehabilitation unit. I am also the owner of a health-oriented business offering aquatic exercise for clients with arthritis and other degenerative diseases.

Although I have listed my accomplishments already, I do not feel that I am finished. There are still more areas and fields of learning to cover. I just can't stand being stagnant when it comes to learning new things. I become uncomfortable and feel that I'm missing something if I am not gaining knowledge about something or someone. Remember that old cliché that our parents always told us, "You're never to old to learn"? I honestly believe that. There are so many areas yet to be tapped into. Well, I'm off to meet another challenge. This time, I think in investments. Please! Come and join me. Or better yet, surpass me.

PART III

HOW CONTEMPORARY STUDENTS IN GRADUATE AND PROFESSIONAL SCHOOL ARE SUCCEEDING

Surviving in Graduate School Even If You Have a Writing Problem

MAYSA AKBAR

Doctoral Candidate, Clinical Psychology, Saint Louis University

As a doctoral candidate in clinical psychology, writing, instead of the development of clinical skills, became the most difficult part of my graduate career. This essay describes the origin of my difficulties and my initial reaction to it. I discuss the steps that I took to cope with the situation and address the difficulties I encountered. I provide suggestions drawn from my own experiences, which may be of assistance to other students of African descent confronting similar circumstances.

My academic career began in the public school system in the inner city of New York. Budgetary constraints, lack of resources, and inadequate instruction plagued most of my early educational opportunities. Nonetheless, I was nominated and accepted into the advanced placement (AP) English class at my high school. While I did not receive AP credit, I received an "A" in the course. In my mind, the difficulty was not with English or writing, but with taking standardized tests.

When I graduated with honors as class president, I was faced with the reality that fewer than 20 percent of graduates from my high school pursued higher learning opportunities. I was one of the fortunate students granted the opportunity to attend state university, which signified a way out of the inner city. I was the first person in my family to attend a four-year college. As a minority in a predominantly White university, I struggled academically because of the multiple-choice test format used in most undergraduate psychology courses. I soon discovered that my strength was in my ability to write (creatively).

While in college I developed a profound love for working with children, specifically because during my childhood key individuals assisted in my growth and contributed to my development. Providing support, encouragement, and therapeutic understanding were precisely the interventions I wanted to provide for others—hence my decision to major in psychology and minor in education and women's studies. As a sophomore, I was one of thirty students chosen to teach the Introduction to Women's Studies course. I was nominated for several honor societies, began the first psychological association for minority students, and often received the student of excellence award. I graduated cum laude from the university and gave the commencement speech, which I wrote, for my graduating class.

Promptly after graduation I began my graduate career. I went to a historically Black university and majored in community psychology. Academically, most of the course work entailed writing papers and essay exams. I wrote several psychological reports and completed a thesis. During this time I was very comfortable with my writing and academic skills. My professors and instructors provided limited feedback on my written work. Thus my perception that my problem was taking standardized or multiple-choice tests continued.

After receiving my master's, I decided to pursue a doctorate at a predominantly White private institution. After years of academic success, critique of my writing began. In fact, I was identified in the program as a "problem writer." During my first-semester, first-year evaluation, my adviser informed me that a professor had commented that the "flow" of my writing could improve. I was not initially upset by this feedback but instinctively knew that my writing would be closely scrutinized from this point on. This is precisely what occurred.

The next semester I had a paper due in my adviser's class, which I took to the university's Graduate Writing Center several times. I was told that the grammar was correct and that the content was appropriate given the guidelines provided. When the paper was returned, I received a 9 out of 10 for the content but a 6 out of 10 for the writing. Ironically, the recommendation was that I should consult the writing lab. My first perceptions that I would be singled out for scrutiny were confirmed. Emotionally I felt that no matter what I produced, it would not be good enough. As I processed the feedback, I began to feel defeated, I questioned my abilities, and my self-esteem lowered. I felt that it did not matter that I worked diligently and took the extra step of going to the writing lab; I could not be successful in this environment.

I was confronted with several questions that I would have to answer if I were to survive and complete my dream of obtaining a Ph.D. in psychology. I had to determine whether there were problems with my writing or whether this was "perceptual bias," as it is termed in the social psychology literature. If there was perceptual bias operating, how could I address this issue? If it was my writing, what was wrong, how could I correct it, and why was I discovering it now?

Intuitively, I decided to return to the writing lab and discuss the feedback with the writing assistant. The assistant provided feedback on the editing suggestions made by the instructor and concluded that there were no errors of grammar or content, rather issues of style. At that point, I decided to discuss the issue with the instructor providing the feedback. I indicated that prior to submitting the final draft of my paper, I had frequently visited the writing lab. She was shocked to discover that her recommendation had not worked. She noted that the writing lab was probably not familiar with the writing criteria in psychology and suggested that I take a writing course in the English department. There was no guarantee that the instructor in the English department would be any more familiar with psychological writing than the Writing Center personnel. Thus, my dilemma remained.

After consulting with peers and professionals in the discipline, I formulated several steps to prevent this situation from recurring. First, I decided that I would have to improve my own editing skills and practices. I no longer submit any written work without editing a hard copy, and I resist the temptation to edit on the computer. Second, I ask a peer, colleague, or professional in my discipline to edit all my written work. Third, I requested precise clarification of critiques regarding my written work. I use this information to gain insight into the types of stylistic issues I am likely to encounter as I proceed in the field. Finally, I inquire about reviewing and resubmitting my work to obtain a higher grade. I have realized that the deficits in my early educational background are likely implicated in the critiques I now receive. Yet I have also learned that they do not represent an insurmountable obstacle. My ultimate goal is to learn from each experience.

My message to my fellow graduate students is to accept feedback, but with a caveat: you cannot give up, internalize, or become consumed with negativity. You must deliberately evaluate the information and messages received, obtaining feedback and input from those more neutral and more experienced. The input and feedback you seek should be specific to your discipline. It is important to understand that the styles and requirements for writing vary by discipline. Those outside of your field may be unaware of and unfamiliar with the standards by which your work will be judged and therefore unable to assist you in identifying weaknesses. Finally, you must know yourself and be confident in your abilities. This will allow you to accept feedback and perceive it as an opportunity for growth, whether or not it was an area you originally perceived as a limitation.

"A" Is for Average

On Being an Average Medical Student

CAMILLE T. CADE
Medical Student, Pediatric Anesthesia,
University of Maryland School of Medicine

When I walked into the University of Maryland auditorium for orientation on that first day of medical school, numerous thoughts and questions danced through my mind. Would I make any real friends? Would these strangers whom I would soon call classmates and colleagues attempt to undermine me in class for a few extra points with our instructors? Would these same classmates turn into my professional network system after medical school? Undoubtedly, these were important questions, which were all ultimately answered. However, more interesting than the questions I asked myself were the statements—no, proclamations—that I had made to myself prior to even arriving at the university. Those proclamations helped me to make it through that first day. I thought, since I was smart and had faced no overwhelming academic challenges during my undergraduate experience, it was understood, at least by me, that I would be stellar—and lead the class. Further, I could never have any academic difficulty, because I was smart—and that was that. I would obviously make all As and honors in my coursework, and in my free time (which would be copious) I might even consider getting a part-time job. I would do community service and continue to be the overly committed, high-functioning individual that I had been for the past four years at my Alma Mater. These were my assumptions—but now I realize my fantasies. That first day was both frightening and invigorating at the same time. My confidence was strong and fierce based on my undergraduate experience. Yet I was still afraid of what the future held for me and desperately sought an acceptance and a feeling of belonging that I had taken for granted previously in college and with my family.

And so began the next chapter of my life. Now that I look back on that day, everyone in the class probably had similar feelings and questions. But the only person's feelings and thoughts I was acutely and finely in tune with were my own. As I began taking classes, I quickly developed several acquaintances, began my "old faithful" study routine, and was off. Everything was moving along smoothly—until the first test. I was still at the top until that examination. That was the first exposure I had to reality, or at least what would be my reality for the next two years. My fantasies were permanently destroyed with that first exam, and I was left with only the realization that I would have to work harder than I had ever imagined in the past just to be average. This idea, that I could not afford to take anything for granted, including my intelligence or my past experience of being a top student, was a difficult concept to grasp. However, in time, I came to embrace it and use it for motivation throughout the next two years of my journey through medical school. This precept was critical to my development as a physician, and more important, as a young, upwardly mobile, and ambitious Black woman in America. I would have to work hard at everything in order to be average and acceptable. I would have to work harder than almost everyone else to be successful, and so I did.

All who apply and are admitted to medical school undoubtedly have been told that they are smart. There are probably not too many students who have been called average all of their lives applying to medical school. Medical school applicants have excelled in most projects that they have undertaken and have experienced very few, if any, setbacks or failures. When preparing to enter medical school, one must also prepare to be surrounded by a class full of individuals who are just as exceptional. All of these remarkable individuals have to come to the realization, as I did, that they are now just average in comparison with their classmates. There is nothing wrong with being average in this crowd of high achievers. It helps one to step up to the plate and meet the challenge of the many tests ahead. These tests are meant not only to evaluate your knowledge, but also to assess your values and everything else that you hold dear. You learn quickly to prioritize your day and your life.

As a third-year medical student looking back over and reflecting on my past two years, I am pleased by all that I was able to accomplish over those first two years through God's grace. There were many victories, as well as many defeats. I never made it into the top 10 percent of my class; however, I believe that I still did pretty well for myself. I came to think of myself differently after that first test. Realizing that I was really no smarter than most of my other classmates, I decided to work hard to make the largest possible impact on my community as a medical student. I decided that this meant that I should do well in medical school. By "well," I mean putting forth 100 percent effort in everything. Doing well also entailed giving back to those who needed me through community service, and encouraging others by telling my story. I share my experiences with others when they begin to lose their confidence and sense of self when they hit the hard reality that they are not at the top of the class like they were in undergraduate college. I explain that they are still intellectuals and can achieve success even after an academic defeat. Most important, my relationships with God, my family, and friends have been strengthened during my matriculation in medical school. I now know that through these not-so-secret weapons, and with the knowledge and confidence that I brought to medical school, I can face any difficult situation in my future. I know that ultimately I will be successful in my career field, and most important, this average medical student will achieve victory in life.

On Being a Great Student

NICOLE D. COLLIER
Master's Candidate, Elementary Education, Florida State University

Are great students born or made? I believe we can all be great students. A great student is one who exhibits the qualities of a good student *and* knows how to be a good learner. There is a very clear difference between being a good student and being a good learner, and being truly successful academically and beyond rests in the integration of those two concepts.

Admittedly, I had a head start in the academic realm. I had two parents who were both college-educated and provided me with positive learning experiences at a very young age. One loved words and the other loved numbers, and soon enough, I loved them both. I took initiative to learn new things simply because they interested me. Reading and writing were probably my two favorite pastimes. But I also enjoyed a good bike ride through the neighborhood or a short footrace in the heat of the day.

As I got older, I still had support from home, but I began to take more responsibility for my own learning. I did pretty well academically in middle school, and I also participated in cheerleading, band, and regular preteen stuff like hanging out at the mall. I believed then, as I do now, that part of academic success comes from activities done outside of the academic setting.

In high school, I ended up ranking comfortably in the top five of my graduating class. Success in high school was due to continued interest in learning, innovative teachers, and continued participation in extracurricular activities. I didn't usually look at my homework as a chore, but as an activity to keep me from being bored. It was more independent practice than anything else, but I found enjoyment in getting the answers right. I liked doing well, being successful, making As. That's what drove me to do it—I *liked* doing it. I had support for doing it, but the main impetus came from within. Maybe it was because I was lucky enough to have a good educational foundation, but I always had the motivation to learn—I always saw the value in knowing.

BEING A GOOD STUDENT

But everyone cannot have the same background I did. Everyone does not have the same home environment or the same intrinsic motivation. Even so, being a great student is still within reach. The first step to becoming a great student is to be a good one. I finished my bachelor's degree summa cum laude. Is it because I'm a genius? No. It is because I exhibited the qualities of a good student. The most important thing to that end is to *make your education your number one priority.* You cannot have more than one number one priority. Some people think that school and fun can both be number one. Many of those people fail college the first year. Others think that school and a relationship can both be number one. Many of those end up taking classes two and three times because they were spending time with someone while they were supposed to be in class or in the library. Make school your number one priority. Everything else can be tied at number two.

My definition of a good student involves three additional tenets: (1) Go to every class on time, meaning anywhere from five to fifteen minutes early. (2) Sit as close as possible to the front in every class, or in the place you feel affords you the fewest distractions and the best view. (3) Finish all assignments on time, following all directions exactly as given. Finish early if possible.

Be punctual. By the time the professor is ready to begin class, you should be, too. Cease walking in just as he or she is starting, picking your seat from those that are left over, and risking not being able to see or hear what is going on. While you are digging through your bag and pulling out paper and pen for notes, you're already missing (or have missed) the beginning of the lecture. Class then becomes a game of catch-up. It's stressful and unnecessary. And worst of all, it's unproductive. Should you be the lone nerd in your classes? No. Draft a friend (preferably in the same major) to brave the world of "good studentship." There were small groups of us who ate breakfast together so we could all walk to our classes together—and pick out our seats in the front row (center). Believe it or not, being in class early meant more time for gossip anyway!

As for homework, always write down all details of the assignment and always turn it in on time—early if possible. The most complex, complicated, and lengthy assignments are the ones you should start on as soon as possible. That way you are not waiting until the last minute. This is crucial, and you will have time to turn it in for comments and feedback from the instructor. And if it's good, you're done! And if it isn't, you don't have to go reinvent the wheel, since you know exactly what needs to be done. It's a win-win situation!

Yes, I was that student everyone hated. Most of my classmates were stressed about doing this, that, and the other, and there I was—done! And the great thing is, I had plenty of time to party. All work and no play makes Nicole a dull girl. I had time to play cards with my friends, attend the frat parties every Friday and Saturday, and become an active participant in a sorority. I also had plenty of time to participate in extracurricular activities, which continued to be just as important as the academics.

Is all of this going to guarantee you straight As? No, but you will certainly be a more likely candidate. Are grades necessarily an accurate reflection of knowledge? No. I will be the first to tell you that success for many undergraduates (depending on their major) is based in appearances (neat, timely homework, good attendance, meaningful class participation, etc.). You won't remember half the things you memorize for tests. The knowledge you will truly retain is only that which you deem relevant. Did I learn anything while pursuing my undergraduate degree? Yes! But a lot of it came from—I cannot stress this enough—extracurricular activities. Those activities don't really have anything to do with graduation requirements, but they do give you the opportunity to get to know yourself and others better, and they give you the chance to use your new knowledge outside of the classroom. The application of knowledge is critical to a deeper understanding. Memorization and regurgitation can be a first step but certainly should not be the last.

ORGANIZE AND PRIORITIZE

After you've made school your number one priority and you've learned to deal with being on time and sitting in your new seat, you still have the issue of homework. The key here is time management and organization. Some people study for hours and hours nonstop. Many times they study for hours because they have waited until the last minute in the first place—not necessarily because it's difficult material to master (this does not apply across the board, but often). For Monday-Wednesday-Friday classes, do your homework Monday night; however, do not wait until midnight. Then do it on Wednesday and on Friday when classes meet again. Don't wait until Monday morning at 2 A.M. to squeeze it all in. If you do, you will end up rushing, and you will not do your best, you will not get a full night's rest and you will be sluggish or sleepy Monday morning. This may cause you to run late for class, creating a pattern.

Time management is not just about setting a schedule, though. It's sticking to it as well. Change it when necessary, but not because you have procrastinated. Here's a tip: build in chill time! For every forty-five minutes of work you do, take ten minutes to talk and five minutes to use the bathroom or get a snack. Or work for an hour and a half and take a twenty-minute break or whatever works for you. Legislate breaks. That makes sticking to your schedule more reasonable. If you're on a roll, keep working, but don't be afraid to take a little down time when you need it. But if you do your homework all along, you're not pulling marathon sessions, so it becomes infinitely more manageable. You're more relaxed, you have more free time ... you're being a good student.

BEING A GOOD LEARNER

I was a good student all the way through college, but I did not find the key to being a good learner, hence a great student, until I began graduate school. I think students in grad school have a serious advantage because they are more mature and have a more clearly defined sense of direction and commitment to a field. Additionally, the busy work of the undergraduate is replaced by rigorous reading and discussion. My field is education. Some of the things herein will apply more directly to education majors, but many are valuable for students in all disciplines.

Being a good student is the easy part. More than anything else, it requires devising routines and sticking to them. Being a good learner, however, involves more thought and deeper reflection. While being a good student involves punctuality, proper seating in class, and commitment to excellence, being a good learner also requires you to absorb and reflect upon the knowledge, applying it in a new way, and adding it to your store of information. The key to being an effective learner is knowing what you want to accomplish. It is important to have a "big picture" in mind. What type of educator do you wish to be? What do you want your students to learn? You should develop a teaching philosophy to use as a road map for your learning. Ask yourself what type of change would you like to effect? Or what is it about the status quo you think is effective? What works and how can you build upon that to make it better? The answers to these questions help guide your learning. All of the information you acquire should be applied toward those answers.

For instance, one of my major goals is for my students to be problem solvers. In today's information age, it simply is not enough to memorize and regurgitate facts. The amount of information and new knowledge available increases exponentially daily, even hourly in some instances. However, if my students are problem solvers, they know how to determine the information they need, where to locate it, and how to apply it. Therefore, when we discuss things in class, or as I take notes, I ask myself, how can I use this information toward helping my students become problem solvers? How is this information related to my philosophy of teaching? When given reading assignments, don't just read the material and take notes, but actually take time to reflect and see how this can fit into your philosophy, into your road map, into your goals.

Good learners do what is necessary to make sure they have a clear understanding of the knowledge and how (and in some cases if) it fits in with their belief systems. To that end, it is imperative to take time to discuss various issues with your peers. This discussion can help you solidify your thoughts on a variety of topics, or investigate viewpoints you may otherwise not have considered. There are countless theories, strategies, and materials out there. It is impossible to believe in them all, as many of them are in direct conflict with each other. It is impractical to try them all because there are many ways to get to the same place. How can you begin to sort through this maze of information? By discussing it with your peers. Challenge their beliefs and defend yours and vice versa.

Good learners don't just take information and store it haphazardly. They file it carefully in their mental file cabinets, making sure they know exactly where to find it. And when necessary, they make sure they move it, so that the new knowledge is always readily accessible—actually connected—to prior knowledge. To further that concept, good learners see the connectivity of the world, meaning they readily see the connections between various facts and ideas. Learning to see connections will make it easier for you to file new information as you see the relevance in seemingly unconnected ideas. It will help you look at a problem from a fresh perspective, giving you the opportunity to generate new knowledge—the ultimate goal of many who pursue graduate degrees.

Once you are exhibiting the qualities of a good learner, you begin to truly appreciate the knowledge you acquire for what it is—a new lens through which you view life.

PUTTING IT ALL TOGETHER

Being a great student means successfully merging the qualities of a good student with those of a good learner. Good students make education their number one priority, are mentally and physically prepared for class, and manage their time effectively. Good learners create mental road maps, take time to reflect, and make connections between ideas. Learning to do all of these things in concert with each other will not only help you be a great student academically, but also help you be a great student of life.

Adapting to Life as Graduate Students

Getting Up to Speed on Information Technology

FELICIA DOSWELL, HOPE HARLEY, TRACY LEWIS, AND CHERYL SEALS
Doctoral Candidates, Computer Science, Virginia Polytechnic Institute and State University

GLENDA SCALES
Assistant Dean of Distance Learning, Virginia Polytechnic Institute and State University

Two keys for success in graduate school are becoming information literate and improving communication skills. To sharpen your level of information literacy, there are several skills you should acquire. All graduate students should have good competency in the use of educationally related software tools, like word processors, presentation software, spreadsheets, and the Internet. As the Internet continues to play an ever-increasing role in our lives, new graduate students should quickly familiarize themselves with the basics of using and searching for information on the World Wide Web (WWW). Indeed, many professors use the WWW to disseminate class notes, homework, and announcements to their students. At some point in your academic program, you may even take a course offered completely on line. A growing number of universities are offering this option, known as distance education, to their students.

You should also be comfortable with accessing information at your school library. As a graduate student, you will share much more of the responsibility for your learning. Familiarize yourself with the journals and periodicals in your research area, and find out if your library maintains current subscriptions to them. Your library may participate in an interlibrary loan program, making it possible to access the lending materials of a consortium of libraries. Many university libraries now have their card catalogs available on line, making it even easier to find materials on a given topic anytime of the day or night.

Your success as a graduate student will ultimately depend upon not only your ability to find information, but also your abilities in communicating that information to others. Whether oral or written, good communication skills are a necessary asset. Effective communication is required if you are to share your research ideas with the larger community of scientists in your area. Take advantage of opportunities to submit papers to conferences, journals, and the like. Your submissions may not always be accepted, but the reviewers often provide valuable feedback on both the content and the writing style of your work.

We began this brief journey with keys to success that we think all graduate students should possess. Next, we will share some initial experiences of a new student as she begins her graduate studies. We then share some resources identified by other graduate students here at Virginia Tech that have made their academic lives a bit easier. Finally, we will share some personal experiences from our own tenure in graduate school.

SCENARIO ONE

The Life of a New Graduate:
How One Graduate Got Connected

Hi, I'm Sandy. When I began looking for a place to spend the next four years, I did a lot of on-line investigation. I didn't have the money to travel to all the schools I was interested in. I looked at the campuses on line and explored the events and my program at each school that I was seriously considering. I even applied to these schools on line. I used the following site to get college applications: http://www.collegequest.com/cgi-bin/ndCGI/CollegeQuest/pgGateway, http://www.collegelink.com/html/index.htm, and http://apply.embark.com. These sites also provided helpful information about financial aid. After doing a careful investigation and getting financial support, I was off to graduate school!

Now I'm a new graduate student at Virginia Tech. I have met with my adviser and have completed on-line registration for my classes. I don't know anyone and have no idea where anything is, but this will be an exciting challenge. By buying my textbooks early, I found really great discounts on used books. There are even some great places on line for textbooks. Try www.Varsity-Books.com, www.bookswap.com, and www.textbooks.com. Most of these services give students a big discount because they cut out the go-between.

Once I had my textbooks, I needed the proper tools to get my work done. Nowadays, that means having ready access to a computer. Investigate the computer resources available to students in your department. You may be required to buy your own computer. Virginia Tech gives the minimal requirements for student computers at http://www.compreq.vt.edu/specs. html. With this knowledge, I could get exactly what I needed without paying for a lot of frills. Find out if there are loan programs available to assist students in purchasing a computer. Make sure you have a network interface card or ethernet card. This software device enables your computer to work with your school's computer network. They are not always included with new machines.

Once my computer was up and running, I made sure the computer came with a suite of software that would meet all my basic computing needs (e.g., Microsoft Office or Corel Suite). This software should include at minimum a word processor and spreadsheet software. The final component to make my computer complete was to make sure that a Web browser and Web page creation tools were included with my software package. With most computers some standard browser is included (e.g., Netscape Navigator or Internet Explorer).

Next I had to find out how to get connected to the Internet. There were two options available: ethernet or modem. Luckily, my apartment had an ethernet connection, which made logging in to school a breeze. I just picked up the software in the school's bookstore, called up the local phone company, and got connected.

Now I'm ready to get cracking this semester. With my computer I can explore the Web, and my professor has our class notes, announcements, assignments, and old class notes on line. This is really helpful. I even looked at a couple of other schools that have similar classes, and they have more examples. This was a great find for me. During my studies and research, I have had several occasions to use the Internet for research. I have used it to find information, remembering to use a reliable source because some of the information found in cyberspace can be misleading. I also used the Internet to do some on-line surveys to help me collect some data. Well guys, it was nice talking to you, but I have to get back to my homework and research.

My years of graduate school have been very successful, and I owe my success to being a self-starter and a self-motivated learner. I also had to honestly assess my strengths and weaknesses and be resourceful enough to search out things and individuals to help me mitigate my deficiencies. The last task for me at Tech is to complete an electronic thesis and dissertation. With the skills that I learned while here it will be a piece of cake. Now am I ready to enter the job market very well prepared, and I will set up an electronic portfolio on my Web page that consists of a resume, publications, research, and the like. I used on-line tutorials to help me set up my Web pages and learn html (see http://www.vt.edu/vt98/featured/compute.html). This experience has taught me that getting up to speed on the information superhighway and being a self-motivated learner will help me be successful in graduate school.

In our efforts to identify the technology needs of graduate students, we posed questions to the body of the Virginia Tech Black Graduate Student Organization (BGSO). We will summarize the statements of the group. We received responses from graduate students both old and new, in both master's and Ph.D. programs.

1. Describe a key learning experience related to technology. What information or technique did you discover that saved you time and energy?

In designing Web pages for a class, on-line html tutorial session helped me learn some basic html language. Learning the Microsoft suite (software) enabled me to do word processing, spreadsheets, and PowerPoint presentations. Some students liked using VTnet modem pool, which is cheaper than industry alternatives. Netforum provided a forum for threaded discussions to occur between and among classmates and groups when working on projects. This saves time with respect to class, as we could read the responses of others prior to coming to class, thus devoting class time to discussion of ideas (as opposed to having to hear them and then discuss them). It also saved a lot of time when working with groups, because in many cases we could use Netforum in lieu of actually coming together, which can be a coordination nightmare for a graduate student. Another student really liked e-mail with Eudora. This software package was very prevalent on campus. He also enjoyed participating in the "Sharing the Knowledge," a BGSO-sponsored series on word processing, presentation, and Web software. This really helped him make the technological transition from undergraduate to graduate school at Virginia Tech.

2. What sorts of technology do you utilize to complete your assignments?

Some of the technology used for assignments are the following:

(a) Software: Microsoft suite (Word, Excel, Access, PowerPoint), Claris, Page-Maker, and PhotoShop
(b) Statistical analysis packages: MiniTab, SAS
(c) Superhighway: WWW, Internet, library databases, e-mail, Eudora, Netscape
(d) Equipment: scanner, digital camera

3. Have you had any particularly interesting experiences, positive or negative, on the Information Superhighway? Please explain.

Most of the experiences of the group were positive, with a warning to be careful; not everything you read is true. There were two negative comments expressed, that some e-mail services leave your mail open for viewing in the history and too much forwarded mail!

4. What essential information would you give to a new graduate student?

If you don't have a computer background, take a class for your own benefit. I recommend that all graduate students get familiar with the technology on campus, whether it's e-mail, SAS, or whatever. There are a lot of good classes available. Subscribe to your school modem pool for Internet access at home instead of the more expensive alternatives. Take advantage of any opportunities you have to learn all you can about technology (this includes attending classes, workshops, and seminars). This will not only help you as a student but make you more marketable in your profession and career.

5. Is there any other information about your graduate experience that you would like to share?

Words of wisdom: know thyself, be disciplined, seek and share the knowledge; get a network of friends to share your college experience. A mentor would be helpful. One student said, "I am having a great experience at Tech because I have exposed myself to a variety of people and experiences. All will be beneficial when I get a faculty position at a major research institution."

PEARLS OF WISDOM AND REFLECTIONS FROM THE AUTHORS

The final section of this work is a bit more personal. Our goal is to provide our readers with some sense of the life-changing experiences we have encountered while in graduate school. We believe these brief excerpts are similar to what many graduate students encounter. Graduate school provides you the opportunity to stretch yourself in ways you may not have imagined. You will grow not only educationally but also spiritually and emotionally. The graduate school experience opens doors of opportunity that might otherwise be closed. Don't take these opportunities lightly! We should appreciate and take advantage of each one. We are, after all, a part of W. E. B. Du Bois's notion of "the talented tenth." Higher education should not be taken for granted, for it is a privilege, not a right.

PEARL ONE

As a new graduate student, you may feel overpowered by the task in front of you—that of completing a thesis or dissertation. Initially your direction will be quite clear. You must first complete required course work. Depending on your background, you may need extra materials in some areas. Don't be afraid to go to your professors for assistance. They will refer you to other references and sources of help.

By all means, try to form a study group. The thought of staying up all night to finish an assignment may not sound appealing, but it's not so bad when you have the company of others. During the first three semesters of my graduate studies, I spent many, many hours toiling through the night. Fortunately, I was not alone. My study partners and I worked diligently, pausing to take breaks now and then. Sometimes our breaks just meant a brisk walk outside in the night air or a trip to the soda machine. Other times, we would take a trip to the local Wal-Mart. Taking a break from a particularly complex problem often enabled me to see the problem in a new light upon my return. My friends and I pulled many all-nighters. As I look back on those experiences, I can't help but smile. Yes, we thought we were suffering then, but we were also developing bonds of friendship that I will treasure for the rest of my life. So, work hard. During your breaks, take some time to get to know your partners. You'll be glad you did.

In the computer science department here at Virginia Tech, Ph.D. students are required to successfully complete a qualifying examination. Two three-hour sessions of questions dealing with algorithms, programming languages, and operating systems determine your worthiness to pursue further research. We are allowed to sit for the exam twice. I failed on my first attempt. I was really not shaken by this failure. My weaknesses were revealed. I knew what I had to concentrate and focus on for the next time. My second attempt at the exam was successful. Everyone said it would be all downhill from there. That was not the total truth.

After you have completed your course work, the real work begins. If you don't already have an area and topic in mind, now's the time to talk to professors and attend research group meetings. Some professors will have ideas already in mind for dissertation work. This can be a definite plus. It will cut down on the amount of time you spend searching for a topic. In addition, you don't have to convince someone to be interested in your work. It is very important that your adviser be interested in your work. Let me reiterate that last thought. It is very important that your adviser have an interest in your work. Your adviser will be your key ally in helping you define and refine your research ideas.

In the early stages of your research, you may feel overwhelmed by the amount of reading you'll have to do to familiarize yourself with the literature in your chosen area. Your adviser will probably provide you with pointers to the classic papers in your area. As you read, begin a research journal to keep track of your thoughts and ideas, other references you need to find, and so on. You will also have to develop a bibliography sooner or later, so you may as well add your references to it while they are freshest in your mind. It's okay if a paper or article does not make sense the first time (or maybe even the second time!) you read it. I find it helpful to first glance at the summary and conclusions. Then I read the entire paper, rereading sections as necessary. Beginning with the end in mind makes it a lot easier for me to understand and digest the concepts and ideas being discussed. After reading a paper, I try to summarize the main ideas in a few sentences. If this is difficult, then I probably need to reread the paper again.

During this phase, many graduate students suffer from feelings of anxiety, guilt, and even boredom. Don't worry, these feelings are all normal! What you must do is find a way to overcome these feelings and continue toward your goal. Instead of comparing your work to that of others, establish a network of fellow graduate students whom you feel comfortable talking to and sharing ideas with. When you do hit an obstacle or feel otherwise lost, talk to your adviser about possible next steps. Keep in mind that if you knew everything necessary to get a graduate degree in your field, you'd have one already! You should feel comfortable in admitting to your adviser that you are having problems. Your adviser is not a mind reader and cannot provide assistance if he or she is unaware of your problems.

Personally, I found it difficult to maintain a sense of balance in my life. Graduate students who are married may feel guilty about not spending quality time with their spouses and families. In my case, my husband and I were also separated by physical distance. He resides in Greensboro, North Carolina. His travel schedule and my all-nighters in the lab meant that occasionally several days passed between our conversations. There was even a six-week period during my qualifier preparation when we had little or no communication. Understand that you will have to sacrifice time with your family to be successful in graduate school. You will need the support of your loved ones. Be sure to discuss the ramifications of your decision to attend grad school well in advance, so everyone has time to become adjusted.

Graduate student life can also be detrimental to the waistline. Staying up until the wee hours of the night, eating junk food, and then crashing for a few hours before class will eventually result in added pounds. Try munching on fresh fruit and vegetables instead of pizza and Coke. Better yet, incorporate some sort of exercise program into your daily routine. Finding time for exercise can be hard, but it's also an excellent way to relieve stress and give your mind a chance to focus on less intellectual issues. At the very least, park a little farther away than usual or take the stairs instead of the elevator.

All in all, my graduate experiences have been pleasant. Although I would not like to repeat them, I must admit that I have learned a lot, and not just about computer science. I have grown tremendously as a person. Graduate school will stretch you in ways you may not have imagined. Hang on and enjoy the ride!

PEARL TWO

The most important resources needed while attending graduate school are computer technology, time management, a useful adviser, and fellow graduate students. My graduate experience is from the viewpoint of a graduate student who returned to school after working for four years. I am currently working on a Ph.D. in computer science. In addition to being a graduate student, I also have the title of wife and mother to a one-year-old. I started school where I was working near the campus, and my husband was located two hundred miles away. During that period of time I was the typical graduate student (except for the marital status), where I would be on campus all day. However, after finishing my course work and subsequently having a child, my resource needs changed, so that I needed to work at home more. This required a computer and Internet access, which I already had available. I have recently moved to where my husband resides, which has resulted in a stronger dependence on computer technology. The computer technology is crucial for maintaining contact if you happen to be some distance from campus and your adviser.

Ironically, the items I listed as important are the things that were beneficial before the lifestyle changes. The next couple of paragraphs will further explain the items I listed as significant.

Computer Technology

Computers are an integral part of attending graduate school. Students must have access to the necessary technology at work or at home, including hardware (either UNIX, IBM compatible, or Macintosh personal computers), software, and network connectivity. As a graduate student, you are expected to know how to compose and print a research paper with appropriate figures and tables using standard word processing software. If you own a computer, you should know how to install it, load software onto it, and use the modem. In addition, the following skills should be acquired before you begin your degree program.

1. Basic computer systems knowledge. This means that you can do such tasks as save to a floppy disk, find a file, create a directory or folder, and start a program.

2. Information retrieval skills. You need the ability to use the on-line catalog and common bibliographic databases found in many libraries in order to find research material.

3. Internet information skills. Most likely your department or school will have a lab where you will have access (hopefully twenty-four hours a day), and this lab should allow access to the Internet. However, to be able to work from home, you need a modem on your computer and you must obtain Internet access, either through your school or an Internet service provider. With this capability, you should be able to transfer files, connect to other computers via telnet, and find information on the Web.

4. E-mail and bulletin board skills. You should know how to use e-mail and electronic bulletin boards. Most graduate students use their e-mail and Internet access for personal and research activities. They keep up with friends and family through e-mail. They perform research activities using Internet search engines and other research tools available. In addition, professional discussion lists provide the opportunity to receive job postings, notices of conferences, and calls for papers.

5. Multimedia skills. If you are a graduate teaching assistant, you may have the opportunity to use the multimedia technology available in the classrooms. This technology includes a VCR, overhead projector, and computer for showing film clips or displaying slides or PowerPoint presentations. Ph.D. candidates and other students who are required to do presentations will need these skills as well.

Time Management

In order to be successful as a graduate student, you must manage your time properly. Keep the following things in mind when budgeting time.

1. In addition to your weekly study hours, include time to do chores (such as laundry and grocery shopping) and run errands (doctor visits, taking care of children). Also, budget time for departmental or group meetings, exercise, and office hours.

2. Plan for things that are periodically scheduled such as monthly class reports, conference or journal papers, conference dates, and qualifying or comprehensive exams required by many degree programs.

3. Be aware of due dates, especially at the end of the semester. You do not want to have four reports due the same week that you have three exams.

4. Plan for the unexpected items such as illness or family emergencies. You will most likely experience at least one illness and family crisis during your graduate school experience. How will you handle them as they come? Ensure that in the event of such an occurrence you inform your professors of your situation. This includes your research adviser.

5. Include time for yourself such as exercise, a movie, or a chat with friends. This is important to maintain your sanity and keep you from becoming overwhelmed with all of the requirements of graduate school. Try to eat properly and get enough sleep. These are usually the first things that students, including myself, disregard when other things need to be accomplished. However, your health depends on these two basic things.

Adviser

Your adviser is very important in gearing your graduate work, especially for a Ph.D. candidate. Advisers have firsthand knowledge of how to successfully complete a graduate degree. My first bit of advice here is to determine whether you are allowed to choose your adviser at the beginning of your graduate career. This is important in forming an early relationship with him or her. Your graduate adviser aids you in setting the course work needed for your particular professional endeavor. She or he provides feedback about your research ideas and accomplishments. If you are lucky, your adviser will also give you moral support when necessary. Although an adviser performs the listed functions, you must keep in mind that sometimes the professors have gotten their degree many years ago and may have forgotten the position of a graduate student. In addition, they probably received their degree from another school, and therefore the experience is not equivalent. This is where your fellow classmates and senior graduate students become helpful.

Graduate Students

Senior graduate students are the best resources to have before you choose a school to attend and while you are attending that school. They will have taken many of the classes that you will enroll in and have knowledge of the professors' methods of teaching and testing. Since they have been through the process of finding a topic, they are good persons for discussing research ideas. Furthermore, they may be the best persons to communicate your concerns, as they know the atmosphere of the department.

Your fellow classmates are a vital resource in that they are the persons with whom you will need to form study groups, and you may end up working in research groups together. Please do considering working in study groups! They are a valuable asset for providing discourse on class topics as well as feelings and emotions about your academic program. In addition, each group member provides experiences (from other schools, industry, etc.), which you and the others may not have. My experience is that just having someone to talk with, who understands my plight, has saved the day many, many times.

Remember that effective communication is an important component of your professional development. Keep track of your professional contacts; they will be very valuable. If you would like to stay in contact with us or become part of our mentoring network, just send e-mail to cseals@vt.edu. Be sure to include your name, e-mail address, major, and the degree you are pursuing.

USEFUL LINKS ON THE INFORMATION SUPERHIGHWAY

I. Buying Books on the Internet

VarsityBooks.com	www.VarsityBooks.com
BigWords.com	www.BigWords.com

BookSwap	www.bookswap.com
Books on Tap	www.booksontap.com
Collegestudent.com	www.collegestudent.com
Barnes and Noble Bookstores	www.textbooks.com

II.   APPLYING TO COLLEGE ON THE INTERNET

CollegeQuest	www.collegequest.com/cgi-bin/ndCGI/CollegeQuest/pgGateway
CollegeEdge	apply.embark.com
CollegeNet	www.applyweb.com
CollegeLink	www.collegelink.com/html/index.htm
E-Apps	www.eapp.com/firstfl.htm
XAP	www.xap.com

III.   BUYING A COMPUTER

VT Requirements http://www.compreq.vt.edu/specs.html.
http://www.vt.edu/vt98/featured/compute.html.

IV.   MOTIVATIONAL

The Daily Motivator http://www.greatday.com

REFERENCES

Pottinger, R. (1999, Fall). Choosing a Ph.D. program in computer science. *Crossroads: The ACM Student Magazine, 6*(1), 6–13. http://www.acm.org/crossroads.

Roach, R. (1999). A textbook case. *Black Issues in Higher Education, 16*(15), 18, 19. http://www.BlackIssues.com.

Terrell, K. (1999). Applying to college online: Some schools and students find E-Applications easy and economical. *Black Issues in Higher Education, 15*(14), 34, 35.

How to Win a Seat in Medical School

JASON W. HAMMOND

Medical Student, Orthopedic Surgery, The Johns Hopkins School of Medicine

Think of the application process as a game. It is your job as the applicant to win the game. The only way to get that spot at your dream medical school is to sell yourself. Everyone has an individual way of presenting him- or herself. But the trick to impressing the interview committee is to imagine yourself in the mold that they have for an interviewee. The great thing about this, though, is that you can present yourself in an endless number of ways, but there is one unifying theme that has, in my experience, stood the test of time—*be different.* Whatever you do, whatever school you want to go to—be different.

All potential applicants to medical school know the statistics. When I applied for medical school, I was told that sixty-four thousand students took the Medical College Aptitude Test (MCAT). Of those students who took the examination, sixteen thousand were granted an interview with medical school admissions boards. Unfortunately, fewer than five thousand students each year are accepted to a medical school. Just imagine how many minorities are in that pool. With numbers like that, if you do not stand out from the crowd, your application can get washed away like loose swimming trunks at the beach.

The best thing to do when you are applying to medical school is to think about all of the usual things that the "normal" medical school applicant emphasizes to get accepted. The usual triad is grades, MCAT scores, and research experiences. Just imagine if you were a member of the medical school admissions committee and had to read thousands of applications from students who fulfilled these three criteria exceptionally. You would, most likely, not be too impressed with all of those high grade point averages and MCAT scores.

In talking with admissions officers at various medical schools, and especially the dean at Hopkins, I found that they are most impressed with that fourth groundbreaking, smashing quality about you. They want to know about that one experience that you had that sets you apart. Remarkably, the one thing that everyone is impressed with is studying abroad. International studies provide you with an interesting topic to make a part of the interview. Additionally, the topic provides the interviewer with additional questions to ask outside of the usual academic norms. In my interviews, most of the time was spent talking about my experiences abroad and not about my grades or MCAT scores.

I would not be surprised if my experiences abroad got me interviews that I otherwise would not have gotten. Why? I think it was because I stood out like a sore thumb in the application pile. I had enrolled in a program called *Semester at Sea* offered by the University of Pittsburgh, in which I took college courses on a ship and traveled to eleven countries around the world. I also knew I had to do research, so I decided to do it at a university in Peru through a program offered by the University of Alabama. The theoretical and practical opportunities afforded me by these experiences were outstanding.

Medical schools committees ate that up, and the best thing about that is that I got scholarships for both of those programs, and so can you. The good thing about undergraduate programs is that people are eager to assist you financially to ensure that you can participate in these programs to study or do research abroad. It's a win-win situation. You get the experience of a lifetime, and you can use that as a catapult to boost you into medical school. However, that is not the only answer. I studied abroad, but maybe you have some talents besides being an excellent student that will help you to stand out from the crowd. Maybe you were able to get some of your undergraduate research published along with your mentor's work. You can do anything you like to make yourself stand out, but you have to be proactive. You have to start long before that first interview. Remember that you have a goal in mind and a game to win. I have given you the rules to play; now go straight to medical school, do not pass go, and do not collect two hundred dollars.

Life after Sports

The Participant Observer

JARRETT DAVID IRONS

Master's Candidate, Sports Management and Communication,
The University of Michigan–Ann Arbor

As the years passed, I continued to get better in football. Even though I was very focused on my academic success, it was obvious my mind-set had changed. I did not value education as I did before. Looking back on it, football started to consume me and most of my thoughts. It became very difficult for me to juggle football and school. One was going to suffer, and football was not. I found myself going against everything I believed in. It was a known fact in my upbringing that education is more important than football. I still conceded to the rigors of playing big-time college football. Because of my weakness toward coaches and the pressure of wanting to succeed, I became totally engulfed in football. I was 80 percent dedicated to football and 20 percent toward education. As a result of this dedication, my junior year I was elected captain of the football team by my teammates. This was the greatest honor I had ever received. For my peers to have that much respect for and trust in me really meant a lot. I was one of five players historically to have been elected to be captain as a junior at the University of Michigan football program. I was entering the period of my life that I call "the limelight era." The limelight era was the time when I started to receive attention from the press, newspapers, magazines, and television. It seemed as though I was getting interviewed every day of the week. This attention I was receiving was more than I ever expected. These were some of the perks that came with being captain.

As a result of my playing football, I was elected First Team All–Big Ten and First Team All-American. At this time, I was feeling on top of the world. I was captain at one of the best universities in the country, All–Big Ten and All-American. I was happy and life was great. Even though I received these accolades and my grades dropped, I still found a way to achieve my goal. I graduated from the University of Michigan my fourth year and went on to pursue my master's degree during my fifth. This was a great accomplishment, but I did not value it as much as my accomplishments in football.

As I entered my fifth year, high expectations would be something I would have to contend with (athletically). I had done so much during my junior season that my fifth year could not help but be great. At the start of the season, my picture was plastered on the cover of six sport magazines ranging from *Sports Illustrated* to *Sporting News*. Also, Nike decided to promote and sell my number 37 jersey to the public. It was the first time Nike featured a linebacker's number for its seasonal jersey. It was a great feeling to walk into stores and see my Michigan jersey hanging on the rack. Even though it was my jersey, I did not receive any money from its sales. Nike claimed the jersey did not have my last name on the back, meaning that the company was not obligated to pay me anything. Despite my name not being on the jersey, many fans knew that the number 37 jersey belonged to me. As a result, there were many number 37 jerseys sold around the country. During this season, I was the most publicized player on the team. With this publicity came more pressure and responsibilities for me and the team. This pressure enticed me to play even harder.

During my fifth year I was elected team captain for the second consecutive year. Our team went on to have a good season, and I led the team in tackles. As a result of my play on the field, I received numerous awards that year. These awards ranged from linebacker of the year to defensive player of the year. I also became the second leading tackler in University of Michigan history. After this season, I put myself in a good position in terms of the National Football League (NFL) draft. The media had me rated the number one linebacker in the country entering the NFL draft. Looking over my career, I had proved that I was a tough, consistent player as well as a great leader. Viewing my accomplishments, one would think that many NFL teams would fight over who would draft me.

Before a player enters the draft, there is a series of events he must endure, for example, participating in the NFL combine. The combine is where all of the top players go and meet to perform for the NFL owners and coaches. It is equivalent to a business job interview. During the combine, players would have to endure psychological evaluation tests, meet with numerous teams, undergo grueling physical examinations and physical workouts. In my opinion, the combine is nothing but a continuation of a series of tests. Even though it was a difficult task, in order to get drafted high, I would have to compete well at the combine, and I did. I then expected great things to come. Looking over my credentials, I won all of the top awards, had a great career, and did well at the combine—not to mention that the analysts were predicting me to be taken high in the draft.

On draft day, I was very calm. I had every reason to be. Many of the NFL teams were calling to let me know they might take me. Even though I was calm, many emotions were running through my body. I remember sitting in my living room watching the draft with my family (father, older brother, and younger brother). I could feel the anticipation in the room. Mother could not even watch the draft with us. She went to her room and continued to read one of her romance novels. Well, the draft got under way, and the first round was going fast. As I sat there, I remember thinking I could be one of the players to get drafted in this round. In my heart I knew I was good enough and had proved that through my career. The first round concluded, and my phone had not made a sound. While still being calm, I kept a positive attitude about my situation. I knew I had a better chance of being drafted in the second round—still a great accomplishment. However, this round was quickly over, and my phone was still quiet. I was alarmed but remained calm. I was very confident that the third round was going to be my time to go. I tried not to think of not getting drafted in the third round. Whichever round I did not get drafted, the next round seemed to be the next best. There are seven total rounds in the NFL draft, but only the first three rounds were presented on the first day. As half of the third round went by, I started to get nervous. Why hadn't I been drafted yet? What was going on? Unfortunately, I did not get drafted in third round. I was devastated. Even though I was not taken on the first day, I still had four more rounds to go. I remember not sleeping very well that night. I just could not get over the fact that I did not get drafted on the first day. I remember my father saying, "Don't worry, you will get drafted tomorrow. It does not matter what round you go."

Surprisingly, the next day I woke up with a great attitude. I had a great feeling that today was going to be my day. Still sitting in the same spot as the day before, I started watching the draft. The fourth round went before my eyes and still no phone call. I started to get mad. I could not understand why I was not drafted up until this point. Before I knew it, we were halfway through the seventh round. At this point I was dazed and confused. I could not fathom the fact that I was not drafted. I remember the puzzled look on my father's face when the last player was taken. He was confused over the events that had taken place. He just kept shaking his head and asking "Why?" It was hard to see my father like that, but it almost killed me when I entered my mother's room. I remember her sitting there reading one of her novels. The way she was sitting, I could tell she was bothered. She just knew I did not get drafted. I came in and sat on the floor staring at the ceiling. As I sat there, nothing came out of my mouth. I wanted badly to say something, but I did not have the strength. My mother slowly put her book down and started to cry. "It's not fair; it's just not fair," my mother said. "After all you've accomplished as a player and a person. How could they not draft you?" It hurt me deeply to see my mother this way. Regardless of how I was feeling toward the draft, it could not compare to the experience of seeing my mother cry. My mother is my heart, and to see her in pain like that really killed my spirit. Likewise, it was killing her to see me in pain. I remember her saying it's hard to understand how you could do everything you were asked as a player and not be rewarded. All the time, sweat, blood, and tears, and for what? To this day the thought of her crying still sickens my stomach.

Ironically, when the draft ended, many of the NFL teams started calling to invite me to their training camp. At this point I was fed up with football. First the teams did not draft me; now they wanted me to try out. There were about fifteen teams trying to contact me. They all expressed how sorry they were for not drafting me and how they loved me as a player. It seemed as though they were trying to "suck up" to me to get me into their camp. I really did not care about them calling, as my mind-set was totally numb. I remember getting upset with many of the teams because they were trying to pressure me into coming to their camp as a free agent. A free agent is a player who has the choice of which team to play for, whereas when players are drafted they are obligated to the particular team that drafts them. From that standpoint, free agency sounded like a good thing. However, there was a catch. Players that are drafted have more financial bargaining power than players who are free agents. It is also easier for drafted players to make the team than nondrafted players. Eventually I decided to play for the Arizona Cardinals. Out of all of the teams pressuring me to come to camp, Arizona was the one to let me take my time to decide. After the disappointment with the draft, I just did not like the idea of being pressured. I was emotionally hurt and drained.

By the time camp started, I had accepted the fact of being a free agent. I welcomed the notion of having to prove myself all over again. When training camp started, there seemed to be a chip on my shoulder. I wanted to show what a big mistake these teams had made by not drafting me. Training camp was six long weeks of hard, grueling torture. However, I loved being in football pads again with the opportunity to play. Throughout training camp I started coming into my own. I was playing well, just like I did my whole career at Michigan. As training camp went on, I remember receiving a phone call early one morning. The person at the end of the phone told me the head coach wanted to see me. He told me to bring my play book. I started getting nervous. "What did the head coach want with me? Did I do something wrong?" As it turned out, the Cardinals were cutting me from the team. I remember being disappointed and mad. The head coach told me that I was good enough to be on the team but that I was not what he was looking for. I could not understand this. I was playing very well and I fit into the scheme of the defense. Unfortunately, it was not for me to understand.

Even though it hurt, it did not compare to the feeling of not being drafted. I had a feeling that I was going to get cut; that is how my luck was going.

Even though I was at a low point, I began to reflect on my life as a person and my purpose. I stopped asking myself why and started believing that things happen in this world for a reason. With this, I only had two options. I could either go back to Texas and hang out with all of my buddies I grew up with, or I could go back to the University of Michigan to finish my master's degree. Even though I was bitter, in my heart I knew what I had to do. I could not start something and not finish.

Going back to Michigan was going to be one of the hardest endeavors I would ever endure. I was a football icon in the state of Michigan. How could I face those people knowing that I had failed. I had been playing organized football since the second grade. Socially I had been viewed as an athlete in the eyes of others. Subsequently football became my identity. I was known and regarded as an athlete and loved the fact that people respected me. In the back of my mind, I felt like people would not respect and look at me in the same way as before. Essentially, I was embarrassed and did not want to face the fact that football was over. Through time, regardless of my feelings about not playing football, I knew my life was going to have to move on. Closing the door on football and opening a new chapter in my life was not going to be easy. Graduate school became my transition. Even though I had always had a plan for life after sports, I never thought sports would end so soon.

In contrast, life went on and I began to make the career transition that all former athletes experience. In essence, I was better prepared for this transition. Regardless of whether football worked out, I had put myself in a great position. I always believe in having choices and not being restricted to one situation. Since I had already received my undergraduate degree, this allowed me many different opportunities. For example, I could either further my education or test the job market. Regardless, I had control to do whatever I wanted to do. As stated before, I chose to go the academic route.

Looking back on my situation, it makes me happy the way things worked out. I am proud of the fact that I have become more than just a football player. I believe the key to my transition was the attainment of my college degree. This gave me the confidence and belief in myself outside of football. As a result, I began to develop an entirely new identity. My identity transformed from football player to scholar. In essence this was my transition out of football.

Reliving these experiences in my life has drawn me to the question, how or why have I made the transition out of football? Why is the transition out of sports so difficult? My situation is similar to that of many of the collegiate athletes playing today. They have been socialized and identified as athletes and nothing else. I especially see this dilemma among African American male student athletes. In my opinion, many athletes would have a better chance of a more positive career transition if a college degree was attained.

How to Move through Your Graduate Program Successfully

JERLANDO F. L. JACKSON

Doctoral Candidate, Educational Leadership and Policy Studies,
Iowa State University

> Ability is of little account without opportunity.
>
> —Napoleon Bonaparte

Graduate education is increasingly becoming more normative in the American society. The master's degree today is what the bachelor's degree was in the past. African Americans are lagging behind their counterparts (i.e., White and Asian Americans) in obtaining graduate education. This is directly reflective of the present trend of African Americans obtaining undergraduate degrees. Naturally, if the number of African Americans obtaining undergraduate degrees is scant, then the number awarded graduate degrees will be low as well. The following essay will discuss general strategies for negotiating the graduate school system and learning strategies for students pursuing degrees in the discipline of higher education. It should be noted that discussions are from the perspective of African American students at predominantly White institutions (PWIs). Presently, the overwhelming majority of graduate programs in higher education are located at PWIs. The remainder of the essay will provide a detailed discussion of eight steps on how to successfully matriculate: admissions, financial assistance, organization, time management, playing the game, developing competencies, and preparing for the future.

The first step in successfully matriculating through a graduate school program is being admitted. Therefore it is important to choose the best graduate program for you and your interest. Identification of the university and department of study is difficult. This step requires determining the components needed to succeed in your career. Things to consider are program reputation, types of institutions, support systems, opportunities, and the experiences of other African American students in the program. It is important that you consider program reputation so that your degree will be reinforced by the higher education community's perception of your educational process. An emphasis should be placed on the type of institution from which your degree is awarded (i.e., research, doctoral granting, and master's granting); future opportunities can be fostered or stifled based on this criterion alone. Support systems are key for your survival in graduate school; whether the university has a strong mentor program for graduate students can make a world of difference. Institutions that provide opportunities to apply what you learn will cultivate a meaningful educational environment. Before attending an institution, find out how African American graduate students have managed in the past. You do not want to be enrolled in a department that creates a hostile environment for African Americans.

The second step in successfully matriculating is obtaining resources to help finance your education. A key deterrent for African American students in finishing their educational process is attributed to financial difficulties and not academic difficulties. There are a number of ways to finance your education: fellowships, scholarships, graduate assistantships, and financial aid. It is very crucial that students entering graduate school secure an assistantship or pertinent work-related experiences, because the discipline is practitioner-oriented. Therefore it is key that students not finish their degrees without securing appropriate work experience. Fellowships are awarded on a merit basis, either by professional organizations or by individual institutions. Scholarships are awarded on the basis of merit as well. Graduate assistantships come in several forms: graduate administrative assistantships (GAAs), graduate teaching assistantships (GTAs), and graduate research assistantships (GRAs). GAAs work in the administrative areas of the institution. GTAs assist professors by leading discussions, supervising laboratory activities, and grading papers. GRAs provide assistance with research projects. Choose the assistantship according to your professional interest. Last, financial aid consists of federal student loans (i.e., Perkins and Stafford loans).

The third step occurs once enrolled at the institution: *organize*. Develop a checklist of milestones to be accomplished during your tenure as a graduate student. Your list should include the following: read the graduate handbook, choose a major professor, complete a plan of study, choose a thesis or dissertation topic, develop a course work schedule, and plan for written and oral exam schedules. Before your arrival to campus, read the graduate handbook. It provides the policies and procedures for faculty and students in reference to graduate education. During the first semester, schedule meetings with all the faculty in your department. Before each meeting, obtain information about the professor you will be meeting with (i.e., research interest, time commitments, and professional experiences); this information will allow you to pick the best major professor for your interests. Choose a major professor who will provide opportunities for you to present at conferences and publish articles. If at all possible, complete your plan of study (POS) the first semester, but no later than the second semester. The POS is your contract for graduation. You want to be clear on what is required of you as soon as possible. Next, it is never too early to pick a topic or at least an area for your thesis or dissertation. It would be advantageous to gear class assignments around your topic so that half of your work will be done when it is time to officially start your culminating assignment. Last, find out the written and oral exam processes. The more you know about these exams, the better you will be prepared to take them.

Time management is very important in graduate school. You will have more things to do than time to do them. Organization is key in time management. There is a plethora of things to be done in a day (i.e., class, work, study, meetings, appointments, etc.). The object of time management is to get as much done in a day as possible. The only way to effectively accomplish this is through the organization of tasks. Maintaining a schedule is also important. Investing in a weekly or daily planner is wise; relying on memory alone will not suffice. Recording things that need to be done will help your day or week run smoothly. Set goals to be accomplished! Each week you should set goals or things that need to be done by the end of the week. The best time to set these goals is at the beginning of the week (Sunday or Monday morning). After setting your goals, you should then fill in your planner accordingly. Keeping a daily to-do list to coincide with your schedule, goals, and other objectives is a good idea. After figuring out what needs to be done for the day, prioritize the list in order from most to least important. You may find that even after making a to-do list you are still unable to get everything done. Those objectives then become priorities for the next day. At the end of the week compare your to-do list with your weekly goals to assess your time management skills.

Playing the political game of the department is very important, but it is the most overlooked component of graduate education. Our White counterparts are acculturated their whole lives to playing the game; we too must be cognizant of it as well. Playing the game entails building networks and coalitions. This discussion will focus on three areas: peers, faculty, and professionals. Interact with colleagues to develop a support system for class work and projects. Also, join study groups to give yourself added exposure to course work outside of the classroom. Interact with your professors outside of class to obtain greater insight pertaining to course work. Make sure you have a clear understanding of what professors are expecting of students in reference to assignments, papers, and projects. Determine the types of professors you have and what they place the most importance on: lectures, class participation, written work, and class discussion. Identify their style; then give them exactly what they want. Furthermore, establish a positive rapport with professors in order to be recommended for special projects. Last, interact with people working in your field to give practicality to supplement course work. Establish these links to enable you to stay current in your field.

Higher education is a very broad field. Some departments specialize in certain areas (i.e., student affairs, education policy, and faculty preparation), while others offer a broader curriculum for preparation. If there is a specialization you seek, be sure you apply to departments that offer that specialty. Although you may want to specialize in a particular area, higher education professionals should be versed in all areas. The first year in your program, I would recommend reading across the discipline. Publications such as *Black Issues in Higher Education* and *The Chronicle of Higher Education* will expose you to the current issues and concerns relevant to higher education. You should also become familiar with academic journals such as *The Journal of Higher Education, Education Administration Quarterly*, and *Educational Leadership*. Read journals in your specialty area, such as *The Journal of College Student Development, Journal of Black Studies, Educational Researcher, Urban Education*, and *Theory into Practice*. Supplementing a reading routine of this nature with your class assignments will give you a better understanding of the higher education arena during your first year. After you are comfortable with the area, then zero in on journals of interest. Also schedule weekly meetings with your major professor to provide additional insights into the information you are learning.

Next, start preparing for your future so that you can be marketable in higher education. It is very important that you do this, because you will have a lot of colleagues to compete with in the job market. Making yourself marketable is the key to your success. The more marketable you are, the better your chances at securing the career position for which you are aiming. Your hands-on experience will be an excellent marking tool. Internship opportunities, assistantships, and full-time experience will help to open doors for future employment. Joining professional organizations will be very important. Membership in associations relating to your area of study is a plus. These organizations usually allow students to join at discounted rates. You will receive journals and be able to attend conferences that will allow you to stay abreast of changes and new findings in your field. Networking is an important component of attending conferences. Presentations and paper presentations will enhance your marketability. Writing a paper is no longer just writing a paper. You should gear your papers and projects toward your specific area of study. This not only broadens your knowledge but also allows you to share your research and ideas with others through presentations and forums. You should go one step further and attempt to get your work published. A great deal of importance is placed on these activities in the academy. By the time you finish your degree, your resume should be filled with experiences.

Last, know exactly what you need to get the position you want. In some fields a master's degree may be sufficient to get the position, while in others, a terminal degree is necessary. Remember, the majority of people working at the university have terminal degrees. When perusing the journals mentioned before, there are advertisements for positions in them. Look them over; they will tell you exactly what universities are seeking. You can then set out during the course of your graduate career to obtain these requirements. Upon completion, you will continue to pursue your goals, because some of the requirements you will have to seek once you are done with your degree.

REFERENCES

Anderson, T., Lott, R., & Wieczorek, L. (1998). *Improving time management for the working student.* (ERIC Document Reproduction Services No. ED 422 127).

Boyle, P., & Boice, B. (1998). Best practices for enculturation: Collegiality, mentoring, and structure. *New Directions for Higher Education, 26*(1), 87–94.

Guddemi, M. *How to plan, organize, and implement a playday.* (ERIC Document Reproduction Services No. ED 350 076).

Ibarra, R. A. (1996). *Enhancing the minority presence in graduate education VII: Latino experiences in graduate education: Implications for change.* (ERIC Document Reproduction Services No. ED 397 764).

Kotter, P. P. (1985). *Power and influence.* New York: Free Press.

Nettles, M. T., & Perna, L. W. (1997). *African American education data book: Volume I. higher and adult education.* Washington, DC: Frederick D. Patterson Research Institute of the College Fund/UNCF.

A review of the directories of higher education associations (ASHE, NASPA, AAHE, and ACPA) did not list any historically Black colleges or universities as member organizations.

See *U.S. News and World Report* Exclusive Rankings by Schools and Departments. A review of the Web sites for departments of higher education will provide the variety of program curriculums available.

St. John, E. (1998, July). Loan debt: A new view. *Black Issues in Higher Education,* 16–17.

ESSAY 8

The Key to Graduate School Success

BOBBY J. JONES

Master's Candidate, Business Administration, Oklahoma City University

The commitment to further one's education can be quite a challenge. This commitment requires dedication, determination, and—most of all—discipline. I believe that in today's society it is vital for African Americans to achieve the highest level of education possible. Education is the stepping stone to an enriched occupational career and can serve as a mentoring opportunity for young African Americans. I'm very privileged to share both the positive experiences and the obstacles that I had to overcome in order to achieve my master's degree.

Upon completing my bachelor of science degree at Grambling State University (GSU), I was convinced that my college days were ended. Once I entered the workforce, I realized that in order to enhance my career and to be competitive on a higher level, additional education was essential. I procrastinated for over fifteen years after my undergraduate degree was obtained before enrolling into the School of Business at Oklahoma City University. Upon entering the program, I immediately realized that time had taken its toll on my study habits. Things that I once grasped with ease as an undergraduate now appeared to be much more challenging. In order to succeed in this curriculum, I immediately came to the conclusion that I needed to readjust my life and concentrate on "the business of school."

One of the major tasks of a graduate student is to focus on a field of study. Students must prepare themselves academically prior to entering a particular field of study. The more knowledge students have about the curriculum, the higher their success rate will be. For instance, prior to enrolling into the graduate program, I had to prepare myself for a whole new field of study. As an undergraduate at GSU, I obtained a bachelor's degree in computer science with a minor in mathematics. Therefore, most of my skills and expertise were associated with the technical aspect of the business world versus the management aspect. In order to become more knowledgeable in management, I enrolled in a junior college. There I completed several economic and accounting courses. These provided me with an enhanced knowledge of business management and proved to be a valuable asset in the master's program.

Time management is an area frequently overlooked by graduate students. Time management is critical when students are faced with family obligations, eight-hour-a-day jobs, and school in the evenings. There are several ways to overcome this problem. The way that I chose to deal with it was to record the activities of every hour into my Day Runner planner. This provided me with the advantage of knowing exactly what I had to do and where I had to be at any given hour of the day. When students try to organize their assignments and appointments without using some type of structured method, they have a tendency to become overwhelmed with the number of activities to be accomplished. Therefore, some assignments and appointments may be neglected. I strongly encourage students, whether they're pursuing higher education or striving to complete high school, to take time to plan and schedule their daily events and activities.

Another area that is sometimes overlooked by graduate students is the ability to communicate effectively. During my undergraduate studies, I was notorious for studying alone and was very hesitant in addressing unclear subject matters to the instructors. I discovered that it is imperative that students and instructors have an open channel of communication. This benefited me tremendously. I would stay after class and have one-on-one sessions with the instructors. I also constantly consulted with classmates on various assignments. We would form study groups in which we would review each other's work and ensure that each member had a detailed understanding of a particular topic. There were times when we were required to perform joint projects, problem analyses, and presentations. This form of communication made the assignments more enjoyable and provided a valuable lesson in how to work with people of diverse backgrounds and cultures.

Graduate students must be dedicated and very serious about their objectives. Many sacrifices will have to be made in order to obtain the end goal. For example, during my school years, I was, and am still, a sports fanatic. I can recall many times when there were National Football League Superbowl parties, National Basketball Association championships, and various other sporting events that I wanted to view. But there were only so many hours in a day. Therefore, I placed my focus on school projects, assignments, and exams; the extracurricular activities simply had to be put aside.

Becoming a successful graduate student is not an easy task. However, by preparing oneself with the necessary organizational, communication, and scholastic abilities, the task will be far more enjoyable and less stressful. I was fortunate to be surrounded by a cast of professors and students who were serious about education. I was blessed to graduate with a 3.99 grade point average. As an African American male, I have learned that if students, minorities in particular, truly devote themselves to achieve their goals, they will be respected for what they know, instead of the color of their skin.

To all African Americans who are seeking a higher education, I strongly suggest you go the extra mile to obtain all the knowledge that you possibly can. It may mean spending extra time in the library, taking prerequisite courses, visiting the Internet, or just associating with your peers on different subject matters. But one thing is certain: once your education is achieved, no one can take it away from you.

The Essentials for Graduate Success

BERNADETTE M. LUMAS

Master's Candidate, Social Psychology, Howard University

Graduate school success is determined by intelligence, initiative, motivation, and persistence. Your GRE scores and undergraduate transcript are not always the best predictors of your success in graduate school. Although mastering the skills necessary to get good grades and high GRE scores is truly helpful, the essential indicators of success in graduate school are more inclusive. They include the ability to organize and balance multiple activities while meeting deadlines, networking with academic professionals, satisfying personal relationships, and maintaining a grounded sense of self. Graduate school success requires that individuals realize and build on strengths and weaknesses, enabling them to get the most of their graduate experience. As an African American graduate student, I am proud to say that I have successfully completed my first year of graduate school. I must be honest and admit that I have encountered many challenges within this new level of formal education. Reflecting back on my first year, I realize that my graduate school success is a result and function of my ability to successfully transition through life. I am delighted to share the essentials of my graduate school success and feel confident that these essentials will be positively reinforced by your mentors and peers.

First, as an undergraduate student, you will find it important to have a comprehensive understanding of your field of study. Ask yourself, "What are the demands and expectations of my field?" It is imperative that you, as a young scholar, begin to conduct and publish research early in your career. The benefits of your undergraduate research experience will include a strong, lasting relationship with faculty mentors, exposure to the process of conducting and publishing research in your field, and an indication of your talents and abilities. With this experience, you are setting the pace as a young scholar and building on your existing knowledge base by focusing on and contributing to a chosen field of study. This early exposure will shape your focus on the program and university most compatible with your career interest.

Take control of your graduate education by working hard in and out of class. The academic transcript is an undisputed measure of graduate school success, but you must also work hard at being a presence in your department and university community at large. Ultimately, the department is there for your benefit and use. Make it a point to ask questions, give constructive feedback, utilize available resources, and contribute to the overall camaraderie of your department. Your active involvement will give you a greater understanding of departmental and university policies and procedures. Exerting control over all aspects of your graduate education will keep you focused on your ultimate goal—the graduate degree.

Be involved! Your involvement in the department, campus, community, and professional organizations will profoundly enhance your graduate school experience. Make every activity or initiative an intellectually fun-filled experience. This involvement will allow you to develop important contacts with peers, faculty, and professionals influential in your respective field of study. Getting to know faculty and professionals is key and resourceful, because they are your future colleagues. In my experience, faculty and professionals are enthusiastic to serve as mentors for those students who display determination, dedication, and strong academic work ethics. Networking is a vital part of your graduate experience and crucial in terms of postgraduate opportunities (i.e., research grants, postdoctoral fellowships, etc.).

The most essential factor to graduate school success, yet often overlooked, is to maintain your health and happiness. As a prospective African American graduate student, you have decided to embark on a path that is both strenuous and rigorous. If you do not have family or friends in the immediate area, it will be necessary to actively build relationships with others in your community, church, and school. Family and friends are two of God's greatest blessings. Surround yourself with beautiful, positive, and committed people—in other words, build a reliable support system. There will come days where having a friend to run an errand can relieve a mountain of stress. Before you and I can uplift the well-being of our communities, we must first take care of ourselves and remain healthy and happy, both physically and mentally.

I strongly believe that these essentials will remain a challenge throughout a graduate experience, but it is up to the students to maintain a balance ensuring their successful transition through their program and into their professional career. The notion of balance is an absolute essential in the pursuit of your graduate education. Maintaining this balance will maintain your focus. Focus will drive you to complete your degree in a timely manner with many rewarding academic and personal relationships developed throughout this experience. As young African American scholars we are preparing ourselves for the responsibility of educating and improving the quality of life for our community and the next generation of minority scholars to come. We must constantly remind ourselves that we are major assets to our respective fields of study, and by being successful in graduate school we are laying the foundation for our success in our chosen careers.

Predominantly Black to Predominantly White

Making the Transition to Graduate School

JAMES L. MOORE III
Doctoral Candidate, Counselor Education,
Virginia Polytechnic Institute and State University

Progressing from undergraduate to graduate education is a tough journey for any student. The experience is often mixed—challenging, distressing, and rewarding. For African American students who graduate from predominantly Black institutions (PBIs), the changes are especially perplexing. Where are the African American students, faculty, and staff? Where do they hang out and fellowship? How many African American brothers and sisters do I have in my department? Will I be fully funded? Finally, where do the brothers go to get their haircuts?

These are common questions that are, consciously and unconsciously, asked; at least, these were the questions that I had when I initially matriculated in graduate school at Virginia Tech. Of course, after weeks of investigating and perusing the campus, my questions still went unanswered until, fortunately, I bumped into another African American graduate student, who happened to be the president of the Black Graduate Student Organization (BGSO). At that time, the president (a brother) invited me to the organization's first meeting, which I eagerly attended. I discovered, what I already had assumed, that the Black presence was virtually invisible in regard to faculty, staff, graduate and undergraduate students, and surrounding communities. To me, this was evident when I noticed that the domestic workers whom I encountered were not people of color. Perhaps this was common for some, but for a small-town South Carolina native this was highly unusual.

Nevertheless, at the meeting I also discovered that many other incoming graduate students had the same questions, especially the brothers and sisters who had attended PBIs. It was evident by the questions and attendance that they wanted to meet other African American graduate students. When the meeting adjourned, many remained talking and exchanging phone numbers and e-mail addresses. Naturally the new graduate students connected and developed stronger ties with individuals in their respective fraternity, sorority, and departments. However, the BGSO still availed as the collective voice for African American graduate students, as well as one of the main programmatic groups for African Americans.

In my opinion, such organizations are critical for helping reduce feelings of isolation and inadequacy at predominantly White institutions. Although African Americans have made great strides, they still endure the same historical challenges related to racism, discrimination, and oppression, even in graduate school. Graduate school is nothing but a microcosm of society. Frequently I hear anecdotal stories from friends and colleagues all around the country that illustrate both overt and covert racism. Howard and Hammond (1985) suggest that stigmas of inferiority follow African Americans everywhere they go, from the classroom to the workplace. The stigmas are reinforced, for example, every time affirmative action is mentioned or associated with African Americans. Because one is African American, it is automatically assumed that all African Americans are unqualified and receiving hefty stipends. Speaking from experience, this is most often not true.

BGSOs provide a temporary escape from mainstream stigmas and academic pressures. Here at Virginia Tech, the BGSO sponsors forums, programs, and events where both African American graduate students and faculty can engage with one another intellectually and socially. The organization's members and associates (e.g., faculty, staff, and neighboring schools) share vital information related to African Americans and graduate students. I guess it was fitting to have "share the knowledge" as its motto. Every time I check my e-mail, people are sharing information related to "us" on the BGSO e-mail listserv.

While working on my bachelor's degree (in English education) at Delaware State University, a PBI, I took things for granted. It never transpired that I would, in many instances, be the only African American in my cohort group, classes, or program, including master's and doctoral students. In all honesty, I had expected to see more African Americans around campus, if not in my department. Perhaps these assumptions are directly or indirectly related to my wonderful experience at Delaware State University.

Delaware State University provided educational, leadership, and mentoring opportunities that, I believe, helped me to excel in graduate school. Initially I consulted heavily with other graduate students at Virginia Tech and with my mentor, Dr. James Scott King, at Delaware State University. In my opinion, it is critical that African American graduate students get the best advice possible in regard to graduate school, even if it requires having a mentor outside the university.

For first-generation graduate students, I believe some of the best mentoring and advice will come from those who have already pursued and obtained advanced degrees. Sometimes seeking advice from invalidated sources can be detrimental. Although I love my parents dearly, I realize that they may not be the most qualified to provide the best-informed advice. However, I do not dismiss what my family has to offer because they provide unwavering prayer and support in my ability. In many instances, prayer and support are the very things needed to persist through the program.

Stephen Carter, in his book *Reflections of an Affirmative Action Baby,* profoundly articulates that African Americans are constantly judged on a continuum: the first Black, the best Black, and the only Black. In my mind, this suggests that we, as a people, are still going places where none of us have yet to go. For instance, there are departments at Virginia Tech that have just recently graduated an African American doctoral student. From talking with graduate students from other schools, this is not unique to Virginia Tech, because other universities are having some of the same problems.

After four years in graduate school and near completion of my doctorate, I think that I am qualified to give advice about making the transition to graduate school, especially from a PBI to PWI. To prospective African American graduate students who are considering attending a PWI, I suggest the following points: Make sure you are genuinely interested and passionate about your respective degree program. Come expecting to be successful. Establish both short- and long-term performance goals. Familiarize yourself with the requirements for obtaining a degree. Get to know your adviser, faculty, and other graduate students in the department. Be proactive rather than reactive. Identify mentors on campus or off campus. Develop a strong support group. Join organizations in which leadership competencies can be developed. Familiarize yourself with resources in your department and around campus. Stay abreast of the literature in your field. Engage in class discussions and study with classmates when possible. And don't limit yourself.

After accomplishing these points, I expect that you will excel right through your respective programs. The bottom line is that the African American graduate student must take responsibility for his or her success or failure. Let us continue the legacy of our predecessors by obtaining advance degrees, in spite of the obstacles. I wish you much success as you pursue your advanced degree!

REFERENCES

Carter, S.L. (1991). *Reflections of an affirmative action baby.* New York: Basic Books.

Howard, J., & Hammond, R. (1985). Rumors of inferiority. *The New Republic,* 17–21.

Some Reflections and Insights for African American Graduate Students

CHARLES E. OSIRIS

Doctoral Candidate, Higher Education Administration,
Florida State University

I was born and raised on the south side of Chicago, Illinois. From the educational mire that was (and is) the Chicago public schools, I emerged with aspirations of higher education. Through encouragement, trials, tribulations, and successes I have arrived at the threshold of doctoral studies. I write this essay as I am nearing the end of my first year of doctoral studies in higher education administration at the Florida State University. I hope that some of the reflections and insights shared in this essay will be of some benefit to African American students considering doctoral studies.

In many ways it can be considered a declaration of war for African Americans to pursue higher education. This is particularly true when the goal is a terminal degree. Simply stated, these citadels of higher learning were never intended to serve African Americans. The historical barriers that have existed over time to keep African Americans in a state of ignorance and submissive confusion are present in more pervasive forms in 2001. As George Wallace once stood blocking the threshold to Southern higher educational opportunity during the Civil Rights movement, institutional racism now sits all so subtly as an immovable barrier to educational opportunities today. Attacks on African Americans' intelligence, on affirmative action, and on our humanity are ever pressing as we embark upon a new millennium.

As an African American man, I am more than remotely aware of the overall educational crisis for people of varied hues in the United States. I am particularly aware of the crisis in our communities surrounding aspirant

African American men's educational opportunities. Many researchers have exposed the societal, educational, and personal challenges that face African American men. As a result, we are most often resilient survival victims of family breakdown, high school and college dropout, police brutality, incarceration, unemployment, and underemployment. We are victimized by homicide, stress, and various psychological and sociological factors that adversely affect our abilities to cope in a society that challenges our humanity and manhood at every crossroad.

I arrived on the campus of a predominantly White institution (PWI) to pursue a Ph.D. despite the odds, not to capitulate to them. I came to this environment aware of the challenges, but more importantly, aware of the many supposedly impregnable obstacles that my ancestors have overcome so that I might have an opportunity to struggle toward progress—so that you and I may have the opportunity to choose the road to achieve the goals that we desire. We are the heirs of a community of successful struggles! It is with this knowledge that I press on with due diligence to contribute righteously to the continued struggle of our peoples and of all people.

Predominantly White campuses can be dangerous and alienating for African Americans pursuing any degree program in graduate or professional school. At the doctoral level the dangers and alienating factors can feed upon your fears if you allow them to. It has been critical for me to develop a strong community of support to help me through my studies. A community of support is critical, because you will need support in times of challenges to share in your struggles and in times of joy to celebrate your triumphs. One of the primary factors that causes African Americans to discontinue degree programs is a lack of a strong support network. I cannot overemphasize this point. The times when I have struggled most have been when my community of support was weakest. Your community can and should consist of people from various areas of your life, including other Ph.D. students to commiserate with, friends not connected to academe to help you maintain perspective, and family and loved ones for the support that only they can provide. Of critical importance to your community of support are faculty that care about your success and can identify with your struggles and concerns. One of the critical factors that lead to doctoral students' lack of direction and low morale is minimal contact with faculty who can provide effective mentoring at critical junctures throughout the doctoral process. Jacqueline Fleming refers to the need for students to have access to a wide network of constructive relationships with people who will support, encourage and inspire them. The African adage "It takes a village" is very true as it relates to pursuing a Ph.D. for African Americans. Remember, as a people, we have found that our successes have most often come from collective (communal) efforts more so than individual efforts.

Though our successes have come from collective efforts, it is critical that as a doctoral student you assume personal responsibility for your educational enlightenment and for seeking the terminal degree. It is important that from the beginning you learn the complexities of performing effective research and developing a research agenda. As a scholar you will confront many challenges, but what is equally as important as your personal success is that you develop a research agenda that will in some critical way improve or enhance the African American experience. Throughout your doctoral studies and your career, you will need to have a critical understanding of our collective experiences in the United States and learn to translate those experiences in productive ways that can enrich life as we know it.

One of the ways you must begin to develop this perspective is to read diligently about the African American experience. This will be of supreme importance to help foster an intellectual balance as you consume your doctoral program studies. You cannot counteract the misinformation, frustrations, and barriers that are in place without a practical understanding of what has been and what is possible for African Americans throughout the African diaspora. Therefore, when you read Fleming's *Blacks in College*, Carter G. Woodson's *Miseducation of the Negro*, bell hooks's *Teaching to Transgress*, Joseph White and James Cones III's *Black Man Emerging*, Lee Jones's *Black in America: When a Ph.D. Is Still Not Enough!* and a host of other literature that reflect on and translate our experiences, you will know that the struggle you are involved in is a collective struggle, not merely an individualized one. Knowing that others have achieved against greater odds and succeeded will provide the impetus for your success. May all the fortitude of the ancestors guide you toward excellence. Believe that you can accomplish anything that you commit your energies to. Doctoral study is as much a socialization process as it is strenuous academic activity. You can achieve all that you desire. The knowledge of our historic successes as a people is a road map toward present and future success. May the spirit of Sankofa light your path toward scholarly achievement.

Lessons Learned That Were Vital to My Success as a Doctoral Student

MIRIAM E. PHIELDS

Doctoral Candidate, Counseling Psychology,
University of Maryland–College Park

As a fifth-year graduate student, I am working at my predoctoral internship at the University of Maryland Counseling Center. The completion of this predoctoral internship and defense of my dissertation will mark the end of graduate school and my ascension to Dr. Phields. My specific areas of interest include African Americans' mental health concerns and the psychosocial and behavioral factors related to preventable health concerns, particularly HIV/AIDS. For example, my dissertation focuses on developing an emic model of African American women's gender identity. Before I started my doctoral program, I earned a B.A. in organizational behavior and management from Brown University, worked for eight years in the field of HIV/AIDS, and earned an M.A. in counselor preparation from Seton Hall University. My interest in a doctoral program in counseling psychology evolved from my work experiences in HIV/AIDS.

My interests have grown out of my personal and professional experiences as well as my desire to advocate for and contribute to the study of mental health within the context of the minority experience, primarily that of African Americans. Because one of my professional goals is to promote the use of mental health services by minorities, particularly African American men and women, a concomitant goal is to contribute to the study and provision of culturally competent services by mental health service providers.

Mental health in the African American community is rarely a priority as compared with other more immediate needs. The stigma associated with psychological needs and services further discourages African Americans from seeking services. Black psychologists are scarce, and many African Americans do not feel that their needs will be adequately addressed by non-black therapists. I have hoped that my addition to the field of counseling psychology will help alleviate, if only by one, the scarcity of Black psychologists. I believe that with more minority practitioners, minorities will be more readily encouraged to seek psychological assistance. Moreover, psychology within the context of the minority experience has only recently been explored by psychologists and requires further research.

As I began my first year of a five-year doctoral program in counseling psychology at the University of Maryland, earning a doctorate appeared to be a far away goal. I anticipated a great deal of schoolwork and very little social life, but graduate school turned out to be much more than reading, writing papers, and taking tests. In graduate school, I learned several lessons that were vital to surviving and succeeding in graduate school and that will be invaluable throughout my professional life. I will discuss just a few of these lessons below.

LESSON ONE

Initiate and use a support group of other African American graduate students or other graduate students of color. As a Black graduate student in a predominantly White university and graduate program, I often found that my perceptions of the material or classroom discussions were different from those of my White classmates. I began to wonder, "Is it I?" I found it helpful to have a group of Black peers with whom I could conduct "reality checks" and validate my experiences of prejudice, ignorance, and racism. An informal group of supportive peers of color provided a necessary and safe place to vent my frustrations without fear of alienating White classmates or other costly consequences. I was fortunate (blessed) to be part of a research team composed of African American women. In addition to discussions about racial identity research, this group was a source of support, research experience, information/resource sharing, and new strategies for surviving graduate school. I encourage Black graduate students to seek out other Black graduate students (and graduate students of color) inside and outside their graduate programs for camaraderie and support.

LESSON TWO

Identify and cultivate African American mentors and or role models in addition to other mentors and role models. In addition to the program requirements, I found balancing competing priorities and setting priorities for what I wanted to get out of my graduate school experience to be challenging. Cultivating relationships with African American faculty and staff was helpful in figuring out which experiences I needed to obtain to get my preferred jobs as an African American woman. These mentors and role models shared with me their experiences as African Americans in the positions that they hold and the nuances of surviving and thriving. In addition, they were able to warn me about potential pitfalls and to help me to anticipate potential barriers or difficulties.

LESSON THREE

Do what you love—within the parameters of finishing your degree in a reasonable time frame. One's love (or at least strong interest) for a subject or field is necessary for survival and success in graduate school. Graduate school can be an enjoyable and challenging experience. It can also be a long and difficult process, and even longer and harder if one doesn't love the work involved. I have found that I'm more productive, persistent, enthusiastic, and energized when I tackle tasks that interest me. I made a conscious decision to study, research, and specialize in areas that I love. My love for my work has carried me through comprehensive exams, thesis, dissertation, and sleep deprivation. I love what I do, and I can't wait to graduate so I can do my work unencumbered by courses, tests, and papers.

Don't Let Anyone Tell You That You're Not Smart Enough

TINA D. PIPKIN

Master's Candidate, Social Work, Florida State University

My name is Tina Pipkin, and I'm a thirty-seven-year-old single mother of six. My oldest son is a third-year college student at Florida A&M University. I have three teenagers attending high school, one attending middle school, and a ten-year-old attending elementary school. I am a second-year graduate student at Florida State University (FSU) majoring in social work. I serve as director of a Faith-Based Residential Program for Substance Abuse. When I came to college about five years ago, I was stepping out on faith. I had not seen a school campus in about fifteen years. I had gotten expelled from high school and settled for obtaining a GED. Needless to say, I was scared because of my last academic experience. I was scared because a teacher had told me that I was not "smart enough to go to college." I had to learn how to endure the ups and downs of life. Faith was my key. I had to believe that I was deserving of an education and that I was smart enough to get it. I could have rolled over and allowed what people say cause me *not* to pursue my dreams, but I had something inside that would not let me quit. Then I met Dr. Brenda "BJ" Jarmon at a community event where she was the guest lecturer. She gave me the reassurance to continue with my faith, endurance, belief, and perseverance.

As students, we all have things that we must endure. I believe Black students' need for endurance becomes compounded when the majority of the general society believes that Black students are incapable of persevering. You must not fall prey to what others believe about what you can or cannot accomplish. Your success is not predicated on what others believe, but on what you believe. The Bible says, "I can do all things through Christ." For example, when I met BJ, I had been clean from drugs for about a year. She didn't know that I had been on a ten-year crack binge prior to this. I asked her for her help to assist me with getting into FSU, and she gave me her word that she would help me. Well, the rest, as they say, is history. Today, BJ is my mentor and has been since our brief encounter some years ago. She has made a tremendous impact on my academic life as well as my personal life. She has been the one that God has used to broaden my horizons for my future. No longer do I have drug dealers and gang members for companions and friends. Through her I have met people whom I have grown to trust, admire, and love—people who have become my mentors, and who have literally helped me to change the course of my life.

Obtaining a mentor is very important to one's graduate school success. Allow me to share some of my other mentors with you. The first is Dr. Na'im Akbar, who challenged me to change the way I looked at learning information I found no interest in. He said, "Tina, you want to learn everything you can about what other people are saying in the area of your studies so that when you begin to do your own research and write papers and books, you will have the knowledge of knowing what has already been done in order to address the so-called experts in your specialized field of study." I appreciate him for that, because I was beginning to become discouraged with learning material that, in my opinion, had no relevance and no power to assist our people with their journey through life's difficult moments.

Dr. Asa Hilliard, who continues to speak blessings into the empty spaces of my being, is another chief mentor of mine. When I told him that I was thinking of pursuing a Ph.D., he told me that I was already Ph.D. material. He said that I had learned lessons that some people will never learn and that these lessons are so vital to the continuity of life. I thank God for him! The lesson I learned was "to thine own self be true."

Dr. Robert Franklin is another one who has touched me immensely. He was so moved by the recounting of my life experiences that he advised me "to keep doing what I've been doing because it's working." You can't imagine how important it was to have someone come along and validate me after all my life I had been told by people that I trusted that I wasn't good enough to go to college. Yes, mentoring is very important to one's success in graduate school. There were many other mentors like Dr. Lee Jones, Drs. Sharon and Dana Dennard, Dr. Len Worley, Pastor G. V. Lewis, Pastor Jack P. Leland, my "Between Friends" book club members, and my church family.

Being blessed with the opportunity to begin an academic career in higher education after being kicked out of my high school district some fifteen years earlier has been one of the most rewarding and self-fulfilling personal goals I have ever accomplished. Although I have had some pretty degrading and sad experiences as a graduate student, I would not trade these experiences for anything in the world. Why, you might ask? Once I realized that I had a wealth of life experiences but I had very little structured academic knowledge,

I wanted to know more. I needed to know more, and I had a burning desire to know more. Subsequently, I openly shared my experiences and beliefs in hopes of learning even more. I have had real-life experiences to contribute to my belief systems, which cause me to question Caucasian professors who set themselves up to be knowledgeable about lives of Black Americans but can direct me to very little in the literature, their research, or their personal work. This frustrated me immensely! In pursuing academic knowledge at a predominantly White university, I've discovered my professors know very little about me as a Black mother, Black person, Black citizen, or Black human being!

In attempting to share my experiences, I felt like everything I knew was being challenged. I was beginning to question my own healing process from my experiences, yet I knew what my experiences had taught me. You see, I was raped, domestically abused, a former crack cocaine addict, and a victim of another violent crime, just to name a few of my life experiences. Therefore, my suggestions for success in graduate school, especially if you are at a predominantly White institution, is to gain all the knowledge that you can. Learn all that you can, but do not think just because it is being taught it is the absolute truth, because it may not be!

Do your homework. Be assertive and study the issues for yourself. Learn what Black Americans and other minority scholars have said about the field in which you are studying. Find out about the culture of the people you are desiring to work with. Additionally, the spiritual component is extremely important in the Black culture, and yet in most academic arenas, it is talked about and taken into consideration very little. My philosophy is "whatever works for you." Just because you are unfamiliar with something does not make it wrong. It just means that you learned something that you didn't know that works for someone else.

If you are an older student with the responsibilities of raising a family, please don't sacrifice your children. Get some balance. It would be unwise to work all day, be on call all evening, at the library all night, and expect to have holistically healthy children. Use the few years that you have been blessed with to instill in them road maps for living wisely. Someone said that "time heals all wounds." I beg to differ. Time is neutral. Attention to your wounds during the course of time is what heals wounds, not time alone. First and foremost, I would say, "to thine own self be true." Do not underestimate the power within! Surround yourself with positive people on and off campus. Getting connected with God through prayer is a must too! Again, it is extremely important to have a mentor. In soliciting and selecting a mentor, find someone who has your best interest at heart—someone who will teach, guide, and nurture your progress, someone who will be honest with you, even if it hurts, someone you can cling to for support, someone you respect and admire, someone you can trust and depend on, someone who will correct you when you get off track. Ultimately, learn in order to teach, and teach in order to learn.

Building Relationships during the Graduate Experience

CRAIG POOLER

Program Management Analyst, Federal Trio Programs,
United States Department of Education, Washington, D.C.

This is actually my first year in graduate school. It has been over five years since I completed my undergraduate degree. I have just completed my first semester of graduate school. In the beginning, I did not know if I could cut the mustard. After being out of the mix of writing papers and so forth, I had to ask myself what are some of the things that I must do that will allow me to be successful in graduate school. I would assume that most individuals entering graduate or professional school would ask the same question. Upon asking myself this question, I begin to reflect back on my undergraduate experience. As I reflected, I wrote down a couple of things I thought were conducive to my success on the undergraduate level. Everything I wrote down revolved around the ability to effectively communicate with others. I am applying the same process now on the graduate level.

Graduate school should be looked at in terms of a relationship between you the student and the program being pursued. The program involves all individuals within the institution who have a direct and indirect effect on the student's success. What is the most important factor in any type of relationship? Communication! Understanding what you want and expect out of the program is essential. I continually ask myself, what do I want to accomplish within the program? Of course, the answer continues to be that I want to master the subject and receive a high grade in the courses. How and to whom do I convey this message? Obviously to the professor, but I believe others play a key part in helping me convey this message. For me, those others are the dean, professors, and classmates.

Communicating with the dean of your program allows you the opportunity to gain some inside track information on financial assistance that may not be readily available, as well as changes that may be occurring within the program that students may not have been made aware of. For instance, the dean of my graduate program is the one who informed me of the courses to take that will aid in my receiving a dual degree in a limited amount of time. The dean's advice has saved me from having to take four additional courses that were previously recommended for a dual master's degree within my program. This will save me both time and money. Communicating with my professors on a regular basis outside the classroom has proved to be just as beneficial.

Communicating *effectively* with your professors is usually the main factor determining success in a particular course or not. When I say *effectively,* I'm asking if you as the student have a clear understanding of what is required of you in each particular course. Depending on the size of the class, it is to your advantage to take time at the beginning of the semester to schedule a one-on-one conference with the professor. I recommend that you use this time to go over the syllabus and ask questions you have related to the course. For example, at the beginning of the semester, the professor briefly went over what would be on the class final. To say we were all confused would be an understatement. We all had interpreted the professor's brief explanation differently. I visited with the professor during her conference hours. Here I was able to inquire in more detail about the class final. From this visit, I got a better understanding of what was required on the final, and this gave me the chance to get a jump start on my final project. This was beneficial to me because I knew in advance I was going to have a couple of conflicting days the last two weeks of class because of my full-time job. This brings out an important point. If you know in advance that there may be a conflict in your schedule, an early conference will give you the opportunity to make arrangements with the professor to cover any assignments that will be due during your absence.

You may not always have the time to meet with the professor in person. Here are some alternative ways in which you could communicate with your professor. Most universities have free e-mail accounts for faculty and students. This has become the preferred way of communicating in today's society. I use e-mail to send assignments ahead of time to my professors to solicit their comments. The good thing about e-mail is that you can send and receive e-mails from anywhere that has Internet access. If you do not have access to a computer that has Internet, I would suggest calling your local library for computers that are Internet accessible. I recommend to those who do not have an e-mail account to log onto www.hotmail.com. Hotmail.com is a free e-mail access provider. For those individuals who prefer speaking to the professor but who aren't able to make conference hours, there is the traditional way of calling your professor during the professor's conference hours. After a couple times of visiting and talking with your professor, the professor may feel comfortable about giving you his or her home telephone number. If permission is given by your professor, inquire as to what hours calls should be made.

Another suggestion is to group up with some classmates and exchange phone numbers and e-mail addresses. In fact, professors encourage students to communicate with one another within and outside the classroom. It really helps when you can depend on a classmate to take good notes in your absence and vice versa. In some classes you will find classmates who are advanced in the program. They usually are a semester or more advanced in their studies. These individuals have provided me with an abundance of knowledge regarding courses and professors. For example, a few of my classmates have informed me of what to expect from various courses, the teaching style of various professors, and techniques to use to successfully pass those courses. I must admit that talking with my classmates has also helped me generate some excellent ideas in regard to choosing a topic for a course assignment.

As you can see, it is the simple or rather basic things that play a major part in a student's success. Before concluding, I would like to recommend a few more tips that will make the semester more enjoyable. Schedule shorter but frequent review sessions. Read two or three pages of the required textbook each night before you go to bed and when you wake up. Read well in advance. This will help lighten your reading assignment when a couple chapters are assigned at one time. Keep a small notepad on you and by your bed for jotting down thoughts that come to you relating to the course. You will find this little notepad to be of value as you explore and develop any class assignment. If you use some of these suggestions, you will definitely feel less stressed and develop relationships that will prove to be conducive to successfully completing the program.

Prescription for Persistence

What Graduate Students Need to Know

RODNEY B. PULLIAM

Doctoral Candidate, Public Administration and Policy,
Virginia Polytechnic Institute and State University

> Education is our passport to the future, for tomorrow belongs to the
> people who prepare for it today.
>
> —Malcolm X

Persistence has always been the cornerstone of the African American experience. As descendants of slaves, we are heirs to an inner dogged determination and spirit to survive despite all odds. As graduate students, we must
constantly call upon that spirit to sustain us in our academic endeavors.

Today, in higher education, particularly with African American graduate
students, persistence is an indispensable trait to possess. Even the most intelligent person can fail without persistence. It does not come by study, but
it surely comes by a willingness to succeed beyond what the reasonable person would endure. Persistence sustains you when graduate advisers seem to
work against your best interests, when the better research projects seem to
go to your European colleagues, when departmental funding runs out upon
your inquiry, and when your colleagues receive special mentoring from professors while you simply get help.

The question must then be asked, "Just what is persistence?" I have
learned through my years of graduate education, a master's degree, a law
degree, and currently a doctoral degree, that persistence is a combination of
my belief system, persistence, and perseverance. These three factors work in

concert to help strengthen you during the difficult periods of graduate education.

BELIEVE

You must have a strong belief system. You must have strong convictions concerning your ability and potential. For example, if you truly believe in yourself, then it becomes more difficult for you to accept defeat or failure. Moreover, it becomes more difficult for you to allow anyone else to validate your graduate education experience.

PERSIST

You must be persistent. I often remember former Virginia governor Douglas L. Wilder talking about persistence in many of his speeches. Governor Wilder would say, "Persist, persist, persist, until you win." He did just that in becoming the first African American governor since Reconstruction. Persistence is not simply surviving or hanging on, but it is a drive or longing to accomplish a goal or task. Persistence is like the mosquito that continuously buzzes around you until it bites. It buzzes and hovers around you in spite of your futile attempts to swat it. It hovers until it accomplishes its mission—drawing blood.

Finally, persevere. You must continue on with the determination not to give up or give in. You must develop your resolve to accomplish and complete goals, particularly when the prevailing winds of anguish, defeat, and despair blow your way.

A prescription, generally speaking, is a direction usually written by the physician to the pharmacist for the preparation and use of a medicine or remedy. The prescription that I list serves as merely suggestions stemming from my personal experience. This prescription does not propose to cure all ills but will certainly help improve your academic experience and maybe your life as well. In your academic experience, however, you must play the role of physician in diagnosing your academic development.

I offer five points to graduate students as a prescription for persistence: (1) Do not be afraid to go it alone. (2) Know who you are. (3) Truly examine your strengths and weaknesses. (4) Validate yourself. (5) Recognize that you did not come to stay; you came to leave.

DO NOT BE AFRAID TO GO IT ALONE

In life, there will be times when you must go it alone. The truth of the matter is that there are certain obstacles people will not endeavor to overcome. Many people are not willing to put forth the requisite amount of effort required to become successful or to win. You must.

Your life's goals may be called into question by either family members or friends. Often, this challenge may simply be the result of their fear of the unknown, fear of success, or outright jealousy. You must not listen to those voices nor allow them to occupy too much of your mental and physical energy.

There is an old adage, "You can never go home." I believe this. Home will never be the same once you are exposed to new things. Education and your learning experience have enlarged your worldview. Your friends no longer speak your language. The old happening things at home are no longer exciting. The stark reality is that you have changed. Your world is now much broader than your friends'. You cannot allow anybody to derail your goals. Also, never worry about the person who says, "You must think that you are somebody." I am suggesting that you are somebody ... with something to do.

KNOW WHO YOU ARE

To know who you are requires self-reflection. This self-reflection should include those things in life that you hold to be dear and important to you alone. You must know what drives you to achieve your dream. Once you find that energy force, harness it and move forward.

In addition, self-reflection demands that you call upon your ancestral legacy for strength as well. It requires a recognition of your linkage to a glorious past with great African men and women who dared to be different and who, in spite of the dangers, conquered the unconquerable. Even if your knowledge of African history and its triumphs is suspect, reflect on your grandparents' accomplishments. In spite of all their struggles, they still purchased homes, raised families, and possibly provided for your parents' education. Retrieve that "struggle" story and make it yours. Getting to know yourself will help you to solve the mystery of who you are and allow your mind to transcend what you have previously believed to be your limitations.

EXAMINE YOUR STRENGTHS AND WEAKNESSES

In order to be successful in graduate school, you must perform a personal diagnostic examination on yourself. I am not referring to some mechanistic self-evaluation, but you must critique yourself in order to build upon your shortcomings. Also, while improving upon your weaknesses, do not forget to maintain proficiency in your strength areas.

If you did not regularly study as an undergraduate or if you always completed papers at the last minute, for example, then organization may be your problem. You must organize your schedule to allow sufficient research, study, and writing time. You must be honest with yourself in planning and scheduling. Failure should not be the first day of reckoning with respect to planning. Proper planning will still allow time for many of the positive things students enjoy: exercise, relaxation, and study.

If you want positive change to occur from examining your strengths and weaknesses, you must place emphasis on two aspects of your consciousness—attention and intention. Attention energizes and intention transforms. Whatever you put your attention on will grow stronger in your life. Whatever you take your attention away from will wither. Intention, on the other hand, triggers the transformation of energy and information. Putting both forces to work carries your examination process forward into action.

VALIDATE YOURSELF

You must determine what determination, hard work, and success mean to you. Do not accept someone else's view of the world. You are the best evaluator of your efforts. Only you know where you have come from to get where you are today.

In law school, where type A personalities abound, I found that one of my greatest assets was the fact that I did not let anyone validate my law school existence. I validated my own experience. I knew why I was in law school. I realized the daily responsibilities that I faced. I did not rely on anyone to make me feel valued. No one could make me believe that my success as an attorney hinged on being in the top 10 percent or making the law review. Obviously, those persons lived in another world! My goal was to get as much out of law school as possible to become the best attorney that I could be. Do not allow yourself to get caught up in someone else's hype.

YOU CAME TO LEAVE

The goal of graduate education is to finish. Thus, when you begin a graduate program, map out your courses starting from day one through graduation. In this respect, if deviations occur, then you can make appropriate adjustments.

Do not become so comfortable with your school environs that you do not wish to leave. Realize that you came there to leave, not to stay. You should take the approach that anything that stops you from leaving is thereby an enemy. It must be defeated. Visualize graduation, walking across the stage and seeing widening smiles on your parents' faces. Your singular goal is to get it and get on. Your life is ahead of you.

CONCLUSION

To achieve as a graduate student in higher education, one must be committed to a task. This commitment requires persistence. Persistence can be rooted in your spiritual faith. It can also be birthed in the knowledge of your purpose as an educational pioneer in your family. It must, however, be rooted in something.

If you remember the four points discussed above, they should serve as a guide to help you weather the storms of academia. You must not quit nor be afraid of success. You must continue to tear down the tall timbers of academia so that future African American graduate students can find shelter in the land you cleared for them. Remember, to whom much is given, much is required.

REFERENCES

Chopra, D. (1994). *The seven spiritual laws of success.* San Francisco, CA: Amber-Allen Publishing, p. 70.

Flake, F. (1999). *The way of the bootstrapper: Nine action steps for achieving your dreams.* San Francisco, CA: Harper, p. 28.

Some Factors to Consider in Graduate School

LENWARD T. SEALS III

Doctoral Candidate, Physics, Georgia Institute of Technology

If you think that graduate school will help you enhance some aspect of your career either academically or professionally, then there are a number of factors that I think you will probably have to consider.

The first will be what do you want from your education. To state this more clearly, the question will be, what do you want to do with your life, not necessarily for the next thirty years, but for the next five or ten. This is pertinent to whatever follows. I think there are many factors dictating success or failure, but satisfaction with the product is a major factor.

Second, I feel that it is important to understand what it is that you are seeking from your degree. Again to oversimplify, what level of education do you feel is important to fulfill the role you have laid out for yourself? That could be a master's degree, a Ph.D., or a specialty degree. It is equally important to determine your degree as it is to determine the program you want to enter. This will again be determined by your road map for the next five to ten years. After entering the job market, you might find the environment more dynamic depending on your type of industry. However, you want your education structured so that you are able to adapt quickly and instinctively to the changes that you might face, even if you feel it is beyond the scope of your formal education.

This brings up the next point, which is choosing the right graduate school. This may not necessarily mean the Ivy League, Big Ten, Southeastern Conference (SEC), or Atlantic Coast Conference (ACC); it may be some of the regional or local universities where you live. A big factor is cost. You may not want to spend the hundreds of thousands of dollars that it might take to attend one of the top hundred schools. Your background is also a factor. You might just need a degree to advance in your current position and not necessarily need a top-ranked program. Alternatively, you might be highly competitive and motivated, but for some reason you are satisfied with your current status. It is important to understand this, because if you decide to pursue an advanced degree or other graduate or professional degree, it will require a large time commitment in a region of the country in which you may not desire to reside. College is the time for new experiences, but you will want to do all that you can to make the best of it.

After picking a college for graduate school, the next step is to apply for admission. You want to apply to as many colleges and universities as you can afford or have a desire to attend. You might not always be the first choice of the school to which you try to matriculate. It happens; get over it and develop a back-up plan! I think it would give you an advantage over others to have a good grade point average and other distinctions, which would help in the selection process. Determining what type of work you want to do can also be helpful.

Once you are in graduate school, you should try to learn the system. Talk to the teaching assistants and research assistants. Try to understand what professors expect. They may be a valuable study resource for old exams and other intangible information. You will also have to be resolute and hardworking. This is important; it is your future.

For the Ph.D., the most important aspect is to pass your comprehensive exam and choose a thesis adviser. It is important to develop a relationship and a plan with him or her. This part of the program is fluid and can vary greatly with the individual, so it is important to state your expectations.

Beyond that, all I can do is say good luck.

Faith without Works Is Dead

XANTHE Y. SEALS

Doctoral Candidate, Developmental Education, Grambling State University

Faith without works is dead. This is true in every aspect of life. As for me, it is the golden rule of graduate school. Ultimately, without work there is no reward. Without vision there can be no insight into the desired outcome. Without sowing the good seeds of academic pursuits, there will not be the bountiful harvest of academic excellence. It is important that as a graduate student you understand what is expected and what you have to do on an individual level in order to accomplish the task at hand. Everyone is different; we all have different strengths as well as weaknesses. Have you ever heard of the old saying "accentuate the positive"? That's exactly what you need to do. Don't overcompensate for your weaknesses, but if you have talents in specific areas, develop ways to utilize them to their fullest. Also, work on your trouble areas; they can always be strengthened to a certain level of mastery. In the end, you want to develop and evolve into the best person that you can. No one is perfect, but we all can be improved into a better, more productive version of ourselves. However, in graduate school the ultimate goal is to become a graduate professional in every sense of the word.

Graduate school isn't easy and it's not for everyone. Although you can form contacts with professors and networks with other graduate students, they cannot do the work for you. They can provide you with priceless knowledge and insight that can ease some of the pains and stresses of your journey, but they can only take you so far. You have to make a decision, the sooner the better, on whether a graduate or professional school degree is in fact what you truly desire. If it is not, there will be many times when obstacles seem too great or personal life stresses become too much. If you're not sure a graduate degree is what you want, you'll probably cave in under the pressure or you will not have the reserves left to make it through that last long mile to graduation.

As a doctoral candidate, there are some things that you may need to understand as well as address. At this point in your academic career, your parents probably won't be supporting you or will be providing you very little assistance. You probably will work as a teaching or research assistant at the university that you attend. You're probably getting paid enough to make it, but not enough to live. If you're lucky, you're medically insured by the university you attend, and if you are, this doesn't have anything to do with dental insurance. So this means no new car, no new house, and no shopping sprees.

If you are married, or thinking about getting married or having children, graduate school can be increasingly difficult. Some schools have married student housing and some schools don't; either way you want to get increased funding for your spouse, your kids, or your living situation. This isn't the military, where all your needs are taken care of so you can focus on the task at hand. So it is imperative that you make a plan, and also plan within that for the unexpected. Untimely things will always occur, you and your dependants will get sick, and your car will need repairs, regardless of whether it's new or not—it will still cost you in one form or another. Unfortunately your studies will not wait until the latest crisis has passed or until your broken heart has time to heal. Also, your significant other will not save the argument until the semester break. You have to deal with life, as well as death, as a graduate student; it will not wait until you graduate. You will lose contact with many people, and you will miss many of your friends' weddings as well as holiday and spring break vacations. You will be trying to play catch-up on other work, or you will be too tired or too broke to participate.

Don't get me wrong. Graduate school has been the single most rewarding experience of my life. I have learned more about everything and have become attuned to what I'm truly made of. This experience has made me become aware of many skills that I didn't even know I had. It has allowed me to sharpen skills and to become a greater thinker as well as doer. Graduate school isn't just trials and tribulations; it is full of accomplishments and triumphs, but it doesn't come without a cost. Unfortunately, most feel in the end that the cost is too high. Marriages may have to wait, relationships may end, marriages may be brought to the breaking point and in some cases broken. It is a sad reminder that life continues while you are in graduate school; it doesn't wait until you're ready to deal with it. You may have to let many things go. That doesn't mean everything. You can make time for the important things as well as some rest and relaxation activities, because we all need downtime. Don't believe what others say, if they tell you that you can't burn yourself out, because you can. You can drain yourself to the point where you can't write, work, or even think clearly. It is important as a graduate student that you don't spread yourself too thin. Again, this point is different for everybody; you don't need to spread yourself too thin. Too many commitments can spell disaster for a graduate career, and you may not be able to recover from them. At best, you many complete some things and not complete others. At worst, you will do sloppy work on all fronts, everything will go lacking, and nothing will get done. Avoid that by making a plan and sticking as close to it as possible. Nothing can be laid in stone, but if you stick to the plan, you will make it through just fine.

As for your choice of graduate profession, money is important but it is not key. You need to go into a field that you feel comfortable with, and it helps if you like it. This will make those study and research hours go faster. However, the single most important thing I can tell you as far as academics is about picking an adviser. This decision can either make or break your graduate career as well as your professional career. Make sure you think it through and determine whether you can work with this adviser. Consider whether this adviser can help you achieve your goals. Graduate school is like any other place worthy of note; it is very political. You need to trust that your adviser will lead you where you want to go. A lot of times you will need to yield to your adviser's experience and knowledge of the situation instead of your own emotions, especially in departmental and committee matters. So it helps if you trust your adviser and have an understanding of how he or she thinks and responds to situations as well as students.

Graduate school is a very rewarding as well as challenging experience. Make the best of it and put into it what you want to get out of it. Treat it like a job for now that will become a stepping stone or a stumbling block to your future success. Embrace the experience and enjoy the journey. Good Luck!

Some Traits of a Successful Graduate Student

LESTER SPENCE
Master's Candidate, Political Science, The University of Michigan–Ann Arbor

Looking back on my graduate and undergraduate career, I see a path that wound through many different spheres: through dormitory life, through involvement in political activities, through fraternal life, through nine years of pickup basketball (three days a week, like clockwork), through marriage, and through parenthood. Indeed, sometimes it's hard for me to see how I came out relatively sane! Throughout it all (and I have to add that I'm not quite through yet), I think there were a few things that separated me from the pack. What I'd like to share are some of my experiences in the hope that you too can get something out of them.

First, it is important that you know something about me. You see, I didn't enter college with a 4.0 grade point average from high school. Though I did take honors courses, I ended up with something closer to a 2.0 than a 4.0. Furthermore, though I have fond memories of my high school, if I had listened to my high school teachers and counselors about where I should have gone to college, the last place I would have ended up is at the University of Michigan. But please don't think that I'm in any way tripping on the teachers who didn't think I could cut it in a school like the University of Michigan. My confidence and clarity of vision grew as much from people telling me what I couldn't do as it did from people telling me what I could do. Most of my success, however, did not come solely from a strong academic background.

Now with that out of the way, let me explain what made me the student I am. One of the first things contributing to my success was my confidence and my vision. When I first came to the campus, through a summer program designed to bridge the brief, but important, period between high school and college, I should have been nervous. But I knew that this was the beginning of a grand adventure and a great opportunity. Nobody here knew my past; that is, the professors didn't know how I had performed in Mr. Fogel's physics class back in high school. The slate was totally clean. Not only that, but for the first time everything was on me—and not just which classes I took, but also whether I attended those classes regularly. Rather than scaring me to death, I found this knowledge liberating. That summer experience helped me to realize the possibilities that awaited me as well as what I was capable of achieving. It was finally my time. *My* time. And I took advantage of it with the help of a couple of teachers who recognized my potential. Not only did I study what I was expected to study, but I also studied outside of the class, pursuing my own interests. To me it wasn't just about reading what Orwell had to say about language because it was an assignment for English composition. Instead, it was about absorbing knowledge of those things I wanted to study. I can still remember brothers and sisters asking me, "What class is that for?" in reference to a book I was checking out. When I said "no class," they tripped, as if unassigned reading on my own was akin to catching typhoid fever. But I kept a book with me at all times. On the bus I was reading. While in the waiting room at the doctor's office, I was reading. Sometimes, even between pickup games I was reading.

Not only did I read on my own outside of class, I also wrote on my own outside of class. I kept a journal, at first just recording my day-to-day life, but eventually branching out into political essays and thoughts about culture, about America, and about my place in life. I can't tell you how much those two simple activities helped me to grapple with my role in the world and helped me to deal with school. The number of drafts I had to write for assigned papers dwindled, while my ability to bring a variety of different ideas to the table in class discussions increased. My ability to speak knowledgeably and confidently increased as well. I grew from being a person who shied away from speaking in public to being able to speak with authority on a variety of topics.

In hindsight, these activities were what I call "tighteners." To illustrate what I mean by this, consider a constant in my life over the past eight years: I've played basketball three days a week like clockwork. As I've grown older, I've been able to actually study the game and apply its lessons to my life. In pickup games as well as in the pro arena, the only way to be a good point guard is to know how to dribble with your left as well as with your right hand. You have to make sure your game is "tight." If you have to dribble with your right hand for a half-hour every day, and then switch to your left hand and dribble for another half-hour, then that is what you have to do in order to tighten your game. This is what I'm talking about when I speak about tighteners. When I was reading on my own or writing on my own it was the academic equivalent of dribbling a half-hour with each hand each day until things were " tight" academically.

I was also blessed with a number of mentors. A few of them were professors who took an interest in my development and who helped me in numerous, untold ways. Here is where the various programs designed to help African American students really aided me. I really appreciated the support I was given by the staff and the faculty. The professors I encountered through the program that helped me get into Michigan in the first place saw something in me that I didn't even know I had. Their aid helped me immensely in terms of my confidence and my work ethic.

Also among those who looked out for me were graduate students I'd met after pledging Omega Psi Phi fraternity. Even though I was doing well academically, in fact getting higher grades in college than I had received in high school, I knew that someone giving me "the hookup" could only serve to benefit me more. I learned from those willing to show me how they did it the type of information that they had found helpful to them. For instance, I didn't think there was any way for me to afford graduate school, and so I didn't give it much thought despite my strong undergraduate record. But one of my fraternity brothers who was a graduate student in chemical engineering told me about fellowships and teaching and research assistantships, in addition to scholarship awards that allow a student to earn money while in graduate school. I didn't know that I could actually make money writing journal articles until an English professor told me. And when I was messing up, these same people had the integrity to tell me about it; with only a couple of exceptions I had the good sense to listen to them. These brothers (and a few sisters too) looked out for me in ways that I can never truly repay, and in ways I'll probably never fully know.

I got involved in political activities on campus in my freshman year and the year after I joined the fraternity. I became even more involved in campus affairs. Here also is where the support staff designed to aid African American students at Michigan kicked it. Though I'd butted heads with several administrators, including some who were African Americans, I was always able to count on them to help me with programs I'd designed or for advice about becoming a better scholar. This support continued long after I had left my undergraduate years behind, gotten married, and started a family.

College can be expensive, and there were times when I held two jobs to support myself. Though I am not sure that most people would tell a prospective student that the key to success is to become an activist and get two jobs while juggling a full credit load and a pickup basketball career, I have to say that these activities aided me. I became a much more disciplined and well-rounded person spiritually, socially, physically, and mentally. I learned not only how to organize my time but also how to organize people. I learned not only how to keep my mind fit but how to keep my body fit as well. I am now in my final year of graduate school, and I juggle not only my dissertation but also family responsibilities. When asked how I do it, I just shrug because I've tightened my game to the point where I can do it with the level of skill that a pro point guard can dribble a basketball. It's to that point where I don't really have to think about it; I just do it.

So basically I've taken both the negative and the positive things that life has thrown my way, and taken from them bits and pieces, strategies and tactics, in order to accomplish my academic goals. I'd like to conclude with a final word of advice. Contrary to popular belief, the world is yours. Whether you know it or not, you've been given the keys to life itself. Figure out what you want to do, plan how you want to get there, and work on your game. Do this, and when it's your time to fly, you'll have a crowd watching you ascend.

Knowing Yourself Will Enhance Your Graduate Study

LEON P. STRAYER

Doctoral Candidate, Higher Education Administration,
Florida State University

Knowing yourself is the key to success as a graduate student. We enter a graduate or professional program coming from different areas in our lives. Some of us enter the program directly after our bachelor's degrees, while others enter graduate school after gaining experience in the professional world. Having a clear perspective on my career options allowed me to understand my role as a graduate student. After I graduated with my bachelor's degrees, I taught first grade for two years. When I decided to pursue graduate school, I realized that I was a professional going back to school to gain and refine my leadership, organizational, and interpersonal skills. Once in the program, I applied what I learned as a professional to my new career as a graduate student. It was almost as if this role held me accountable for my actions, thus allowing me to stay focused on achieving the master's degree.

Those students who are admitted directly after their undergraduate careers will gain and refine leadership, organizational, and interpersonal skills, but perhaps there will be a different perception of their role in graduate school. Students may become extremely motivated to finish their degree programs in order to experience the workforce for the first time. My essay focuses on sharing my experiences as I began graduate school after working for a period of time. Realizing where I came from prior to graduate school and what experiences I gained allowed me to stay focused.

Goal setting was important for me. I found that graduate school course work was more demanding and time-consuming than undergraduate work.

I spent less time in the classroom but more time on class assignments. Simple goals like reading for two hours in one textbook and reading for one hour in another were obtainable and manageable for one study session. Completing these goals gave me confidence and reassured me that I could keep up with the academic demands of a master's program. I made personal goals for particular courses also. Some of those goals were driven by my desire to earn good grades. Other goals consisted of learning how to apply and connect the curriculum throughout all of the courses in the program. Most of the courses in my program were coordinated to make a connection in one class so that I could recall that information in another.

Encouragement helped me succeed in graduate school. When those goals became overwhelming and intimidating, I gained encouragement from a close network of friends. This was important for my success. It was important that they were African American, since I attended a predominantly White institution. I established a core group within my academic field or department that complemented my graduate school experiences. It was inspiring to be among intelligent, highly motivated, and enthusiastic graduate students who shared similar goals. My peer group helped me define what scholarship and academic success were. Learning from my peers, collaborating with my peers, and challenging my peers provided that continuous intellectual stimulation outside of the classroom, thus making me a better student. We formed study groups, assigned each other parts of the reading, note taking, and research to disperse the responsibilities and lighten up the workload.

Without getting overly involved on campus, I participated in a limited number of activities and organizations. Your academic department may recommend a national organization to join. Take advantage of the low student membership rates, and gain national networking contacts, current literature about your field, and opportunities to attend conferences that provide professional development and job interviews. Involvement will help you manage your time as well as provide an opportunity for leadership and interpersonal growth. This involvement may become the source of gaining your peer group. If your university offers an orientation for Black graduate students, I recommend attending. Some of the people that I met in our program have become part of my transitional foundation of adjusting to graduate school and my new environment. They have become a part of a core set of friends from whom I gain insight, trust, criticisms, and friendships. Also, maintain contact with colleagues attending other universities, especially if they are enrolled in the same graduate program. Collaboration, dialogue, and comparison and contrast between graduate programs will enhance your graduate school experience. You gain a different perspective on current issues in your major area of study, as well as discover what other universities are doing to prepare their graduate students for the workforce.

Another important relationship to have is a faculty member, administrator, or professor who is a mentor, more specifically, an African American mentor or someone whom you can closely relate to. Confirmations that I received from my mentors about my progress as a graduate student motivated me to work harder, overcome the challenges, and continue to pursue my goals. My mentors provided a model of professionalism and success as well as guidance and experiences that helped me complete graduate school successfully like they did. Working with mentors helped me refine my study habits, organization skills, and professionalism as a graduate student—goals that I want to achieve in the program.

This is an exciting part of your life. Maintain a healthy lifestyle of exercise, good diet, close friendships, knowledge of a personal philosophy, and a strong spiritual foundation. A combination of these will become your foundation for who you are and will oftentimes answer why you are in graduate school. You will then make the right decisions that involve your professional, personal, and educational goals.

Hard Times

Traveling on the "D" Train Day to Day,
Dreaming of Life as a Ph.D.

SCYATTA A. WALLACE

Master's Candidate, Developmental Psychology, Fordham University

PREPARING FOR GRADUATE SCHOOL [*]

I had no idea what I was getting myself into. I remember my undergraduate research adviser kept telling horror stories of her life as a graduate student. "You're at the bottom of the totem pole, lower than an undergrad." It didn't sound very promising. But she seemed happy, and as a woman of color, she believed that she had made the right choice. So I shrugged off my anxiety and called to say, "Yes I will be coming." That summer, before graduate school, I didn't do much preparing. I saw old friends, relaxed, and had fun. I worked in a psychiatric hospital to make money and also to get some experience. In all, I was anxiously awaiting the beginning of my journey toward a doctorate degree.

I wouldn't do much differently, except I would advise students embarking upon graduate school to talk to as many graduate students and faculty about their experiences before applying and definitely before accepting admission to any school. There will not be any other summers to spare, so get as much rest as possible during the summer.

The First Year

The first two weeks before my program I received a huge package from my research adviser (at my institution, students are assigned one their first year until they are acquainted enough with the program to properly chose whom they want to work with). The package included articles and book chapters of her work. I was to read them and comment on what she wrote. The first day was intense; I had to figure out everything. Where were my classes? What were my classes? The bookstore didn't have any of the materials I needed. And my adviser was ready to begin immediately. By the end of the day I was depressed. Had I made the right decision? Was I cut out for this type of work? "Bottom of the totem pole," was all I could think of. Again, I shrugged off my anxiety and decided to push on.

That first semester was rough for many reasons. The workload was increased and the degree of difficulty greater than undergraduate work. In addition, what was expected of me was markedly different from what it had been when I was an undergrad. Even more, class participation was necessary. I had to thoroughly understand the content and critique the literature based on the knowledge of other works and past experiences. Therefore, reading the materials took more time. Academically, though, I didn't feel trapped. I knew I could adjust to the changes and work things out. However, there were subtle things that I didn't realize were necessary until my adviser pulled me aside and gave me some much-needed advice. Unfortunately, proper mentoring for students of color is rare. One-on-one contact makes a world of difference between succeeding and just floating through the program. I was lucky. It is important to try to find someone who will provide this experience for you. My adviser told me to get to know my fellow students. "You will need them for a lot of things, and you will be with them for at least the next three years. Study with them, review research opportunities, and share your stories. They are your support network." My adviser further told me, "Talk to the professors. Get to know them. They are the ones who control your fate. They need to know that you are interested in their work. They need to meet with you individually to see that you are bright and articulate. And most of all, they need to be aware of your accomplishments and research interests. Before a paper is due, go to them with a draft. Ask them questions before exams. This shows initiative."

At the end of the year, when I received a copy of my yearly review, I saw exactly why I was given this advice. The department wrote personnel a detailed account of how it felt I was progressing in the program. It often commented not only on my academic progress but also on my professional, mental, and social progress. This was kept in my records for use when writing recommendations.

The most important thing to do during your first year is to focus on doing well. Study very hard. Good grades will help secure money for the duration of the program. It also helps to decrease stress when you know you are doing well.

- Read, read, and read. Read not only what they give you to read but also works by people of color, as well as by those from other disciplines. This will always make your work stand out. As you read, begin to see which areas interest you the most and which authors you most agree with and admire. Begin to follow them and keep up with their work.

- Get acquainted with people in your program and your institution in general.
- Venture out and get to know your community. Locate the leaders, find out what places people of color frequent, figure out what the city or town has to offer. You don't have to see it all in one year, but gather the information.
- Begin to soul search and tailor your life goals, not just academic, but personal goals as well. If you are not already doing so, practice a faith. Prayer and meditation go a long way in keeping you focused and happy, especially in a place as hostile and stressful as graduate school.

Course Work

I was lucky to have an exceptional undergraduate education. I was taught how to write effectively and master psychological concepts. However, because the majority of my classes were large, I was not prepared for the close interaction and increased attention I would receive as the only African American graduate student in my program. It is very difficult as people of color to be so aggressive and draw attention to our accomplishments. However, this is essential in graduate school.

As stated earlier, getting acclimated to graduate-level course work can be stressful, but it is feasible with some careful planning. Organization is the key.

- Read all the materials ahead of time; pick points that are particularly interesting to you and highlight them during class.
- Address all your questions about the material with the professor.
- Meet in as many study sessions as possible with your classmates.
- Always turn in a draft and outline of your papers to professors for their feedback.

Research

The reason I applied to graduate school is because of my love for research. I felt very secure about my research abilities and ideas. Upon my initial assignment to my adviser, I made this known. I presented my ideas and my adviser was interested in pursuing the research. This led to a three-year relationship in which I was integrally involved in multiple research projects. Although I felt comfortable jumping right into a research experience, I could never have predicted how exhausting and complicated it would be. It has been especially difficult because I do research on African American and other ethnic group adolescents. There is a paucity of research available, and much of the mainstream work is inadequate. It uses only theoretical models, which are based on White middle-class standards, and often does not include variables that underscore the experiences of African Americans. So, in addition to learning basic research skills, I had to become extremely creative and novel in how I approached my research (which means double the amount of work). This was especially true because my adviser is White.

Research is an integral part of your education. It is considered equal to your course work and helps to steer the direction of your professional path. However, unlike the course work curriculum, obtaining a research track is never clearly defined and takes a lot of personal initiative.

- Very early in your graduate school career, find out the research interests of the faculty and determine whom you would like to work with. Approach that individual and let him or her know your interests and make sure you present your knowledge of the research field.
- Always be willing to do the grunt work. Although it may seem tiresome, it is a rite of passage in the field. In addition, it teaches you a lot about self-discipline and the realities of research work. It takes time and money to be able to hire graduate students, such as yourself, to do the odd jobs necessary to pull off a research study. Most new faculty have to suffer through these duties alone, with all the other responsibilities academe provides. So take the time now to master these skills, and your work will be easier for you in the future.
- Let your research adviser know you are interested in the work and that you want to learn more. Look up the literature and present your ideas to him or her. It is very rare for a professor to give assistants opportunities unless they ask for them. Be assertive.
- Over time, learn what your strengths and weaknesses are and ask for assistance in developing your research skills.
- Most important, ask to coauthor a paper with your adviser, but be prepared to work! You will need lots of extra time to review the literature and draft the articles. But, like anything else, this exercise gives you much-needed practice in a skill that is vital to your success as a professional.

Comprehensives

One of the most difficult experiences of my graduate school journey was studying for the Ph.D. comprehensives. I was terrified of failing. The massive amounts of information I had to learn immobilized me. I was unable to get it together for a long time. Finally, with the help of my classmates, I was able to buckle down and get to it.

One of the first things to understand about the comprehensives is that this is just another exam. Getting over the fear of the title will do a lot to curb your anxiety. I studied in a group with my classmates, and that was my only saving grace. We provided each other with much-needed support. Because there is so much information to cover, in our initial meeting we devised a list of all the possible topics that we needed to cover. We then divided each topic among ourselves and assigned a date to review each topic. Topics were assigned based on each person's expertise. Each person had to review the literature about the topic and condense it into an organized report for the group. What a relief! Suddenly the task wasn't so bad. During our biweekly meetings, each person presented his or her report, and we reviewed the material until everyone understood it. During the final month, we decided not to meet until the final week. I then took this month to condense the reports into index flash cards. I wrote theoretical concepts, terms, names, and dates on one side and then the explanations on the back. I reviewed a topic each day until I felt comfortable enough to move to my final task. I took old comprehensive questions and answered them. I would review my answer and fill in the missing information. The night before the exam we met for dinner to ensure that no one was at home studying or, worse, having an anxiety attack. Our comprehensives are two weekends in a row. So the following week we didn't meet, but we called each other to check in. This was the best strategy; all of us passed and felt much closer as a class.

- Another thing that saved me was taking the comprehensives as soon as I was able to. Putting them off will only delay your process, and if most of your other classmates have taken it, you won't have much support.
- My only other advice is to stay calm and take at least three months to study. Be consistent and study with a group.

Right now I am teaching and working on my dissertation. This is another major learning experience. However, I do see the light at the end of the tunnel. I feel that I have learned and experienced so much that has prepared me for this last hurdle. The most important lesson I've learned is to put God first. He has led me in the right direction and provided me with many blessings and mentors along the way. Also, staying close to my family and friends has helped me realize that there is a world outside of the research lab. They have forced me to take my head out of my pile of journal articles and go to the park, watch movies, and see the sights of the city. In addition, staying in touch with my community has kept me sane. Graduate school as an African American can be draining. You often feel torn. The process can be brainwashing; your true self can be left behind. Volunteering and giving back is a great way to stay in touch with that self, as well as helping to do your part in healing the community. I have made a vow to keep my life in balance— staying involved in my hobbies and extracurricular activities and making time with myself alone. There is very little time available, but I make it stretch because work will never end if I let it. There is harm in living a life with all work and no play. I've been lucky in that my university, although all White, has been very supportive of my work and interests. I have been allowed a healthy amount of autonomy, but I still received proper guidance, including financial support. I still, however, sought others in my community, at professional meetings, and in other disciplines as role models. They have provided me with a balanced outlook on my career path and have assisted me in dealing with obstacles that have come my way, obstacles I did not feel comfortable revealing to my department.

It takes extreme self-discipline to get a dissertation written, but the years spent doing course work and studying for the comprehensives have helped me to get this far in one piece. The most important thing to remember is that this is another part of life's journey. It is a learning experience. Take time out of your graduate school life to pay attention to what you have learned. It helps to build strength of character and will help boost your self-esteem. I know I will finish and one day attain this coveted degree because I have come this far. I know that if you stay focused and determined, one day you too will be a Ph.D.

Constructing Identities

The Black Graduate Experience

KERRIE COTTEN WILLIAMS

Doctoral Candidate, American History, New York University

In the fall of 1992, I entered New York University (NYU) as a full-time graduate student in the history department. I graduated from Dillard University in the spring of that year, and I was aware that I was making a major transition in my academic life. However, the change for me was not just institutional. I was now making a move from New Orleans to New York, from a small historically Black college to a major urban university. Upon arrival in New York City, I understood immediately that I no longer belonged to a cohesive group of undergraduates who were bound to the ideal of communal space and familial support. I entered the NYU history department as one of only two Black graduate students under the guidance of the only Black faculty member in the department. The ability to survive this new transition centered on my desire to build my own community of mentors, peers, and allies, engage my role as a graduate student, and finally reach back to the support group that helped me to get to the position I now occupied.

The major difference I discovered between Dillard and NYU was that the latter lacked a real sense of community between students, faculty, and staff. I had come from a place where there were many people concerned with my intellectual growth. I was raised in my small college environment to be a responsible and respectful member of a larger body of folk. In New York I found that I was severely detached from my core, my center that consisted of family and friends. There was a serious contradiction in my new life. New York University offered me a challenging academic environment with a seemingly endless wealth of resources for historical study. New York City was the very metaphor of living history. The Schomburg Center, Greenwich Village, Lincoln Center, Chinatown, and Harlem were a subway and a transfer away from my Brooklyn apartment. Each day offered a new cultural experience that deepened my awareness of difference in ethnicity, race, class, and gender.

Even though my exposure to new experiences expanded my notions of identity and community, I lacked a community of my own. My total existence was my small apartment and my department at the university. I was unable to connect with my fellow graduate students because there was no real sense of cohesiveness within our group, which was due mainly to age differences. My inability to get ahead of my tremendous workload reflected my growing alienation. I soon discovered that I needed to integrate into a network of students who would propel one another in the critical thinking necessary to tackle the reading assignments that seemed endless. Once I was able to locate several students who had the same needs as my own, I became much more involved in my academic growth. They challenged me to join organizations that addressed my interests and concerns as a Black scholar.

In New York I created my own resource network, but my mentor, friends, and family were a constant source of guidance and support. Even though I found myself more involved with the university, I knew that the support group I had as an undergraduate was essential to my success at NYU. Ultimately, my ability to remain in New York hinged on the stability of this important mix of folk. I needed the constant push of my mentor to get through the first year of graduate school. Within that year, I was challenged to go beyond what I thought were the limits of my own critical thinking. My professors introduced me to new theoretical paradigms I found intriguing and complicated. I had to adjust to the reading load, which consisted of thirty to forty books per semester. I wrote and churned out papers and reviews at an exhausting pace. I became a better scholar, but I also became disillusioned with the whole "Ivory Tower" experience. What was my role as a graduate student within my own Black community in the South? What good did it serve me to learn abstract ideas and arguments when I was really concerned with more tangible issues that surfaced in the lives of people I knew and met every day? I began to see myself as a detached student who had no real place or purpose other than the classrooms in which I sat.

My confidence in who I was and what I was capable of accomplishing gradually faded. However, I was able to work through this period by consulting my mentor. She and my family members redirected my attention to the skills and abilities I possessed to make it to NYU. Their presence in my life helped me to ground my goals as an academic. My role in the community rested on my position as a valued contributor as a teacher. I felt more in control of constructing my own identity by embracing those individuals who were a part of my life before graduate school. If I had not reached out for my core, I would not have continued my studies in New York. I need their support and presence in my life to anchor me.

Making the Right Decisions in High School Can Enhance Your Chances for Success as an Undergraduate and Graduate Student

TOMEKA K. BROWN

Computer Technology Major, Grambling State University

For as long as I can remember, obtaining an education has been one of the common topics of conversation in my parents' and grandparents' homes. My mother and grandmother are perhaps no different from anyone else. They wanted their children to receive a high school education, to attend college, then to graduate, and above all to have a relationship with God. I truly believe that their influence greatly attributed to my success in high school. Some of their advice has been "Education comes first," "Don't try to grow up too fast," "Act like a lady," "Don't be disrespectful," and "Always let God guide your life." These parameters have served to shape my personal goals. During junior high, wearing makeup was the fad. My friends wore it. So, naturally, I wanted to wear it also. My mother repeatedly told me that I should not try to grow up too fast. I did not understand then, but now I realize that growing up too fast can lead to other problems, including drug abuse or an unwanted pregnancy.

During my high school experience, I was confronted with many challenges. Some were dealing with peer pressure, making decisions, and becoming responsible. One of the challenging decisions I had to make at the end of each year was to decide what courses to take. Most students preferred an easier course load just to get by. However, I selected courses in high school that I knew I needed in order to be successful as an undergraduate in college and later as a graduate student. These courses included algebra II, trigonometry, and geometry as well as science and mathematics. Computer technology, the field I have chosen to pursue, is very competitive; therefore, I needed the curriculum that I chose to prepare me for the stiff competition. In addition to these courses, I had to make decisions about other courses.

Other crucial decisions I made involved peer pressure. My freshman year in high school was the worst. I was trying to "hang" with the right crowd or the clique, but I was with the wrong crowd. For example, during my freshman year, my peers and I frequently attended many parties. I knew that drinking would be involved; however, I had already decided that I would not drink. My peers encouraged me to drink. This was indeed pressure. They talked about me and said that I was "chicken" and that they had thought I was cool. I realized that many of my peers were not my friends. I am happy to say that I stuck to my decision not to drink. If it were not for my parents' advice, I would have made many mistakes.

Because of my parents' spiritual guidance, I made the right decision. If it were not for them, I would not be as focused in high school as I am today. As I entered the tenth grade, I again saw that people who claimed to be my friends were not really friends at all. If they had been my friends, they would not have encouraged me to do wrong. It doesn't matter what grade you are in, peer pressure will always exist, especially in high school. Although my mother encouraged me, my father did also. As a law enforcement officer, he constantly reminded me about the consequences of drinking and taking drugs. I tried to do the right things to succeed in high school.

During my freshman year in high school, Mrs. Morgan, my English teacher, became one of my mentors. Although I had very good teachers, Mrs. Morgan was different from all of my other teachers; she inspired me. She was always there for me. She was a very patient and understanding individual. She inspired me when I was in the ninth grade when she told me that I was very intelligent and that I could be successful in whatever I chose to do in life. I could go to her and talk to her about any problem, because she was always willing to listen and offer advice. She wanted me to be successful, and I didn't want to let her down, and I didn't. She always told me that she believed in me and that I could do anything if I put my mind to it. Her vote of confidence motivated me and kept me encouraged when I was down.

The best advice I can give to other high school students is that they should not allow their peers to think for them. They should depend on themselves. Therefore, students need to become self-reliant and not depend on others for their success. They must do it themselves. It is important that students learn to rely on themselves. Self-reliance is being confident in one's own abilities. My definition is self-explanatory. In my family, I was taught to be self-reliant. If students depend on themselves, they will go further in life. If I had depended on others to do everything for me, I would not be where I am today. I do not mean that students shouldn't depend on others for some things. No one can do everything by him- or herself. Again, becoming self-reliant is a part of becoming responsible, responsible for your actions and decisions. Finally, I am confident that I will be successful when I enter undergraduate and graduate school.

Preparing for Graduate School

An Undergraduate's Perspective

OCTAVIA R. DANIELS

English Education Major, Grambling State University

When one thinks of "the college experience," parties, clubs, fraternities, and sororities immediately come to mind. These are the expectations that are commonly associated with life as an undergraduate. The typical freshman thinks of college in terms of "no rules," "no parents," and "no discipline." However, while seeking fun and new adventures, a high percentage of undergraduates fail and never achieve college success. I must admit that I too came to college with some of the same misconceptions of college life—no rules, no parents, and no discipline. But I soon realized that this view of college can lead to a dead-end road. I thank God that I awakened from this daydream and began to take my college life seriously.

This wake-up call eventually led to my doing something that hurts even today. This something involved thrusting my pompous and dogmatic attitude aside. I had to reevaluate and query myself. "Am I living up to *my* standards?" "Am I in control of *my own* thought process?" "Am I focusing on my goals?" "Am I reaching toward the expectations of my senior class in being voted Most Likely to Succeed?" To my astonishment, I wasn't doing anything to achieve my goals. Something had to change. I promised myself that I would be able to answer "yes" to these questions later on in life. After identifying my strengths and weaknesses, I set goals and strategies for how to achieve them. I was now able to get back on track.

I began slowly getting back on track, one accomplishment at a time. Although there were many distractions, I remained focused, remembering why I was at Grambling State University. In my pursuit to fulfill the promise that

I made to myself, I began to value the importance of an education—an undergraduate degree. As an education major I would have to be a perfectionist in my area of concentration. I realized that I was learning for myself as well as the students who would fall under my wings. At the end of my first semester of college, I had made several rewarding accomplishments. I was an honor student, and I was nominated and named a National All-American Scholar by Dr. Helen Richards-Smith, dean of the Honors College.

After these accomplishments, I began to place more attention on my goal to attend graduate school at Howard University. From conversations with various graduate students, I knew that a satisfactory grade point average would be a major requirement. Therefore, earning and maintaining a 3.0 grade point average became my number-one goal. However, from my past experiences I knew this would be no easy task. Although the road to graduate school would be long and difficult, I knew that I had what it takes to travel the road to success. I started to search around campus for resources that would somehow connect me to the world of graduate school. After weighing my options, I registered for the work-study program. God allowed one of his angels to pay me a visit, because I was assigned to work in the School of Graduate Studies and Research. It was there that I received guidance and advice from Dr. Vernon L. Farmer, dean of the Graduate School, and Dr. Evelyn Wynn, an English professor. A day did not pass that I didn't learn something new. Under their leadership I became familiar with research and publishing, knowing that as time progressed I would eventually turn to writing and publishing myself. This early experience would certainly help me to become an established writer.

In my preparation as an undergraduate for graduate school, I've learned numerous lessons and secured valuable advice. One of the lessons learned is that one's undergraduate academic performance determines whether or not you'll reach the graduate level. I've been told of various cases where a low grade point average ruined a person's chances to continue education on the graduate level. In my desperate need not to fall in this category, I decided to take no shortcuts and accept no shortcomings. One thing that I have learned at Grambling State University is that my actions as well as my mistakes will follow me.

I advise all students to take their education seriously. It is better to miss a party than to miss the chance of obtaining a degree. Although they may want to experience all that college has to offer, they must not forget their reason for attending college and what it takes to make it. As I implied before, the glory days are only temporary, but reality is forever.

ESSAY 24

Preparing for Graduate Study
While in High School

JERRY L. FARMER II
Criminal Justice Major, Grambling State University

While in high school it is important to have someone whom you can count on to keep you on the right track. You can't always depend on your peers to do this. One of the hardest things for high school students to do is to trust an adult. I have found, however, that adults are often the best individuals to advise you during a problem simply because of their experiences. I can remember an incident when many of the Black students in my high school viewed me as a "nerd," perhaps because I made better grades, talked differently, and dressed a little nicer. Their view often frustrated me. One day I decided to have a talk with my math teacher, who was one of my mentors, about this problem. She gave me some advice that I will never forget. She said, "Just because someone tells you that you are different, don't let that get you down. Just pick your head up and show them differently." During the remainder of the school year I decided to mingle with my classmates so that they could get to know me better and I could get to know them better. Toward the end of the school year, I observed a change in their attitude and behavior. Many of them began to realize that I was no different than they were. A number of them began to devote more time to their study, which resulted in an improvement in their academic performances.

During my high school days, I had a lot of supporters, but my biggest supporter, without question, was my mother. She stuck with me through good times and bad times. She was always there when I needed someone to talk to. Along with God, she was the shining light in my eyes that guided me to success in high school. She helped with my homework whenever it was necessary, she attended my sporting activities, she comforted me when I was depressed, and she helped me solve problems I could not solve myself. I am convinced that without my mother's guidance and support, I would not have achieved the level of academic excellence I did in high school.

Although my parents divorced when I was a young child, I never forgot my father. My father has spent his entire career in the United States Air Force and has advanced in the ranks as an officer. I have no doubt that my decision to join the Air Force ROTC at Grambling State University was greatly influenced by my father. My father was clearly my career role model.

During my high school years, there were a number of other factors that contributed to my success. Having a clear mind and logical understanding about what I wanted to do in life was one of those factors. Many high school students do not have a clue as to what they want to do in life, and they usually do not figure it out until their senior year, which can be a big mistake. I figured out what I wanted to do in life by taking a good look at what I wanted to do best. However, I did not limit myself to what I though I could do best. I am convinced that you can accomplish anything that you want to if you set your mind to it. Remember you can do anything that you want to because nobody knows yourself better than you do.

Another factor that contributed to my success in high school was my commitment to studying so that I could master the course content in the curriculum. I realize that students sometimes regret having to take certain high school courses for a number of reasons. Perhaps this is so because they are not strong in a particular subject, or because the course lacks interest, or maybe the students are simply not interested in certain courses. However, I had to overcome these attitudes and look at the big picture, which was being successful in high school, so I could go on to college. I knew prior to attending high school that I would not like every course that I would need in order to prepare for college. I now realize that what we need to be successful in life isn't always going to be things we enjoy. When this occurs, you will just have to "suck it up" and take the tough courses whether you like them or not, if you want to be successful as an undergraduate and graduate student.

There are also a number of tasks that I performed that contributed to my success in high school. For example, completing homework assignments, reading for pleasure, not just for assignments, studying for tests beforehand, getting familiar with computers, and always maintaining a positive perspective on different views. I am convinced that if students perform these tasks, they will have a successful high school experience and will be prepared to go on to college for undergraduate study and then graduate or professional school.

Conclusion

FREEMAN A. HRABOWSKI III

President and Professor of Education, University of Maryland–Baltimore County

Finally, most of us already know that people living and working in the twenty-first century will see more dramatic changes than humankind has ever witnessed. Consequently, I talk with colleagues a great deal about how young people can best prepare to succeed in such an unpredictable world. Meanwhile, students on college campuses frequently talk about their dreams and anxieties related to career and life choices. For Black undergraduate and graduate students, the challenges may be even greater given issues related to race and under-representation in a variety of fields, including especially the sciences, engineering, and technology.

In conversations with Black students, I emphasize that the skills, values, and habits they acquire and practice in college will be the same ones they will use to succeed in life, both professionally and personally. The importance of reading, problem solving, asking questions, and knowing where to go for answers is also stressed. Further emphasis is placed on the significance of working hard and working to be the best, setting high standards, following through, being dependable, and knowing how to work well with others.

Whether a Black student is preparing for a career in science and technology, business, or one of the human-service areas (e.g., education, health care), both technology and communication skills will be critical. Consequently, we should encourage those who are not majoring in science and technology areas to take a variety of courses in either computer science or information systems to supplement their major course work. Students should be encouraged not only to become technologically literate but also to learn how to use technology within their academic disciplines and career fields. Health care professionals, for example, with strong computer skills can excel in informatics, and faculty who are comfortable with technology will play a special role in higher education institutions, where computers are becoming increasingly important. A student's ability to speak and write clearly and confidently in standard English also is critical, whether the student is completing a term paper, lab report, master's thesis, or doctoral dissertation, applying and interviewing for a job, or making a presentation once on the job. Initially, grades and ultimately job performance will be heavily dependent upon these skills.

We should also encourage Black undergraduates to become involved in hands-on research or practicum experiences as soon after the freshman year as possible in order to help them understand more about potential postgraduate or career fields and to help them determine whether their strengths and interests are compatible with the demands of a particular field. As part of these applied experiences, we should urge Black students to identify potential mentors, both Blacks and other professionals, who are already working successfully in a profession of possible interest to them. In addition, we should emphasize the importance of being open to having new experiences, meeting new people, and learning how to interact effectively with people from diverse backgrounds.

We are fortunate at the University of Maryland, Baltimore County, where Black students often are at the top of their classes, competing against students from all over the world. Many were attracted to the university's Meyerhoff Scholars Program for high-achieving minority undergraduates in science and engineering, and we also now have a Meyerhoff Graduate Fellows Program. Other programs similar to the Meyerhoff Graduate Fellows Programs include the Ronald E. McNair Scholars Program, the SREB Doctoral Scholars Program, the McKnight Doctoral Fellowship Program, and the Ph.D. Project. From these programs, we have learned about effective strategies for supporting Black students' academic success and personal development. Some of these strategies include (1) seeing a vision for oneself; (2) taking advantage of group study and finding student peers with common values and the "right chemistry"; (3) understanding that tutoring is useful not only for passing courses but also for excelling in them; (4) sitting up front in classes and asking questions of instructors; (5) getting to know faculty and staff who are willing to give support, not only in the classroom but also out of the classroom (e.g., serving as references in the future); (6) taking the time to relate internships and research experiences to course work and vice versa, taking time to reflect on what it means to be high-achieving and Black in American society; (7) focusing on standardized test performance, because admission to many graduate and professional schools requires strong test-taking skills; (8) developing a strong support group with other students of like minds who are serious about their studies and aspirations; and (9) listening to and learning how to evaluate the advice of others.

We also have learned about some important personal skills and values that students should strive to develop. These skills can help Black students strengthen their academic performance and career preparation. They include (1) knowing not only one's strengths but also those areas in need of improvement; (2) identifying strategies for motivating oneself to continue working hard; (3) developing a "thick skin" and the willingness to welcome constructive criticism and learn from it; (4) developing leadership skills by being involved in extracurricular activities and learning from the successful leadership practices of other students; and (5) engaging in community service to help others less fortunate and, equally important, to learn about oneself and develop character. This last point is especially important because Black children need young role models who can strengthen their support systems.

When talking to groups of Black undergraduate and graduate students, I discuss the skills, values, and habits they should develop while emphasizing the need for staying focused on one's work and one's dreams. The discussion sessions often end with me asking Black students to recite Langston Hughes's poem "Dreams." Afterward, we say together, "Focus, focus, focus."

Index

About the Editor and the Contributors

THE EDITOR

VERNON L. FARMER is acting assistant vice president for Academic Affairs and dean of the School of Graduate Studies and Research at Grambling State University. He is a professor in the Department of Educational Leadership and former department head and director of doctoral studies in the College of Education.

THE CONTRIBUTORS

MAYSA AKBAR, Doctoral Candidate, Clinical Psychology, Saint Louis University

JAMES A. ANDERSON, Vice Provost for Undergraduate Affairs and Professor of Counselor Education, North Carolina State University

MOLEFI KETE ASANTE, Professor of African American Studies, Temple University

LIEUTENANT GENERAL JOE N. BALLARD, Commander, U.S. Army Corps of Engineers, Washington, D.C.

WILTON A. BARHAM, Professor and Head of the Department of Educational Leadership, Grambling State University

C.O. "BRAD" BRADFORD, Chief of Police, Houston

LISA PERTILLAR BREVARD, Dean of Humanities and Associate Professor of English and African World Studies, Division of Humanities, Dillard University

TOMEKA K. BROWN, Undergraduate student, Computer Technology Major, Grambling State University

WARREN W. BUCK, Chancellor, University of Washington–Bothell

CAMILLE T. CADE, Medical Student, Pediatric Anesthesia, University of Maryland School of Medicine

CARLOUS CAPLE, Assistant Professor of Instructional Technology, North Carolina Agricultural and Technical State University

DONALD R. COLE, Associate Dean of Graduate School and Associate Professor of Mathematics, University of Mississippi

NICOLE D. COLLIER, Master's Candidate, Elementary Education, Florida State University

WILLIAM C. COLLINS, Adjunct Associate Professor of Psychology and Director of Comprehensive Studies, The University of Michigan–Ann Arbor

WILLIE CURTIS, Associate Professor of Political Science, United States Naval Academy

OCTAVIA R. DANIELS, Undergraduate student, English Education Major, Grambling State University

ELIZABETH K. DAVENPORT, Assistant Professor of Education and Coordinator of Center for the Professional Development of Teachers, Texas A&M–Kingsville

LAWRENCE F. DAVENPORT, Deputy Chief Administrative Officer, United States House of Representatives, Washington, D.C.

JAMES E. DOBBINS, Professor of Psychology and Director of Postdoctoral Training, Wright State University

FELICIA DOSWELL, Doctoral Candidate, Computer Science, Virginia Polytechnic Institute and State University

ANTHONY ECHOLS, Senior Statistical Analyst, General Motors Corporation, Detroit

MARTIN O. EDU, Associate Professor and Director of Graduate Program in Mass Communication, Grambling State University

CHARLES J. ELMORE, Professor and Head of the Department of Mass Communications, Savannah State University

BETTY J. FARMER, Associate Professor of Nursing, Grambling State University

JERRY L. FARMER II, Undergraduate student, Criminal Justice Major, Grambling State University

LAWANNA GUNN-WILLIAMS, Professor of Psychology, Grambling State University

JASON W. HAMMOND, Medical Student, Orthopedic Surgery, The Johns Hopkins School of Medicine

PAMELA V. HAMMOND, Dean and Professor of Nursing, Hampton University

S. KEITH HARGROVE, Associate Professor of Mechanical Engineering, Tuskegee University

HOPE HARLEY, Doctoral Candidate, Computer Science, Virginia Polytechnic Institute and State University

ADA HARRINGTON-BELTON, Assistant Professor of Curriculum and Instruction, University of Southern Mississippi–Hattisburg

WHITNEY G. HARRIS, Director, Office of Diversity and Affirmative Action, Eastern Michigan University

C. KEITH HARRISON, Associate Professor of Sports Management and Communications, The University of Michigan–Ann Arbor

BARBARA J. HOLMES, Associate Professor of Communication, University of Colorado–Denver

FREEMAN A. HRABOWSKI III, President and Professor of Education, University of Maryland–Baltimore County

JARRETT DAVID IRONS, Master's Candidate, Sports Management and Communication, University of Michigan–Ann Arbor

MARILYN M. IRVING, Associate Professor and Chairperson of the Department of Curriculum and Instruction, Howard University

GLENDA J. ISLAND, Coordinator for Grant Development, Grambling State University

JERLANDO F. L. JACKSON, Doctoral Candidate, Educational Leadership and Policy Studies, Iowa State University

BRENDA JARMON, Associate Professor of Social Work, Florida A&M University

PATRICK O. JEFFERSON, Attorney-at-Law and former Dean of Student Affairs, Dillard University

DAVID A. JETT, Assistant Professor of Toxicology, The Johns Hopkins Medical School

IRENE H. JOHNSON, Interim Dean of the School of Graduate Studies and Professor of Counseling, Alcorn State University

JOHNNYE JONES, Vice President for Academic Affairs and Professor of Biology, Jarvis Christian College

BOBBY J. JONES, Master's Candidate, Business Administration, Oklahoma City University

LEE JONES, Associate Dean of the College of Education and Associate Professor of Educational Leadership, Florida State University

LINDA LACEY, Associate Dean of the Graduate School and Professor of City and Regional Planning, University of North Carolina

TRACY LEWIS, Doctoral Candidate, Computer Science, Virginia Polytechnic Institute and State University

KELI DREW LOCKHART, Practicing Psychologist and President of the New York Chapter of the Association of Black Psychologists

ANNE PRUITT-LOGAN, Scholar-in-Residence, Council of Graduate Schools, Washington, D.C.

BERNADETTE M. LUMAS, Master's Candidate, Social Psychology, Howard University

OCTAVIA MADISON-COLMORE, Assistant Professor of Counselor Education, Virginia Polytechnic Institute and State University

PAULINE E. "POLLY" MCLEAN, Associate Professor of Media Studies, University of Colorado–Boulder

COLONEL SAMUEL E. MIMS, United States Army (Ret.)

JAMES L. MOORE III, Doctoral Candidate, Counselor Education, Virginia Polytechnic Institute and State University

CAROL MOSELEY-BRAUN, United States Ambassador to New Zealand and former United States Senator of Illinois

CHARLES E. OSIRIS, Doctoral Candidate, Higher Education Administration, Florida State University

ERNESTA P. PENDLETON, Program Analyst for Academic Affairs, Division of Academic Programs and Research, University of the District of Columbia

MIRIAM E. PHIELDS, Doctoral Candidate, Counseling Psychology, University of Maryland–College Park

TINA D. PIPKIN, Master's Candidate, Social Work, Florida State University

CLIFTON A. POODRY, Director of Minority Opportunities in Research, Department of Health and Human Resources, National Institutes of Health, Washington, D.C.

CRAIG POOLER, Program Management Analyst, Federal Trio Programs, U.S. Department of Education, Washington, D.C.

ALVIN F. POUSSAINT, Faculty Associate Dean for Student Affairs and Clinical Professor of Psychiatry, Harvard Medical School

RODNEY B. PULLIAM, Doctoral Candidate, Public Administration and Policy, Virginia Polytechnic Institute and State University

HAKIM RASHID, Associate Professor of Education and Psychoeducational Studies, Howard University

GLENDA SCALES, Assistant Dean of Distance Learning, Virginia Polytechnic Institute and State University

DELORES W. SCOTT, Vice President for Student Affairs, Virginia Union University

CHERYL SEALS, Doctoral Candidate, Computer Science, Virginia Polytechnic and State University

LENWARD T. SEALS III, Doctoral Candidate, Physics, Georgia Institute of Technology

XANTHE Y. SEALS, Doctoral Candidate, Developmental Education, Grambling State University

WILLIAM E. SEDLACEK, Assistant Director of Counseling Center and Professor of Education, University of Maryland–College Park

EVELYN SHEPHERD-WYNN, Assistant Professor of English, Grambling State University

DOROTHY V. SMITH, Conrad Hilton Professor of History, Dillard University

LESTER SPENCE, Master's Candidate, Political Science, The University of Michigan–Ann Arbor

LEON P. STRAYER, Doctoral Candidate, Higher Education Administration, Florida State University

SANDRA L. TERRELL, Associate Dean of Robert B. Toulouse School of Graduate Studies and Professor of Speech and Hearing Sciences, University of North Texas

MARGARET DANIELS TYLER, Chief of Staff, Norfolk State University

LIEUTENANT JUNIOR GRADE DIALLO SIKOU WALLACE, United States Navy

SCYATTA A. WALLACE, Master's Candidate, Developmental Psychology, Fordham University

NEARI F. WARNER, Acting President and Provost and Professor of Education, Grambling State University

HOMER B. WARREN, Associate Professor of Marketing, Youngstown State University

ELVIRA M. WHITE, Assistant Professor of Criminal Justice, Grambling State University

BRUCE D. WILLIAMS, Attorney-at-Law and Police Lieutenant, Houston

KERRIE COTTEN WILLIAMS, Doctoral Candidate, American History, New York University

MAJOR MARGARET WILSON, United States Army Reserve, Shreveport